The Fight for Time

STUDIES IN SUBALTERN LATINA/O POLITICS

Series editors: Raymond Rocco, University of California, Los Angeles, and Alfonso Gonzales, University of California, Riverside

The Fight for Time: Migrant Day Laborers and the Politics of Precarity
Paul Apostolidis

Specters of Belonging: The Political Life Cycle of Mexican Migrants
Adrián Félix

The Fight for Time

Migrant Day Laborers and the Politics of Precarity

PAUL APOSTOLIDIS

OXFORD
UNIVERSITY PRESS

OXFORD
UNIVERSITY PRESS

Oxford University Press is a department of the University of Oxford. It furthers
the University's objective of excellence in research, scholarship, and education
by publishing worldwide. Oxford is a registered trade mark of Oxford University
Press in the UK and certain other countries.

Published in the United States of America by Oxford University Press
198 Madison Avenue, New York, NY 10016, United States of America.

Library of Congress Cataloging-in-Publication Data
Names: Apostolidis, Paul, 1965– author.
Title: The fight for time : migrant day laborers and the politics of precarity / Paul Apostolidis.
Description: New York, NY, United States of America : Oxford University Press, 2019. |
Series: Studies in subaltern Latina/o politics |
Includes bibliographical references and index.
Identifiers: LCCN 2018024333 (print) | LCCN 2018028943 (ebook) |
ISBN 9780190459352 (Updf) | ISBN 9780190933180 (Epub) |
ISBN 9780190459345 (pbk. :acid-free paper) | ISBN 9780190459338 (hardcover :acid-free paper)
Subjects: LCSH: Foreign workers—United States. | Foreign workers—Latin
America. | United States—Emigration and immigration—Economic aspects. |
Latin America—Emigration and immigration—Economic aspects.
Classification: LCC HD8081.H7 (ebook) | LCC HD8081.H7 A66 2019 (print) |
DDC 331.5/440973—dc23
LC record available at https://lccn.loc.gov/2018024333

9 8 7 6 5 4 3 2 1

Paperback printed by Sheridan Books, Inc., United States of America
Hardback printed by Bridgeport National Bindery, Inc., United States of America

To my children, Anna and Niko,
with joy and hope.

Contents

Acknowledgments

I AM MORE grateful than I can say to a great many people whose various collaborations with me were crucial to this book. Above all, my heartfelt and infinite thanks go to the day laborers who spoke at length with my assistants and me about their working lives and their hopes for Casa Latina and Voz's MLK Center.

At Casa Latina, I thank the many coordinators who welcomed us warmly into the community and provided us with essential opportunities to conduct research, above all Hilary Stern and Araceli Hernandez, with whom I worked out the initial research program, as well as the following individuals: Gabriel Aspee, Amanda Chavez, Veronique Facchinelli, Emily Gaggia, Raul Garcia, Esteban Ginocchio-Silva, Marcos Martinez, Deborah Purce, Daniel Silva, and Leonardo Ulate.

At Voz, my thanks go especially to Romeo Sosa, whose enthusiasm for this project I have always deeply appreciated and with whom I collaborated in designing our field research and planning the *Jornaleros* screenings. I also especially thank Francisco Aguirre, whose courage, humor, and gentleness inspire me and whose friendship and assistance I have greatly valued. In addition, I am grateful to Ignacio Paramo, Paul Riek, and Justin Shear for facilitating our fieldwork at the MLK Center.

In the broader network of day labor organizations and worker centers, the following leaders took the time to share their analyses, visions, and experiences with me in interviews: Pablo Alvarado, Loyda Alvarado, Yesenia Castillo, Omar Henriquez, Adam Kader, Omar Leon, Nadia Marin, Marlom Portillo, Eric Rodriguez, Valeria Treves, and Paul Zilly. I am also very grateful to Nik Theodore for our discussions of this project and for his own essential research with day labor organizations.

It has been a true pleasure to work with Angela Chnapko, who has consistently been an insightful and engaged interlocutor, and an excellent editor in all ways. My thanks also to two anonymous reviewers for the provocative and careful comments they provided.

Several friends and colleagues deserve special acknowledgment for their indispensable contributions to this project. Romand Coles was a constant intellectual companion throughout, always willing to swap ideas, read drafts, bolster my enthusiasm, and push me in theoretically and politically challenging directions. My development of the project additionally benefited from crucial conversations with the following individuals, most of whom also commented on draft material and whose own work enriches the book in both explicit and inexplicit ways: Cristina Beltrán, Joseph Carens, Jodi Dean, Hagar Kotef, Raymond A. Rocco, Abel Valenzuela, and Kathi Weeks. Sustained conversations with Noah Seixas shaped the discussions of occupational safety and health issues in this book, and I am also grateful to him for inciting my interest in day labor, connecting me with Casa Latina, and introducing me to vital domains of public health research. I further thank Michael McCann for giving me the privilege and the opportunity to share my analysis of occupational safety and health matters in day labor with a dynamic group of scholars at the University of Washington's Harry Bridges Center for Labor Studies, as well as for his valuable comments regarding the project.

Major portions of this book's analysis took shape during several years in which I had the good fortune to participate in a remarkable intellectual community at the Institute for Social Justice at Australian Catholic University in Sydney. I thank the following friends and colleagues for sharing their penetrating reflections in work sessions on papers that became chapters, in panel sessions and lectures, and in many casual conversations: Linda Martín Alcoff, Rajeev Bhargava, Akeel Bilgrami, Joseph Carens, Costas Douzinas, Naser Ghobadzadeh, Kiran Grewal, Lia Haro, Emilian Kavalski, Nikolas Kompridis, Jennifer Nedelsky, Jacqueline Rose, Allison Weir, and Magdalena Zolkos; thanks also to Paula Gleeson and Lisa Tarantino for all their work enabling these vital discussions.

Discussions with participants in the Radical Critical Theory Circle seminar in Nisyros, Greece, sharpened both the critique of precarity and my arguments about its political implications in pivotal ways; thanks especially to Darin Barney, Andreas Kalyvas, Regina Kreide, and Artem Magun.

During the course of this project, Robyn Marasco, Sara Rushing, and Joan Tronto all provided insightful discussants' comments on conference papers that formed the basis of chapters for this book. Thanks also to Jules Boykoff for his incisive feedback on a draft chapter. This book further benefited from stimulating discussions with a number of other individuals whose remarks about the project stayed with me and helped shape my arguments: Anna Agathangelou, Lawrie Balfour, Jane Bennett, Angelica Bernal, Rebecca Brown, Susan Buck-Morss, Craig Burowiak, Samuel Chambers, Anita Chari, William Connolly, George Ciccariello-Maher, Joshua Dienstag, Lisa Disch, Michaele Ferguson,

Ricardo Gomez, Katherine Gordy, Margaret Kohn, Joseph Lowndes, Keally McBride, Kirstie McClure, Tamara Metz, Paul Passavant, Holloway Sparks, Peter Steinberger, Chip Turner, Andrew Valls, and Juliet Williams.

I am grateful to the following colleagues at Whitman College for their helpful comments on my work as well as for many informal conversations about this project: Susanne Beechey, Shampa Biswas, Aaron Bobrow-Strain, Phil Brick, Arash Davari, Jack Jackson, Timothy Kaufman-Osborn, Bruce Magnusson, Gaurav Majumdar, Jason Pribilsky, and Elleni Centime Zeleke. This book's critique of precarity, especially aspects of gender, also benefited greatly from discussions with Jennifer Cohen. I thank Whitman College for providing research funding and sabbatical leave-time that were essential to the completion of this book; thanks also to the Department of Politics for additional funding for student research assistants.

From this project's earliest stages, a growing roster of students at Whitman College contributed invaluably to this endeavor. Most of all, I am tremendously grateful to Ariel Ruiz and Caitlin Schoenfelder for their reliable, meticulous, critical, and spirited efforts as primary research assistants with the fieldwork. Their dedication to this research and to achieving justice for day laborers was indispensable to the project. In addition, I thank the following students who served as research assistants in other important ways: Pedro Galvao, Gennie Jones, Diana Madriz, Madelyn Peterson, Leslie Rodriguez, Paloma Romero Lopez, Julia Stone, and Annie Want.

This book culminates in a discussion of convivial politics, and I want to acknowledge the many people in my near and extended family as well as numerous friends—on the East Coast, on the West Coast, and in Argentina and Greece— with whom I have enjoyed much precious convivial time, without which a lengthy project like this would not have been possible.

This book is dedicated to my children. I thank Anna for the gift of our conversations about ideas and for her assistance with the bibliography, as well as for the inspiration I get from witnessing her jubilant and vigorous engagement in intellectual life. I thank Niko for his own joyful spirit and tenacity, his boundless curiosity about life, and his sage advice about reducing the word count.

Finally, inexpressible thanks go to Jeanne Morefield for being my rock throughout a turbulent and precarious phase in our life together, for our innumerable discussions about this project, and for the example she sets of devotion to work like this and to feeding the intellectual and political communities that give it life.

The Fight for Time

Introduction

THE MATURATION OF neoliberal capitalism has yielded a curious conundrum: even as the social circumstances of the world's populations become ever more vastly dichotomous and unequal, in certain ways the fates of working people everywhere have become more densely interwoven. At one and the same time, working people's experiences have come to resemble one another more closely and have acutely diverged.

The damage wrought by neoliberal transformations of working life has been exceedingly partial and sometimes narrowly targeted. The continually growing burdens of employment reductions, wage and benefit cuts, corporate restructuring, finance-driven accumulation, social welfare retrenchment, deunionization, and workforce casualization have fallen hardest on the least fortunate in terms of class, racial, gender, and national privilege. Social commentators and academic theorists often usefully gather the panoply of losses, stresses, and humiliations that stem from these social-systemic transformations under the conceptual rubric of "precarity." These problems, ranging from daily punches in the gut to dwindling hope for long-term personal security, familial well-being, and social justice, have by no means been distributed equitably. Indeed, it is central to neoliberal logic that social disparities, and hence competitive and self-preservative motivations, should deepen and proliferate aggressively.

Yet precaritization also has projected tendrils and sent down roots within multiple class strata well above the bottom, among white as well as nonwhite people, in the lives of men and women alike, and in the United States just as in societies victimized by US empire in decline. If precarity names the special plight of the world's most virulently oppressed human beings, it also denotes a near-universal complex of unfreedom. In critically attending to these strangely juxtaposed situations and drawing their political consequences, there is the potential to make things turn out differently. Precarity can have a politics, and that politics can espouse radical desires and imaginings.

This book searches for portents of such radical hope in the words and practices of day laborers. These beleaguered and impoverished migrants inhabit social quarters quite remote from the spheres of labor that tend, for good reasons, to kindle the most excitement among critical theorists on the lookout for a constituency that could form the nucleus of a new workers' mobilization. If, for instance, communicative value-generating processes define capitalism's current formation, as Jodi Dean argues, then it makes sense to hinge expectations on the radicalization of knowledge workers.[1] Insofar as digital innovations comprise the leading edge of capitalist expansion, "info-producers" who perform "cognitive labor" would seem the most fitting candidates for leadership in any new mustering of working-class political spirit.[2] Others reason that given capital's growing reliance on logistics to ensure optimally timed transfers of material commodities and technical information between globally networked ports, warehouses, and retail outlets, attractive opportunities exist for strategic intervention in logistically structured "domains of struggle."[3]

Developing anticapitalist theory and molding practices for constructing alternative social forms certainly require investigating workers' political potentialities in these tactically advantageous domains. Nevertheless, a different perspective on dominant social tendencies must also be sought by engaging the reflections and experiences of people cast to the banks by capitalism's rushing currents of innovation. As Walter Benjamin advised, it is often amid ruins strewn across revealingly disordered landscapes by societies bent on progress that theorists can discern the telltale marks of domination and the stirrings of hope.[4] Without such illuminating signs, critique and resistance in the face of power will lack not only a genuinely universal scope but also critical bite. In other words, the warrant for paying sustained attention to the thoughts, acts, and communities of the hypermarginalized goes beyond simply taking stock of tactical assets that particular groups could lend to others' mobilizations. The rationale is also more than a matter of principled respect for the dignity of the most woefully downtrodden individuals. Lingering sympathetically and critically with those mired most deeply in society's ruts is also necessary because general social phenomena invariably look different from the vantage points such tarrying makes possible, as this book demonstrates. With surprise, at times with shock, we come to know otherwise the warp and texture of the social world that vastly inclusive systems—of labor, work's ethics, public spaces, or social temporalities—generate for all classes and cultures of workers when we try out the viewpoints of day laborers and others at the extreme margins.

This book provides a new and politically redolent critique of contemporary precarity through intellectual collaboration with migrant day laborers. Of course, others before me have elaborated, derided, and wrestled with the concept of precarity. Rather than catalog such prior interventions, I begin this account by offering a series of general theses or propositions regarding precarity today. This preliminary exercise unfolds various ways in which precaritization at once singles out specific groups of people for uncommonly deplorable treatment and makes work-related experiences isomorphic for populations throughout class, racial, and gender hierarchies. These theses also provide opportune moments to acknowledge preceding accounts of precarity's qualities, antecedents, and effects. In addition, exploring these propositions about precarity furnishes an avenue for introducing day laborers' circumstances, considering why their idioms of work-life and organizational struggle merit special attention, and offering some initial meditations, in a heuristic and exploratory spirit, on several key concepts that later chapters address systematically, following day laborers' leads: time, movement, isolation, suffering, and collective struggle.

Thesis 1: Precarious Workers Are Suffering

There is a diffuse awareness today that people who work in the most benighted occupations suffer grave threats to their lives, bodily integrity, and emotional stability as a result of their jobs. Regular albeit discontinuous news stories about industrial disasters in the global South offer familiar touchstones for this phenomenon. Emblematic of such reports was the brief coverage of a dilapidated garment factory's collapse near Dhaka, Bangladesh, in 2013. The building's cave-in killed over one thousand workers and drew scrutiny of their dismal wages, which were at planetary lows.[5] As is customary with media cycles, the public gaze soon shifted to other matters but then returned abruptly to Dhaka when further reports emerged about a spate of factory fires in the same region.[6] Neither Walmart's sanctimonious promises to embrace new safety standards in the plants supplying its megastores, nor Disney's holier-than-thou severing of ties with Bangladeshi producers, seemed to have altered daily realities for Dhaka textile workers. Such news stories resonate with periodic reports about intolerable working conditions elsewhere—women clothing workers in Cambodia who faint by the dozens due to extreme heat and overwork;[7] Foxconn iPhone assemblers in China who see no exit from infernal laboring conditions apart from suicide;[8] Latin American migrant meatpacking, dairy, and farm workers in the United States exposed to constant injury, wage theft, and poisoning on the job.[9] Cumulatively, such reports foster an ongoing, low-grade perception that employers across the world are treating workers disgracefully and that these problems are inevitable. Intervallic evocations of shock enable an overall schema of normalization.

The odious suffering of precaritized workers thus has become a matter of public consciousness that is, itself, distinctly precarious. Both formations of precarity feature a similar temporal tension. On the one hand, the mainstream media supply routine reminders of low-wage workers' abysmal employment conditions; there is a continuity and predictability to the stories' publication, just as the grinding abusiveness of workers' job-situations remains a constant. On the other hand, precarity is made to seem a matter of astonishing events, such as a long-serviceable building suddenly collapsing or a conflagration bursting out unexpectedly. A "breaking" story about workers dying en masse qualifies as "news" because it is supposedly about something extraordinary, just as the report itself is intense but fleeting. In short, the suffering endured by precarious workers involves not only hazards of life and limb but also the social death associated with the commodification of their circumstances: the mortifying effects of temporalized media rituals that stave off serious engagement with workers' experiences by making them objects of public consumption.

But who exactly qualifies as a precarious worker consigned to a suffering existence? The better question might be: who *does not* belong to the vast population of the precaritized? As Lauren Berlant argues, precaritization inflicts suffering on not only the indigent and racially abjected but also much wider swaths of the working population, although it reserves its greatest wrath for the former groups. Berlant underscores that what matters is not just the depth of suffering but also its affective structure: the ways certain emotional, relational, and corporeal habits become ingrained and reinforce one another under specific sociohistorical conditions. She sees a particular affective syndrome as characteristic of precaritized work-life, in which people's fantasy-filled struggles to thrive or just survive economically ironically diminish their capacities to do either of these things. She calls this predicament "cruel optimism," and she contends that it applies "across class, gender, race, and nation: no longer is precarity delegated to the poor or the *sans-papiers*."[10]

Another news genre illustrates how precaritization in this form—protracted self-debilitation through work that registers in anxious psyches, overtaxed senses, constricted hopes, and worn-down bodies—radiates throughout the economy. In the early twenty-first century, reports abound about emerging technologies and management-techniques that are making work environments hostile and displacing masses of working people from their jobs, even as they promise to tailor work to individuals' dreams and desires. One exposé probes Amazon's "Darwinist" white-collar work culture, where employees' mutual ratings through social networking combine with intensive job-performance data-collection to foster a cutthroat and mercilessly stressful milieu.[11] Uber, we read elsewhere, adapts algorithmically contrived stimuli from video games to induce drivers to extend their hours beyond the point of exhaustion.[12] Airbnb relegates most who try to earn a living through the online rental economy to a perpetual gauntlet of temporary gigs and ultimately magnifies affluent people's advantages rather than redistributing wealth downward, as the company's celebrants claim.[13] Popular apprehensions mount as a torrent of reports project the termination of whole categories of employment, from the most stingily paid supermarket checkers to lawyers and financial advisers, due to accelerating innovations in artificial intelligence.[14] Precarity thus stamps its imprint on declining mental and physical health prognoses for working people in virtually all industries. It augments this misery, furthermore, through the peculiar malice of encouraging fantasy in the pose of resignation to these cruel circumstances of self-incapacitation as less bad than completely going under.[15] Only superficially disputing such resignation, in turn, is the compensatory fantasy suggested by the news media that major institutions are always ready to respond to breakdowns in the "normal" social order, not least (although perhaps at most) when the media themselves break stories about new crises of precarity.

In sum, precarity is written on the bodies and inscribed in the psyches of suffering workers the world over. Precarity means injury, illness, sudden death, and foreshortened life, including attenuated life from the constant and growing anxiety about when the next lethal threat will target the worker's already pummeled body, heart, and mind. Precarity portends these maladies especially for non-white people, women, low-status workers, and residents of countries outside neoimperial America. Yet precaritization as suffering extends to many more privileged populations through structurally encompassing dynamics. The dominant venues of public communication intrepidly hide both these inclusionary features and the narrowly concentrated forms of working people's misery precisely through granting them publicity. Public discourses enlist time and temporality as field generals in the ongoing campaign to reassure us that the problems we see all the time are mere aberrations, thereby compounding the suffering of precarious workers.

Thesis 2: Precarious Workers Are out of Time

Precaritization not only advances through time-calibrated rubrics for translating workers' suffering into public discourse—it also arises through workers' day-to-day experiences with distinctive temporalities of action and affect. The analysis of social time-patterns has been central to the critique of capital since Marx famously dissected the working day and proclaimed its strategic manipulation as the secret of capital's genesis. From today's perspective, Marx's intervention appears less a solution to capital's riddle than a provocative starting point for contemplating the ever more widely proliferating and variegated forms of capitalist domination rooted in temporal flows and formations. Critiques of post-Fordism and postmodernity by André Gorz and David Harvey, respectively, highlight some particularly crucial transformations in work-related time since the mid-twentieth century.

For Gorz, unprecedented temporal "discontinuity" results from the ascendance of "economic reason" through post-Fordism's advance, especially as firms boost profits by replacing permanent full-time jobs with temporary and part-time employment arrangements.[16] Work time becomes disjointed in an everyday sense, as workers constantly shift gears between multiple jobs that they perform for shorter durations during the same day or night. Furthermore, argues Gorz, short-term and independently contracted employment breaks up people's work time trajectory over a personal life-span.[17] Workers who experience such fragmentation are thrust "out of time" in at least three related senses. First, they lack time to do much else apart from working or going to and from whatever jobs they have at the moment. Second, workers must perpetually carve out time in the midst of their present work-lives to find and prepare for the next job they will need when the one at hand expires, even as the concentrated effort any given work-activity requires is becoming more and more taxing; this not only aggravates time's diminution in quantity as a disposable resource but also spells the overburdening of time in everyday life with an excess of activity. Third, because modern mythologies that ground social belonging and political citizenship in stable full-time employment remain hegemonic, people whose work-lives fail to correspond to these ideals end up feeling, and being viewed as, out of sync with "normal" society.[18] These modes of social-temporal dysfunction disproportionately implicate women, who continue to shoulder the bulk of domestic care responsibilities and hence must squeeze another entire category of work into these multiply constrained circumstances.[19]

Precaritized workers also are "out of time" inasmuch as their jobs block them from consciously and collectively intervening in capitalism's globally distributed and historical temporalities. In part, the problem is that workers are caught in the prevailing social condition of time's condensation into a present with neither forward- nor backward-looking trajectories, which Harvey describes as follows:

> Accelerations in turnover times in production, exchange and consumption . . . produce, as it were, the loss of a sense of the future except and insofar as the future can be discounted into the present. Volatility and ephemerality similarly make it hard to maintain any firm sense of continuity. Past experience gets compressed into some overwhelming present.[20]

As subjection to such temporal compression, precarity signifies imprisonment within a self-contradictory formation of time that is both homogenized as a relentless presentism and replete with fragmentation and flux. For Harvey, these temporal constraints also correspond to a form of spatial confinement: even as globalizing capital surmounts obstacles of time and space, "the incentive for places to be differentiated in ways attractive to capital" grows.[21] As a result, working people are increasingly subordinated to locally specific regimes of labor control. People's temporalities of work therefore become disconnected across varying geographical regions, even though their labors aggrandize an ever-slimmer set of corporations, whose activities increasingly conform to a uniform worldwide beat. Immersed within divergent and place-specific temporal rubrics of labor, and even though they *are* capital in the classic sense theorized by Marx, precaritized workers nonetheless occupy practical conditions of everyday life that systematically impede their apperception of capital's structural and historical dynamics.

Considering the multiple ways that precarious workers are out of time suggests further aspects of precaritization's dual structure as both aimed at certain exceptional groups and pervading the general population. Even working people fortunate enough to hold full-time, long-term jobs increasingly face management techniques, ideological inducements, and technical interventions that intensify the productivity for capital of each moment of their day. As Franco "Bifo" Berardi, Kathi Weeks, and Christian Marazzi each show in different ways, the activity of work has saturated people's everyday lives in several key respects. Technological devices such as smartphones now make it possible for any tiny stretch of time in any part of one's day to yield bits of surplus-value-enhancing work.[22] Meanwhile, an ever-more insistent "postindustrial work ethic" bids us to use every opportunity to "grow" our individual value as "human resources," in a world where firms' stepped-up reliance on "immaterial" and "affective" labor makes *any* human activity or encounter potentially convertible into economic value.[23] This reconstituted work ethic gains irresistible force, moreover, from exhorting us not only to do our jobs dutifully but also to *love* our work and to seek ultimate fulfillment from working[24]—so, why would we *not* want work all the time? Yet we also end up working incessantly even when we think we are relaxing or just having fun. Businesses coax consumers to provide surplus-value-producing labor routinely and for free, such as through social network-based product or service evaluations that spread information—that is, advertising—about companies' offerings.[25]

These social patterns of desire and behavior comprise general forms of precaritization insofar as they make people throughout society feel that, and act as if, they are never working hard enough, no matter how hard they try. To be sure, some groups experience this predicament with more material urgency than others, just as some grapple disproportionately with post-Fordist time's rampant discontinuities and postmodern time's self-contradictory compressions. Yet

Cameroonian day laborers who wait on edge for highly uncertain, dismally paid, and micro-term construction jobs at Casa de Maryland's Silver Spring worker center, decompressing now and then by going on Facebook, render services to capital not unlike those of white millennial techsters clustered at northern Virginia start-ups, regardless of whether the latter are permanent staff or independent contractors. Throughout the employment hierarchy, working people are *running* out of time and *living* out of time, notwithstanding the greater abilities of some to approximate standards to which all aspire. Likewise, the suffering produced by this temporal drain and arrhythmia imposes itself on the working population at large through generalized syndromes of anxiety and depression even as it expands most alarmingly among migrant workers and others at society's distant margins.

Thesis 3: Precarious Workers Are on Their Own

Capitalism has long been indicted for creating a world where people live in atomized, hostile dissociation from one another. Yet critics of capitalism also have traced dialectical switchbacks by which capitalism's need for temporarily stable worker-collectivities counteracts its own fostering of anonymous individualism. For instance, Marx and Engels envisage modern factory floors as sites where industrial workers can recognize their world-making power as a class; Gramsci ruminates on prospects for forging counterhegemonic projects among culturally distinctive and geographically localized constituencies that economic-structural developments endow with special historical consequence; Harvey underscores capital's inevitable dependence on relatively fixed spatializations of production, markets, and legitimation regimes. The historical formation of human collectivities catalyzed by capital's relentless pursuit of self-expansion, at least at times, has thus provoked a series of unintended opportunities for convening anticapitalist associations.

Precarity in our time immeasurably deepens workers' individual segregation from one another while ruthlessly eliminating possible loci for forming communities of any sort, let alone solidarities of resistance. Capital's centripetal effects with respect to human interrelationality have metastasized as temporal disjunctions and desynchronizations have proliferated. Lacking a contiguous space-time of work, contingently, multiply, and sporadically employed workers no longer have even the ambivalent basis for cultivating subversive associations that regular jobs once offered. Gone are the ballasts such interpersonal and political relations once could find within a fairly consistent set of colleagues, a familiar institutional culture, and a steady organization of work featuring stable procedural "games" one could learn to play skillfully over time.[26]

The consequences of these developments, once more, are felt most acutely by those in the worst jobs. Thus, migrant meatpacking workers endure bitter isolation in the midst of densely populated but insanely sped-up cattle disassembly operations, in which perpetual panic and sense-numbing noise foil any attempt to speak to coworkers. Rapid employee turnover, as mega meat companies churn through the "disposable" migrant workforce, further undercuts efforts to kindle solidarity, or even just sustained acquaintances, among workers.[27] Meanwhile, household domestic workers' ranks swell as neoliberalizing states offload social-reproductive responsibilities onto women and as companies' wage and benefit cuts induce women to take on more wage-earning activities for longer hours. On the job, women who do domestic work find themselves marooned and alone in the intimate spaces of their "despotic" employers' homes, sometimes lacking even an informal network of fellow workers with whom to commiserate over routine abuses and humiliations.[28] Migration as such also freights those who relocate continents away from those they love with weighty burdens of loneliness and loss, while the ever-present fear of capture by immigration officials terrorizes the unauthorized into avoiding social contact and seeking solitary refuge in what Mexican migrants to the United States call *la vida encerrada* (living shut in or encaged).[29]

Nevertheless, the atomizing instrumentalities of precaritization operate at all levels of the class, racial, and gender hierarchies, and for lawful citizens and the unauthorized alike, if not in equivalent manners or proportions. Dean's emphasis on knowledge workers' decisive implication in communicative capitalism as a class notwithstanding, the mechanisms of expropriation she describes apply throughout contemporary society. Insofar as the population at large eagerly performs the "searching, commenting, and participating" online that companies convert "into raw material for capital" in the form of "Big Data,"[30] people everywhere, at every rung of the social ladder, are working for communicative capital. Correspondingly, all of us undergo precaritization through this ubiquitously extractive process in the sense of being left on our own. Dean characterizes the social milieu spawned by newly dominant profit-making strategies as "a setting of communication without communicability" in which "the content of our utterances" loses importance in direct proportion to the capital gains achieved through our words' quantification.[31] As this general "decline in a capacity to transmit meaning" gathers pace,[32] isolation spreads in the form of a pervasive disability to have meaningful, language-mediated interactions with anyone outside our own heads.[33]

Consigned to a form of *la vida encerrada*, albeit likely without the physical abuse and everyday terror that shape many migrant workers' existences, mass populations dispossessed and atomized through the communicative "enclosure" movement also know they are on their own in the struggle not just to survive but, more specifically, to prove their own worthiness to survive. Such "responsibilization" furnishes key contours of the dissociative individualization that is precaritizing all reaches of society. Wendy Brown succinctly defines neoliberal responsibilization as an array of techniques aimed at "forcing the subject to become a responsible self-investor and self-provider."[34] Enthusiastically devoted participation in protocols of outcomes-maximizing "governance" supposedly ensures not just the individual's sustenance but also that person's perpetual increase in value as "human capital." This, in turn, promotes value's nonstop growth in society at large in a way that relieves leading institutions of accountability for the vast risks their ventures precipitate.[35] Similarly, Maurizio Lazzarato sees the hallmark neoliberal figure of the "indebted man" as emerging through disciplinary practices that induce individuals always to strive to appear deserving of credit through conscientious labor and ceaseless self-valorization. The cancerous growth of hyperindividualized and monetized conscience tracks the degree to which such diligent "work on the self" also becomes "an injunction to *take upon oneself* the costs and risks of the economic and financial disaster."[36] Of course, migrants face more daunting and distinct pressures to prove themselves trustworthy and hard-working, and to "pay their debt" to society for violating border laws, even as their personal liabilities balloon with the ever-increasing costs of coyotes' smuggling services. Still, in important ways, the trope of the self-reliant and industrious immigrant, on which migrant advocates reflexively lean and which most migrants strive to emulate, expresses but one permutation among others of the broader phenomenon of responsibilization.

In sum, precaritized workers are hoisting heavier, more isolating, and more densely moralized burdens of economic self-sufficiency, as firms cut wages and casualize jobs, states slash social programs and retract union rights, and debtors' obligations mount while capital's financialization expands. As their private encumbrances become more unwieldy, workers also feel the weight of the world pressing down on them as never before. Ever more segregated and alienated from others by work processes—whether in manufacturing or services, as paid employees or unconscious drones in the communicariat, and for legal residents and national citizens just as for unauthorized migrants, although more intensively for the latter—precarious workers are on their own as they face the moral injunctions decreed by the responsibilizing culture.

Thesis 4: Precarious Workers Are on the Move

The precaritization of work-life is tightly intertwined with the growing geographical mobility of people across the globe. In absolute numbers, as of 2015, more people were migrants than at any other time in the history of migration recordkeeping—over one billion people in total, including 244 million international migrants.[37] Although migrants have comprised about the same proportion of the world's population over the past few decades, this figure has more recently crept upward, from 2.8 percent in 2000 to 3.3 percent in 2015.[38] International Labor Organization (ILO) data show that migrant workers comprise "about two-thirds of the total international migrant stock" and that migrants "have higher labour force participation than non-migrants, particularly due to higher labour force participation rates for migrant women relative to non-migrant women."[39] In North America and the Arab states, migrant workers make up particularly high proportions of the total working populations.[40]

It would be inaccurate to say that work's precaritization is causing migration to increase, pure and simple. Violent conflicts have recently displaced record numbers of people from their communities of origin, in particular from Syria. People fleeing war and destruction in Syria generated a 55 percent increase in the worldwide number of refugees between 2011 and 2015.[41] Once people are on the move, violent clashes in destination locations aggravate migrants' hardships and propel further efforts to find refuge elsewhere, as has happened with Somalian and Ethiopian refugees in Yemen.[42] In addition, to say that work is becoming precaritized implies a previous situation in which work was more stable, better remunerated, and more capable of securing normative identities associated with the work society. Although such conditions and expectations have hardly been limited to advanced capitalist countries in North America, Europe, and Australasia, they have been far more deeply embedded in these societies than in developing countries of the global South.

Yet the standard distinction between economic migrants and refugees, and hence the sorting of migrants into laboring subjects and victims of violence, needs to be critically interrogated, for at least two reasons. First, war distributes its effects in dramatically unequal and class-specific ways. Second, refugees and "asylum seekers" work for self-supporting income more commonly than many people assume. They also usually work for little monetary reward, under hazardous circumstances, and in informal arrangements, just as do most "economic migrants." In Jordan, for instance, over 40 percent of the massive and growing population of working Syrian refugees in 2014 labored in construction, which is rife with job-related injuries and illnesses the world over.[43] Among Syrian refugees in Jordan who were working for pay, a full 99 percent worked in informal occupations and most worked longer hours than Jordanian citizens.[44] Syrian refugee workers also netted significantly less money than native Jordanians, with most camp residents earning below the statutory minimum wage for non-Jordanians, which in turn was roughly 30 percent lower than the rate for Jordan's citizens.[45]

Precarious work also *does* impel people to uproot and relocate themselves for multiple reasons and with mounting frequencies. The temporal discontinuities and compressions analyzed by Gorz and Harvey have spatial correlates. Tenuous ties to any given job, whether in terms of inconsistent hours, limited hours per week, or brief contract durations, weaken people's desires to stay in one place rather than moving elsewhere to seek work. The condensation and presentism of temporal experience propelled by accelerating capital turnover erodes people's abilities even to imagine enduring bonds with particular places. Such temporal speed-up also imparts a quicksand-like quality to the ground underlying strategically devised place-specific economies because the progression from initial success to capital's overaccumulation, crisis, and exit becomes that much swifter—and when that happens, people leave, too. In turn, capital benefits handsomely from and thus promotes mobile workforces of precaritized migrants. Not only have major business sectors such as meatpacking and other agricultural industries come to rely structurally on migrant workers; in addition, the inflation of global migration rates has fueled the growth of an entire "migration industry" (with its own precaritized workforce) that profits from facilitating, interdicting, incarcerating, or deporting workers on the move.[46]

Strangely, precarious workers' ever more hectic and frequent movements to other locations are often accompanied by obdurate forms of stasis. Berlant suggests that precaritization in this sense creates yet another affinity between the degraded conditions of the most oppressed and the problems of more privileged social constituencies. Recent films about unauthorized migrant workers and those who take advantage of them illustrate this paradoxical coinciding of movement and immobility: they depict "the constant movement of people and things through national boundaries, temporary homes, small and big business, and above all an informal economy," yet no one gets anywhere in the sense of upward mobility.[47] The immobility that oddly twins with precarious workers' wanderings can also be a bodily attribute. It is discernable, for instance, in the sedentary habits encouraged among those who lack the wealth to avoid standing in line, whose jobs prevent them from walking around at will, and whose haphazard work schedules make the idea of regular exercise regimens laughable. In certain ways, as Judy Wacjman acerbically notes, "Speed for the few is contingent on others remaining stationary."[48] More precisely, all but the 1 percent face the spatial conundrum of precarity that melds stubborn fixity with perpetual motion, although the intensity of this conflict varies for different groups of precarious workers.

Thesis 5: Precarious Workers Are Fighting Back

Assaulted frontally and on every flank by forces that wreak so much suffering and cause such extensive isolation in precarity's time-spaces, precarious workers often battle tendencies toward acquiescent fatalism and respond to the powers that assail them with courage and inventiveness. Precaritized workers' political counterthrusts have taken many different forms and yielded ambiguous results. Following the world financial crisis of 2008, Greece became a focal point for those seeking signs that precarious workers could mobilize to contest both national and international neoliberal regimes. Activists initiated radical-democratic circles of protest and deliberation in Syntagma Square in Athens that thousands attended. Those who gathered repudiated European austerity demands, launched militant demands for social policies to counteract precaritization, and audaciously asserted the constituent power of ordinary people just a few meters outside the walls of parliament. Migrants contributed in energetic and gutsy ways to this Greek activist culture. For Andreas Kalyvas, the 2008 "insurrection" witnessed "a real rupture: a new subject appearing into the public realm, the *rebellious immigrant*, politicized and public, claiming a political life."[49] Embracing both deliberative and confrontational modes of action, and refusing to confine themselves "to the civil and private spheres of social life and economic production," immigrants numbered among the hundreds arrested for causing civil disorder and joined in debates about defining the rationale for the uprising. [50]

More ambivalent assessments have greeted the institutionalization of Greek popular-democratic energies through the SYRIZA electoral coalition, as with similar attempts to create more formal vehicles for radical upsurges in other countries. Initially celebrated worldwide as the first genuine repulse of neoliberalism's advance in Europe, SYRIZA's 2015 victory was soon followed by disillusionment as leaders' actions belied their denunciations of international creditors' austerity demands. Analysts of Spain's leftist Podemos party have similarly criticized its detachment from the most radically democratic currents in the Indignados popular movement.[51] Events in other regions have been even less encouraging, as popular-democratic revolts in Turkey and the Middle East have met with brutal repression. Already by the time of SYRIZA's watershed moment in Greece, the Arab Spring seemed a very long time ago, as did the previous gains of the neo-Bolivarian left in Latin America.

Disaffection and disappointment with momentous struggles to reignite a powerful and spirited left politics thus abound at this book's writing, although these sentiments are also alloyed with a growing, albeit at times desperate, sense of expectation that the world stage is being set for left resurgence. On the one hand, the deflation following the dissolution of Occupy and other radically democratic and anticapitalist thrusts to reappropriate public spaces has more recently been mixed with dread upon witnessing the racist Right's expansion, as indicated by Brexit in the United Kingdom, Trumpism in the United States, and nativist parties' advances throughout Europe. In this sense, the kernels of a left politics of precarity that had seemed to sprout shortly after the start of the new millennium, including the EuroMayDay movement and various other protests in France staged in the name of *la precariat*,[52] seem to have produced shoots either stunted by opportunistic compromise or bent toward the sickly phosphorescence of the new fascism. On the other hand, socialism has gained renewed currency in the United States in the wake of the Sanders presidential campaign, especially among millennials, while a formidable new sanctuary movement has networked progressive urban leaders with migrant justice organizations to challenge Trumpist nativism. Brexit may have passed, but Labour in Britain then tacked left, elevating Jeremy Corbyn to party leader. In Europe, some newly emerging left parties have treated antimigrant parties' alarmingly swelling numbers in parliaments as opportunities to forge new constituencies from the detritus of social-democratic and green coalitions. Across the globe, people are increasingly defining action in response to climate change as a matter of taking stands against capital and welding the environment's defense to the mobilization of displaced and exploited workers. Both climate-oriented political activism and counterorganizing against antimigrant hate also face the imperative of responding to the distinctive phenomenon by which precaritization for the world's general population twins with exceptionally lethal forms of precarity for the world's poorest and most vulnerable people.

The political ferment among precarious workers, especially migrants, thus argues against any simplistically disconsolate narrative that would see recent left insurgencies as culminating merely in repression, sellout, and right-wing counterorganization. Taken together with the first four theses, the tenuous yet proliferating materialization of precarious workers' political struggles then prompts a basic and urgent question: how can working people craft a politics of precarity that addresses both acutely marginalized groups' uncommon predicaments and social syndromes that enwrap mass constituencies? Proponents of such a politics face the core challenge, in other words, of configuring an autonomously collective force that is at once formidable and elastic and that stays bifocally attentive to the ubiquitous and the exceptional. We need a politics that merges universalist ambitions to change history, which are indispensable to structural change, with responsiveness to group differences that matter because minimizing them means leaving some people out whose contributions are essential and whose demands for freedom are nonnegotiable.

Other pressing questions follow from the prefatory meditations on precarity in the prior sections: How might a politics of the precaritized give workers' suffering its due without valorizing it in ways that make it seem acceptable or even laudable? How, in addition, might a politics of precarity forge collaborations among workers who suffer in very different ways and with varying intensities, even while sharing certain politically significant miseries? How might organizers among the precaritized nurture the relational attachments crucial to any political cause even while precarity relentlessly isolates and displaces individuals? With legions of precarious workers on the move and with capital itself ever a moving target (yet always seeking provisional points of fixity), how can workers develop alternatives to capitalist spatial logics? As spatial flux mounts among precaritized workers, how might antiprecaritization efforts splice together place-making elements with other components that tap the transformative energies of migratory mobility? In turn, if anticapitalist struggle has quite frequently been in some sense a fight for time, then how should this fight be updated and retooled today? How might precarious workers' organizations invent more self-conscious, more affectively dynamic, and more politically galvanizing strategies for grappling with the temporal dimensions of precarity?

Finally, what organizational forms can best equip working people to strike back against precaritization in all its multiple and varied guises, and what substantive priorities should those organizations adopt? This issue increasingly absorbs the attention of political theorists, who have offered widely divergent proposals in response, of which the following are illustrative examples. Jodi Dean advocates refocusing on the mass party as "a basic form of political struggle" that operates affectively, psychologically, and across "different organizational terrains" to build and unleash the "collective power" of "the people."[53] Michael Hardt and Antonio Negri warn against reinvesting hopes in "a vanguardist revolutionary party" but affirm the need to reflect critically on organizational implications of the radical "critique of leadership" in recent liberation movements, such as Zapatismo in Mexico and Black Lives Matter in the United States; they call for the creation of "institutions without centralization" and "organizations without hierarchy."[54] In contrast to Hardt and Negri's embrace of "nonsovereign" organizational forms, Ali Aslam sees transformative promise in social movements' "micro-practices" for "democratizing sovereignty" and rejuvenating popular hopes for attaining political freedom through the state.[55] He concentrates on social movements inspired by the Tahrir Square protests, analyzing their affectively stimulating efforts "to cultivate responsiveness and vitality among citizens habituated to low-intensity citizenship" and accustomed to satisfying "their desires for agency in their identities as consumers."[56] Romand Coles shares Aslam's regard for the transformative effects of microaffective energetics. Rather than focusing on movements, however, Coles highlights even more localized efforts to forge "a radically democratic habitus," in part through organizational forms and tactics that co-opt the neoliberal "politics of co-optation" such as action research programs at public universities.[57] Thus, there is no shortage of difficult questions about the social scale, structural attributes, internal power-distribution, core practices, and relation to neoliberal culture of organizations we might envision to advance a politics of precarity.[58]

A Sojourn with Day Laborers

Day laborers' activities and commentaries make up the focus of this book, and these workers have much to say regarding the questions just posed. Faced with endemic suffering that comes from poverty, insufficient work, and the hardships of migration; often alone as they wait to get hired or work exceedingly brief jobs with no steady location or consistent coworkers; awkwardly positioned in urban spaces that expose them to daily harassment and intimidation; desperately out of time, in all the ways I have described—day laborers also have grounded robust forms of common life and political solidarity in the muck of their suffering and loneliness, forged innovative and atypical political spaces within cityscapes on digital capitalism's cutting edge, and converted the scattershot-yet-continuous drumbeats of precaritized time into opportunities for developing new organizational forms for autonomously collective action. Those who seek answers to the questions about precarity formulated in this introduction should consider taking a sojourn among day laborers and listening to how they think about time, space, suffering, community, politics, and work.

A sojourn: a detour from what might seem like more urgently needed inquiries with workers central to the digital and logistical economies; an extravagant expenditure of time in an era when none of us has time to spare; a tarrying with the temporary, at which the word's etymology hints (with the antecedent Latin *subdiurnare*[59] and Old French *surjurn*,[60] words related to Latino day laborers' self-designation, *jornaleros*); an irresponsible digression from *work*, shirking the social-scientific labor of dutifully scrutinizing policies, institutions, and populations more obviously decisive for the shape of the polity; a search for contemplative repose and reinvigoration through transitory relocation elsewhere. It is perhaps the most heartrending, and heartening, contradiction in the lives of day laborers that even as they express with poetry and grim precision what it means to face necessity's relentless pull and the obligation to work without rest, they are creating social spheres where work is not all, where there is time for freedom, and where the people's precarity catalyzes the precaritization of capital's rule.

I was initially drawn to learn more about day laborers while finishing an earlier research project about migrant workers employed at a large meatpacking plant owned by Tyson Foods.[61] A corporate titan whose beef, chicken, and pork products dominate world markets, Tyson operated a cattle slaughterhouse and beef-processing plant near my home in eastern Washington State that generated job-related injuries and illnesses with astonishing frequency. The broader factory culture was rife with unfair, degrading, and illegal labor practices. Banding together at first quietly but then with growing boldness and numbers, immigrant workers at this plant ultimately staged the largest wildcat (i.e., unauthorized) strike in decades, took control of their local union (Teamsters Local 556), democratized its internal operations, and launched challenges against Tyson on multiple fronts. Interviewing the Tyson workers gave me a gruesome familiarity with the mechanisms that systematically expose migrant meatpackers' bodies to disfigurement, pain, and death. I also learned that for migrant workers, bodily endangerment and its psychological comorbidities are hardly confined to meatpacking—they permeate all reaches of the low-wage migrant laboring world. Particularly energetic efforts to tackle job health and safety problems, I then found, were underway among day laborers, who were studying occupational safety and health (OSH) problems and developing training activities through the nontraditional labor organizations they called worker centers, while also calling badly needed attention to a wide range of other deplorable working conditions in many areas of the low-wage labor economy.[62]

Worker centers, I soon realized, were quirky places that fomented power among day laborers in ways both similar to and different from the processes of solidarity-building I had witnessed among Tyson workers in their Teamsters local union. Above all, I noticed a puzzling contrast between the significant political influence worker centers seemed to exert and the dolorous poverty, acute marginalization, and personal crisis-states of most members. The Local 556 unionists had been fully employed individuals with stable homes and families, notwithstanding the personal agony and turmoil that resulted from the injury mill at the plant, and they were also mainly legalized migrants. Day laborers at Seattle's Casa Latina and Portland's Martin Luther King, Jr. Day Labor Center (MLK Center), the two worker centers where I began new research, were in much more dire straits. About half the workers were homeless; virtually all were legally unauthorized; many were "food insecure," as the delicate euphemism puts it; many struggled with substance abuse; their family and personal lives were often a wreck, or at least under severe duress; almost all were men who had migrated from Latin America, and the minority who were trying to support families abroad or in the United States seemed unable to do so consistently; they moved locations constantly, although at irregular intervals, largely because they lacked stable jobs. More than a few day laborers told me they had relocated temporarily to the Midwest to work in meatpacking but then left due to injuries, pain, or stress from those jobs. Skeptically, I wondered: if, unlike the stalwarts who doggedly waged Local 556's decade-long fight despite the brutality of their jobs and the company's vicious attacks, these workers had quit and moved on, then what were the chances day laborers could contribute much insight about contesting neoliberal capitalism? How, indeed, could anyone in circumstances so thoroughly precarious be expected to develop an activist will, a critical consciousness, and a commitment to common struggle?

Casa Latina and the Voz Workers' Rights and Education Project (Voz), the MLK Center's parent organization, held precious assets Local 556 lacked, however. The worker centers were gradually and methodically sending down roots in their urban communities, which was ironic because their very physical structures were visible testaments to day laborers' wobbly and transient existence. In 2008– 10, when I conducted most of the fieldwork for this book, both organizations operated out of run-down trailers perched tenuously in the shadows of the downtown viaduct (Seattle) or just off the freeway's edges (Portland). Yet Voz and Casa Latina were also forging enduring relationships with local groups: Latino advocacy organizations; nonprofit associations; social-justice-oriented churches; municipal officials; university research shops; student organizations; service learning courses—even labor unions, despite the obstacles to cooperation imposed by competition for construction jobs. Like most other worker centers in the United States, these organizations were in the process of growing beyond initially underfunded and "undernetworked" origins into groups with more stable membership bases and denser community ties.[63] Although Latino small businesses and churches had at first rallied to the Tyson workers' cause, that support had waned over time, and the reformed union's later efforts to build new community bases, ambitious though they were, did not survive Tyson's eventual busting of the union. Brilliant as it flared up in the "hot shop" atmosphere at the plant, and instructive for the critical analysis of race, class, migration, and power under neoliberalism, the meatpackers' movement never implicated itself into a larger and more durable solidarity network. Casa Latina and Voz were also tossing out lifelines far beyond their respective cities when I started my research and have continued to do so avidly. At that time, under the leadership of the National Day Labor Organizing Network (NDLON), which Voz and Casa Latina helped found, day labor organizations were embracing more militant antideportation activism.[64] The intensifying political vitality of the immigrant rights movement, which day labor groups had fueled since their inception, thus further infused these organizations. By the time of Donald Trump's election, Casa Latina and Voz had assumed indispensable roles within the political infrastructure pursuing migrant justice in the Pacific Northwest.

Popular Education and the Constellating of Theory

Still another important difference between migrant worker activism via Casa Latina and Voz centers in comparison to the Tyson mobilization was that worker centers organizers had a more autonomously developed *theory* of transformative social action. Worker-activists in Local 556 had eagerly embraced principles of rank-and-file democracy borrowed from Teamsters for a Democratic

Union (TDU), a long-running effort to build leadership from below within the International Brotherhood of Teamsters. Viewing union governance and legal action as scaffolding for worker-leadership development rather than the realms of elites serving passive clients, these migrants had made the union the animated body of the workers-in-struggle. Moreover, through shared narratives that linked the battle at Tyson to harrowing experiences of migration, workers had recrafted the TDU approach as their own intellectual creature. The day labor centers, however, drew on a theoretical disposition with organic antecedents in Latino migrant and Latin American working-class activism, and with a less embattled, more intuitive, and more palpable presence among participants. This was the theory and practice known as *popular education*. Casa Latina, Voz, and their network partners celebrated a theoretical culture oriented by popular education, although this culture was often more a manifestation of taken-for-granted common sense and habitual affect than the result of intentionally elaborating and implementing a conceptual model.

Here was a new opportunity and growth challenge for me, as a researcher and theorist. In my earlier project, I had advanced an egalitarian approach to social theory by seeing migrant workers' narratives as bases for developing a Gramscian critique of hegemony's reliance on ordinary people's common sense. Yet those workers, although appropriating TDU concepts and attitudes in ways that resonated deeply with Gramsci, had never conceived of their own stories and struggles in Gramscian terms. Day labor organizations possessed a more home-grown intellectual account of their own activities. In addition, their popular-educational culture spoke directly to methodological issues regarding how one might relate academic theory to vernacular speech and how social research can help motivate popular action for radical social change. In this situation, engaging day laborers and worker center organizers as intellectual collaborators implied an obligation on my part—and a prospect I found exciting—to draw upon popular education in crafting the interpretive procedures and categories for my analysis.

Proceeding in this manner gives this project affinities to other critical and political theorists' recent interventions, to which it may be helpful to compare this book. Like Romand Coles, I immerse theory within activist contexts as a way of sparking theoretical ideas about how to undertake radically democratic action in the face of neoliberal capitalism's profoundly antidemocratic and socially oppressive onslaught.[65] My explorations of precarity in day laborers' bodily experiences and thought-worlds further synergize with Coles's avid engagement with affective politics in Arizona migrant collectivities of resistance. Coles and I also share a curiosity regarding modes of transformational action that are densely imbricated within congealments of domination yet strike out beyond them. Recent investigations by Raymond A. Rocco and Alfonso Gonzales also meaningfully resemble what I seek to accomplish here. Rocco gauges the demo-cratic electricity that circulated through Latino and migrant informal-mutualist networks in East Los Angeles in the 1990s, in the wake of massive job flight and social program cuts. His fieldwork propels an alternative conception of "asso-ciational democracy" that overturns theorists' common assumptions about the proper institutional foci and practices of democratic action.[66] Gonzales fashions an incisive account of the "anti-migrant hegemony" orchestrated by the US "homeland security state."[67] He does this, in part, through conversing with Latino migrant workers in Southern California warehouses as well as with deportees who confront life-threatening circumstances upon their forced relocation to El Salvador. With all these scholar-activists, I hold a common commitment to doing research that takes an active and self-reflective role in migrant workers' struggles on the ground and that produces theory from within those contexts.

How, exactly, to do this, is a complicated question that admits of multiple valid answers. My approach derives its specific orientation from the popular-educational culture percolating among day laborers today, and thus I strive to be studiously attentive to these workers' thoughts and situations of everyday life. In the pages ahead, readers will find a series of sustained, fine-grained, carefully wrought encounters with thematic elements of day laborers' commentaries about searching for work, performing day labor jobs, interacting with employers, and participating in worker center communities. To some, this might seem like a form of ethnography because it prizes meditation on the specificities and idiosyncratic wrinkles of people's everyday speech as well as their micro-level, habitual, corpo-real, and communal practices. Especially since so many anthropologists conceive of ethnography as immersed in intersubjective relations with the people whose lives are at issue, and sometimes in political struggles alongside them, family resemblances abound between my project and ethnographic research.[68] Also, within political science, a small but feisty contingent of scholars has recently taken up the banner of ethnography to demand greater recognition of research that employs qualitative methods, in a situation where quantitative inquiries still enjoy the greatest prestige in the discipline.[69] I am grateful to have found soli-darity among these researchers for the kind of analysis I carry out here.

Nevertheless, what I offer differs from most ethnography in two related respects, and understanding these differences helps convey what makes this proj-ect methodologically distinctive. First, an investment in theory is fundamental to this book. By "theory," I mean both (1) the critical elaboration and exploratory reformulation of general social-analytical concepts that proceeds self-consciously in the context of historically based, critical-theoretical textual genealogies, al-though not necessarily with the goal of extending any one particular strand; and (2) the characterization of social phenomena in analytically stimulating or reflective ways by people who are not usually recognized, and typically do not regard themselves, as "theorists." Rather than primarily seeking to satisfy a curiosity about the complexities of people's vocalized and lived experiences and subordinating theory to the probing of such nuances, I aim to activate mutually enlivening moments of contact between popular conceptions and scholars' attempts to describe and account for precarity in social-structural terms. The point is to see how ordinary migrant workers theorize both their own specific circumstances and more broadly ranging social predicaments in distinctive ways that at once resonate with, diverge from, and can spur critical rearticulation of notions of precarity suggested by those who theorize in academic registers—and vice versa.

Second, this book has metatheoretical ambitions, which are to sculpt a subtly contoured figure of *how* to conceive of and call forth this resonant relation while also modeling how to fashion such a figure by reflecting on migrant workers' own theoretical culture. I thus hope to furnish a stimulating example of how similar critiques could be carried out with other groups in other contexts, taking up whatever cultures of theory such groups honor and practice. In addition, I hope to foster more critical appreciation for the political-intellectual resources offered in this respect by popular education—that is, concerning how to enact encounters between academic social critique and popular understandings of power, such that these juxtapositions embody a spirit of intellectual equality and emanate political vibrancy. This intention fosters a kinship between this book and the work of James Tully, whose call for theorists to pursue "public philosophy in a new key" I affirm. Tully encourages theorists to "establish pedagogical relationships of reciprocal elucidation between academic research and the civic activities of fellow citizens."[70] For Tully (and for day labor leaders, as the final chapter discusses), citizenship is thus a practical rather than narrowly legal designation.[71] The category also includes academics and activists alike, and it accentuates dialogical relations of mutual learning, just as popular education does.[72]

The principle of reciprocity oriented my field investigations for this project, which centrally comprised individual interviews but also included participant observation at the Seattle and Portland worker centers. Two bilingual research assistants and I conducted seventy-eight interviews in total with day laborers at Casa Latina (in 2008) and Voz's MLK Center (in 2010).[73] I worked out the interview questions through processes of mutual accommodation with coordinators at each center, settling on paths of inquiry meant to yield useful information for these organizations while also furthering my academic aims and with an overarching ethos aptly described by Tully's notion of public philosophy.[74] The interviews explored workers' experiences seeking jobs at the centers, on day labor corners, and in other fields of work; their encounters with employers, occupational safety and health concerns, and other working conditions; the general circumstances of workers' everyday lives and needs; workers' conceptions of community membership at the centers; and workers' thoughts and experiences regarding political action through the centers or otherwise. At each center, systematic and extensive participant observation in the context of regular volunteer work at the worker center complemented the conduct of interviews. I describe our volunteer activities in detail in chapter 1. For the most part, my assistants and I taught English classes at the MLK Center; we took employers' calls and dispatched workers at Casa Latina; we supplemented these efforts with many other activities in both locations. Through these endeavors, we all came to feel part of those communities, enjoying day-to-day friendly acquaintances with workers, staff, and other volunteers. The interview process further strengthened these ties, inasmuch as we performed them at the center or a few steps around the corner, with the aid of coordinators who ran spirited lotteries for the interviews and vocally played up the importance of these conversations, and also because the interviews, themselves, for which we paid workers twenty dollars apiece, materially wove together the political-educational aspects of the center cultures with these organizations' economic activities, in characteristic ways that I explore in depth in chapter 5. As I discuss further in chapter 1, all these personal experiences provided a concrete basis for listening attentively to the workers' interview-commentaries in the analyses that unfold in chapters 2–5 and for attributing various social-critical and political provocations to them, despite certain misapprehensions that doubtless exist in the pages ahead. Importantly, we treated the question protocol as a basic organizational tool and a flexible spur to relatively open-ended exchanges: we engaged with participants on topics they brought up as significant even if our questions did not cover those issues. We also made a point of asking participants not just to describe their experiences but also, following the core thrust of popular education, to share their thoughts about the reasons behind problems and the forms of action that could address them.[75]

In a sense, this book participates in popular education by conducting preparatory activities for it, although my theoretical and metatheoretical interests also mark the project at hand as different from an exercise in popular education per se. As the next chapter argues, Paulo Freire's early texts offer compelling reasons to view the critical correspondences I evoke between workers' themes and academicians' concepts as vitally conducive to the popular-educational process of "conscientization" (*conscientizaçao*). My discussions of day laborers' themes partly seek to provision organizers with fruitful material for "dialogues," in the Freirean sense of interactive and affectively charged discussions through which oppressed persons identify problem situations in their lives and develop a critical sense of how they can transform these conditions. I have conducted experimental dialogues informed by workers' themes that confirmed my characterization of these themes as intellectually and politically generative for day laborers, as I recount in chapter 4. On the whole, however, this book seeks to lay groundwork for popular education, through analytical procedures critically drawn from popular education, rather than practice popular education—which, as any organizer with Casa Latina or Voz will tell you, would consist in reiterated dialogical interactions in real time among people in the flesh. This also means that in this project, I am the one responsible for the interpretations here of what day laborers seem to be saying. Only in the case of workers' themes regarding occupational safety and health, and even then, through just one workshop, have I exposed my readings of day laborers' commentaries to workers' critical scrutiny in an organized and methodical fashion, although I have discussed my analysis casually with coordinators, workers, and volunteers on numerous occasions. Nonetheless, Freire's writings suggest the distinctive value of the novel form of critique I unfold here as a prelude to popular education. Furthermore, as the next chapter contends, radically transforming precaritized conditions not only requires practicing popular education among local groups of working people; it also demands efforts to knit those endeavors to much larger embodiments of collective action. Envisioning the terms of such connections is precisely the point of combining popular-educational priorities and perspectives with interventions in critical theory.

Apart from my methodologically oriented critical recuperation of Freire, the chapters that follow foreground an eclectic assortment of theoretical writings selected because of the luminosity each acquires when placed in proximity to day laborers' themes, to which it reciprocally lends a distinct glow. My textual archive is weighted somewhat toward autonomist Marxism but, on the whole, is purposefully not confined to any particular school of thought, much less any canonical theorist or theoretical construct (thus differing, for instance, from the way my analysis of the Tyson workers' narratives sought to rearticulate Foucault's conception of biopolitics). Instead, this archive brings together a cluster of theoretical texts chosen because of each one's capacity to resonate, in its own way, with workers' commentaries, such that the two forms of theorizing disclose more about precarity jointly than each could do by itself. That said, my successive pairings of workers' themes and scholars' concepts do yield a tenuously coherent account of precarity: as both lamentable condition and political opportunity; as both targeted at the hyperoppressed and extending throughout society; and as having certain key temporal, spatial, bodily, and ethical aspects. What makes thinkers as diverse as Kathi Weeks, Lauren Berlant, David Harvey, Franco "Bifo" Berardi, Hagar Kotef, David Weil, Nicholas De Genova, Raymond A. Rocco, Anna Lowenhaupt Tsing, Cristina Beltrán, and Romand Coles all capable of contributing to this theorization of precarity, in particular, is their common ability to join day laborers in revealing the defining *temporalities* of precaritization in ways that simultaneously suggest political tactics for contesting these time formations and time deformations. This, then, is theory as the provisional and politically entangled construction of thought constellations rather than as the developmental extension of a theoretical tradition that subjects itself to dutifully rigorous self-critique. As the charting of constellations, such theory inevitably partakes of the fortuitous. This situationally configured theory is also especially attuned to the singular rhythms of historically generated currents surging in the present, and better outfitted for illuminating, by faint starlight, courses through and beyond them.

Day Laborers and Counterprecarity Politics

This book aims not just to rethink precaritization but also to help fight it. The passion for *political* research that animates this effort echoes similar expressions of resolve in writings by Coles, Tully, Dean, Gonzales, and others, albeit with the distinctive sonorities that my particular style of engaged theory emits. This commitment to research that gains a critical edge from its conduct within contexts of political struggle, rather than from any inevitably misleading pretense of detached objectivity, also links my endeavor to important undertakings outside political theory. Some might consider the project at hand a species of "militant research," for example, and I would affirm this association. As Glenda Garelli and Martina Tazzioli explain, the qualifier "militant" signifies the dislodging of research from the depoliticizing snares of "its incorporation within the academic practices of a '-Studies,'" such as "migration studies" or "labor studies."[76] These theorists also intend the moniker of militancy to evoke historical associations with the practice of collaborative research developed by Italian workerist movements during the 1960s that later gained adherents in Argentina:

> Militant researchers sought workers' direct engagement in social research, to sift through the transformations that occurred within the system of production and to come up with new strategies for workers' struggle. The explicit goal was to overcome the distance between the researcher and the target of the research (hence the name *conricerca*/co-research); to craft a knowledge practice stripped of the "comfort of 'critical distance' with regards to the object" (as [the Argentinian organization] Colectivo Situaciones would later put it), and thus to stage a mode of enquiry rooted in a particular point of view, i.e. that of the workers' struggles. It was a political goal: making certain knowledges part of, and tools for, social and political struggle.[77]

My effort to situate research squarely within determinate fields of political and social struggle also connects this book to Aziz Choudry's explorations of "the knowledge about systems of power and exploitation developed as people find themselves in confrontation with states and capital," whether in the Quebec student movement, antiausterity organizing in the Philippines, or elsewhere.[78] I have written this book as a participant in day laborers' and worker centers' struggles to demand justice on city streets, in the sequestered spaces of employers' homes, and against the deportation regime. More precisely, this text has emerged in the midst of an as yet only partial politicization among ordinary day laborers, as organizers strive to spin the straw of precarity into the gold of power. I proceed with the task of envisioning such political activation and exploring its possible links to wider forms of solidarity, upon the premise that intellectual collaboration with day laborers is indispensable to this endeavor.

Strategic considerations also underscore the value of investigating day laborers' working worlds and political initiatives for any broad-scale attempt to contest the forces of precaritization. In part, this value stems from the fact that day labor organizing is happening in rapidly mutating global cityscapes that day laborers are physically building and that therefore depend on their cooperation with the capitalist forces engineering these changes. In other words, day labor *is* a strategically significant aspect of the current economy, even if these workers do not perform communicative or digital labor. Residential housing construction throughout the United States now structurally relies on migrant day labor, even as commercial real estate construction continues to depend on traditionally unionized workers in the building trades.[79] Day labor also has been thoroughly integrated into the burgeoning economy for home improvement projects that renovate, enlarge, and beautify people's dwellings and yards. The home remodeling and residential construction industries, in turn, connect the work of day laborers to the enormous growth of Home Depot and other such retail companies. The significance of day labor for contemporary urban capitalism also goes beyond providing an easily exploitable labor force for dynamic industries: these economic-sectoral activities are hardwired into the most frenetic circuits of financial capital via the mortgage and consumer-debt industries. Furthermore, the home improvement retail firms help solidify the recently evolved capitalist strategy of boosting accumulation by relying on logistics-enabled "just in time" supply chains.[80] In addition to all these material implications of day labor for capital today, furthermore, business activities in the areas of home renovation and construction bolster American fantasies about the family and the livable city in an era when a bewildering array of socioeconomic forces have rendered these ideologies fragile. In sum, migrant day labor is implicated in post-Fordist, globalized, digitized, logistical, financialized capitalism in intricate and extensive ways that are belied by these workers' socially marginal status.

Similarly, as I have noted, the political vigor and sway of day labor groups contrast strikingly with day laborers' socially peripheral condition, and this curious incongruence reflects day labor organizations' tactical ingenuity and catholicity. The one nationwide study of day laborers, conducted in 2004, found a median hourly wage among day laborers of just $10 and monthly earnings that ranged from $500 in slow seasons to $1,400 during peak periods.[81] Just under 120,000 worked or searched for jobs as day laborers on any given day, in a tremendously fluid labor force that individuals enter or exit daily; it was also a small labor force, representing less than 1 percent of total employment in 2006.[82] The study further found that three-quarters of day laborers were unauthorized migrants, mostly from Mexico (59 percent of all day laborers) and Central America (28 percent) and that 60 percent had lived in the United States for six years or less.[83] Other research notes that even though day laborers typically experience egregious violations of basic fair labor standards, few are even aware that they have any rights under labor law much less disposed to seek legal or political redress for these injustices.[84] Nevertheless, by inventively combining direct action, community organizing, policy advocacy, and other modes of struggle, day labor groups have wielded far greater power than day laborers' humble numbers and marginal circumstances would lead us to expect. During the second Obama administration, for instance, day labor groups and their coalition partners mobilized blockades of ICE vehicles and hunger strikes that successfully pressured the initially reluctant president to grant a temporary deportation reprieve to millions of undocumented youth and then to propose a similar stay for their parents. Simultaneously, day labor organizations deployed other tactics to advocate for comprehensive immigration reform, including congressional lobbying and internet-enabled mass petition campaigns.[85] These groups' work-targeted initiatives have evinced a similar strategic versatility, tacking among First Amendment–based lawsuits defending workers' rights to solicit jobs in public spaces, the patient assembling of urban coalitions to gain municipal funding for worker centers, shoe-leather-on-pavement organizing to set wage floors at day labor corners, and boisterous pickets outside the homes of employers who short workers' wages.[86]

Day labor groups' organizational forms also hold provocative implications for a politics of precarity, in ways that speak to the heated debates about this issue among political theorists and social activists alike. At a time when the traditional labor movement can no longer make even a dubious claim to represent the US working class and even in countries where unions historically have achieved far greater institutionalized power, the future of working-class solidarity depends significantly on the growth of alternative workers' organizations such as worker centers. To be sure, unionism maintains or is even increasing its vitality in various places and industries, and some unions have built strong memberships among precaritized workers despite their lack of a consistent employer or workplace. Migrant workers have been motor forces behind not only the spread of worker centers but also much union rejuvenation, as impressive campaigns among low-wage security workers, hotel workers, janitors, and garment workers illustrate.[87] Nonetheless, the exploding variety of work-arrangements, especially in terms of work process and employment temporalities, spatial locations and fluxes, and legal governance, demands fluid and inventive organizational responses. Migrant workers have acted as innovators in this respect, too. The National Domestic Workers Alliance (NDWA), for instance, surged in strength after its 2007 founding and a decade later counted over sixty affiliated organizations and more than twenty thousand members.[88] Pressured by the NDWA, California, New York, Illinois, and several other states have passed "domestic workers bills of rights" mandating minimum wages and establishing unprecedented fair labor standards for these workers. Through transnational alliances in pursuit of global-level institutional action, in turn, the NDWA and allied groups from other countries pushed the ILO to issue a first-ever Convention and Recommendation on domestic workers' rights in 2011.[89] Migrant warehouse workers in Southern California have accomplished similarly startling results through novel kinds of worker organizations. Inventively mixing organizing along commodity chains with direct action, lawsuits, and labor coalition-building in a campaign that began in 2008, Warehouse Workers United brought Walmart to heel, forcing the corporate giant to improve its workplace standards.[90]

Worker centers offer another response to the pressing need for organizational ingenuity that brims with future promise. This book partly aims to demonstrate how and why worker centers show such potential as organizational vehicles for antiprecarity politics, particularly in the last two chapters and especially in ways that day labor organizations manifest. Here at the outset, however, a few basic considerations are worth noting. One is that worker centers have grown rapidly in numbers and have established themselves as pivotal participants in the migrant justice and workers' rights communities in most major cities, in fairly short order. In 1992, just five worker centers existed; by 2013, there were over two hundred. The great majority of these organizations also serve and are firmly grounded within migrant communities.[91] In my reflections on the fifth thesis, I underlined that countering precaritization demands spatially attuned, place-making politics among working people who are perpetually "on the move." Worker centers promote just this sort of action: they ground organizing in specific urban communities and thus furnish essential local tethers for workers who are otherwise prone to severe spatial, temporal, cultural, occupational, and personal dislocation.[92] In addition, worker centers have been organized among a wide variety of ethnic-national groups. Even though most people involved in US worker centers (and almost all who attend Casa Latina or Voz's MLK Center) are Latin American migrants, large numbers of West African migrants populate the Casa de Maryland worker centers near Washington, DC, Chicago's Latino Union worker center has seen an influx of Polish migrants,[93] and influential worker centers exist in the Korean and Filipino communities of Los Angeles.[94]

As day labor groups exemplify, worker centers also have built networks on multiple geopolitical scales, thus striving to keep pace with capitalism's global kinesis, its fueling of worker transience, and its decimation of the union movement in the United States.[95] Worker centers have forged sturdy ties to "popular organizations in the countries from which workers have migrated."[96] They also have joined in global "movement building" through the Excluded Workers Congress, which worker centers helped found at the 2010 World Social Forum and which has brought day laborers together with domestic workers, farmworkers, restaurant workers, and other highly precaritized working people.[97] Along with these ventures, the day labor network has developed cooperative arrangements with unions that have intensified traditional labor's focus on workers who are "on the move." Increasing coordination between unions and worker centers in California during the 1990s created momentum for the adoption in 2000 by the American Federation of Labor and Congress of Industrial Organizations (AFL-CIO) of an unprecedented resolution to promote immigrant rights and to prioritize organizing migrants.[98] By the time of the massive immigrant rights marches of 2006, NDLON and the AFL-CIO had established a formal partnership.[99] A 2015 report commissioned by the Labor Innovations for the 21st Century Fund reaffirmed worker centers' and unions' commitment to "Building a Movement Together."[100]

Just as worker centers provide a politicizing form of grounding for migrant workers on the move, so likewise, they furnish environments for grappling creatively and politically with the myriad ways in which precaritized workers are "out of time." Again, this book makes the case at length in the later chapters that these organizations operate this way for day laborers—and that worker centers have untapped wellsprings of this sort for precaritized workers in general. To begin this line of thought, however: one of the first curiosities that sparked my enthusiasm for conducting research at day labor centers was noticing how these organizations seemed to refunction the embattled time of everyday life for those who attended. Workers congregated at Casa Latina and Voz's MLK Center during awkward pauses in their work activities and work searches, more often just waiting around than expeditiously getting dispatched on jobs. Yet at the centers, this waiting time could become something other than merely dead or suspended time. To be sure, I saw plenty of workers who just kept to themselves, seemingly preferring to be left "on their own" as they sat in boredom with the slim hope of hearing their names called in the job lotteries. Other workers, however, joined in animated conversations about all sorts of topics, from World Cup matches to free trade agreements, soup kitchen hours, and weather reports. Overlaying these lively informal interactions were (loosely) organized activities: English classes, arts projects, know-your-rights workshops on immigration enforcement, and worker assemblies that usually featured vibrant debates and moments of humor. Sometimes, a worker pulled out a guitar and began singing and playing, either to himself or with others listening. In my very first visit to Voz's MLK Center as a volunteer English teacher, I was abruptly assigned a minor role in a slapdash "theater of the oppressed" exercise that coordinators cooked up to prod workers into reflecting on stubborn racial and ethnic tensions among them. As the exercise progressed, I heard and saw workers transition from play-acted griping about the filthy habits of "peasants" from Guatemala's highlands or Mexico City "delinquents," to accelerating hand-clapping in unison as the contrived character of the exercise dawned on those assembled, to candid discussion about how to combat unfair preconceptions that sapped the community's power. What struck me on this and other occasions was not only the diverse range of affects such activities encouraged, and not just the fact that the centers seemed able, against stiff odds, to nurture a common spirit and a sense of abundance among deeply isolated, poor, and discouraged migrant workers. It was also how intentional, improvisational, and informally connective activities emerged within mundane time-gaps in the precarious work-economy—and then *remade* the time of everyday precarity into novel, unpredictable, and politically generative temporalities.

In sum, taking a sojourn among day laborers not only furnishes intellectually enlivening prospects for reworking critical theories of precarity while feeding popular-educational efforts to ignite theory-on-the-ground among the oppressed, but this apparently digressive journey also carries real political stakes for the fight against precaritization. The stakes derive from day laborers' crucial participation in urban residential construction and home improvement economies, with their multiple material and ideological vectors. Augmenting the need for this sort of study are day labor organizations' strategic ecumenism, tactical versatility, and outsized influence in the worlds of public policy and migrant justice activism. Signs also abound that worker centers and the day labor network have much to teach, and a great deal to offer in practice, in the effort to develop dynamic and sustaining time-spaces of political action for workers who are out of time, on the move, and on their own as they suffer the effects of today's precaritized working world.

Stages of Critical-Popular Exploration

The chapters ahead pursue this critique of precarity in partnership with day laborers and other critical theorists through a series of steps. I first develop and justify my approach of critical-popular analysis in chapter 1, in dialogue with Freire's theory of popular education. Crafting a procedure for critical social research to participate meaningfully in social and political transformation, this chapter reconstructs from Freire's early writings a conception of fieldwork among oppressed groups that sheds light on structures of power and names these power formations in politically galvanizing ways. Freire calls such nominative activity the articulation of "generative themes"; chapter 1 elaborates the qualities that enable themes to "generate" critical consciousness and political action and suggests how researchers can recognize such themes in interview transcripts. After specifying how such research can equip local groups of oppressed people to tackle social-theoretical and political labors through popular education, this chapter also takes on a further challenge: delineating a complementary process of *critical-popular* investigation that discloses larger-scale opportunities for radical worker solidarities by staging encounters between particular groups' generative themes and structurally oriented theories of social power. The chapter then concludes by reflecting on how best to construe the relation between generative-thematic inquiry and political action. Here, I argue that militant and receptive affects stimulated through both Freirean popular-educational dialogue and demand-politics, as conceptualized by Kathi Weeks, can reconstitute political subjectivities in radically transformative ways within localized contexts. Critical-popular insights, in turn, coax into view the broader-scope and audaciously utopian implications of such mutations.

Three chapters then follow that take up day laborers' major themes regarding their circumstances of work and work searches, as voiced during the interviews. Chapters 2–4 thus construct a differentiated account of contemporary precarity guided by day laborers' reflections in conjunction with resonant conceptions drawn from recent social-theoretical writings. These discussions accentuate the temporal, ethical, and corporeal dimensions of precaritized work-life as well as the antiprecarity political priorities that various juxtapositions of theme and theory bring to light. Each chapter also attends to certain masculine qualities of the workers' themes and considers how these gendered features limit the significance of day labor as a synecdoche for precaritization writ large. As I discuss in each main portion of the analysis, other research often suggests how women migrant workers—for instance, the domestic workers who are becoming increasingly influential leaders and participants in worker centers and the day labor network—would likely frame the temporalities, bodily constraints, and ethical dilemmas of precarity differently, while still probably pointing to many of the same problems. One important implication of this study is thus that additional critical-popular inquiries with women migrant workers, as well as with more racially and ethnically diverse worker-center communities than those at Voz's MLK Center and Casa Latina, would help further elaborate a politics of precarity capable of attracting widespread commitment and mustering radical energies.

Chapter 2 explores the ironic pairing of "desperation" with "responsibility" as themes through which day laborers characterize their everyday trials seeking highly uncertain and fleeting employment stints as unauthorized migrants. Probing these themes uncovers a hallmark structure of time in everyday life that re-emerges in related forms in this book's subsequent generative-thematic investigations: a conflict between time's stifling uniformity and immutability, as the urgent need for work never subsides while the worker's anxiety steadily mounts, and abrupt, frequent, and unforeseeable shifts in everyday temporal experience with each job lottery, each new gig, and every altered set of employer predilections. Further complicating this temporal conundrum is an imagined time-trajectory associated with workers' striking claims of personal responsibility to ensure their own economic sustenance and success through hard work. Shifting the gaze from workers' commentaries to social theory, I then ponder how this ironic syndrome of "desperate responsibility," which avows fidelity to personal duty under conditions that preclude any meaningful choice about whether to act dutifully or not, applies exceptionally to migrant workers who are uncommonly vulnerable to economic crises and to deportation. Yet with the ascent of affective and digital labor, along with a post-Fordist work ethic that grounds all personal satisfaction in work but disables such fulfillment by making work incessant, the theme of "desperate responsibility" designates a predicament stretching far beyond the forlorn world of day labor. This brushing together of workers' themes with theories of neoliberal crisis (David Harvey), the deportation regime (Nicholas De Genova), the contemporary work culture (Kathi Weeks), and labor's new psychopathologies (Bifo Berardi) thus generates insight into specifically temporalized and moralized structures of precarity. It also clarifies the political orientations needed to address these problems, especially more militant opposition to an increasingly desperate work culture and a vicious deportation apparatus.

Day laborers who attend worker centers often also seek jobs on street corners, and for most day laborers, looking for work on the corner comprises an indelible episode in their personal stories of migrating and straining to find economic footing. Chapter 3 thus delves into our interviewees' accounts of "fighting for the job," as they put it, in these perilously tense and arbitrarily policed urban time-spaces. This generative theme connotes a distinctly embodied experience of temporal contradictions mapped out initially in chapter 2. On the corner, protracted temporal stasis, registered by the worker's motionless body and its slow evacuation of vitality, gets punctuated at random intervals by outbreaks of frantic physical combat, as day laborers compete for jobs when employers arrive. Nevertheless, day laborers strive to mitigate this temporal predicament by envisioning the corner as their launching pad toward a future path of steady upward mobility enabled by entrepreneurial time management. In one sense, I show, day laborers' split body-time on the corner reflects matrices of legal and cultural power in neoliberal societies that govern subaltern people's habits of mobility, induce violations of liberal norms, and legitimate state interventions to control and expel such people. Yet "fighting for the job" also fittingly characterizes a more widespread problem: working people's self-defeating tendency to substitute dreams for weakly approximating economic stability and upward mobility in place of hopes for material improvement and viable collective strategies to enable such success. By juxtaposing workers' themes with Hagar Kotef's critique of liberal mobility-governance and Lauren Berlant's analysis of precaritized subjectivity, this chapter thus yields a sharpened sense of precarious body-time in both exceptional and near-universal modes. In addition, I find provocations for rechanneling workers' fighting spirit into militant refusals of work and repudiations of deportation in Voz's documentary film *Jornaleros*, in which day laborer-musicians stage transformative incursions into the corner's vexed time-space.

Day laborers' imperiled body-time also involves constant exposure to workplace health and safety hazards, and so chapter 4 takes up workers' themes on this issue: their notion of facing "risk on all sides" and struggling to keep their "eyes wide open" for emergent dangers. In bodily threatening work, the temporal contradiction between stultifying continuity and ruptural discontinuity reproduces itself in still other ways for day laborers. The fear and prospects of injury never abate and the pain from untreated maladies never ebbs, even as new hazards arise without warning and sometimes wreak sudden bodily harm. In response, day laborers often embrace practices of responsible bodily stewardship and try to control everyday flows of work time more autonomously. Yet these individualist strategies ironically intensify workers' embroilment in the very protocols of risky work they strain to avoid. This predicament of precarity, too, has its exceptional and synecdochal dimensions. From one perspective, it is the special lot of impoverished nonwhite migrant workers whom the deportation regime drives into the most dangerous jobs and presses into silence before callous or abusive employers. From another point of view, the burgeoning "risk on all sides" and the imperative to keep "eyes wide open" for dangers apply to working people throughout the economy. Day laborers put words on virtually all workers' vulnerabilities in an age when work-environmental health and safety threats are climbing, especially as subcontracting and other employment-restructuring moves relieve the largest companies of responsibility for workers' bodily integrity. Day laborers also express with sober lucidity how worker-subjects in all sectors reinforce these processes by adopting ideologies of personal responsibility, such as those propagated through corporate employee wellness programs. These critical-popular vantage-points emerge from positioning workers' themes alongside David Weil's study of post-Fordist employment relations and Lauren Berlant's critique of embodied subjectivities wrought through interactions of dangerous work with public discourses about nonwhite workers' unhealthy bodies. From these viewpoints, we can glimpse another essential facet of an antiprecarity politics: the need to take sides unequivocally against capital's transmutation of financial risk for the very few into corporeal risk for the great many.

Chapter 5 continues the close reading of day laborers' comments but shifts the focus toward workers' remarks about their community-building efforts through Casa Latina and Voz's MLK Center. This chapter thus bridges the critique of precarity in the book's middle parts with the formulation toward the book's end of an antiprecarity politics that can be—and is being—practiced by people thoroughly entangled in the hardships and contradictions of precarious work-life. In the midst of these difficulties, many workers narrow their vision for worker-center community life to the promotion of work opportunities through strict discipline and top-down authority aimed at insulating hard workers who deserve those chances from obstacles created by idlers and drunkards in their own ranks. Preserving participants' unity as a workforce, in ways implicating deceptively complex Latino or *mexicano* racial and ethnic identities, becomes the mantra for day laborers who view worker centers this way. Many other day laborers, however, convert these apprehensions about security, work, and division into motivations for reaching out to one another through informal networks of conviviality and mutual care, which in turn form a vibrant practical basis for workers' autonomously collective action both within the centers and in the wider urban society. By constellating workers' themes regarding this inventive style of convivial politics with resonant concepts in contemporary radical-democratic theory, we gain a vivid sense of the processes by which a politics of precarity can gather momentum. This exercise both leans on and critically modifies Raymond A. Rocco's notion of associational citizenship, Romand Coles's vision of embodied democratic resonances, Cristina Beltrán's critique of the Latino unity ideal, and Anna Lowenhaupt Tsing's conception of indeterminately emerging and socially symbiotic possibility within burned-over terrains of neoliberal capitalism. Here, critical-popular reflection signals a temporally and affectively capacious politics that mingles briefly enduring but intense events of defiant public assertion with patient community organizing and adroitly spontaneous responses to sudden onsets of personal crisis among vulnerable members. In tandem with democratic theorists' thought-figures, day laborers' generative themes also signal an innovative style of Latino politics with the potential to rework, in more cosmopolitan and politicized ways, a specifically neoliberal variant of the preoccupation with unity.

The final chapter closes the book by synthesizing a set of provisional objectives for a politics of precarity, assessing how day labor organizations' activities promote these goals and could do so more consistently, and advancing a novel demand to guide the building of broad solidarity against (and through) precarity: a demand for worker centers for all workers. The exceptional forms of precaritization illuminated in chapters 2–4 spotlight the domination effects of the deportation regime. In response, NDLON and the worker centers in its network have developed an ingenious and effective blend of strategies that defuse mechanisms by which the homeland security state fuels the temporal conundrums of desperate responsibility, the fight on the corner, and the battle to ward off bodily risk on the job. These practical initiatives manifest and bolster a lively politics of conviviality among ordinary day laborers while also opening up unprecedented time-spaces of bodily action wherein democratically enlivened and provocatively unauthorized alternatives to the protocols of (neo)liberal mobility governance can take shape. Day labor organizations, I suggest, should pursue such activities with more explicit attention to refashioning the temporalities of precaritized work-life for day laborers and others in their circles. In turn, working people's organizations at large should embrace a multipronged antiprecarity politics, the core components of which spring from this book's critical-popular inquiries: the refusal of *work*, in clear-eyed recognition of work's desperately all-consuming and psychophysically deathly character today as dominant social practice and fundamental ideology; the carving out of unprecedented *spaces* for embodied social interaction in contravention of neoliberal mobility-governance; the militant reclamation of the people's *time* from capitalist and state powers that are stealing it with mounting rapaciousness and remorselessness. If all working people could gain access to worker centers like those that are inspiring such utopian effulgence amid cavernous precarity for day laborers, such a politics could well find masses of adherents and assume more fully developed form in our common precarious world.

1

Generative Themes

FREIREAN PEDAGOGY AND THE POLITICS OF SOCIAL RESEARCH

MIXING WITH PRECARITIZED migrant workers—greeting them as a *compañero* of a sort, lending a hand in their organizations, working with them as a researcher—offers rare opportunities to hear and see how precarity is lived in US society today. Politically engaged scholars who theorize the conditions of precarity and the pathways toward resisting it need openings like this to make their work count. Day laborers' and other migrant workers' organizations involve their own innovative forms of critical-intellectual activity, and researchers should spring at the chance to probe the distinguishing traits of precaritization together with such workers. How to do this, in a way that attunes analysts to the conceptual distinctness and political fecundity of the things deeply precaritized working people say, and that makes something constructive out of affinities between these ideas and notions derived from critical social theory? How to do this, without imperiously translating the former into the latter's terms and thereby perpetuating historically entrenched colonizing and racist practices, but also with an eye toward the differently contextualizing suggestions of academic theory and the hints they provide of solidarities perhaps only dimly glimpsed by migrant workers caught up in their own specific struggles?

This chapter crafts a process for reflectively listening to day laborers' commentaries about precarious work and antiprecarity politics, and for exploring affiliations between such comments and concepts drawn from scholarly critiques of precarity. Pursuing this process both evokes and presupposes a lively attentiveness to intellectual currents within the day labor movement. Following this course also means practicing a powerful strategy for performing critical theory in the company of those usually denied recognition as thinkers, let alone "theorists," and thereby unleashing new opposition to the forces driving precaritization for

legions of working people. My approach centers on a renewed scrutiny of popular education, the intellectual lodestone that sparks organizing, mobilizing, and
community-forming among day laborers.

Theories of popular education have informed a vast range of political education and mobilization efforts in many parts of the globe. These endeavors include workers' organizing in Melbourne, activism among Massachusetts welfare
recipients, Venezuelan school reform efforts, and political work among undocumented immigrants in Birmingham, England. In the United States, popular
education animates the day labor movement and most worker centers as well as
the migrant justice movement more broadly. Popular education defined the mission of the very first efforts to spark self-organizing among day laborers, which
the Coalition for Humane Immigrant Rights of Los Angeles and the Institute of
Popular Education of Southern California (IDEPSCA) initiated around 1990.
For IDEPSCA coordinators Raul Añorve and Pablo Alvarado, who later became
executive director of the National Day Labor Organizing Network (NDLON),
popular education provided migrant workers with both a path to English and
Spanish literacy and a route toward collective power. Both were literacy educators
who had learned and practiced popular education in their native country of El
Salvador. In Los Angeles, they sought to make language education the seedbed
for the growth of political activation and leadership among day laborers. They
did this by rooting educational interactions in workers' concrete experiences of
work, joblessness, and social marginalization, through pedagogies that facilitated
workers' development of their own vernaculars for expressing their struggles.[1]

This chapter considers the following questions about the politics of social research that is intellectually in tune with day laborers and involved in popular education: what methods of research with highly marginalized and impoverished
groups harmonize with the priorities of Freirean political pedagogy? Through
what research approaches can politically engaged scholars help set the stage for
small-scale popular-educational dialogues among the oppressed and excluded?
How, in turn, might research keyed to popular education also call forth critical energies such groups share with broader social constituencies, thereby
further promoting social transformation on the grand scale to which the popular-
educational tradition aspires? What might Paulo Freire's theoretical writings dare
researchers to do in these respects?

The chapter at hand critically excavates from Freire's earlier writings an approach to conducting and analyzing interviews with migrant day laborers that
matches this politically inflected methodological ambition, which I shall refer
to here with the short-hand notion of "critical-popular research" (my own ne-
ologism). Especially in the youthful stages of his lifework, in the context of his
responsibilities directing Brazil's national literacy program and then leading

literacy initiatives in Chile and New York City, Freire reflected in detailed and practical ways about how a researcher might invite subaltern persons to express their ideas and then incorporate those notions into processes of social analysis. The latter, in turn, were meant to be interwoven with ongoing political action. In light of Freire's reflections on these issues, I ask: if scholars want to understand how day laborers think about their jobs, their searches for work, and their efforts to build community and solidarity among themselves, then how should researchers approach interviews with workers about these topics? How should scholars interpret the material on the printed page when interviews are transcribed? What warrants might there be for conceiving of this interpretive process in ways that bring workers' conceptions into contact with existing attempts to theorize the dynamics of precarity on broad social scales? What possibilities might such exercises disclose for sparking the transformative process that Freire calls *conscientizaçao*, or "the *development* of the awakening of critical awareness," among not only day laborers but also other groups of workers whose joint participation with migrants in large collective endeavors is indispensable to truly radical social change?[2] How might such a research procedure invigorate rather than subvert the dialogical ethos of intellectual equality and reciprocity? How might this approach also lay groundwork for large-scale political action to combat the forces of precaritization?

Conducting interviews and reflecting on the mutual resonances between workers' commentaries and critical social theory does not amount to "doing" popular education as such, although my academic work here strives to feed popular-educational endeavors in tangible ways. I feel immensely fortunate that over the course of my field research, I was able to join in a number of popular education workshops coordinated by day labor organizations and other groups collaborating with them, including organizations from Mexico and El Salvador. Inspired by these experiences as well as by Freire's writings, I made several initial attempts to conduct popular-education sessions with workers and volunteers at Casa Latina. This book benefits from these experiences and experiments—and they have underscored for me that popular education crucially involves real-time, embodied, vigorously dialogical interaction among relatively small groups of people who gather with a distinctive intentionality and spirit. That said, critical-popular research can add something important to the mix by inquiring in an uncommonly systematic way into the problems about which day laborers are preoccupied and the language such workers use to express those concerns. Research in this mode also can bring to light how communities and populations beyond the more familiar circles of migrant worker justice organizing might share similar versions of those concerns, in ways that portend untold possibilities for forming collectivities of popular resistance.

One practical way my research procedure sought to enable *conscientizaçao* among day laborers (and others) was by writing the interview protocols in close

conversation with the organizers of the worker centers where I did my field research, Seattle's Casa Latina and Portland's Martin Luther King, Jr. Day Labor
Center (MLK Center), which is run by the Voz Workers' Rights and Education
Project (Voz). In this sense, the research contributed to the "development of
the awakening of critical awareness" on the part of workers because it directly
addressed topics that the organizers thought would provide effective contexts for
such a dawning, while leaving plentiful latitude for workers to redefine the issues under discussion. I also thereby hoped to counteract both the power effects
of my own social position as a professional scholar vis-à-vis the worker center
coordinators and the power imbalances between coordinators and day laborers
who frequented the centers. In addition, our interviews sought to instigate
conscientizaçao in a more immediate sense: the organizers urged that we phrase
the questions in ways that addressed workers as persons capable of critically
analyzing social problems for themselves. By responding to this invitation, even
if with lingering self-doubt, workers experienced themselves at least tentatively as
persons who could speak as critical social analysts.

The discussion that follows focuses on a further problem regarding the politics
of this research: how to devise a method of *interpreting* workers' commentaries
about their everyday work-lives that can advance the process of *conscientizaçao*,
and not only for day laborers but also for other working people implicated in the
social circumstances these workers reference. I argue that this methodological endeavor benefits from critically recovering Freire's conception of the "generative
theme" and that the search for such themes should be the main objective when
analyzing workers' comments. In the broadest sense, a generative theme refers to
an idea signified by a word or phrase that has the potential to catalyze, among
both the speakers who originally enunciate it and those with whom they enter
dialogue about it, new depths of social critique and unprecedented experiments
with political action. As we shall see, for Freire, the generativity of the theme
stems crucially from its aesthetic qualities: a distinctive artfulness, grace, or
poetry; a palpable concreteness with which a phrase evokes practical everyday
situations; a potent emotional impact; a ready conduciveness to visualization.
Moving beyond Freire but maintaining a spirit compatible with popular education, I then argue that a theme's generative potential also springs from its resonance with self-consciously critical, theoretical accounts of the social problems
that weigh especially heavily on the marginalized groups whose participation
in popular education is being sought. This resonance suggests new conceptual
possibilities rather than merely confirming what those commonly recognized as
intellectuals or theorists already think.

Construing research with day laborers as centered on the effort to identify
generative themes thus holds out the promise of assisting these workers' exertions,

on their own and in cooperation with others from different social locations, to understand power relations more critically and contest them more effectively. In addition, this interpretive approach is especially well suited to radical politics amid the multiple, interwoven predicaments of precarity that I outlined in the introduction. Puzzling questions about time and temporality, in particular, come to the fore when we think about how conversations with day laborers can become attuned to the peculiar political-intellectual challenges that characterize scenes of precarity, and vice versa. As I discuss later, precaritized circumstances signally involve the extreme *fragmentation* of everyday cultural experience, largely as an effect of neoliberalism's advance. This creates a historico-practical warrant for a type of discursive engagement that stems immanently from this aspect of precarious conditions: for social critique that takes fragmentary forms, such as we find in the themes articulated by day laborers and in the juxtapositions that can be provisionally constructed between such themes and theoretical concepts to which the themes speak.

To maximize the historically immanent, transformative potencies of generative themes also requires thinking somewhat differently than Freire does about the valences between such themes and political action. In the chapter's final section, I elaborate a conception of these relations focused on Kathi Weeks's feminist-Marxist conception of the "utopian demand."[3] For Weeks, this fragmentary form of utopian vision and political assertion embraces militancy rather than persuasion. It also insists upon a concrete, immediate form of institutional change. I argue here that the critical and affective energies unleashed by a politics of the demand yield crucial pedagogical opportunities that should be played against the different affects and reflective exertions associated with popular-educational dialogue in the Freirean mode. Not a facile leavening of "theory" with "practice" in a manner that presumes a too-simple distinction between these two enterprises, as Freire seems to do, this dialectic between dialogue and demand assumes that the ideas, dispositions, and subjectivities that emerge in the context of struggle-in-solidarity matter intensely for the vitality of dialogical engagement. It also recognizes the tentative coagulations of militant commitment within scenes of dialogue as crucial elements of political action rather than mere preludes to such action.

Conscientizaçao and Research: Prioritizing the Fragmentary

The basic thrust of popular education, as envisioned by Freire, is to "make oppression and its causes objects of reflection by the oppressed."[4] Freire emphasizes, however, that impoverished, excluded, and marginalized people are often skeptical about both the value of social reflection and their own abilities to engage in it. This is why he conceives of popular education as a laborious but liberating process for developing "the awakening of critical awareness."[5] Let us first consider what exactly Freire means by such an awakening and then take up the question of how social research could contribute to this process.

For Freire, a person manifests a critical wakefulness of mind by exhibiting certain habits of thought, asking certain kinds of questions, and seeing society in certain ways. Most fundamentally, someone with an awakened awareness sees social processes as amenable to the transformative action of ordinary, oppressed people. Such a person understands the problems she encounters as "limiting situations" rather than as ordained by fate or completely beyond her ability to influence or alter.[6] The individual can point to concrete instances, in historical or current affairs, when circumstances have changed through the agency of ordinary people. Viewing these events, he can identify particular persons from among the ranks of the oppressed as exemplifying such transformational capacity.[7] When the individual considers her own abilities to struggle in similar kinds of successful ways to make a difference, along with the abilities of others like her and people she knows, she voices confidence in herself rather than "self-depreciation," and she affirms others' capabilities instead of disparaging her fellows.[8] The person furthermore sees himself not only as an individual but also as belonging to a collectivity that is engaged in the task of transforming the world, and he articulates a staunch and vigorous sense of commitment to that cooperative undertaking.[9]

The awakening critical consciousness thus displays an altered and enlivened relation to self, others, and world, in Freire's view, and it is within this context of transmutation that the participants' *social-analytical* capacities gain expression and fortitude. Having a critical awareness about social conditions not only means understanding intellectually and believing fervently *that* they can be changed through the agency of subaltern people. It also means orienting one's mind toward appreciating the processes through which these circumstances have been and can be transformed, including but not limited to the exertions of oppressed persons and groups. For Freire, this implies seeking the causes for existing situations, especially those that are not readily apparent, and thus cultivating tenacity and patience in analyzing the reasons behind the existence of social problems, as popular analysts "begin to direct their observations towards previously inconspicuous phenomena" rather than just the obvious things in the foreground.[10] The fundamental matter, once more, is that through popular education, participants become actively engaged in analyzing *for themselves* the relations of power that structure the world in which they and others live, rather than being told how this world operates and why it functions in such ways.

Importantly, Freire views the independent and creative construction of an analytical vocabulary as vital to oppressed persons' intellectual autonomy in this respect—and it is through identifying such a lexicon that Freire sees academic research making a crucial contribution to political pedagogy. For Freire, culturally and socially marginalized persons should try to explain social affairs with the aid of analytical concepts and categories that are neither simply imposed on them by others nor merely borrowed wholesale by them from others. Instead, popular education must give priority to the terms participants use to describe their social circumstances, to explain why various problems exist, and to envision strategies for addressing them. As a species of shorthand for denoting this linguistic activity by ordinary people, Freire refers, in *Pedagogy of the Oppressed*, to such people's ability to "name the world."[11] With its resonant theological overtones, Freire's phrase calls to mind a sense of "naming" as speech that is bound up with the active creation (or genesis) of the world in a radically new manner. It is thus fitting that Freire designates as "generative themes" the kinds of vernacular expressions that he believes harbor the most abundant energies for catalyzing *conscientizaçao*.

Freire develops his notion of the generative theme in *Pedagogy* and other early texts, and it is precisely in relation to the discovery and development of generative themes that Freire perceives a vital role for academic research within a more encompassing process of popular education. Such research, in his view, should aim at identifying generative themes and exploring their potential critical and political implications. In the next section, I derive from Freire's texts a critically synthetic conception of what generative themes are and how to recognize them through research. Before proceeding to that discussion, however, it is useful to distinguish the endeavor of inquiring into generative themes from other major approaches to the commentaries by subaltern people that academic field research commonly elicits, such as research participants' remarks in interviews. Illuminating these contrasts highlights the distinctive features of research geared toward generative themes. It also suggests certain ways in which an inquiry aimed at generative themes is particularly well suited to the activation of critical intellectual work and political counterforce in the contemporary situation of precarity.

In the first place, a procedure focused on generative themes does not conform to standard social-scientific precepts for treating interview material as "data" that conveys what is empirically the case, such as the simple facts or tendencies regarding a situation of domination (e.g., "Most day laborers experience serious job-related injuries") or about how certain kinds of people view their circumstances (e.g., "Most day laborers believe employers have workers' best interests at heart"). Instead, an approach geared toward identifying generative themes asks: what elements of what the person says suggest the potential for her to *change* what happens to her, and to do, think, and feel things *differently*? In posing these questions, moreover, the generative-thematic procedure makes explicit—and opens to criticism—the social relations of knowledge-production rather than glossing these over or reifying them as the norms of a standard, acknowledged academic methodology or discipline (e.g., ethnography or political science). The procedure deliberately asks: what kinds of responses are these novel terms of discourse likely to call forth from other people beyond the research participants, and with what consequences for changing whom society understands as intellectually and politically capable persons?

Additionally, hunting for generative themes amid the records of interview conversations differs from a more critically astute approach, compared to standard empirical procedures, that focuses on issues of narrativity.[12] This alternative, poststructural approach begins by recognizing that social science and political theory embed their accounts of social phenomena within narratives that *lend* these stories a sense of the real rather than unproblematically reporting that which is real itself. As Lisa Disch contends, academic texts share precisely this feature of narrativity in common with the personal life-stories and narratives of social events that workers, women, and others produce. Thus, people's stories are to be seen neither as forms of "merely subjective" (read: limited, particularistic, self-interested) expression nor as some kind of preciously authentic self-revelation, both of which ostensibly need to be interpreted from the putatively detached, objective, generalizing vantage point of "science" or "theory" in order to inform a critical account of society.[13] Rather, ordinary persons' narratives about their own life circumstances and the larger worlds in which they exist should be treated as counternarratives that can be juxtaposed critically with extant theoretical or empirical stories, leading to the sharpening and reformulation of both types of narratives.

An interpretative method that conceptually apprehends the material in terms of narratives clearly has advantages over the more traditional, empiricist approach. These include taking a more capacious and welcoming attitude toward the epistemologically creative, world-framing activities of excluded and disregarded persons as well as explicitly engaging in the politics of counterhegemonic discourse-creation. Undoubtedly, narrative analysis of interviews with day laborers and other marginalized migrant workers would yield insights into many phenomena that matter for the analysis at hand, helping to characterize those moments when workers manifest an awakened critical awareness. Indeed, my own previous research with migrant laborers relied principally on discerning and analyzing workers' narratives as its main method of critique.[14]

Yet the precaritized predicament of fragmented temporal experience, which I have emphasized in this book's introduction, produces no little friction with a methodological approach that privileges the narrative form. Narrative aims to cobble, lash, or weld together assorted pieces of experience into some kind of whole, at least of a provisional sort. It also aims at establishing temporal continuity, sequencing, and forward momentum. Stories of the people's power, of the ability of the oppressed to challenge and defeat those who exploit and mistreat them, are undoubtedly essential to mobilizing popular social movements and currents of resistance. Nevertheless, our times also require an approach keenly attuned to the ways that precaritized time intrepidly undermines people's very abilities to think, feel, and act in the temporally contiguous ways that narrative analysis presupposes.

The ascendant temporalities of *work* driven by communicative capitalism have been particularly influential in bringing about the fractalization of everyday experience. Ironically, argues Franco "Bifo" Berardi, individuals dedicate their whole selves to work more passionately than ever today, just when their work activities tend to lose any degree of cohesiveness that could ground, in practical experience, the corporal and intellectual materialization of a coherent self. Labor processes for "cognitive" info-workers ruthlessly disaggregate productive operations, to the point where each worker serves up only tiny, disconnected fragments of work at intermittent intervals that are determined in wholly heteronomous fashion.[15] Berardi's meditations intersect provocatively with those of Jodi Dean, who sees the data translation and commodification of online content, the production of which is especially the task of knowledge workers, as having radically atomizing effects for these producers. For Dean, this happens because the transmutation of "messages," which would call for interlocutors on substantive matters, into "contributions," which circulate as exchange value, corrodes people's abilities to circulate and collectively ponder ideas by dissolving the relatively stable symbolic systems that such interaction presupposes.[16]

Meanwhile, the pervasive discontinuity of work appears in associated but different permutations among the most precarious workers. As I discussed in the introduction, this core feature of precarity, like the others, appears in exceptionally acute forms in the lives of the most violently subordinated groups even as it pervades the neoliberal economy. Andrew Ross, for instance, notes that the microdissection of labor processes experienced by info-laborers in Silicon Valley has an analogue in the gigantic factories in China where industrial workers manufacture electronics commodities under hyper-Taylorized regimes of labor division.[17] As the next chapter discusses, work's extreme fragmentation is also a defining, mundane experience for day laborers, who never know from day to day what type of work they might be told to do, what the conditions of work will be, or whether they will work at all. Domestic workers, too, face the constant fluctuation of tasks and demands, physical and emotional alike, which stem from the extreme informality and intimate-sphere locations of their jobs.[18] Overall, in every quarter of the labor economy and throughout the increasingly blended realms of productive and reproductive work, and in especially intensive ways for the most vulnerable groups, precarious work-life has fractured—even pulverized—the daily-experiential bedrock for cultural productions that privilege continuities of form.

The procedures of critical-popular research must respond to this political-cultural atmosphere and must germinate to some extent from within it, if they are ultimately to feed effective organizing against the forces that structure precarity. The metatheoretical logic guiding my line of thought here stems more from Theodor W. Adorno than Paulo Freire. In a multitude of writings and in regard to a wide assortment of cultural phenomena, Adorno argued that the splintering and decomposition of critical subjectivity by the polit-ical, economic, and cultural-ideological forces of late capitalism generated an historically specific demand for certain kinds of cultural expression. For Adorno, whereas aesthetic forms that negatively manifested the subject's dis-solution harbored a slim but significant potential to call forth new critical capabilities, artistic forms that presumed the endurance of these capacities merely reinforced domination by perpetuating the fantasy that late-capitalist institutions had not so gravely damaged the very possibility of critical thought and action.[19] In the present conjuncture, as autonomist theorists like Berardi, Christian Marazzi, and Maurizio Lazzarato have contended, the individual's ability to organize time-flows coherently for herself (and even to experience heteronomously imposed, stable unfoldings of time), whether on the job or in patches of unpaid time off the wage clock, has come under frontal attack.[20] This does not mean, *pace* Adorno, that there is no place for cultural-political strategies, such as those involving narrative innovation, that strike back fron-tally by directly and positively attempting to revive the human faculties that are being assaulted. It strongly suggests, however, that such strategies must be undertaken in critical tension with still more crucial efforts that operate in a mode that is decisively *immanent* to the negative sociohistorical conditions that maintain.

Freire's conception of generative themes signals a critical-interpretative approach that responds more pointedly to the vexed decomposition of precaritized time than either the empiricist or narrative-analytical procedures. The immanently critical potentiality of generative-thematic inquiry resides precisely in its fragmentary character along with its insistence that the ca-pacity to *originate* new conceptions and contestations of power lies *within* the bits that are its basic stuff and *among* the persons who proffer them. To pursue an examination of generative themes thus means to show self-restraint in relation to the powerful desire that the world be storied that animates the labors (and pleasures) of narrativity, a desire that precarious temporalities have both intensified and rendered less possible to fulfill. (The curbing of this desire does not require jettisoning narrative altogether, however, as I explain in more detail below when I consider possible relations between generative themes and social theory.) Likewise, generative-thematic analysis refuses to let discursive material be reduced to data that authoritative experts could then busily set about manipulating. Such an approach would reflect uncritically the paradoxical situation, which I have also stressed in the introduction, according to which productive activities are not only scattered into disconnected bits of work time but also subjected to more rigidly hierarchical control and temporal homogenization.[21] Let us now more closely examine Freire's notion of the generative theme and his ideas regarding research processes aimed at bringing such themes to the surface.

Searching for Generative Themes: Research Tactics and Generative Qualities

Freire views the search for generative themes through processes of "research" by politically engaged academic "specialists" as an important part of the overall pedagogy of liberation.[22] He thus sees these explorations as consistent with the pedagogy's mission of fostering the critical and emancipatory activities of the oppressed on their own behalf, by their own powers. In a 1968 essay about redesigning agricultural extension programs in Brazil as vehicles for popular education, Freire writes:

> To know the peasants' manner of seeing the world which contains their "generative themes" (which, after being taken, studied, and placed in a scientific setting, are returned to the peasants in the form of problem themes) implies a search. This in turn requires a methodology which should be, in my opinion, dialogical, problem-posing and conscientizing. Research into the "generative themes," and education as a gnosiological condition, are different stages of the same process. If one offers the peasants their own theme, so that in the act of knowing they can dialogue on it with the educator . . . it will "generate" other themes when at a later stage it is apprehended in its relationship with other related themes through the transformation undergone by the perception of reality. Thus one passes from a stage which tends mainly toward the search for the "generative theme" to another whose tendency is mainly educational-gnosiological.[23]

In this passage, Freire validates the role of a certain type of research within a much broader, more ambitious program of popular education. He distinguishes a preliminary "stage" focused on *identifying* the generative themes in oppressed people's discourses from subsequent phases in which *dialogical* pedagogy is conducted, with the themes furnishing material for such dialogue, or what he here rather obscurely calls "gnosiological" education. Although the gnosiological is not a prominent concept in Freire's oeuvre, understanding the term's significance in this text adds depth and multidimensionality to his conception of research on generative themes. In this critique of agricultural extension programs, the gnosiological endeavor denotes an educational process that is not "individual but social," that is politically committed rather than claiming opportunistically to be "neutral," and that instantiates "freedom" by placing educators and students on a level with one another: "In the educational process for liberation, educator-educatee and educate-educator are both cognitive Subjects before knowable objects which mediate them."[24] The concept of the gnosiological, in other words, encapsulates the three core tenets of Freire's theory regarding the process of *conscientização*: it must be a *collective* undertaking, in the midst of dedicated and divisive political *struggle*, accomplished through processes of dialogue that presuppose and enact *radical intellectual equality* among the participants. By associating the search for generative themes with the gnosiological, Freire thus underscores the vital role this research plays within the broader popular-educational effort as well as the consistency of such inquiry with each separate component of the endeavor.

Freire develops his conception of excavating generative themes as a way to address the specific issue of how dialogue can catalyze participants' abilities to interpret their experiences, relations, and world conditions for themselves through experimentation with their own vernacular terms. Bearing this in mind suggests what Freire likely means when he refers to the examination of generative themes "in a scientific setting." Mildly specialized techniques of academic investigation do have a place within Freire's vision of how to conduct research aimed at eliciting generative themes: he writes that researchers learn what possibly generative themes are through "interviews" as well as "informal encounters with the inhabitants of the area," or what social researchers might more commonly call participant observation.[25] Yet in the same text, Freire undercuts any impression that the scientific identification of generative themes and subsequent dialogue on such themes constitute two distinct forms of intellectual activity that, in turn, could be mapped onto hierarchized groups in a division of theoretical labor. Plainly put: Freire refuses to dichotomize between research as the province of specialists and popular dialogue as an activity for everybody else. Recalling his attempt to develop a popular educational agenda for Brazil, for instance, Freire writes: "We needed, then, an education which would lead men to take a new stance toward their problems—that of intimacy with those problems, one oriented toward research instead of repeating irrelevant principles."[26] Here Freire positions research as not only preparation for dialogue but also the aim and animating spirit of dialogical engagement for all involved.

Yet even if the intellectual activities of identifying generative themes and probing them through dialogical interactions are not substantively distinct for Freire, and are equally scientific and research oriented, the immediate tasks in each case are slightly different. The initial investigative stage helps set the popular-educational process in motion by assembling a preliminary set of linguistic elements—nuggets of language, bits of common expression—that people in positions of oppression furnish. How, then, to recognize the fragments of language that show generative promise in the sense of harboring the potential to spark energetic dialogue and bold, critically leavened political intervention?

Historically, literacy campaigns among Brazilian peasants and the urban poor provided much of the ground on which Freire and others started cultivating popular education theory. In addition, as noted at the start of this chapter, many day labor leaders in the United States today began developing their political-intellectual skills and orientations through conducting literacy-oriented popular education in Latin America.[27] For these reasons, it is important to consider how Freire begins to formulate his approach to discerning generative language in his early reflections on the nationwide adult literacy initiative he promoted in Brazil in the 1960s. In the manner of generative themes, Freire argues, the words literacy educators emphasize in their curricula should propel the gnosiological endeavor of collectively actualizing radical intellectual equality within contexts of committed social struggle. It is the job of popular-educational researchers, in turn, to compose an initial lexicon for literacy education by identifying words that adult-literacy teachers can use to provoke a type of literacy education that is highly politicized, in terms of both prompting critical reflection on social power-relations and instantiating relations of radical equality in the concrete learning-space. As Freire specifies, "The educator's role is fundamentally to enter into dialogue with the illiterate about concrete situations and simply to offer him the instruments with which he can teach himself to read and write."[28] Generative *words* are precisely such instruments, by virtue of their embodiment of *themes* that instigate critical and political activity:

> In the practice that we defend, generative words—people's words—are used in realistic problem situations . . . as challenges that call for answers from the illiterate learners. "To problematize" the word that comes from people means to problematize the thematic element to which it refers. This necessarily involves an analysis of reality.[29]

Critically scrutinizing "reality," Freire clarifies elsewhere, means performing "a linguistic analysis that in turn includes ideology and politics" and that strives to construe the ways that public ideas and political actions are structured on a broad social level: "What is important is that the person learning words be concomitantly engaged in a critical analysis of the social framework in which men exist."[30] In sum, the goal of literacy training in the mode of popular education is nothing less than "teaching adults how to read in relation to the awakening of their consciousness"—in other words, fomenting *conscientizaçao* through a process that combines real-time experiences of intellectual equality, the gaining of new practical capabilities for reading, and intensified engagement in analyzing social fields of power and inequality.[31] Field research, in turn, helps prepare the ground for such radically political pedagogy by discerning word-instruments within the people's language that exude generative-thematic potential.

So, once more: how can researchers identify such generative potential when they undertake fieldwork with oppressed and excluded persons? Considering Freire's reflections on literacy education, in association with his comments about generative themes, makes it possible to specify a set of characteristics to which researchers should be attentive as they attempt to discover themes with generative potential. In the Brazilian literacy initiative, Freire describes the following process of "field vocabulary research" aimed at detecting generative words, which he labels "Phase 1" within a multiphasic program of popular education:

> One selects not only the words most weighted with existential meaning (and thus the greatest emotional content) but also typical sayings, as well as words and expressions linked to the experience of the groups in which the researcher participates. These interviews reveal longings, frustrations, disbeliefs, hopes, and an impetus to participate. During this initial phase the team of educators form rewarding relationships and discover often unsuspected exuberance and beauty in the people's language.[32]

As Freire's references to participants' "longings," "frustrations," and "hopes" implies, a distinctive *intensity of feeling* emanates from generative terms. Enunciated by people whose daily lives routinely involve loss and lack, the theme registers an unexpected abundance of feeling, or as Freire puts it, a striking "exuberance." This emotional charge, moreover, fosters a *dynamic of gathering for action*. It is an evocation that implies convocation, enlivened as the feelings kindled travel among the participants and activate their desires to "participate" in some common endeavor, although in the opening stages of dialogue that may simply mean jointly recognizing that most participants share certain severe problems that seem intractable, and about which they feel deeply discouraged.

Freire also proposes that terms showing promise as generative themes deal with *concrete* aspects of people's *situated everyday lives*. Generative themes, Freire writes, are "concrete representations" of conditions that prevail in a certain, delimited historical situation; they are always characterizations "of that epoch" in which the people who voice them live rather than expressions of eternal truths or responses to timeless conundrums.[33] For Freire, the quality of concreteness often manifests in a speaker's preference for tangible, material forms of evocation, such as when a Recife slum-dweller defines the notion of a favela (slum neighborhood) by saying: "In the *favela* we don't have any water."[34] As this example further suggests, the concrete features of thematically promising utterances locate speakers not only in time but also in space. Themes with "pragmatic value" for dialogue, Freire intimates elsewhere, mobilize "linguistic signs that command a common understanding in a region or area of the same city or country," such as a Brazilian favela or its Chilean analogue, the *callampa*. In other words, the ability to evoke a person's and group's peculiar sense of how they live life *now*, in the current moment in a particular place, fills out the theme's emotional repertoire and further signals its pedagogical generativity. In this instance, the theme would invite further examination of what it means to lack a water supply, why this deficit exists, and how the problem produces a shared condition of present suffering, while stirring a collective desire for something better among those who live amid these conditions.

Aesthetic qualities of the language by which research participants put words on such features of everyday life contribute additionally to the thematic generativity of such terms, in Freire's view. This is an important point to stress, given that Freire's conception of political pedagogy has sometimes been criticized as too narrowly focused on cognitive reflection and the development of critical ideas while neglecting aesthetic concerns.[35] For Freire, generativity abides in articulations that possess *poetic* qualities of expression, and Freire's dispersed but suggestive remarks in this regard help flesh out what criteria for aesthetic "beauty" and richness he has in mind. He emphasizes, in particular, that generative terms evince "simplicity of expression, both profound and elegant": they derive from the "simple, poetic, free language of the people."[36] Such terms and phrases are ordinary, yet they are neither trite nor predictable in their effects. Rather, as Freire intimates when he refers to the "unsuspected" emotional plenitude of generative words in literacy education, generative themes possess stylistic elements that make the moments when they are voiced startling.

When Freire discusses the initial phase of research preceding literacy education, he also emphasizes aspects of the way language *sounds* that have provocative implications for an effort to spell out an approach to identifying generative themes through critical-popular research. A signature aspect of Freirean literacy training, as other scholars have noted (and as day labor leaders who were popular educators in Latin America stress), is the breaking down of complex words into syllabic building-blocks, or "phonemes."[37] The idea is to facilitate the experience for language-learners of constructing words for themselves by "recombining" the phonemes into new complex terms of their own design—and hence, in keeping with the politicized ethos of such literacy popular education, to experience themselves in the moment as active creators of their own linguistically mediated social worlds.[38] Significantly, Freire suggests that the sonority and even musicality of language particles are very much in play in this process of recombinatory invention. In Freire's ascription of "phonemic richness" to generative words, we thus might hear (or extrapolate) the notion that the tonalities of certain themes, and the impulses such sonorous features can yield toward linguistic innovation via creative juxtapositions or neologisms, have a lot to do with a theme's generativity.[39] Sometimes, in other words, a generative theme might take the form of a compound word or phrase that results from imaginative, musically attuned couplings of smaller language-elements.

Freire sees the *visual* register of language as even more decisive for the generativity of words and themes in popular education. In Freire's literacy pedagogy, after generative words have been identified through preliminary research, the researchers commence the central dialogical endeavor by creating visual images of the situations named by those terms and engaging participants in group discussion of those words and situations. Freire calls the designing of such images the construction of "codifications," and he refers to the dialogical interpretation of the images as the process of "decodification." Again, the motivation of the exercise is at once instrumental and social-critical. Through decodifying the images based on generative words, participants engage in recombinatory experimentation and thereby "discover the mechanism of word formation"; they also, through the interplay of language and thought, and of sound and vision, "open perspectives for the analysis of regional and national problems."[40] For Freire, working with language's visual registers also can involve creative play with metaphors. Freire has a fondness for quoting statements by peasants to illustrate such aleatory innovation with visual metaphors, recalling, for instance, one individual who sorrowfully described the month of January as "a tough guy who makes us suffer,"[41] and another who, upon gaining ground in his effort to become literate, exclaimed that for him, words now were " 'like puppets . . . I can make them talk.' "[42]

To summarize: by piecing together Freire's dispersed comments about generative themes and generative words from the early texts where he most actively develops these concepts, we have arrived at a differentiated account of the characteristics that suggest generativity when an investigator examines the themes that emerge in research meant to help catalyze popular-educational dialogue and action. A theme's generativity subsists in its *emotional* intensity, fullness, and mobility. Generative themes also privilege *concrete, material* forms of expression over abstract concepts, situating seemingly intransigent difficulties in the *temporal now* and referencing distinctive features of *place*. In addition, generativity springs from the theme's aesthetic attributes of *sonority*, in the sense of provoking musically attuned improvisation and recombination; *poetry*, in the form of spare, elegant plainness that is both familiar and jolting; and *visuality*, in a way that spurs creative re-envisioning of stubborn problems and hopeful experiences, alike.

Theme and Theory

Through identifying generative themes and convening dialogues to analyze and develop them, popular education in the Freirean mode opens new pathways of critical social analysis oriented by the vernacular terms with which subordinated people make sense of their worlds. Having explored the specific processes by which researchers can ascertain themes likely to show generative promise for popular education, another key question must now be confronted: what should the relation be between dialogical work on the linguistic fragments that constitute generative themes and efforts to construct continuities of thought that can represent complex social systems and power relations? How, in other words, to frame an adequate understanding of the relation between *theme* and *theory*?

Part of the answer concerns pursuing dynamics that are internal to dialogical processes for linking themes and decodifications together in ways that gradually induce such conceptual continuities to take shape. Freire characteristically emphasizes this approach to the issue. In doing so, he also sometimes inadvertently demonstrates how difficult it can be, even for thinkers and organizers stoutly committed to radical intellectual equality, to keep one's ideas fully aligned with this principle. We see slippages of this sort when Freire discusses the codification and decodification process: a tension between boldly asserting ordinary people's abilities to analyze and change the world for themselves, on the one hand, and subtly implying the need for better-trained individuals to prearrange these processes as well as their outcomes, on the other hand. Writing about popular education in the context of the agricultural extension program, Freire initially seems to presume that the researchers (who are not peasants) know in advance what the codifications mean and are simply designing an efficient route for participants to reach a foreordained conclusion:

> The "treatment" of the theme researched considers the "reduction" and the "codification" of the themes which make up the program as a structure,

that is, as a system of relationships in which one theme leads obligatorily to others, all joined in units and sub-units within the program.[43]

This depiction of a "program" with a "structure" in which the constituent themes are connected to one another through "obligatory" relations seems to leave little or no room for participants to say for themselves what the codifications mean and how they might interrelate. Yet moments later, Freire returns to his refrain that educators and educands must be coparticipants in popular education, teaching, and learning from one another and consistently subjecting the pedagogical methods themselves to dialogical scrutiny and popular reformulation:

> Thematic "codifications" are the representations of existential situations— situations of work in the fields where the peasants are using some less efficient method of working. . . . The interlocutor-Subjects, faced with a pedagogical "codification" (problem-situation) . . . concentrate on it, seeking through dialogue the significant comprehension of its meaning. . . . [I]t is not the role of educators to narrate to the educates (the peasants) what in their opinion constitutes their knowledge of reality or of the technical dimension involved in it. On the contrary, their task is to challenge the peasants once again to penetrate the significance of the thematic content with which they are presented.[44]

Here there is friction between Freire's prior suggestion that the meaning of the codifications is fixed and known in advance by the researchers, such that the latter can arrange them into a rigid "system" with logically necessary relations among carefully selected parts, and an alternative implication. Notwithstanding the uncritical invocation of "efficiency," the passage clearly affirms the need for a distinctly open-ended, egalitarian exchange among "interlocutor-Subjects" in which educators do not tell peasants what to think but instead "challenge" the latter to explore what they (the peasants) think the themes mean. By ascribing subjecthood to the peasants, moreover, Freire gestures toward his central argument, which receives its fullest expression in *Pedagogy of the Oppressed*, that a sine qua non of popular education is for educators to approach the pedagogical scene with the self-conscious need to learn new things from the students, who have prodigious if beaten-down capacities to teach the teachers.

My primary aim here is not to parse the text and argue for the best way to interpret Freire but rather to underscore that the dialogical labor of splicing together participants' initially separate efforts "to penetrate the significance of the thematic content," one theme at a time, should follow the intellectually egalitarian ethos that stands at the heart of popular education, Freire's occasional equivocations on this matter notwithstanding. Critically modifying Freire's rather flat, one-dimensional conception of narrative suggests one way to do this, in practical terms. As the first of the two passages on codifications quoted above illustrates, Freire tends to use the term "narrative" and its cognates disparagingly. Typically, it serves as a shorthand for the unidirectional mode by which traditionally minded teachers try to "deposit" their putatively expert knowledge into the minds of passively mute students, or what Freire also calls the "banking" educational approach.[45] However, when Freire offers concrete examples of decodification processes in some of his early writings, he occasionally discusses statements by peasants that take the form of storytelling, although in these passages he provides no further metacommentary on the narrative form. The stories related are limited in both scope and duration. For instance, one individual recalls a time when his family's need for water had become so urgent that even though a mass of dead locusts was floating in a pond near the village, he and others fished out the insects and drank the water anyway.[46] From one point of view, this story could be seen as simply an elaboration on the generative theme of "water" in (and absent from) the favela. Yet the brief narrative also offers possibilities of transit to other themes one might well imagine could emerge in that dialogical setting, such as "family" (or responsibilities to family) and "nature" (or just bugs). Drawing lines of connection among such themes, in turn, would amount to nothing less than engaging in *theory*—telling a more complex story about how and why society works in certain ways—by practicing narrativity in the creative and egalitarian intellectual sense I have discussed above in the section "*Conscientizaçao* and Research" with reference to Disch and White.[47]

Freire's own sporadic insertions of concrete stories in his texts thus illuminate certain ways of understanding "narrative" that depart decisively from his unreflective equation of narration with banking education. In doing so, these episodes indicate one compelling response to the more general issue of what to do with the singular thematic interpretations that dialogue participants initially produce. Dialogical exploration of generative themes can lead to further experimental efforts to conjoin individual themes into composites that take the form of stories about the workings of society and thereby assert themselves as theory.

Not only the unintentional implications of Freire's illustrative story-sharing but also some definitive claims in his texts, and in related writings by others, further support this conception of a later-stage dialogical practice that associates various themes with one another—without, however, imposing a fully integrative, preformatted logic. To return to an earlier key point in this discussion: *working with fragments* lies at the very core of popular education. Thus, efforts to combine fragments should be done in the spirit of such work: assembling broader figurations of meaning that refrain from totalizing, and imagining provisional-but-durable affiliations between concepts rather than claiming to disclose iron chains of causality. Skepticism toward projects that aim to dissolve the fragmentary into integral wholeness can draw strength from Freire's consistent emphasis, despite periodic vacillations, on interrupting, deconstructing, and problematizing commonly held understandings of social power-relations through problem-posing education. Freire deserves criticism when he lapses into vaguely Marxist truisms about social theorizing that lag behind the explosive originality of his own political pedagogy, such as when he writes: "Existential experience is a whole. In illuminating one of its facets and perceiving the interrelation of that facet with others, the learners tend to replace a fragmented vision of reality with a total vision."[48] Freire has been justly criticized by many for never elaborating a substantive theory of social power and oppression that would substantiate a claim like this.[49] He himself, however, offers a more supple and promising way to conceive of the dialogical-theoretical challenge—the collective effort to convert themes into theory—when he writes that "themes are generative . . . because . . . they contain the possibility of unfolding into again as many themes, which in their turn call for new tasks to be fulfilled."[50] According to this formulation, far from gravitating toward ever-more-bounded possibilities of social-critical meaning-making, dialogue on themes generates *multiplied* prospects for theorizing relations of social power and domination as well as proliferating avenues for popular political action. As the passage quoted at the start of the previous section notes, furthermore, it is in those later-stage instances when a theme "is apprehended in its relationship with other related themes" that such expanded intellectual and practical opportunities begin to show themselves.[51]

Stepping back from the micrological processes of dialogical interaction, however, a second, distinct route toward construing relations between themes and theory comes into view. Certainly, popular education demands that organizers curb their own impulses to approach dialogue participants didactically, or under the assumption that the organizers' own preferred language for theorizing social power and conflict is the right idiom. Yet the question remains: does this mean, and does the Freirean procedure of unfolding theory through exploring relationships among generative themes in dialogical interactions imply, that there is no constructive relation one might imagine between the themes identified through critical-popular research and already existing bodies of critical social theory, penned by writers who are fortunate enough to see themselves as composing theory legitimately and with some degree of authority? Or, by noticing how such societally recognized theory and the themes of subaltern commentators, like day laborers, speak to one another, could researchers perhaps open up additional, valuable channels of political pedagogy and action that bespeak further dimensions of the themes' generativity?

I understand the practice of *critical theory* to mean the effort to compose accounts of social, political, economic, and cultural formations that strive self-consciously to maximize the critical acuity of their own concepts and categories, that endeavor to be self-reflective about how their own intellectual approaches are implicated in historically specific flows of power, and that seek both to theorize and to help upset patterns of domination. There is a profound affinity between this labor of critical theory and popular education's aim to interrogate the accepted conceptual instruments of sociohistorical knowledge in the context of determined action to transform an oppressive society. Popular education and critical theory, thus defined, share a common ethos that accentuates unyielding self-reflectivity, the constant rearticulation of languages of critique in response to historical changes (especially in the class-, race-, and gender-inflected structures and flows of capitalism), theorization from perspectives of subjection to domination, experimentation with not just the content but also the form of critique, and commitment to radical social and political action.

Critical social theory that views itself as such also has something quite practical and concrete to offer to popular education, notwithstanding the typical inaccessibility of academic theoretical vocabularies to workers who often lack formal education even at primary levels. The core principle of *political-intellectual reciprocity*, which imbues Freire's conception of dialogue in the context of socially transformative action, affirms that all parties to this practice stand to learn genuinely new things from one another. Thus, a crucial dimension of any theme's generativity, which we have not considered until this point, lies beyond its ability to provoke passionate, thoughtful dialogue among people who are already gathered in the room. As I have discussed in the preceding section, the features of generativity emphasized by Freire (i.e., concreteness, emotional intensity, etc.) are well equipped to do this. In addition, however, generative themes may well possess urgently needed potential to foster collective struggle on a much larger social level—the higher planes on which concerted challenges to core social structures of capitalism, racism, and patriarchy become genuinely feasible. Themes articulated by a given group of speakers manifest this other sort of generativity inasmuch as they resonate with experiences that groups from *categorically different social locations* might have in response to the broad social conditions signaled by the themes.

From a perspective focused on the new forms of political solidarity that dialogue could facilitate, generative themes articulated by Latino migrant day laborers in Seattle might, for instance, fairly readily evoke engaged (although neither automatic nor unequivocal) responses from black unionized construction workers, middle-class Latino activists, or Cambodian restaurant workers in the Puget Sound area. Such groups are already on the radar screen of worker center activists seeking to assemble local urban coalitions on important issues like Seattle's fifteen-dollar minimum wage, more reliable state labor standards monitoring, and city funding for worker centers. Yet if the goal is also to organize a much larger movement to change the ways whole industries and metropolitan economies operate, as well as to connect such a movement to allied forces in national and transnational spheres, then it becomes vital to know how the themes identified through critical-popular research could help generate such movement-building. That means thinking in terms of very widely applicable albeit internally differentiated formations of social subjectivation and subordination. Such formations, for example, could include broadly encompassing forms of precaritization that day laborers name but that also implicate white-collar tech workers for Amazon and Microsoft, even if in distinctly contoured ways.

Thinking along such emphatically capacious lines is the pressing concern for most people today who call themselves and are heeded as critical social theorists. The concern has become even more imperative lately because the need to counter the ascendant forces of capitalist brutality and political reaction is intensifying as I write this book. Notwithstanding this urgency, in no sense should reflection on the interconnections between popular themes and academic theory supersede, displace, or defer the slow and rigorously bottom-up process of generating theory through popular dialogue on participants' own themes. Instead, there is value in *both* the endeavor of letting this internal dynamic of popular-educational dialogue unfold and the further task of deliberately juxtaposing popular themes and extant theories to see what associations emerge. Not only are these efforts mutually compatible—in addition, if done properly, the latter enterprise can strengthen the former by instigating pathways of dialogue that counterintuitively relate participants' lives to the experiences of quite different social groups, potentially bringing to light prospects for unsuspected, broad-ranging solidarities.

The question, then, is how the critical-popular researcher can perform this additional analytical labor of brushing theme against theory and vice versa without rehearsing and reinstalling pernicious dynamics of intellectual imperialism and colonization. How to proceed with such critique, without thwarting the intellectual agency of the popular group centrally involved in the research in ways that Freire and other theorists expose and denounce through critical analyses of empire and colonization? How, furthermore, to avoid undercutting participants' agency right from the start—in identifying generative themes—if the researcher comes from a substantially different social location than the participants, as I do with respect to day laborers, being a white, US-born, English-speaking, highly educated and employed professional?

Several critical practices can help stave off such effects, and here I will use my own work with day laborers as a basis for describing these efforts concretely. Both the initial characterization of generative themes and their subsequent encounters with extant critical theory must be done in ways that, as much as possible, thoroughly engage day laborers' commentaries on their own terms and mingle such terms with theoretical concepts without dissolving the former into the latter (or, for that matter, uncritically folding the latter into the former, although this is not the problem of greatest concern, given historical experience). Of course, the researcher cannot interpret the material at all without consulting categories and concepts he or she already has, so there can be no conceit here about immediately intuiting what the speakers are "truly" saying about their life-conditions and experiences. The researcher will misperceive and misinterpret certain things because of this, and so the question is really how to counteract that tendency. The problem might be phrased as a matter of how to maximize the researcher's ability to *listen well* to the speakers, such that the researcher's sense or judgment that a given parcel of language constitutes a generative theme accords as closely as possible to what the speaker himself would say about this attribution, and so that the suggested approximations of theme with theory yield associations the speaker would at least find plausible and worth pursuing. Several modest, though in no sense fully adequate, measures can help, and I have sought to take such steps in this project.

First, although formal interviews may furnish the discursive material for determining generative themes, the researcher's more extended involvement in the speakers' cause and organizations as a dedicated partaker provides indispensable context for listening well to the voices in the transcripts. Absent the months I spent volunteering at Voz and Casa Latina and joining in related activities with the day laborers and coordinators of these organizations, in ways pivotally informed by my research assistants' vigorous involvements in these communities in shorter-term but intensive ways, I would not even have minimal confidence in my capacity to make sense of what workers said to me and to my assistants in the interviews. Counterbalancing the alarming urgency of this historical moment is the against-the-grain imperative to let unpredictable processes of field research take their course so that one gradually acquires a sharper sense of the problems people mundanely face and how they tend to act and talk with respect to those issues. As I noted in this book's introduction, I do not profess to have performed anything like a full-scale ethnography with day laborers, so my contextualizing experiences of these kinds are more limited than some ethnographers would likely advise. Nevertheless, my claim to do a baseline responsible job of listening to the transcripts hinges significantly on my own and my assistants' active and reasonably extensive participation in everyday activities at Voz's MLK Center and Casa Latina. At Casa Latina, where I continue to be a volunteer as of this writing, I mostly fielded calls from employers and set up day labor jobs for workers.[52] In addition, I organized two health and safety workshops for day laborers (in 2010 and 2017) and one for volunteers (in 2017); attended social events with workers, staff, and volunteers; observed workers' leadership-building sessions; joined in dialogue circles about protecting migrant families from immigration enforcement; participated in a training session for the center's ICE-raid rapid response network; contributed to an occupational safety and health training grant proposal (in 2010); helped rewrite the volunteer training manual, partly by adding material on popular education; and joined the eighteen-person Casa Latina contingent (mostly workers) at the weeklong 2017 assembly of the National Day Labor Organizing Network, during which I talked with workers and coordinators over meals, participated in workshops with them, and rode the bus with them to a rally denouncing a California sheriff's cooperation with ICE.[53] My assistant, Caitlin Schoenfelder, spent a summer as a volunteer intern at Casa Latina doing job dispatch as well as ad hoc tasks, such as translating documents for workers.[54] In Portland, my assistant Ariel Ruiz and I taught regular English classes at the MLK Center; we also spent ample time talking leisurely with workers afterward, participating in worker assembly meetings, and observing worker leadership-training discussions.[55] I also collaborated with Voz's worker-leaders to organize two local community screenings and dialogue-discussions of Voz's documentary on day laborers' artistic and musical endeavors at Whitman College in Walla Walla, Washington, where I am on the faculty, in 2014 and 2017.[56] My assistants and I all maintained a systematic practice of writing thorough field notes about our interactions with the Voz and Casa Latina communities, and these notes provided a further rich basis for exploring the themes that, to my eyes and ears, show generativity.

Second, it is not just the experience of taking part in these activities, as such, that I believe has aided my capacity to listen well to the workers. The deeply *politicized* character of my own and my assistants' relations with the day laborers and organizers at Casa Latina and Voz also has helped foster the fragile and perforated, but lively, milieu of affective resonance and communicative connection on which my efforts to distinguish and reflect on workers' generative themes depend. These relationships have been politicized, in one sense, in that when workers describe problems and situate them in social circumstances during our interviews, they are doing so as linguistically savvy political agents who say certain things in particular ways, and refrain from saying other things, in order to induce us to see the world in ways they intend—just as we are asking questions in ways that encourage them to view certain issues as important and suggesting terms for understanding those matters. Power, in other words, saturates the interview context on all sides. Yet far from lamenting this or straining to neutralize it (as if that were even possible) in the manner of so-called value-free social science, this very situation contributes positively to the endeavor at hand, which centrally aims to highlight language that can motivate others to take action to transform society. In short, language as politically and intersubjectively effective rather than as disclosing objective truth is the main focus in this exercise, and this makes the politicized quality of interview conversations an asset rather than a defect.

Another dimension of politicization in our interactions with the workers, in turn, concerns the fact that my assistants and I engaged in these interviews and our other activities at Casa Latina and Voz in an express spirit of *political solidarity* with these centers' day laborers and organizers. This meant that workers had more of a stake in these interactions and were more likely to sense this than if we had approached them in a detached and dispassionate way as outside analysts. Again, my hope was not that this would simply make workers more candid about their "real" experiences than they otherwise would have been. More precisely, it was that by feeling and seeing that in key ways we were on the same side in the same fight, they would be more generously dilatory, comfortably casual, freely experimental, and politically attuned in the ways they expressed themselves.

My approach to structuring the meeting points between workers' themes and academic theory, in terms of both selecting theoretical texts and organizing my writing, comprises a third means for boosting my ability to listen attentively to workers' voices. With regard to the latter strategy, I have sought to make such listening more possible by beginning each chapter with a focus on the workers' commentaries and purposely keeping academic theory at bay for a while. Thus, each chapter commences with the "Phase 1" task of identifying generative themes via close engagement with the interviews and only afterward moves on to the differently creative and critical labor of playing day laborers' themes and critical theorists' accounts off one another to see what new angles on precaritizing processes emerge. In choosing theoretical texts to place alongside workers' themes, in turn, I follow the rule of letting the generative themes guide my judgments about which writings are relevant. This makes the crafting of my theoretical archive more eclectic than it would be if I had sought to develop a particular school of thought (e.g., autonomist Marxism) through an encounter with popular themes. This process also makes the insights resulting from theme-theory juxtapositions less smoothly articulable within given theoretical vocabularies than some readers might prefer—but that is the point. Listening to workers through the mediation of one relatively coherent body of theoretical literature, with its own distinctive matrix of analytical concepts, would foster pressure to adapt theme-based generativities to a preconstituted theoretical language. By deliberately diversifying the academic-theoretical lexicons for the theme-theory pairings, the generativities these endeavors descry with regard to the prospects for mass-scale solidarities among the precaritized can become maximally infused with the day laborers' intellectual innovation.[57]

Fourth, the only convincing way to verify the generativity for popular education and for critical theory of the themes I extract from day laborers' comments, and from the theme-theory linkages I construct, is to test out these themes in live dialogue sessions involving day laborers and others. Dialogically engaged field research of this sort lies mostly beyond the purview of this book, which I have conceived essentially as a venture in the identification of generative themes prior to dialogue, in the manner suggested by Freire's notion of first-phase research and critically prolonged through a series of theme-theory encounters. Nevertheless, I was excited to have several opportunities during the course of this project to organize popular education-based workshops with the worker center community at Casa Latina. In preliminary but encouraging ways, as I discuss at length on chapter 4, these sessions confirmed that the generative concepts and affects of themes from this analysis are more than a matter of speculation on my part. Because of the different compositions of the participant groups, furthermore, it was possible to gain an initial sense not only of the generative character of the themes among day laborers but also of these themes' capacities for resonating with wider social groups. Given Casa Latina's particular concern with promoting workers' health and safety on the job, these issues comprised the focus of the dialogical encounters I conducted there, so I have less basis for confidence in the political energetics of the other themes I discuss. The signs from these trial efforts, however, are quite positive, and at the time of this book's writing plans are in motion to design additional programming in popular education at both Casa Latina and Voz based on the themes (and theme-theory valences) explored in these pages.[58]

Dialogue and Demand

The chapters ahead take up the search for generative themes that I have conceptualized here, as I engage with the commentaries of migrant day laborers about their travels to find work, their struggles to gain employment through worker centers and on city streets, their conflictual interactions with bosses and one another, and their efforts to forge communities of hope and solidarity through worker centers. In these forays into critical-popular research with day laborers, I pinpoint key terms these workers use to characterize their worlds and experiences with arresting emotional intensity, palpable concreteness, musicality, visual fecundity, and poetic elegance. In keeping with the notion that the generativity of such language-bits further hinges on the kinds of intellectual responses they invite from others who are not day laborers, I also juxtapose the themes coaxed out of the workers' comments with social critiques supplied by theorists of precarity. I look for aspects of mutual fortification between these two modes of social representation, as well as prods for the critical sharpening of concepts on all sides: for moments when day laborers' themes add distinct textures and focal points to theorists' accounts of precaritized conditions, and for instances when theoretical renderings of precarity's inner disjunctures can put day laborers' commentaries in a more capacious political context.

Before proceeding, one other crucial issue regarding the role of generative-thematic inquiry vis-à-vis popular education needs to be addressed: the specific relation between critical-popular research and the mobilization of political action to transform oppressive social conditions. How does Freire conceptualize the transactions among ventures in dialogue and organized initiatives to change institutional channels of power and domination? What pressure might we want to apply to his conceptual framework in this respect, especially in light of the particular forms of political action that seem most needed in the present era of precaritization?

When Freire writes about the interface between dialogical interaction and political action, he tends to leave it open as to whether these two endeavors can be categorically distinguished or whether popular education involves the break-down of such a sharp distinction. Consider, for instance, how Freire discusses dialogical pedagogy in this passage:

> [This practice] makes oppression and its causes objects of reflection by the oppressed, and from that reflection will come their necessary engagement in the struggle for their liberation. And in the struggle this pedagogy will be made and remade. . . . It is only when the oppressed find the oppressor out and become involved in the organized struggle for their liberation that they begin to believe in themselves. This discovery cannot be purely intel-lectual but must involve action; nor can it be limited to mere activism, but must include serious reflection: only then will it be a praxis. Critical and liberating dialogue, which presupposes action, must be carried on with the oppressed at whatever the stage of their struggle for liberation. . . . [R]eflection—true reflection—leads to action. On the other hand, when the situation calls for action, that action will constitute an authentic praxis only if its consequences become the object of critical reflection.[59]

One might interpret Freire as saying that reflection and action comprise tem-porally and substantively different moments within emancipatory struggle, such that one "presupposes" and "leads to" the other and vice versa, with this dialectic between two stable poles constituting a larger whole called "praxis." Alternatively, one could read Freire as signaling a more complicated entanglement between dialogue and political action, perhaps even their merging into a single activity.

After all, he writes that it is not following but rather "in" experiences of political engagement that pedagogical innovation occurs, and he suggests that the oppressed change their view of themselves "when," not after, they join in "organized struggle" against their oppressors.

Here, as before, my interest lies less in arguing for one reading of Freire as preferable than in mining his texts for ideas with which to develop a method of critical-popular research, including a compelling sense of how such research could be intertwined with transformative political action. Kathi Weeks's provocative theorization of politics in the mode of the "demand" opens up promising avenues for elaborating the Freirean trajectory that undermines the strict binary between action and reflection. In addition, as I shall show, a critical (partial) synthesis of Weeks's and Freire's ideas suggests how the principle of immanent critique—the marshaling of transformative impulses that spring from within but lead beyond given conditions—could orient not only the conduct of generative-thematic inquiry but also the political activities associated with such intellectual labor.

Weeks develops her notion of the demand as a form of political struggle in the context of critically analyzing the sociocultural significance of work. She proposes a feminist, anti-neoliberal politics that attacks the moral-affective governance of work by the "postindustrial work ethic," which prompts individuals to view work not only as a basic duty but also as the ultimate venue for self-expression and personal fulfillment. Weeks focuses on the temporal implications of this ideological formation, according to which people find themselves devoting every moment to working or enhancing their employability. In response, she calls for radical initiatives "to reduce the time spent at work, thereby offering the possibility to pursue opportunities for pleasure and creativity that are outside the economic realm of production."[60] She emphasizes that such political efforts must include refusing standard pleas for greater "work-family balance," which merely reinforce the hand-in-glove historical relation between capitalism and the patriarchal family. Critically reconceiving a core concept in autonomist Marxism, Weeks argues that the "refusal of work" thus must challenge the work ethic's pernicious government of the entire working day, including reproductive labor in households.

Weeks finds an ambivalent but promising model for the "postwork imaginary" that would inspire such an "anti-work politics" in the 1970s feminist movement that demanded wages for housework, from which she also draws a more general theory of the "demand" as a distinctive mode of political engagement. For Weeks, wages for housework not only advanced a potent critique of the wage relationship as regulating the lives of paid and unpaid laborers alike; it also called into question both wage labor and the productivist work ethic.[61] Beyond reassessing the content of this feminist-Marxist vision, however, Weeks reflects deeply on the movement's preferred *form* of political contestation. By defiantly *demanding* wages for housework rather than choosing more conciliatory approaches, Weeks contends, second-wave feminists were doing far more than proposing policy changes and cultural attitude-shifts about women and work. They were practicing a style of political contestation that has become more acutely needed than ever after the rise of the postindustrial work-ethic because of the ways it evokes and channels the affective energies that have become so central to capital's latest accumulation strategies and matrices of subject-formation.

For Weeks, demand-politics operates through performative and affective modalities that forge novel, autonomously collective forms of social subjectivity. Regarding the demand's "performative dimension" in wages for housework, Weeks writes that the demand "functioned to produce the feminist knowledge and consciousness that it appears to presuppose; as a provocation, it served also to elicit the subversive commitments, collective formations, and political hopes that it appears only to reflect."[62] The "affective charge" of declaring and pursuing the demand elicited these desires for solidarity, insubordination, and radical change in ways that also reshaped participants' patterns of consciousness, but without reinstating deceptively power-laden, artificially "neutral" norms for dispassionately and impartially seeking knowledge. To the contrary: in wages for housework, the demand's "style and tone" conveyed "belligerence," incited "antagonism," and rejected "the possibility of compromise."[63] Activists were neither politely inviting others to join in an open "exchange of ideas," nor making an "effort . . . to be seen as reasonable or to meet others halfway," nor showing any "interest in working within the logic of the existing system and playing by its rules."[64] In particular, those who made the demand renounced supplication for compassionate action to right a moral wrong: "Instead of assuming the position of injured party, these feminists present themselves as a force to be reckoned with."[65] Furthermore, for Weeks, the habitual and iterative practice of speaking in this register *changed* the people involved: it cultivated within them unprecedented yearnings and unforeseen conceptions of themselves and the social order. Through the demand's affective and performative dynamics, those who advanced it both proclaimed "the presence of a desiring subject behind the demand" and shaped themselves into these kinds of subjects.[66]

In elaborating her theory of the performative demand, Weeks points to "generative" and "pedagogical" aspects of demand-politics that resonate profoundly with features of Freirean popular education—and that clarify a conception of action and *conscientização* as contemporaneous and thoroughly intermingled in the midst of demand-pursuits. She describes the demand, for instance, as "not merely a policy proposal but a perspective and a provocation, a pedagogical practice that entails a critical analysis of the present and an imagination of a different future."[67]

Likewise, for Weeks, although the demand is fundamentally an "act rather than a text," it invites and enacts "a mode of political engagement in relation to which textual analyses are also generated."[68] In other words, complex operations of critical thought, reflection, and teaching emerge within and from out of the affectively charged contexts of demand-politics, and together, all these forces foster radically new subjectivities. Weeks's theorization of the demand thus counteracts the idea of a sequential ordering and mutual exclusivity between action and reflection that Freire sometimes implies. Instead, she proposes the more nuanced notion that performative action in demand-politics only *seems* to "presuppose" certain forms of "knowledge and consciousness" when in fact it is bringing them into being.[69] That is to say, the activities of action and reflection are concomitant within the demand and are jointly nourished by the demand.

Weeks has little of substance to say about how people engaged in demand-oriented struggles would participate in pedagogical endeavors that go beyond the activities through which they fight for their demands, however, and in this sense, an attentiveness to Freirean dialogue can offer an important measure of reciprocal critique.[70] In other words, demand-politics not only enacts within itself pedagogical dynamics that correspond to those emphasized in popular education—it also needs the complementary practice of popular education, for two reasons. First, Freirean theory specifies with conceptual precision the *dialogical processes* by which groups of people can wrestle with the pedagogical implications and experiences of their demand-pursuits. Second, popular education ensures the participation of *acutely marginalized, oppressed, and excluded groups* on equal terms in the overall endeavor that combines critique with action.

A further argument for the capacity of dialogue and demand to enrich one another comes from recognizing that just as the affective experiences of demand-politics involve potent pedagogical and critical-reflective effects, so likewise, dialogical exercises in the Freirean mode foster an abundance of affective catalysts to subject-transformation. Participants in popular-educational dialogue do not just ponder abstract ideas about social problems and potential solutions—they also experiment with new affective dispositions and expressions. Dialogue is not only an exercise of the head but also a stretching of the heart and an awakening of the senses. This joyously enlivening attribute of popular education was unmistakable, for example, in workshops run by popular educators from Mexico and El Salvador during the 2017 general assembly of NDLON, in which I participated as a Casa Latina volunteer. The workshops' eclectic affective repertoire featured guitar-accompanied singing, exercises that broke up seated discussions and got people moving around the room, interludes of silent theater and responsive interpretations of bodily poses, mobile formations and reconfigurations of conversation partners to interpret projected images, and tactile manipulations of wall-hung placards—all intermixed with dialogical discussion of various ideas, problems, and experiences. This was a live demonstration, in other words, of dialogue that blends the critical exchange of thoughts with transformative interchanges of noncognitive energies. Such dialogue yields experiences that are at once intellectual and corporeal through setting off rhythms of bodily motion and contact, optical trajectories, aural appeals, and feelings of excitement that mingle in a shared affective-critical topos.

It is also important to note that the affective characteristics of dialogue and demand have more in common than one might expect, given that the militant cast of action to advance a demand could be seen as conflicting with the disposition of generous receptivity to the new and strange that popular-educational dialogue requires.[71] Considering the unfixed and unruly role of affects within each process, however, it seems evident that neither dialogue nor demand-politics can do without *both* receptivity and militancy, and also that receptivity and militancy each gain nourishment from both dialogical and demand-based activities. Within the forceful assertion of demands, the "no apologies" affect implies a counterintuitive receptivity to others. The participant may well be struck by the unanticipated ways comrades act and express themselves in the midst of practical struggle, especially in tensely confrontational moments, in ways that alter the subject's sense of self and conception of the common cause. Defiantly demanding "water for the favela!" alongside my neighbors could well engender a startling and emboldening conviction that we are formidable protagonists in our own struggles and that we are more powerful together than separate.[72] In turn, popular-educational dialogue is partly intended to kindle feelings and expressions of staunch commitment to resolute action that pits the oppressed against their oppressors. Freire insists that participating in the struggles of the poor for liberation requires uncompromising devotion and a single-minded rejection of oppression, even a "conversion."[73] Or, as a Salvadoran popular educator put it succinctly during an NDLON workshop: "If you're not taking sides, it's not popular education." He was standing in front of a drawing with spacious bourgeois homes on the left, huddled masses of people on the right, "houses without people" written on the lower left, "people without houses" inscribed on the lower right, and the word CAPITALISM in block letters at the top.

A critical synthesis of Weeks's vision of demand-politics with Freire's conception of problem-posing dialogue thus helps us formulate an appropriately complex understanding of the relation between popular education and political action. In sum: we should envision demand and dialogue as moving both in tandem with each other and in creative contrast with one another, such that lessons learned and energies released by one form of activity continually reanimate the other and re-establish critical distance on the favored social-analytical categories and strategic goals of the moment. *Pace* Freire, in other words, the dialectic is not between thinking and doing, or reflection and action, or theory and practice. It is between two distinct modes of subjectivation in the midst of different shared endeavors, and each mode effects transformative transits of both affect and critical reflection.

Rather than hypostatizing this dialectical vision, however, I hasten to add the need for a third term to fill out this conception of the interplay between political action and critique in a robustly popular-egalitarian vein. By modulating the dialogue-demand relation with critical-popular inquiry in the form demonstrated by the forthcoming chapters, we can see how the disparate and relatively slender paths toward better futures charted by local circles of popular-educational enthusiasts, and oriented by their audacious yet particular demands, could converge into wider thoroughfares of collective mobilization. In this sense, critical-popular research promises to help actualize the *utopian* aspirations that suffuse Weeks's notion of demand-politics and Freire's theory of popular education alike. Let us conclude the chapter by considering what such utopianism means for these writers and how critical-popular research can augment its chances of materializing in the midst of widespread precarity.

On the Utopian and Critical-Popular Research

Freire and Weeks both aim to rekindle an intellectual-political regard for the utopian at a time when utopianism has come under attack from many quarters, from neoliberal heralds like Margaret Thatcher, who infamously declared that "there is no alternative" to capitalism, to antiutopian theorists of the postsixties Left and proponents of the "ethical turn."[74] Weeks and Freire also construe the basic dynamic of utopianism in parallel fashion. Weeks proposes a utopianism that aims "to think the relationship between present and future both as tendency and as rupture."[75] She thus focuses on how that which is and that which is not-yet transact with one another rather than simply equating the utopian with a vision of an utterly altered world. Weeks borrows intellectual traction for this conception from both Ernst Bloch, for whom a utopian orientation reflects "the commitment both to the real-possible and to the novum," and the Nietzschean "mandate to embrace the present and affirm the self and, at the same time, to will their overcoming."[76] Similarly, Freire approaches the utopian as a mode of intellectual and practical engagement that seeks impulses for envisioning and wanting a radically different future in ordinary people's everyday practices and common-sense ideas. He writes:

The point of departure of the movement lies in the people themselves . . . in the "here and now," which constitutes the situation in which they are submerged, from which they emerge, and in which they intervene. . . . A deepened consciousness of their situation leads people to apprehend that situation as an historical reality susceptible of transformation.[77]

Freire further emphasizes that not only does *conscientizaçao* make utopian aspiration possible, as this linkage between the material present and the not-yet-materialized future—it also imbues this bridging with intense desire, such that "the dream becomes a need, a necessity."[78] For both thinkers, in short, utopianism brings about the confluence of the concrete-immediate with the visionary.

Vital to the utopianism of both demand and dialogue is an ethos of special attentiveness to, and willingness to spend time with, the partial and fractural. As I have argued in the section above on *conscientizaçao* and research, to design a social-analytical approach that draws on Freire's conception of generative-thematic research is to embrace a preference for the fragmentary, in comparison to prioritizing narrative analysis or engaging in social scientific positivism. Such inquiry requires cultivating a sense for the fractional singularities of daily predicaments that participants could conceive of either as immutable or as limiting situations amenable to transformative action, along with a welcoming disposition toward the disjoined and idiosyncratic bits of language people use to describe their circumstances. Weeks similarly roots the utopian potential of the demand in its fragmentary quality. In her view, the transformative energies of demand-politics are so dynamic and fecund because, first, they emerge from action on concrete-particular matters in the time of the now, and, second, they leave wide open the constructions of subjects and visions in the midst of selective struggles. In these respects, the demand differs from two other more readily recognizable utopian forms: the "traditional utopia," which provides a "detailed outline of an imagined better society,"[79] and the "manifesto," which offers a "more minimal" vision but goes further in practical terms by self-assuredly seeking "to fashion its readers into a collective subject."[80] By privileging the fragmentary, in contrast, the Weeksian demand and the Freirean generative theme alike fuel utopian endeavors that combine radical openness with radical militancy and that activate electric interchanges between "actually existing tendencies" and "the political imagination of a different future."[81]

I argued earlier that the search for generative themes constitutes a promising mode of immanent critique in precarious times because by focusing on particularized, fractional forms of expression, this approach takes strategic advantage of the dominant temporal patterns associated with precaritized conditions. That is, this approach converts into a critical asset the key qualities of *experienced time in everyday life* for precaritized subjects. Now, in turn, we can see that granting precedence to the fragmentary also strikes a blow at the neo-liberal *(anti)historical epistemology* that contributes to the sense of time's intran-sigent immutability even as time is constantly, unpredictably shifting gears and running out—the syndrome of being "out of time" that I discussed in this book's introduction. This (dis)order prevails whether one is an info-laborer in the dig-ital workforce, a factory hand in an electronics megaplant, or a day laborer in the informal economy. Yet because those who pursue demands and join in dialogue on generative themes practice the art of suturing scattered elements of the present to future possibilities that seem impossibly remote, they learn how to intervene directly in the paradoxical time-scape of precarity—in both its daily-experiential and its historically extended dimensions. They turn its disjointed cadences and closures of mind into the utopian pulses of a new freedom.

To such an expansion of temporal horizons, in turn, critical-popular inquiry adds a widening of the socioeconomic ambit of popular struggle. A properly utopian impulse does, indeed, emanate more powerfully from concrete-specific desires attached to particular demands than from less situationally rooted uto-pian total-visions or manifestoes, especially in the affective spheres most char-acteristic of the precaritized world. Yet if we are to nurture the hope of lacing together demands and broadening small-scale popular-educational circles, such that general social changes become genuinely possible on the scale of capital's international financial flows and the deportation regime's global apparatus of mi-grant governance, then social critique needs an aspect that locates and palpates the sinews joining the themes of the most severely oppressed to the situations of the people at large. By fostering such amplitude in popular conceptions of who has what stakes in the struggles of others, the critical-popular approach lends uto-pian aspiration further heft and clarity that it urgently needs.

The next four chapters dig deeply into migrant day laborers' commentaries about the features of precarity they meet, grapple with, and sometimes struggle against when they search for jobs at worker centers and on street corners, per-form day labor under dangerous conditions at employers' discretion, and en-gage in the community-building activities at worker centers. I sift through the interviews with the aim of finding generative themes, which in turn cat-alyze improvisatory encounters with critical-theoretical analyses of precarity intended to flesh out the core theme of this book: that building a radically alternative, decapitalized society requires waging a fight for time against the temporalizing dynamics of precarity. Day laborers, as we shall see, offer un-common and keenly unsettling insights into these forces, such that in critical combination with situationally relevant concepts drawn from critical theory, both the exceptional and the synecdochal aspects of day laborers' lives in relation to general syndromes of precaritization begin to show themselves. In the light cast by the generative themes and theoretical provocations stemming from these critical labors, it then becomes possible to imagine the demands that would materially change the conditions of precarity for so many to which day laborers speak so poetically.

2

Desperate Responsibility

THINK FOR A moment about what the phrase "day laborer" connotes regarding the kind of person who works in day labor jobs and the nature of such work. Unlike most other categorical descriptors of workers—say, "car washers" or "electricians," or "attorneys" or "elder care providers"—the idea of a day laborer includes no qualitative definition of any skill or task. Nor does it involve any sense of an industrial context, such as even the vague term "farmworker" conveys, or any information about the types of materials or people with which or with whom the person works. Rather, the single, definitive context in the notion of a day laborer is a quantum of time; work's substantive content is a matter of sheer indifference. The phrase "day laborer" also implies a temporality of work that is not only exceedingly limited in duration but also variable in its rhythms. Each new day job is likely to feel different, in this way, from the one yesterday.

In its less direct undertones, the term "day laborer" carries with it a sense of triviality and the withholding of commitments. These evocations do not necessarily only signify hardship. They can also spell a kind of tentative and even playful curiosity, similar to the way a "day trip" suggests a desire to sample a new place without being constrained to stay there very long. In this book's introduction, I urged readers to accompany me on a sojourn among the lives and thoughts of day laborers. Here it seems that day labor as such can be seen as a sojourn: a fleeting detour from "serious" or "real" work, perhaps one that promises an enjoyment of spontaneity and no-strings experimentation. Kathi Weeks argues that the "tramp" in Western popular cultures, in both male and female versions, impudently defies "both the work ethic and the family ethic" and constitutes "a figure of indulgence and indiscipline."[1] As one form of this figure, the day laborer could be seen as embodying a similar rebellion against generally binding ideologies and disciplines, especially those that organize everyday patterns of time, such that this worker's very precarity comes to signify a new freedom and furnishes the practical basis for forging it.

With this chapter, I begin to unfold a series of instigations toward imagining organized revolt against the forces of precaritization that spring from enlisting day laborers as cotheorists of social power, especially in its permutations related to precarious time. The provocativeness of Weeks's speculations on the tramp figure notwithstanding, such radical impulses do not arise from these workers' direct repudiations of ethicized performances of work or family devotion. As chapter 5 discusses, day laborers are, indeed, cultivating distinctly antiprecaritizing modes of everyday time through their activities at worker centers. For the most part, though, day laborers experience the egregiously untethered qualities of their work-lives as torments that nearly paralyze them in both mind and body, as we shall see in the first section below. They take scant pleasure, if any, in their un-committed and unregulated work. More remarkably, and in no little tension with their panic and dismay over their work-lives, they tend to express keen loyalty to dominant bourgeois ideals about working hard, both as important values in their own right and as means for improving individuals' material circumstances. When I set out to interview workers at Casa Latina and Voz's MLK Center, I ex-pected to hear day laborers voice manifold accounts of dissatisfaction, mistreat-ment, and hardship related to work. I also anticipated that many workers would invoke common tropes about proving themselves as industrious, hard-working immigrants. I foresaw neither that the abuses and miseries endured by these day laborers would be so nonstop nor that, in spite of this situation, these workers would passionately advocate the virtues of personal responsibility through diligent work.

This chapter explores the provocative coincidence of the notions of "desper-ation" and "responsibility" in day laborers commentaries, analyzing these terms and the contradictory figure of "desperate responsibility" they jointly constitute. I focus on those portions of our conversations when participants described their incessant searches for work, the general condition of social fragility they faced as unauthorized migrants, and their treatment by employers when they did day labor jobs. I approach the workers' commentaries in the mode of critical-popular research I detailed in chapter 1: sifting through the interview material in search of generative themes that manifest potential for initiating both critical dialogue and committed, broad-based action to transform social conditions. Freire, let us recall, associates a theme's generativity with its ability to evoke palpable everyday experiences, to convey forceful emotional intensities, and to activate aesthetic sensibilities that are poetic, visual, and aural. By virtue of these qualities, themes can help catalyze dialogical interactions through which participants inquire into why their problems exist and how these situations could be transformed politi-cally. Critical-popular research thus helps set the stage for dialogue and political action alike by making initial inquiries with persons subjected to the harshest forms of social domination, listening carefully to what they say, and identifying themes that evince key signs of generativity.

Lingering patiently with the workers' accounts and listening attentively to their words brings to light a complex and self-conflicting array of temporal pressures, belying what might seem to be the uncomplicated temporality of day labor—a day's wage for a day's work; otherwise, free time. At the temporally vexed meeting-place of work and work's absence where day laborers perch, we find instead a series of divergent and warring protocols of everyday temporal experience. On the one hand, our interviewees saw themselves as caught in the thrall of urgent necessity, such that every moment brimmed with the imperative to stave off personal economic catastrophe by always remaining ready to work, regardless of the type of job or how poorly it paid. In a painful twist, this anxiety-laden uniformity of time was accompanied by the extreme dissociation and perpetual recalibration of temporal routines due to the randomly start-and-stop timing of jobs, the need to keep shifting irregularly from one kind of job to another, and employers' arbitrary discretion over work's pace and compensation. On the other hand, day laborers heavily emphasized their own capacities for positively influencing their individual economic circumstances, above all through a work ethic centered on personal responsibility. Such vaunted responsibility typically implied that "good workers" managed their time at work conscientiously, in contradistinction to "bad workers" whose indolence alienated employers and made other workers suffer unfairly. Moreover, just as the theme of desperation partly reflected unauthorized migrants' perpetual fear of deportation by the homeland security state, so likewise trepidations about detention and banishment infused workers' commentaries about responsible behavior with regard to work. (In turn, my procedure for annotating quotations from individual interviews reflects the need to ensure workers' protection from adverse consequences stemming from their participation in this project, due to their unauthorized status: I use pseudonyms for all day laborers who are not worker center coordinators, the latter already being public figures; I also report only the month and year of the interview, not the exact date.)

After elaborating the core features and nuances of the workers' accounts of struggling to act responsibly in the midst of desperate circumstances, I then briefly discuss how this composite theme offers an attractive point of departure for popular-educational dialogues aimed at inciting the theoretical interest and acumen of day laborers. My subsequent analysis, however, mainly pursues the second path toward exploring a theme's generativity that I described in chapter 1: placing the theme in contact with existing, self-consciously social-theoretical accounts of the precaritizing phenomena to which the workers speak via this theme. As I argued in the last chapter, research that aims to help spark *conscientizaçao* and radical social transformation should provoke those who articulate themes in the midst of concrete local circumstances to engage with one another and proximate allies in politically energizing dialogues, and the identification of generative themes vitally assists such endeavors. Yet critical-popular inquiry also should seek new perspectives on how ambitious and very broad forms of political solidarity could be organized around the problems distinctly named by day laborers, in the hope of posing formidable challenges to the structural logics of power that are precaritizing working people throughout all of society. This further aspiration leads critical-popular research toward the figuration of creative theme-theory juxtapositions.

The most rapidly growing forms of work in the post-Fordist, neoliberalized economy have been the immaterial labor characteristic of jobs in the enormously expanding service industries and the information labor of knowledge workers in the digital job market. These types of work are often heralded as enabling people to find unprecedented personal gratification not only through work itself but also through the enhanced flexibility and autonomy of employees' work schedules. Incisive critiques by Kathi Weeks and Franco "Bifo" Berardi, however, reveal the pervasive forms of domination and subjection entailed by the hegemony of the postindustrial work ethic, in a general social milieu where work simultaneously bleeds into every moment of the day and gets fractured into infinitely small, disconnected bits. Especially when we reflect on the signature temporalities generated by these phenomena, the self-contradictory predicament of desperate responsibility characterized by day laborers appears as a syndrome of society writ large. Day laborers supply language that fittingly names this syndrome. Their theme, in association with theoretical notions drawn from Weeks and Berardi, also exposes unsuspected grounds for solidarity in militantly opposing responsibilized desperation between far-flung and apparently quite disparate social groups—for instance, entwining the fates of hungry day laborers huddled in Casa Latina's worker center with those of absurdly overprivileged Amazon employees in Seattle's exploding high-tech industry.

In thematically theorizing these processes by which day labor takes shape as a synecdoche for widely encompassing social conditions, it is vital not to lose sight of the day laborer's simultaneous positioning as an exception within this society. As I argue in the section on "crisis time, desperation, and deportation," the workers' comments about facing desperate situations with a determinedly responsible ethos also reference their extraordinary yet routine exposure to applications of precaritizing power that are not aimed at most social groups. Such power is deployed particularly through the instrumentalities of the deportation regime but also through certain crisis dynamics of neoliberal capitalism that affect migrants with unusual force, as relevant texts by Nicholas De Genova,

David Harvey, and Gerárd Duménil and Lévy Dominique suggest. As they muster broad-scale, cross-class, and interracial opposition to the generally effective machineries of precarity lit up by the thematic beacon of desperate responsibility, organizers thus must also foster initiatives keyed to the illegalized and extraprecaritized conditions of migrant workers. The militant denunciation of deportation thus becomes a practically essential complement rather than just an ethically generous addendum to antiprecarity organizing. At the same time, more widely engaged forms of militancy gain support from this analysis: against ruling work-norms as not only embodying incomplete aspirations to freedom but also physically and psychologically self-destructive patterns of activity, and for a fight to reclaim the people's time from the capitalist and state forces that perpetually steal it.

Desperate Work, Desperate Time

The workers we interviewed at Casa Latina and Voz's MLK Center often described their experiences doing day labor, looking for day labor jobs, and moving from place to place in search of work as both expressions of, and strenuous attempts to ward off, a life situation of ongoing "desperation." This term kept surfacing in the transcripts in ways that suggested its possible role as a generative theme. Having noticed this, in turn, I was soon struck by how frequently the word also shows up in other researchers' accounts of day laborers' work-lives.[2] What did this general, life-framing condition of desperation feel like for day laborers, as suggested by their own comments about it? What commonplace activities did they associate with the pall it cast over their efforts to find work, maintain themselves, and just live from day to day? How was a desperate sensibility woven through their experiences as migrants—as precaritized workers on the move, searching for better opportunities while fleeing from immigration authorities that were on the hunt for them?

Not all worker centers in the United States operate hiring halls, but worker centers devoted specifically to day laborers tend to do so, and at these places, the morning job lottery becomes an intense focal point for workers' hopes and anxieties. *La rifa* (the lottery) is also a breeding ground for the syndrome of desperation that constitutes one crucial dimension of the precaritized circumstances thematized by these workers. I watched countless lotteries take place at Casa Latina and the MLK Center during the course of my field research, and they followed a fairly predictable protocol. Workers made their way to the center in the early morning hours, typically between 6:00 and 6:30 a.m., and entered their names in the job raffle. They then stood or sat around waiting to hear whether their names would be called, either out in the paved area in the middle of the center's small lot or, if the rain was heavy, under cover in an open-air garage or trailer.[3] Some kept to themselves quietly; others drank a cup of coffee (for a quarter per cup, with one worker monitoring payment), talked casually with each other, or darted into the coordinators' area to ask for help translating English forms or to check their snail mail, which they could receive at the center. At 7:00 a.m. sharp, one of the staff members drew the paper lottery tickets for prescheduled jobs and shouted out the names of the lucky ones, with no little dramatic flair and general applause for each "winner." Later that same morning, additional drawings happened if more employers showed up or called.

Our interviewees described the experience of waiting for the lotteries' results as almost unspeakably stressful. Most workers estimated that on average, they would get hired two or three times a week if they came to the center most days, although they often had gone long stretches, even up to a month, with no jobs at all. Occasionally, however, they had good fortune for several days running. Overall, these day laborers thus felt the overriding sense that their chances of work and basic survival hinged almost entirely on blind fate, the impetuous force of which materialized through the lottery. Jorge Medina evoked both the futility of searching for reasons behind the lottery's outcomes and the tensions that sometimes arose among workers as a result: "It's the luck of the draw. I don't think we can blame anybody—it's just chance.... There are people who get upset because they think the same person [always] comes out in the lottery. I made a point of analyzing that—but it's luck."[4] Several other workers spoke of hearing their names called as winning a "prize," although this was never an honor one earned: to be "awarded the prize," Fernando Sánchez stressed, it made no difference whether one arrived at the crack of dawn or just before the drawing—all it took was "luck."[5]

When the workers discussed what it felt like to be exposed to the vagaries of chance in this way, knowing their prospects were not particularly good even as their needs were urgent, the word they used most often was "desperation." By this term, they signaled a psychophysical state of intense anxiety focused on their urgent need to work and constantly brimming with worry about work's absence. To be sure, my assistants and I consistently discerned a general mood around the times of the lotteries that included aspects of joviality, light-hearted teasing, and good-natured banter. A sense of camaraderie among the workers, which I discuss in detail in chapter 5, comprised part of the climate as day laborers gathered to try their luck in the lotteries. Yet an undercurrent of tension also suffused these mundane events. Such tension was visible in the workers' often taut facial expressions or bodily postures as they waited, and audible in the sometimes-strained tone of the joking as well as the silence of many who held themselves aloof from the repartee of others.

Desperation in the milieu of the hiring process had key attributes of time and space. When I asked Alberto Guerrero why more workers who lost out in the lottery did not attend Casa Latina's skills-training classes, he replied: "It's that sometimes people get desperate because they aren't working. Because sometimes there's work, and sometimes not."[6] Juan Carlos Garza struggled for words to explain what prevented him from coming to my assistant's English classes at the MLK Center when his luck failed in the lottery, even though he had little else to do:

How can I put it—it's the worries. I think that if I had a job where I worked until the evening, I'd get organized enough to study, even knowing that I already had a job. [Now] I'm working but my mind doesn't rest. I'm worried, thinking about it, so my head doesn't let me rest.

For Luís Pérez, in turn, this situation fed a sense of dejection that manifested in vexations of the mind and impediments of the body alike:

There are lots of days all through the winter when the workers are speechless and hopeless [*desesperados*]. . . . The lottery destroys your morale. [Switching to English.] It is very depressing, and I am not the only one. . . . There are other things that we can search [i.e., other ways to find work], but we can't because we need money to leave [switching to Spanish] so you have to have a little bit saved up just to be able to breathe.[7]

Desperation in the commentaries of day laborers thus was defined by both mental and physical decapacitation as well as both temporal and spatial coordinates. Temporally speaking, waiting for the lottery and then enduring lengthy stretches of inactivity in between drawings meant experiencing every moment as saturated with anxiety, as the minutes, hours, and days crawled by at a maddeningly sluggish pace. The everyday time of desperation, in other words, was dually structured in contradiction, pitting the immediacy of the worker's needs against the protracted durations of waiting *and* counterposing the intolerable homogeneity and duration of waiting time with sudden breakups of these continuities whenever the hand of fate graced the worker with job opportunities.

In practical terms, desperation for day laborers meant not only psychophysical inhibition—being unable to draw a breath, speak a word, or gain a moment's respite from the worries in their head—but also a practical self-abandonment to whatever work activities others imposed. Searching for day labor gigs, Garza elaborated, involved the compulsion to clutch at any chance for work that happened to come his way, regardless of what the job entailed or whether it corresponded to his own desires and talents:

> I'm not picky—I'll take whatever comes. I'm not like someone who has a profession, who I've heard can say, "I have this profession" and I'm charging you twenty dollars an hour. . . . I don't put myself in that category—I can work for you for thirty dollars a *day*. Necessity makes me do it. I'd rather earn something than not earn anything at all.[8]

Daniel Rodríguez put the matter even more bluntly: "We do the work that other people don't want to do for the amount they want to pay."[9] In the field of day labor, a day's outing might involve one or more of the following jobs: leaf-raking, weed-whacking, hedge-trimming, spreading mulch, cutting up tree branches with a chainsaw, loading moving vans, digging, pouring or jackhammering concrete, roofing, demolition, carpentry, painting, masonry, sheetrock or insulation installation, and cleaning out a garage.[10] In this context, desperation connotes the extreme alienation of the worker's individuality from the substance of his labor. Ruled by the pressing need for money, he simply cannot afford to heed any personal inclinations he might have, say, to lay bricks instead of demolishing concrete or moving boxes. As the comments quoted above illustrate, he also must renounce any hopes he might have for distinguishing himself as an individual among others or gaining a sense of social equality through his work. To the contrary, work becomes both a marker and a means of his social abasement, his forfeiture of individual distinction, and his renunciation of self-fulfillment in any way other than via the cash nexus.

This manifestation of desperation as self-subjection to the "necessity" of doing any job at any wage further complicated the temporal matrix in which these workers were entangled. Workers' jobs varied from day to day, and each new job possessed its own ensemble of technical requirements, ample or sparse provisions of equipment, and idiosyncratic encounters with employers, not to mention other uncontrollable factors such as the weather's effects on outdoor work. Together, these assorted conditions gave every job assignment a unique temporal cast, such that the worker was driven to readjust to new and different temporalities of labor virtually every time he went out to work. Nor was the duration of work necessarily stable from job to job: although Casa Latina had instituted a five-hour minimum for any day labor stint, no such rule existed at the MLK Center; even with the minimum-time requirement, workers might, or might not, be kept for a few, or many, additional hours or released early. In describing the circumstances that yielded these disorienting uncertainties and perpetual time-shifts, the workers particularly underscored the role of ever-mutating social relations of employment. Chapter 4's focused discussion of occupational safety and health issues considers in detail workers' comments about the jarring variability among different employers' demands. Here my point is simply that with these demands constantly in flux and commonly centered on matters of time—how quickly (or slowly) the *patrón* ("boss") pushed the worker to work, how much break time (if any) the employer allowed, how frequently the employer disrupted the worker's work rhythms to give orders or voice cautions—day labor meant always recalibrating one's activities to newly emerging and never-predictable temporal exigencies.

In certain ways, the perpetual shifts and retemporalizations of work in day labor epitomized much longer-term norms of experience for the people we interviewed—although precisely this *regularity* over time of work's extreme *ir-regularity* activated a temporal counterflow, thus structuring the worker's general temporal experience in contradiction. Our participants, individually and collectively, had done a dizzying variety of jobs in constantly but haphazardly changing places throughout their lives, including preadult years and time prior to migrating to the United States.[11] (They also rarely did day labor, itself, as a regular practice but rather took it up and abandoned it at irregular intervals, when other opportunities fell through or arose, respectively.)[12] Such changes required them to adjust, again and again but with little foreseeability, to altered temporalities of labor and life. Especially extreme fluctuations occurred when workers switched to farm work or forestry from manufacturing jobs with scientifically calibrated time-specifications for mechanized tasks, especially meatpacking and fish-processing. Time disturbances of a different order ensued when workers were laid off or when they quit jobs they found too physically debilitating and thus switched abruptly from bouts of work at a feverish pitch to periods of unemployment, boredom, and temporal laxity. Edgar Medina, for instance, described how he had worked nearly around the clock harvesting Christmas trees during the previous winter, sleeping only for an hour or two each night in a car; by the summer of 2010, however, he was hanging around Voz's day labor center with too much time on his hands, waiting in vain for his number to be called in the lotteries.[13]

Still further permutations of desperation's temporality for day laborers stemmed from the endemic problem of wage theft. This ongoing problem meant that for these workers, the desperate need for money and hence for work of any kind was shaded by omnipresent uncertainty about how much monetary value the time they spent working would yield. "Wage theft" refers to an assortment of devices by which employers cheat workers of their earned wages, and recent studies have shown that suffering wage theft is distressingly common among day laborers.[14] This is no surprise, given the unregulated status of day labor, the extremely short duration of day labor jobs, the socially isolated character of these gigs, and the secluded residential spaces where most day labor assignments occur. To be sure, our interviewees agreed that most employers paid them as promised, and many also provided other elements of a decent working environment, including paid break time, water, and sometimes a meal. (As a volunteer taking employer calls at Casa Latina, I spoke more than occasionally with employers who either offered to give the workers lunch or asked if that were expected—we said it was at their discretion—and who seemed genuinely concerned about treating the workers fairly.) Nevertheless, employers retained the arbitrary authority to treat day laborers however they saw fit, and many abused that discretion. The threat of wage theft and other forms of mistreatment was ever-present, even if these problems did not occur most of the time for any given worker.

Day laborers at Casa Latina and the MLK Center said they had encountered numerous and varied ploys to deprive them of fair payment for their labor. As Víctor Estrada noted, sounding a common chord, an employer sometimes offered only partial pay, or no pay at all, promising to return the next day but never doing so:

> There have been times that, well, they've paid me half. . . . They tell you they're going to pay later, you know? And they don't pay. One time it happened to me. . . . I worked that day, and he said, "Tomorrow I'll come back for you, and then I'm going to pay you for the whole thing." But he didn't come back.[15]

Other employers were deliberately vague about the wages they would offer, and workers who did the job in good faith received far less than they had reasonably anticipated. In still further instances, the *patrón* peremptorily lowered the wage after a job's rate had been established, sometimes barely minutes after workers had left the center but when it was too late to go back, as in this story told by Cristian Gutiérrez:

> Not long ago I had this contractor. . . . The paperwork said . . . , "Whoever can do paving patios is going to get eighteen dollars an hour. . . ." Well, this guy comes over, picks us up right here, we get in the car and [he] drives right down the block and he says, "Guys, I don't pay eighteen dollars an hour, not even to my best employee. I'm going to give you fifteen dollars an hour—you want it or you don't want it?"[16]

Alternatively, an employer might switch the job to a more difficult or more dangerous task but not pay the worker a correspondingly higher amount. Workers thus recalled getting hired "to remove caulking" but then being ordered to rip out decaying fiberglass insulation, or agreeing to do "digging" and then finding that the employer wanted decorative bricklaying.[17] Yet another tactic was the employer's invention, late in the day, of previously unspecified conditions for completing a job to his or her satisfaction.[18] Denying workers breaks, deducting break time from their waged hours, and forcing workers to work overtime with no augmented compensation were additional tools by which employers robbed day laborers of their justly earned pay.

For our interviewees, wage theft was thus a many-headed Hydra—and it further deranged the temporalities of day labor by exacerbating the instability and unpredictability of time flows on the job. Never knowing from job to job or from day to day whether they would get the anticipated value of their labor time, our participants experienced work temporalities that shifted repeatedly and without warning. Occasionally, workers fought back when employers tried to deprive them of wages they had earned. Some day laborers personally confronted wage-stealing bosses; others sought help from the worker center or, more rarely, the police.[19] Also, as I discuss further in chapter 6, simply going to the worker center rather than the corner to seek jobs was one way to limit exposure to wage theft because dispatchers confirmed wage rates with employers in advance and volunteer attorneys stood ready to retrieve unjustly withheld payments.[20] On the whole, however, workers subscribed to the gloomy view of Miguel Vargas, who stated that when faced with an employer who paid only partial wages or none at all, day laborers had "no choice" but to accept such mistreatment. Here again, a paradoxical confluence of opposing temporalities came into play. Even as the menace of wage theft plunged daily time-flows into disarray, exposure to wage theft also prolonged entrenched patterns of experience that for many day laborers long predated their work searches via Casa Latina and the MLK Center.[21] In the present situation, in turn, wage theft involved the ironic coincidence of the temporalities of mundane, fatalistic expectation (wage theft happened all the time) and wildly unpredictable vacillation (wage theft made it impossible to tell how much money your time would be worth from day to day).

This conundrum regarding wage theft illustrated the more general sense in which daily temporal experience for these workers tended to assume the paradoxical form of *normalized crisis*. Many workers made it graphically clear they faced looming personal catastrophes that could render them homeless (if they were not among the roughly half of our interviewees who already lived on the street), lacking basic utilities (due to unpaid bills), or in other dire straits. For these day laborers, survival itself was in jeopardy. Diego Flores expressed this with hammer-stroke eloquence in responding to a question about what he needed most: "Just work. Working wherever it may be—it doesn't matter where. If you don't work, there's no money, there's no food, there's no house, there's no nothing if you don't work."[22] With time so short and the stakes so high, these workers felt immense pressure to "take advantage of the time" available to earn whatever money they could get.[23] Crisis time, or what one might assume would be the unusual disruption of normal time-flows, thereby took on a bizarrely routine cast. This ordinariness of the extraordinary was reflected in the workers' unwavering obsession, according to some accounts, with matters of money. Ricardo Reyes noted that when workers chatted at Casa Latina, all they ever discussed was, "If you have money, if you don't have money."[24] In sum, desperation juxtaposed the temporal immutabilities of anxious perseveration and a fatalism fed by years of personal experience with sudden outbreaks of crisis, all amid the decomposition of everyday time-flows through radically discontinuous work-chances, working conditions, and wage payments.

The theme of desperation further evoked a set of experiences and reflections vividly related to migration journeys and to everyday life as a migrant in the shadow of the deportation apparatus. The coordinators at Casa Latina and Voz with whom I designed the interview protocols wanted us to avoid direct questions about workers' personal migration histories, preferring that we focus on day laborers' current experiences of working, searching for work, and building community networks at the worker centers. Thus, the interviews did not inquire systematically into workers' migration experiences. Nevertheless, interviewees sometimes shared how and why they had migrated to the United States, which in virtually all cases was illegally, or how being a migrant impacted their day-to-day lives.

Some day laborers noted that desperate circumstances had prompted them to make the dangerous and expensive trek across the border in the first place, while others emphasized the routine difficulties they encountered living and working in the United States. Javier Castillo had left Guatemala after finding it impossible to support his family through their traditional means of farming corn, beans, and rice; he also had taken on wage labor to try to make ends meet but found that he could earn no more than "three dollars a *day*."[25] Juan Carlos Garza's mounting debts in Mexico had driven him to migrate north, as he told my assistant:

> Honestly, I don't like the United States. I'm here because I have the need to be here and I'm forced to be here. . . . Some debts . . . were piling up in Mexico to such a degree that they couldn't be paid off, and so then I thought a solution would be to come to the United States, get the money together, and pay them off that way.

No matter how hard he tried, Garza still could not make sufficient money in the United States to settle his debts abroad and could barely earn enough to ensure that his children, who remained in Mexico, could eat. Javier Castillo's cousin, Raul, underscored how language barriers made it difficult to find work and stoked insecurity among migrants:

> From the moment I came here, I lost my security. And then I went out to work, although when you don't know anyone, you feel like they're not going to give you anything. . . . You feel desperate, you don't know what to do . . . without even being able to greet someone in English, or ask for a permit or anything. It's hard.[26]

Other workers described how their terror of the immigration authorities magnified fears that stemmed from inadequate work and income. Said Javier Castillo: "Being an immigrant, well, everything is harder for you in this country because you go around . . . illegally, and at any moment . . . you can be deported, or the authorities can take you away." For many others, this predicament lay at the core of their recurring and occasionally scandalous mistreatment by employers. Ernesto Durán, for instance, attributed workers' silence in the face of employers' verbal abuse to this dilemma; he also stressed that "people don't complain" when employers steal their wages "because they don't have papers."[27] José Álvarez shared a shocking anecdote about an employer who tricked a day laborer into renting a U-Haul van for him and then "disappeared" with it, assuming (rightly) that the worker could do nothing about it because he had "no papers."[28] Still other workers drew attention to basic practical constraints related to being undocumented that inhibited them from standing up to abusive employers, such as speaking little English or lacking identity credentials.[29]

The inhibitions, fears, and frustrations stemming from workers' migration experiences augmented and intensified the complexly temporalized syndrome of desperation. In part, lacking legal papers aggravated temporal paradoxes I have already explored. Being undocumented induced many workers to take their chances in the job lottery because they were reluctant to seek jobs in publicly visible places or through untrusted mediators. Unauthorized status also further blocked workers from resisting the disorganization of work time caused by employers' unpredictable, abusive behaviors. Furthermore, the condition of lacking legal residence suffused every daily activity with the foreboding sense that at any second, a crisis could erupt that would spell not only acute material impoverishment but also indefinite imprisonment, societal expulsion, or bitter separation from family and friends (although many of these men were already living without such close connections). In this further respect, the temporality of desperation awkwardly welded stubborn continuities of time—the never-ending bracing for impending catastrophe—with real onsets of crisis—when individual workers actually were arrested, detained, and deported, or when this happened to someone they knew.

Anyone familiar with even the broad outlines of migrant women's experiences as foreign domestic workers will notice that the account of desperation our interviewees provided has distinctly gendered characteristics. The growing scholarship on domestic workers, supplemented by instances from the handful of interviews we did with women in Casa Latina's fledgling domestic workers' employment program (which had become much more firmly established several years later), along with other minor elements of our field research, suggest what certain gendered qualities of the theme might be.[30] I engage in these considerations, however, knowing that this is no substitute for a full-scale exploration of how women domestic workers would articulate the features of desperation in their work-lives, and whether they might introduce a different vocabulary to talk about similar struggles. Significantly, one woman at Casa Latina who spoke directly to the theme of desperation, Diana Ortiz, expressed the temporality of incessant anxiety in terms of her ability to care for her children:

> Those of us who are new arrivals are in a little bit of desperation because we say, "OK, there went another day." Tuesday comes, and that's two days; Wednesday comes and it's half the week [gone by]. Thursday comes, and the end of the week is getting close. Saturday comes, and what are you going to give your children to eat? And you have to leave your children for a long time, and I think they get really bored. From Monday to Friday all shut up inside, and even Saturday and Sunday.[31]

Ortiz's comments share affective traits with those of male workers, for instance in the way her syntax creates a sense of how constant both the lack of work and stress over not working are. Although many men similarly worried about whether they could provide food for their children, however, these men almost never mentioned doing this as a matter of direct personal care. Nor did any of them relate such efforts to concerns about who would take care of their children from day to day. Such considerations suggest that for women domestic workers, temporalized experiences of desperation may be both magnified and distinctly contoured. At the same time, the long-term separation from children and other family members colors migrant domestic workers' day-to-day experiences with still a different kind of desperation, although it remains unclear whether they would use this term to describe such painful experiences. This was evident at a Casa Latina women's leadership training seminar I attended where many participants wept as they talked about the distances dividing them from children in their countries of origin, or as they listened to others discuss such hardships.

How much deeper and more tangled might the plight of migrant-worker desperation be when, beyond the mutual shearing of immutably stultifying and discontinuously disorienting temporalities described by the men, the most immediate needs of one's own children are at stake? How much more acute might the disturbing unpredictability and self-conflicting character of everyday time-flows feel when, precisely by pursuing work as an iron-clad necessity, one must relinquish so much control over what happens to one's children?

Migrant women's exposures to mistreatment by men comprise another set of experiences that undoubtedly would affect how such women would put their own circumstances of desperation into language. One domestic worker at Casa Latina told us she had migrated to the United States not only because of poverty but principally because her husband had physically abused her for years; studies in the United States and other countries have shown a variety of complex connections between women's migration and intimate partner violence.[32] In addition, as discouraging as the daily lottery was for the men, women's experiences of coming to the center and waiting for work seemed to be worse, in two respects. First, there were very few women and they felt like, and often were treated as, outsiders to the masculine scene where lottery numbers were drawn with bravado and winners received hearty thumps on the back. We asked the men how they felt about women's inclusion in the centers, and although few said outright they wished the women would leave, most betrayed some hesitancy. When this issue came to the fore shortly after our field research and Casa Latina began building the women's employment and leadership programs in earnest, it became clear that many men resented the women's presence at the center. Some men also harassed the women, sexually or otherwise and with varying degrees of severity, despite the staff's efforts (in an organization predominantly led by women) to discourage such behavior. In short, the temporality of desperation took on more troubling features when the daily dread of having no work further involved the gendered structuring of hours spent at the center as time when women felt unwelcome, were denied or only grudgingly granted social recognition, and stayed ever on edge because of routine harassment.

These aspects of our research at Casa Latina provide glimpses of the ways a focused effort to do critical-popular research with domestic workers likely would enhance and complicate the account provided by male day laborers of what they called their desperate situations. At the same time, much of what we learned from our limited interviews with women aligned with concerns expressed by the men. For women and men alike, searching for day jobs and performing them under wholly uncertain and constantly fluctuating conditions involved long histories of exposure to wage theft, the perpetual need to adjust and readjust to employers' shifting whims, and anxiety about work's absence and transience that saturated the turbulent flows of everyday time. As Diana Ortiz's trepidations about her children implied, furthermore, women shared—albeit in different ways—in a certain disposition we found to be so common, and in some ways so self-contradictory, among the men. This was the tendency to avow the inestimable importance of personal responsibility even while mired in utter desperation, and it is to that jarring juxtaposition of themes that I now turn.

Desperate Responsibility

Caught amid swirls of ordinary crisis-time, subject to the job lottery's caprices, living daily with the incoherent sense that nothing ever changed even as the ground constantly shifted under their feet, day laborers often voiced the sense that their lives were at the mercy of forces completely beyond their control. Yet as intense as this sentiment was, just as pronounced was their characteristic emphasis on their capacity and obligation to demonstrate personal responsibility. However improbably, given the social constraints they faced, and often with a touch of irony, our participants saw themselves as able to influence their prospects and conditions of employment in various ways. They believed they could reap tangible benefits from thinking and behaving in what they deemed responsible ways. They also frequently saw responsible action as a moral duty they were proud and obliged to fulfill out of regard for others and for their own integrity.

Workers at Casa Latina and the MLK Center often contradicted their own and others' insistence that whether and how they worked was completely in others' hands. Instead, multiple participants told us, center members had to work hard and show a responsible attitude toward their jobs, to ensure a steady inflow of employers. As Roberto Fernández said: "For them to come here and hire us, we have to do a good job for them so they see that good workers come from here. If we do the job hard and well, and do the best we can, then they will come to hire us."[33] With enough individual pluck, others noted, one also could generate more job opportunities beyond those available through the lottery, as Pedro Santiago explained: "People come here who like my work, and . . . when I go to work I give them my number. Later that person recommends me to another person."[34] For Luís Pérez, building an individual employment network comprised his sole motivation for coming to the MLK Center: "This is the reason that I'm here—to make those contacts. Not to work for two or four hours a day—I'm here to get contacts." Fernando Sánchez similarly contended that by consistently doing "*el* hard work [English in original]" he and others could "get ahead" in the sense of gaining upward mobility. Even workers who doubted they could significantly elevate their class status through "responsible" work still believed that by showing such diligence, they at least could meet their basic needs, stabilize their circumstances, and support dependents.

Many workers who stressed this theme of personal agency and responsibility gave their comments a moralistic tinge by contrasting their own dedication to hard work with the negligent and self-destructive attitudes they imputed to other day laborers. A common trend was to distinguish categorically between "good" and "bad" workers: those who earnestly tried their best, exercised self-discipline, and satisfied their employers; and those who wanted money without working for it, preferred to talk idly or carouse, and leeched off others' efforts. Héctor Molina expressed this contrast succinctly and contemptuously: "Unfortunately, many people really do put effort into their work and others don't. There are some who just go to a job and don't do the work or don't take any interest in the job. Then some [employers] don't come back."[35] As this comment illustrates, our interviewees often cast the obligation to exert themselves faithfully on the job as both a matter of individual uprightness and a duty to others, in the sense that everyone's employment chances would decline if the indolent behavior of some discouraged employers from coming to the centers. In particular, workers often disparaged the "delinquents" among them for having a "problem" with alcohol or drugs, which disposed them to scoff at hard work and to make trouble, for instance by sneaking beers in the porta-john or on the job.[36] Other workers faulted some of their fellows for dishonestly accepting jobs for which they lacked the requisite skills and then slowing their coworkers down.

One frequent complaint from participants who cast themselves in the role of the "good worker" (as nearly all did) was that the "bad workers" took a completely irresponsible attitude toward *time* on job assignments. Antonio Soto thus criticized fellow workers for "watching the clock" instead of putting their minds and bodies into their work:

> One time I went to work with a young guy . . . and we started working and he didn't do anything. [The job was] to break up the soil, and he kept turning around every which way, looking at the clock to see what time it was—asking what time it was and when we would be finished; what time they were giving us a break; what they were going to give us to eat. And we hadn't done anything at all. . . . Just a really bad guy.[37]

Roberto Mendoza was likewise frustrated with colleagues who shirked hard work and slowed down the job's pace, sometimes even resorting to juvenile deceptions, as in the following humorous anecdote:

> I've gone to work with people who just want to sit there talking. If [the employers] tell you that it's a six-hour job, they want to do it in twelve. That is another reason why the [employers] don't come back. If the employer takes two or three people to do a job, there can be one person who is

working but the other two are smoking or walking around without doing anything. . . . For example, we went to work with the [contractor] who lays wood floors. The other guy was just saying crude things and banging on the floor with a hammer—like, to make the employer think that he was doing the work, by making noise. . . . That is not OK. If you want the employers to come to the center, you have to work.[38]

Sean Garcia voiced similar irritation at a coworker who failed to show up for a job, leaving Garcia to do the job on his own. Garcia noted (in English) that this gave him the chance to show what a dedicated and efficient worker he was, but also compromised future employment prospects:

The guy I was working for was tired and wanted to take a four-hour nap. . . . I got the truck loaded in an hour and a half. He thought I was joking! He took me to another site and took another nap. I finished the work. That is the difference of when you have good workers and when you don't. . . . I am pretty sure we lost this dude because of the other guy that was supposed to work with me. If he [the employer] ever comes back, I know he will ask for me first. . . . We not only have to go and do the job right, but in a hurry too.[39]

Here Garcia memorably augmented an invocation of the good worker / bad worker dichotomy with his image of a lazy boss, in contrast to the diligent worker who uses his time productively—and who readily levels moral judgments at coworkers when they fall short of these standards, in ways that highlight the speaker's own time sensitivity and moral superiority.

Beyond increasing job opportunities, personal responsibility was said to help workers avoid job-related injuries, boost their incomes, and ward off wage theft— even as workers typically acknowledged their endemic impoverishment, the stubborn frequency of wage theft, and the constant vulnerability of their bodies to work-related impairments. Alejandro Delgado invoked time-conscious, safety-conscientious work as the antidote to a sense of "desperation" when he criticized fellow workers for prioritizing waged work-hours over their own physical protection:

They work and what they want is the clock—the eight hours, the six hours—and they go around that way, you see, desperate, just looking at the clock. . . . They are worried about lunch; they don't pay attention to the job or, sometimes, the risks there are, that sometimes you go into the forested areas, in the gardens . . . [and] you don't know if there is a snake or if there are animals there. . . . You have to look, to be safe.[40]

With obvious self-approval, other workers lauded responsible behavior on the job as a reliable means for evading wage theft. Echoing several others' irritation at workers who complained that employers cheated them of fair payment, Sean Garcia said flatly (in English): "People are not going to pay someone who doesn't do the job right.... I never had that problem with any employer; I always got paid and they want me back most of the time.... I think that if you do the work, the employers will pay you." Garcia thus implied that if a day laborer suffered wage theft, he probably deserved it.

For the day laborers we interviewed, the point was not just to act responsibly but also to *show themselves* to be responsible individuals through culturally and racially attuned practices meant to elicit positive acknowledgments—and corresponding rewards—from those with more elevated places in the social hierarchy. Many participants stressed this when they used the common expression *echándole ganas*, which essentially means "giving it your best"—putting your heartiest effort into the task at hand; doing something well, proudly, and with evident satisfaction. Workers often professed their dedication to this ethic in ways that highlighted their abilities to "read" white employers' predilections and strategically appeal to them. Noting his commitment to *echándole ganas*, for instance, Arturo González elaborated that he sometimes earned nearly fifteen dollars an hour, well above the ten-dollar norm in Portland; when asked why, he replied: "Because I do a good job for them. [Switching to English.] Clean and neat, [switching to Spanish] that's what the employer likes, that it be clean and neat. I like to work [switching to English] neat."[41] González's code-switching suggests that he not only strove to execute his task properly but also sought to respond skillfully to his white employer's distinctive expectations in a way he wanted that individual to notice and remunerate.[42] Other interviewees who vaunted their own racially attentive canniness in legibly demonstrating a staunch work ethic invoked the "good/bad worker" dichotomy to drive their point home. Along these lines, José Ruiz bragged that he had earned double wages doing yard work for a *gabacho* (roughly, and somewhat pejoratively, "American white guy") by working hard under messy, muddy conditions while his too-delicate coworker had engaged halfheartedly in the job, not wanting to soil his "tennis shoes."[43]

In attending to these affective dimensions of the work expected of day laborers (and of the work they expected of themselves), it is important again to consider the comparative situation of migrant domestic workers and the different visions of personal responsibility an inquiry into such women's generative themes might bring to light. Affective labor is a structural component of domestic work in ways that go well beyond the dynamics of day laborers' performances of *echándole ganas*. Ayse Akalin notes that in Istanbul, migrant domestics are viewed as desirable employees because such women both have extensive experience caring for their own family members *and* are separated from those individuals by vast distances; separation from family ensures that further care for them will not interfere with these women's jobs abroad.[44] Domestic work also continually tests the worker's ability to interpret employers' desires for "the appropriate kind of affect. . . . from keeping good company to showing kindness, deference, attentiveness, and/ or other expressions of affect."[45] Such manifest demonstration of one's skill for making the employer feel the right way is not merely a strategic performance, however, as Pierrette Hondagneu-Sotelo contends. It also involves forming genuine attachments to the children or elderly persons for whom the worker cares, although these bonds are often severed abruptly and treated as inconsequential, in ways workers find painful, when employers dismiss workers.[46] Furthermore, for domestic workers who live in their employers' homes, the temporal condition of relentless work is even more extreme than for male day laborers.[47] To be sure, housecleaners who do not have live-in jobs are less implicated in such temporally and affectively intensified relations of responsibility. Yet these dynamics still exert special force for housecleaners because they work in intimate household spaces, often amid gendered expectations that their work will reflect a special sensitivity to fashioning the home environment a family needs.

In addition, one needs to ask how our male interviewees define the basic concept of "work" when they talk about personal responsibility and what kinds of work they might be leaving out or downplaying. None of the men associated their dedication to individual responsibility with doing reproductive labor in their own households. Yet for many migrant women, especially mothers with young children, the connection between personal responsibility and care-work in one's own family is quite strong, as Diana Ortiz's comment about feeding her kids illustrates. This, in turn, opens up a critical perspective on day laborers' anticipations that responsible work would yield upward mobility through employment networking. Inasmuch as migrant women view care-work in their own households as a key locus of personal responsibility, they value a form of work that not only goes uncompensated but also affords no prospects of economic advancement via such networks.

Gendered differences like these in the meanings and forms of individual responsibility merit much further exploration. Once more, however, there were substantial continuities between the men's themes and the commentaries of the several women we interviewed. Women at Casa Latina just as readily invoked the good/bad worker distinction, underscoring their own responsible values through favorable comparisons with others whose reprehensible conduct and lack of principle they disparaged. Virtually all the workers, without regard to gender, strongly affirmed the duty to work in their paid jobs in a consistently efficient and responsive manner. By thematizing personal responsibility in these ways, they repositioned themselves as pilots of independently plotted courses through everyday temporal currents rather than being rocked and dragged along by those turbulent flows. In the face of the multiform and pervasive desperation they so vividly depicted, they asserted their individual autonomy and rectitude.

Desperate Responsibility and Popular Education

Taken in the context of the theme of desperation and loosely adapting Freire's conception of "recombinatory" practices in the composition of generative words and themes, day laborers' equally marked emphasis on personal responsibility suggests a composite theme: the contradictory notion of *desperate responsibility*. The contradiction lies in the problem that responsible action presupposes a meaningful degree of free, independent choice among options—but that is precisely what the predicament of being driven by desperation to conform to circumstances beyond one's control seems to preclude. I do not mean to imply reductively that the workers were caught in a snare of "false consciousness," irrationally clinging to a faith in their own autonomy amid practical circumstances that belied that fantasy. The workers who praised the virtues of responsible behavior had seen firsthand that they could marginally improve their situations by taking up this disposition. Thus, addressing the theme through popular-educational dialogue becomes a matter of workers self-reflectively modifying their existing practical conceptions about *how* they, themselves, shape their everyday worlds rather than exposing such strategies as pointless and based in illusions.

Promising directions for popular education thus emerge from the catalytic recombination of day laborers' themes regarding responsibility under desperate conditions. Other comments by our interviewees indicate how such dialogical investigations of social power and domination would have useful points of departure in what some workers are already thinking rather than proposing entirely unfamiliar modes of thought. Scattered but incisive remarks identified social-historical sources to day laborers' desperate circumstances, counteracting workers' own tendencies to naturalize their problems or to depict them as amenable only to individualized and moralized forms of action. For instance, when we asked workers why they thought their chances to work were so inadequate and unpredictable,[48] most answered perfunctorily that it all depended on the weather, but a few blamed the dynamics of the general "economic crisis." Granted, as I learned while fielding employer calls as a Casa Latina volunteer through a whole annual cycle of seasons, weather fluctuations greatly affect how many work orders these centers receive.[49] Nevertheless, a few participants mentioned how layoffs by struggling businesses during the 2008 crisis had led more workers to seek day labor jobs and heightened job competition. Others reasoned that employers who suffered decreased revenues with the economy's collapse were likely to hire fewer workers and to do certain tasks themselves, and that the meltdown had caused homeowners to postpone home improvements. A few day laborers contextualized such microeconomic dynamics within global political-economic trends and class relations. Oscar Morales, for instance, declared that "the lower class and the middle" suffered alike from the combined effects of the housing market crash, home foreclosures, and decisions by "capitalists" to "move their industries" to "Mexico or Asia" to "get cheaper labor."[50] Enrique Jiménez similarly denounced the "neoliberal policy" by which businesses contracted out for "labor power," shed sustained obligations to workers, and intensified employers' "class" power in ways facilitated by government tax policies.[51] Comments like these could be interpreted as freighted with their own desperate fatalism about the inevitability of class domination and subjection, but this was hardly their necessary implication. They at least shifted the themes onto the plane of coordinated social action in which, in principle, workers could imagine themselves intervening collectively.

The preceding chapter's discussion of the features that endow themes with generative potency illuminates a range of other qualities the composite theme of desperate responsibility exhibits that make it an attractive touchstone for Freirean problem-posing education. Among these traits are moments of starkly poetic elegance that evoke concrete-practical struggles. Such moments can be heard, for example, in Flores's rhythmic description of the dire consequences of finding no work ("no money . . . no food . . . no house . . . no nothing"), the reiterative cadence of which fosters a palpable sense of confinement within an obdurate order. Workers also call forth images of scenes of desperation that highlight bodily effects (being barely "able to breathe") and emotional intensities ("My head doesn't let me rest") that lend themselves to the visual exercises Freire advocates. Sharp tensions between these affects and the can-do resolve of *echándole ganas*, in turn, brim with opportunities for dialogical examination. It is easy to imagine lively conversations, for instance, about what gives a worker a basis for believing that "giving it his best" will matter, how everyday experiences of time play into such judgments, and whose responsibility it is when simply doing your best is not enough to stave off desperation. The "good/bad worker" dichotomy also seems ripe for dialogical engagement, especially given Freire's observations about how popular education counteracts oppressed persons' common inclinations to disparage one another in lieu of criticizing the powerful.[52] I did not have the chance to initiate dialogues on these themes before finishing this book, as I did with other themes discussed in the chapters ahead, but there would seem to be abundant value in dialogically investigating the theme of desperate responsibility as a means for theorizing precarity within the communities of day laborers at Casa Latina and Voz.

As I argued in the preceding chapter, however, the critical-popular researcher also should seek portents of any given theme's generativity by exploring its valences with conceptions of large-scale social dynamics proposed by critical theory. Probing these affinities can make visible the outlines of broad popular solidarities that could throttle the engines of society-wide patterns of domination. Juxtaposing popular themes with self-conscious social theory also can attune our ears to evocative, in-spiriting language that could help such collective forces name their grievances and aspirations. How, then, might the theme of desperate responsibility kindle a newly critical understanding of conditions of precarity that (other) theorists have already been trying to describe and explain? If the most conspicuous discursive phenomenon here is the ironic entwinement of desperate submission to heteronomous fate with buoyant avowals of personal responsibility, knotted through with temporal threads, then what mutual light can this thematization of day laborers' worlds and extant theorizations of precarity shed on one another? Also, if precarity, as I have argued, simultaneously targets day laborers and other hypermarginalized groups in exceptional ways and encompasses much broader working populations, then how might this sense of precarity's dual character gain refinement through pondering the theme of desperate responsibility in association with critical analyses of responsibility and temporality in precaritized worlds of work?

Crisis Time, Desperation, and Deportation: Day Laborers as Exception

Rich and suggestive resonances abound between day laborers' conundrum of desperate responsibility and certain accounts of the economic and social crises fueling rampant precaritization in recent years. These mutual reverberations signal key respects in which the theme of desperate responsibility frames a condition of subjection marked out specifically for day laborers and other unauthorized, low-wage migrant workers and imposing ordeals on these groups that most other working people avoid. Consider the unique dynamics for migrants of capitalism's burgeoning tendencies toward crisis in the much-discussed current era of financialization, especially as these involve daily temporalities and spatialities of work. David Harvey argues that, historically, a range of crisis dynamics have stemmed from the pressures capitalists constantly face to increase the velocity of capital's circulation so as to avoid its devaluation. For Harvey, the proliferation of crisis propensities also intensifies over time, especially as financial innovations become more commonly used to stall the momentum toward crisis. The financialization of capitalist processes, moreover, leads contradictions to be "displaced on to some higher and more general plane where they provide the ingredients for crisis formation of a different and often more profound sort," as we have witnessed in the neoliberal era.[53] By this "plane," Harvey means the general sphere of financial trading and investing. For our purposes, it is crucial to note that volatile financial market activity has been highly concentrated in the home-financing sector, as the 2008 crash spectacularly brought to light. The shocks and tremors of that market meltdown were, of course, felt worldwide and throughout all reaches of the economy; these disruptions also enacted and exposed sharp class divisions between "high-risk" borrowers, who tended disproportionately to be people of color and on whom the banks ruthlessly foreclosed, and more affluent groups shielded from such calamities. Yet day laborers and domestic workers have been exceptionally vulnerable to this crisis, its aftershocks, and similar crises. That is because they make up the migrant workforce that staffs the economy of home buying, home improvement, and home maintenance, and that subsidizes the crisis-prone corporate and financial interests invested in this business area with its depressed wages and desperate subservience. Such migrant workers thus feel the force of each destructive phase in this sector as specifically and immediately a crisis of *work*. As Duménil and Lévy point out, crisis tendencies in this sector have been aggravated by the common use of mortgage-based debt to finance home improvement projects.[54] This makes the impacts of crises in this area even more devastating for day laborers, whose jobs involve carrying out such projects for homeowners and contractors.

The consumption dynamics associated with financialization mark out further forms of exceptionalization for day laborers and other exceedingly marginalized, low-wage migrant workers. Financialization, Duménil and Lévy argue, involves the systematic rechanneling of corporate profits toward boosting managers' and investors' incomes rather than investing in increased productive capacities; the seldom-reported heavy borrowing by these same elites further bankrolls their extravagant lifestyles.[55] Likewise, albeit in less lavish ways, reckless borrowing among the wider working masses stokes (unsustainably) the general population's consumption at high rates.[56] Day laborers, by contrast, represent the minorities huddled around society's fringes for whom even debt-financed consumption is normally out of the question and who therefore carry on an existence of forced asceticism in the midst of debt-fueled hedonism. In this context, their desperate worries about whether they will be able to feed or house themselves, along with their frequent ensnarement in migration-financing debt and personal debts abroad, position them as socially exceptionalized, and as significantly more devastatingly exposed to the fallout when tactics designed to delay crises ultimately fail.

The exceptionalizing violence at issue here also pivotally stems from migrant work's implication in both the wider spatial dynamics of neoliberal crises and the huge buildup of border enforcement, detention, and deportation capabilities by the state and associated private industries in response to crisis-led migration. In important respects, day laborers' desperation is keyed to the accelerating spatial and temporal displacements of capital, which moves ever more adroitly and to increasingly far-flung places in its frenetic attempts to avoid sinking into crisis. One could even say these workers are the living presence on US territory of crises in capital valorization that, according to Harvey, capital owners and managers strategically have sought to export elsewhere in the crisis-laden neoliberal environment. The necessary concentration of capitalist activity and circulation in particular locations means that when crisis comes, "devaluation is always . . . place-specific."[57] Capitalist crises thus emerge at discontinuous historical moments across multiple and distinct geographic spaces.[58] When those crises happen, Harvey notes, capitalists usually attempt to find a "spatial fix" (which is also a temporal fix) to place-based crises: "Overaccumulation at home can be relieved only if surplus money capital (or its equivalent in commodities) is sent abroad to create fresh productive forces in new regions on a continuously accelerating basis."[59] This strategy of postponing and desituating crisis, however, only generates the "deepening and widening of crises into global configurations," as was dismally illustrated by the debilitating impact on Europe and the United States when the Greek economy crumbled.[60] Given that spatial fixes are tried (and fail) at an ever-increasing rate, this tactic also produces global crises ever more incessantly and rapidly. The problem is further aggravated insofar as global capital flows increasingly determine interest rates, currency exchange rates, and stock prices, thereby inhibiting national and subnational governments' abilities to regulate these entities.[61] Accelerating crises, in turn, provoke mounting waves of migration, such as the massive displacement of populations into the United States from Mexico and Central America that occurred when neoliberalization in Latin America during the 1980s threw national economies in that region into tumult.

Day laborers today are thus, in a crucial sense, the personified, lingering, and only superficially anachronistic presence on US soil of the US economic crisis of the 1970s and early 1980s that helped precipitate subsequent crises south of the border by virtue of the spatial fixes attempted then (e.g., direct foreign investment in Latin America and the expropriation of Latin American capital by US interests through austerity measures and currency devaluations). Even as new short-term crises break out and abate, day laborers *live* the ongoing, more historically and geographically encompassing crisis-dynamic of neoliberal capitalism *as* a temporally oxymoronic period of perpetual turmoil and sustained catastrophe.

Their everyday conditions of incessant spatial and temporal flux encipher and mime the parallel situation of capital assets that relocate to distant continents almost at the moment a key economic indicator spells trouble and that thereby transport crisis time to a series of continually altering places. Moreover, just as capital, especially in its financialized avatars, loses concrete connections to particular communities with relatively enduring social roles tethered to specific work-related identities, so likewise migrant day laborers come to enact a type of work that approaches the form of *abstract labor*: labor that in its very name ("day labor") loses all particularity and is reduced to a cash-for-time equivalence; labor lacking any substantive relation to the worker's personal abilities and hopes for self-realization; labor cut loose from even somewhat persistent temporal and spatial grounding; labor done purely for money and out of sheer necessity.[62]

Day laborers' motif of desperation suggests that on the level of migrant subjective experience, the correlate of crisis-avoidant spatial fixes is the awkward simultaneity of time's *homogenization*, through work's seamless commodification as well as the individual's omnipresent anxiety about the next looming crisis, and time's *fragmentation*, through multiplying discontinuities as the worker keeps shifting jobs, locations, and temporal rhythms. The migrant surveillance apparatus of the homeland security state, in turn, which defines the structural context for the expulsive reception of those who "live the crisis" of earlier times today, both further intensifies this temporal tension and invites the contradictory response of coupling immersion in desperation with the drive to demonstrate personal responsibility. Nicholas De Genova theorizes the conditions of "illegality" and "deportability" for Mexican migrants (although in terms extendable to other migrant populations) in this way:

> "Illegality" is lived through a palpable sense of deportability—the possibility of deportation, which is to say, the possibility of being removed from the space of the US nation-state. The legal production of "illegality" provides an apparatus for sustaining Mexican migrants' vulnerability and tractability—as workers—whose labor-power, inasmuch as it is deportable, becomes an eminently disposable commodity. Deportability is decisive in the legal production of Mexican/migrant "illegality" and the militarized policing of the US-Mexico border, however, only insofar as some are deported in order that most may ultimately remain (un-deported)—as workers, whose particular migrant status has been rendered "illegal." Thus, in the everyday life of Mexican migrants in innumerable places throughout the US, "illegality" reproduces the practical repercussions of the physical border between the US and Mexico across which undocumented migration is constituted.[63]

De Genova contends that even though the situation of illegality arises in important ways through legal institutions, this condition is not just a legal status but rather a practical matrix of daily existence that conjoins exceedingly precarious work with the imminent threat of deportation.[64] From an allied political-geographical perspective, Sandro Mezzadra and Brett Neilson argue that through these forms of subjugation and subjectivation, the "US-Mexico border" becomes mobile and gains practical, epistemic presence in a proliferating range of locations while also acquiring a series of distinctive temporalities.[65] Temporally, this traveling and self-multiplying border provokes the keen sense for the migrant that every moment is brimming with the danger that one will be snatched from the ranks of the undeported and expelled—or, as De Genova emphasizes in a more recent essay, detained indefinitely without due process and thus consigned to a disorienting, amorphous, and heteronomously controlled temporality of everyday life.[66] One is always barely averting these hazards, as De Genova argues, through providing labor power that is as "tractable" and "disposable" as possible.

Day laborers enrich this line of thought in several respects. First, they accentuate just how extreme the commodification and pliability of migrant workers' labor power can become. Second, they underscore the psychophysical manifestations of the warring temporalities entailed by this structuring of migrant work. Third, day laborers' commentaries throw light on a startling counterdynamic of work's *decommodification*, although not in the familiar sense of removing certain goods from the market via social welfare programs to ensure that basic needs are met but rather by untethering migrant labor power from any stable calibration of wages to work through endemic wage theft. The agonies of time in the situation of illegality, in other words, involve not just perpetual anxiety about capture and banishment, and not only the subordination of work time to full-on commodification, but more precisely a series of clashes between time's homogenization and its escalating fragmentation.

Additionally, day laborers highlight how the formation of these desperate circumstances in migrant workers' lives not only stems from the capitalist state's investments in the technologies and institutions that govern illegality—for example, privately owned migrant detention centers, vastly expanded and militarized border police forces—but also depends on workers' own investments in practical-discursive strategies to navigate this terrifying social terrain. Within the situation of illegality, *visibly* demonstrating personally responsible behavior to white people (when one cannot simply remain out of sight) becomes one of the very few tactics available to dissuade the authorities from applying the full extent of their coercive powers. *Vocally* reiterating the homeland security state's self-authorizing dichotomization between deserving and undeserving immigrants, as day laborers do when they deploy the good/bad worker binary, serves a similar purpose: one announces one's responsible ethos as a desperate measure to evade consignment to the abject population of criminalized migrants.[67] As we have seen, though, the temporal profile of this regimen of daily comportment is contradictory. Trapped in a never-ceasing state of emergency in which any instant could bring the migrant's seizure by the deportation regime, the migrant nevertheless acts as though he can distribute his time extensively and autonomously. He enacts a methodical plan for self-governance over time while in the thrall of an alien governing apparatus that condenses the flow of time, in subjective and objective dimensions alike, into an eternally present near-catastrophe.

This general and ironic figure of mundane crisis thus defines a constellation of precarious circumstances that apply in exceptionally acute ways to day laborers and other nonwhite, low-wage migrant workers. Within this configuration, day laborers suffer exceedingly bare exposure as workers to the ever-mounting crisis-propensities of financialized capitalism, along with naked vulnerability to the deportation regime. The self-contradictory pacing of everyday time for day laborers according to the discordantly jostling rhythms of desperation, in turn, reflects the special structuring of their work experiences by hemispheric capitalist dynamics that simultaneously homogenize and decompose time. These workers anomalously embody the absent/past presence and commonly denied continuity of capitalist crisis even in periods classified by economists as times of recovery or growth. As work that is not just contingent or flexible but rather wholly evacuated of durable substantive content, desperate day labor likewise mimics capital's unprecedented lack of fixity in space and time, as spatial-temporal crisis-fixes accelerate in frequency and forcefulness. Personal responsibility in this milieu, in turn, augments widespread orientations toward entrepreneurial individualism and an exemplary work ethic with survival strategies that show the optimistic countenance of "giving it your best" but, on a deeper level, are desperate measures to forestall social death beneath the always approaching shadow of the racialized homeland security state.

Responsibility in Desperate Times: Day Laborers as Synecdoche

Even as the theme of desperate responsibility signals these exceptional circumstances of precaritization endured by day laborers and other migrant workers, however, it also evokes far-reaching temporal dynamics of precarity that implicate much larger populations and in relation to which day labor stands more as a synecdoche than as the exception. Throughout the economy, even working people who are free of persecution by the deportation regime find themselves increasingly wrapped up in work processes and work-dominated routines of daily life that give their activities the cast of desperation. Yet although these proliferating compulsions are engineered by the most powerful social institutions and function to these organizations' benefit, working people also feel themselves to be more personally responsible for their own economic fates than ever before. How has this unlikely union between desperation and responsibility come about for legions of workers in recent times, and how might day laborers' words speak to these more widely shared predicaments?

Resonances abound between Kathi Weeks's critique of the postindustrial work ethic and day laborers' emphases on their all-consuming drive to work, the profound individual responsibility they feel about work, and the temporal issues of time these orientations entail. According to Weeks, the work ethic in post-Fordist times retains its historical affirmation of "work as highest calling and moral duty" and enjoins the individual to "privilege work over all other pursuits."[68] Within the "new postindustrial work ethic," however, there also lies a novel "element that characterizes work as a path to individual self-expression, self-development, and creativity."[69] Weeks argues that today, work has become *the* self-defining activity that people are told they should relish more than anything else they do. Loving one's job is thus supposed to spring from one's deepest core even though this attitude has become a social command aimed at fulfilling the subjective requirements of work in the post-Fordist economy, with "immaterial labor" as the ascendant basis for capital's productivity and profitability:

> In many forms of work—for example, in many service sector jobs—employers want more from their employees than was typically demanded in the factories of the industrial era: not just the labor of the hand, but the labors of the head and the heart. Post-Taylorist work processes therefore tend to require more from immaterial laborers than their sacrifice and submission, seeking to enlist their creativity and their relational and affective capacities. . . . If originally the work ethic was the means by which already disciplined workers were delivered to their exploitation, it serves a more directly productive function today: where attitudes themselves are productive, a strong work ethic guarantees the necessary level of willing commitment and subjective investment.[70]

In positing the productive character of personal attitudes in the new economic culture, Weeks points to the recent phenomenon in which economic success throughout the growing service sector depends on the affective signals that working people convey to clients, colleagues, and superiors. Referencing Arlie Hochschild's research on service work, Weeks also underscores the slippage between just seeming to display the right attitude and genuinely feeling in tune with that posture, which a work ethic that is geared toward immaterial labor generates. Attaining the latter emotional disposition is unquestionably an asset if one wants to execute the requisite performance of desirable affects.[71]

In this context, the postindustrial work ethic exerts a formative impact on the organization of everyday time for working people: it colors the struggle to show ethical responsibility with the tint of desperation. This contradictory situation is not something Weeks conceptualizes, however, but a politically provocative implication that emerges when we pair her theory with day laborers' generative themes. Especially since the expenditure of affective work is "difficult both to measure and to monitor,"[72] the pressure builds for individuals to overdo their efforts to cultivate the affective demeanors and motivations they need to succeed. An oppressive temporality of constant self-surveillance thus takes shape, and it applies to workers throughout the class hierarchy. Whether someone is an executive or front-line customer service agent, companies use the worker's demonstrated appetite for "putting in long hours" as a proxy indicator of that person's "commitment, which can in turn be a signal of productivity."[73] In response, workers redouble their exertions to prove their dedication. They exploit every waking moment either to work (and to show themselves to be working with gusto) or to practice the affective capacities needed to meet employers' demands (during compensated and uncompensated hours, alike). Especially for workers in occupations with lower wages and less autonomy, such as UPS delivery truck drivers and Amazon warehouse workers (although also for Walmart managers), surveillance through the proliferating technologies of "digital Taylorism" intensify these temporally regulative effects during paid working hours.[74] Yet the generalization of self-monitoring and work activity as 24/7 ethical compulsions extends to working people in all quarters.

Weeks stresses that this temporalized existence deprives people of meaningful forms of freedom, in the sense that they lack both the ability and the motivation even to imagine freedom in terms other than those sanctioned by the dominant work ethic. What day laborers add is the suggestive possibility that this temporalized ethic of responsibility not only thwarts our freedoms of imagination and social action but also lands us all, alike, in a state of *desperation*— whether we are Home Depot executives, Lowe's customer service agents, or day laborers hovering around the edges of megastore parking lots. This desperate condition involves not only limited political-intellectual horizons but also intense suffering: if not, for most, the hunger and imminent threat of homelessness that plague day laborers, then still, for all, the perpetual dread about not working enough and not living up to one's own expectations for showing personal responsibility. Adjusting the frame of Weeks's analysis in this way also makes it strangely possible to see day laborers as epitomizing this self-conflicting dynamic of the postindustrial work ethic even though they explicitly disavow any hope of finding personal fulfillment through their jobs. Recall, here, Juan Carlos Garza's dejected comment that he is not like someone with a "profession" who can choose such fulfilling work and even charge higher rates for it. Yet day laborers are *model* "professionals," from a point of view informed by Weeks's perceptive argument that acting "professionally" is another code word for handing over every instant of one's time to capital through work, the constant readiness to work, and the on-going cultivation of the self's working assets. As Weeks writes: "The professional's relationship to his or her calling entailed an erosion of the temporal boundaries between work and life, and a different calibration of the qualities of emotional in-vestment between the times and spaces of work and life outside it."[75] Day laborers ironically personify such professionalism. They also underscore the affective dis-position of desperation that rules people engaged in this temporal askesis and that subtly suffuses the wider field of production-related affects they strain to display, modulating bright-faced smiles with low-level grimaces.

Placing day laborers' theme side by side with Weeks's analysis also highlights how the culturally mandated overlay of all living time with work demands not only impedes radical reformulations of freedom but also sabotages the post-industrial work ethic, itself. In turn, this exercise suggests how day laborers offer arresting language for turning this contradiction into a political provoca-tion. When individuals find themselves on the treadmill of perpetually trying to feel and manifest personal satisfaction in their work (or, in other words, to show they are *echándole ganas*), to the exclusion of all other activities and in step with orders from above, the temporal logic of the ethic cannot but sub-vert the sense of joyful autonomy it promises. A certain form of abstract labor thus becomes the unwitting focus even for highly privileged workers, just as day labor approaches the form of abstract labor, albeit with a different cast. Instead of personally invigorating absorption in concrete activities that are distinctly one's own, the individual ends up immersed in the constant, vacant endeavor to show others *that* he is working and that he loves it. The contradictory figure of desperate responsibility aptly designates this general predicament in which the manic effort to revel in the substance of one's work deprives one of con-tact with that very substance. This way of naming the problem also invites a political response keyed to the affect of desperation. Acknowledging our des-peration means heeding the sharply painful sense that staying on this treadmill is not just giving us an impoverished form of freedom. Rather, it is allowing us no freedom at all. Our temporal habits of work-life not only yield sorely limited happiness but also negate even those timid satisfactions we allow our-selves. The fight against the postindustrial work ethic, with its sturdy anchors in immaterial production, the neoliberalized state, and popular culture alike, needs the outrage and the resolve to leap off the treadmill that this sensitization to desperation is well fashioned to provoke.

As Weeks points out, the merging of work time with time for living as such poses further conundrums with respect to how wages are calculated, leaving a growing breach between the time people spend working and the activity that is considered deserving of compensation. Here, too, day labor stands as a synecdoche for vastly encompassing social syndromes, and day laborers' themes trigger politically innovative ways of rearticulating the problem. Wage theft among day laborers, in a sense, reflects in a particularly harsh light the recent socioeconomic transformation by which the work time designated for compensation is becoming detached from the actual time people devote to work even though class power-relations still permeate the latter stretches of time. In an economy based increasingly on immaterial labor, Weeks writes, "The time of production continues well beyond the formal working day, the space of production reaches beyond the discrete workplace, and the relations of production extend beyond the specific employment relation."[76] Such production via affect activation on what is supposedly one's private time not only occurs outside regular work hours but is nearly impossible to quantify in a way that would make possible an equivalence relation between productive work and time-based wages.[77] The bald exposure to wage theft that day laborers report and the concomitant untethering of waged time and work time for them speaks to this far more pervasive social trend. Multitudes feel their compensation lifting off from its groundedness in their work time, even as the compulsion to work seeps beyond all temporal bounds.

Theorizing thematically with day laborers suggests that we view this problem not merely as a disjunction or gap but also as a *theft*—and not only of money but also of time. Herein lie prospects for radicalizing the recent cross-class organizing around the issue of wage theft, a problem that occurs throughout the working world, as Kim Bobo, the Chicago-based coordinator of a nationwide network of worker centers grounded in faith communities, and a leading critic of wage theft as a widespread violation of fair labor standards, emphasizes.[78] Read in fertile juxtaposition with one another, day laborers' commentaries and Weeks's critique intimate that what the bosses are stealing is not just fair pay for jobs well done but also the formal temporal coherence and substantive durations of nonwork activity that are essential to freedom. Reframed in this way, the struggle against wage theft must move beyond recovering unpaid wages and punishing employers who stiff workers—because wages were never paid in the first place, nor were ever thought to be owed, for the untold amounts of time the bosses have stolen. The struggle against wage theft thus becomes a fight for the people's time that has been taken from them by force. Naming the fight in this unequivocally militant way, in turn, offers a chance to begin loosening people's self-contradictory embrace of individual responsibility through work under the duress of desperation. It also seems well poised to help galvanize popular support for Weeks's proposed demand for a universal basic income as one route toward restoring the stolen goods, in a political environment where self-destructive attachments to desperate responsibility remain ubiquitous and counteract enthusiasm for such a demand.

Critical-theoretical accounts of the morphing of work-life in the digital age suggest still further respects in which day laborers' syndrome of desperate responsibility manifests an isomorphism with general social tendencies while supplying additional, politically salient reconceptualizing resources. Such analogues involve not only the incessant pressure to work and to make plain one's supreme pleasure in working but also the friction between temporal homogenization and counterdynamics of temporal decomposition. Excluded from what Franco "Bifo" Berardi calls the "cognitariat" and even typifying the digital worker's Other, as workers whose tools are neither linguistic particles nor segments of code but rather shrub clippers and paintbrushes, day laborers nevertheless live out an alternative version of the frantically discontinuous work-culture that is endemic in the information technology industries.[79] As Andrew Ross argues, most work in information technology industries today "is done either by users who do not perceive their interactive input as work at all, or else it is contracted out online—through a growing number of e-lance service sites—to a multitude of taskers who piece together lumps of income from motley sources."[80] Ultimately, this yields "the microdivision of labor into puzzles, stints, chores, and bits, which, if they amount to anything more than distractions, require only fitful bursts of concentration."[81] Just as day laborers repeatedly but unpredictably encounter time's random dissociation into unlike fragments, so likewise, the (dis)organization of work in the digital labor market exposes working people in this realm to a similar blasting into bits of work time.

Berardi probes the psychosocial contours of this temporal tendency by which work processes systematically fracture and dissolve the subject's cognitive-practical coherence, even as they generate a counterdynamic of time's homogenization—again, in ways the theme of desperate responsibility helps characterize. For Berardi, cognitive laborers suffer the toxic combination of the demand for constant attention to the possibility of inserting their moment of work into the network with the relentless speeding-up and particularization of the processes by which work valorizes capital. Portable electronic devices such as smartphones now make it technically possible for individuals to be called to attention at any instant their productive labor is needed while remaining flexibly unemployed during the intervals between such beckonings. In turn, it has become culturally obligatory for such workers to live in perpetual anticipation of the next microjob, whether they are working in the moment or not:

> At every moment and place they are reachable and can be called back to perform a productive function that will be reinserted into the global cycle of production. In a certain sense, cellular phones realize the dream of capital: that of absorbing every possible atom of time at the exact moment the productive cycle needs it. In this way, workers offer their entire day to capital and are paid only for the moments when their time is made cellular. . . . They prepare their nervous system as an active receiving terminal for as much time as possible. The entire lived day becomes subject to a semiotic activation which becomes directly productive only when necessary.[82]

Berardi's nightmarish portrayal of the e-lancer's cyborg-like transmutation might make such info-laborers want to ditch their smartphones and take up jobs doing physical work on concrete objects with low-tech implements like hammers and saws. Yet as our interviews reveal, one does not have to be a cognitive worker to feel such relentless and intensifying pressures to be available to work whenever opportunity suddenly presents itself. Ironically termed "day laborers," as we have seen, these migrants spend most of their days (as well as most hours on days they get jobs) *not* working, but rather anxiously looking and waiting for work. They are, quintessentially, workers who "offer their entire day to capital and are paid only for the moments when their time is made" productive. Day laborers' "entire lived day," like those laboring in the cognitariat, is given over to a discontinuous "activation" that is more physical than semiotic but that similarly "becomes directly productive only when necessary," and only according to terms dictated to them by others. This self-described desperate subordination to work imperatives graphically mirrors the desperation that suffuses the organization of work in the digital economy, not only as a matter of time's disorienting decomposition into pieces but also in terms of the nonstop vigilance and ceding of autonomy this situation demands.

Berardi argues further that this insidious culture of work is not only contrary to freedom but also psychologically damaging. Day laborers' theme of desperate responsibility helps put resonant words to these debilitating circumstances, too, and in ways that suggest a politically significant modification of Berardi's theory. For Berardi, cognitive workers' perpetual alternation between frantic bursts of activity and periods of waiting while on high alert results in a hyperactivity of mind accompanied by a vastly diminished ability to integrate the mounting flow of signs and stimuli. These difficulties, in turn, undermine individuals' capacities to engage in meaningful, mutually receptive interactions with other people.

Contends Berardi: "The hyper-stimulation of attention reduces the capacity for critical sequential interpretation, but also the time available for the emotional elaboration of the other, of his or her body and voice, that tries to be understood without ever succeeding."[83] Thrust into corporeal and emotional isolation within "a competitive society where all energies are mobilized in order to prevail on the other," working individuals end up living in a "psychopathologic economy" in which "the conditions for mass depression," accompanied by "collective panic," prevail.[84] Day laborers expand, concretize, and personalize the critical vocabulary for articulating this much more broadly cast syndrome of psychopathology. They do this when a worker describes how his "head doesn't let him rest" because all he can think about is who will "win" the job lottery, or how his conversations only replay the groove-worn refrain of asking who has money and who lacks it, or how his rampant anxieties trap him inside his own pounding brain and block him from engaging socially with others even when there are easy chances to do so.

By expressing this orientation as desperate *responsibility*, we can add still a further twist to Berardi's diagnosis: the misery that comes from guilt that one has never done enough to fulfill society's work-ethical imperatives. Such wretchedness, moreover, tends to be ironically self-compounding because the more one strains to satisfy these commands and thereby integrate into society, the more atomized one's existence becomes, for the reasons Berardi specifies. It also mingles with a different guilt formation related to the excessive responsibility loaded onto working people through their debt-financed overconsumption habits. On the one hand, as I argued in the section on crisis time and desperation, day laborers stand out as exceptions to this trend, living in dire poverty even as they lay garden beds and beautify interior spaces for the more comfortable people who employ them. On the other hand, day laborers' insistent embrace of personal responsibility in the midst of sheer desperation can be seen as a synecdoche for the broad, debt-based phenomenon of responsibilization under financialized capitalism, just as their incessant anxiety about economic survival encodes the pervasive sense in all social quarters that the next crisis is always close at hand. As Duménil and Lévy contend, the shift that renders sacred the corporate responsibility to increase value for shareholders proceeds in tandem with the piling on of consumer debt for ordinary workers through subprime mortgage lending, other predatory practices, and the vigorous marketing of credit vehicles.[85] Taking on these debt responsibilities is truly an act of desperation for consumers in most spheres of society, given not only that these very practices generate crisis conditions but also that the overall schema eliminates the jobs that would enable individuals to meet their payment obligations in a stable fashion. Indeed, the voracious borrowing habits that have become typical of not only well-to-do households but also, ironically, the financial industry as a whole combine with exploding consumer debt at large to yield a composite image of a society addicted to debt and amassing debt obligations at a rate, and with a compulsivity, that can only be called desperate.[86] Once again, day laborers propose terms useful to political efforts to call out the permanent crisis for what it is—a perpetually and growingly desperate accumulation of impossible responsibilities rather than the supposedly natural oscillation between up-market and down-market trends.

Berardi speculates that poetry may be the antidote to the debilitation of people's "psychic energy" and physical-emotional bonds through raging "semiotic overproduction" driven by "the wired ideology" and the exigencies of capital's financialization.[87] He envisions "the uprising against financial capitalism," along with the "abstract work" and social atomization it promotes, as enabled by a rebirth of poetry, which he conceives of in this way:

> Poetry is language's excess: poetry is what in language cannot be reduced to information, and is not exchangeable, but gives way to a new common ground of understanding, of shared meaning: the creation of a new world.... Poetry is the reopening of the indefinite, the ironic act of exceeding the established meaning of words. . . . A social movement, at the end of the day, should use irony as semiotic insolvency, as a mechanism of disentangling language, behavior, and action from the limits of the symbolic debt.[88]

Uprisings against capital's financialization and struggles to organize such insurgencies into a durable movement can draw real strength from the poetic language of day laborers and from critical-popular recombinatory experiments with such poetry, like those I am suggesting here. Such exercises follow a logic opposed to the stultifying form of "recombination" that Berardi links to financialized capitalism, which merely lubricates the mechanical "compatibility and functional operativity" of social elements rather than undertaking their "composition" into a distinctive collectivity based on "growing together" and "conjoined expectations."[89] The irony exuded by the poetic figure of desperate responsibility exhibits the affective potency needed to focus the attention of pathologically distracted working people on collective projects to fight for time as a battle to regain the basic conditions for psychophysical health. Such irony could sensitize not only the info-laborers on whom Berardi concentrates but also day laborers, as well as countless other categories of workers, to the complex comorbidities in the psychopathologic economy.

Desperate Responsibility and Antiprecarity Politics

At the start of this book, I argued that precarious workers are "out of time" in several distinct ways. These include not only lacking enough time to perform the mounting hours of work that surviving in the neoliberal economy requires of more and more people but also increasingly being deprived of sufficient stretches of temporal continuity to maintain a stable everyday mind-set. Precarity's temporalities, I further suggested, involve living out of step with stubbornly persistent full-time employment ideals, being detached from capital's increasingly global dynamics through subjection to local accumulation regimes, and living in a state of presentist absorption divested of any clear sense that the future could be different.

In view of this critical-popular exploration of the theme of desperate responsibility drawn from the commentaries of day laborers, it is now possible to advance beyond those preliminary propositions and say that precarious time has a distinctive, basic structure. Such time is structured in contradiction. On one side, time's precaritization involves tendencies toward homogenization and immutability. These tendencies include the saturation of each momentary parcel of time with anxiety about impending personal and social crisis; with neurally activated, technologically prompted, and ethically enforced imperatives to remain perpetually on the lookout for the next chance to work; and with brimful regret about never fully meeting our unwieldy responsibilities to work, to wring ultimate fulfillment from work, to earn enough to pay off our debts, and to show others (especially those with power) just how much we love it. These features of temporally precaritized subjectivity wax in correspondence with the growth of crisis propensities in the neoliberal economy as it becomes immersed in financialization while relying on debt creation and immaterial labor as the primary engines of capital accumulation. On the other side, precaritization for working people today explodes time into myriad, disconnected, unlike particles. Fleeting stints of labor begin and end in no predictable sequence, follow few consistent rhythms among them, and leave workers' time sensibilities scattered and incoherent. Psychopathologies bloom as distraction and disruption become the paradoxical norms of work-life, damaging the individual personality as well as the wider web of social and interpersonal relationalities. These temporal dynamics, too, intensify in association with ascendant social-structural forces, especially the rise of semiotic labor in the digital economy along with the larger trend toward the downsizing, subcontracting, and part-timing of labor forces and the declining investment in production that reflect the leading priorities of financialized capitalism.

In the light cast by the ironic theme of desperate responsibility in day laborers' commentaries, the contradictory status of this social-temporal formation stands out in sharp relief. Furthermore, by virtue of this critical-popular juxtaposition of themes and theories, new language bubbles forth for characterizing in politically galvanizing ways the abrasions of precaritized time's clashing components.

A society-wide collective movement to combat the forces and frictions of precarity could gain strength, amplitude, and resolve from polemicizing the humiliating *desperation* of workers impelled to sacrifice every living minute to the capricious calls and slights of capital, such that work-life for everyone gets refashioned according to the model of the lottery. The stark poetry of day laborers' themes also suggests rearticulating the struggle to act and appear responsible under desperate conditions as both futile and *self-undermining* (not just too timid) because of its unrelinquished attachment to a contradictory social-subjective reality. Denouncing the desperate responsibilization of time as not only a loss and a burden but a *theft*, in turn, raises new prospects for sharpening the edges and enlarging the scope of the feisty but limited pushback against wage theft while fortifying calls to reap the radical consequences of the disengagement of wages from work through a basic income. In short, perceiving the multiple and interwoven respects in which day laborers epitomize conditions for working people at virtually all social-hierarchical levels, including many who would doubtless prefer to see their circumstances as safely superior to those of such despised migrants, does more than simply offer badly needed lessons in humility, and even more than highlight unsuspected areas of shared experience and possibilities for solidarity—it also builds pressures toward political radicalization and militancy. Such energies are to be avidly sought and cultivated, if, as I argued in the last chapter, critical-popular research and popular education need the bracing practical context of demand-based politics in order to generate genuine social transformation.

Another core duality of precarious time, nevertheless, also must be kept in view even as working people engage the broad-scale political pursuits that align with the trope of day-labor-as-synecdoche. This further dualism is a matter of the tension (but not contradiction) between such generalizing dynamics and the exceptionalizing forces that uniquely govern the circumstances of day laborers and other persecuted, deeply marginalized migrant workers. How best to envision the relation between forging wide-ranging solidarities against time's precaritization writ large and combating the particular temporal agonies that stem from the singling out of migrant workers for extraordinarily harsh treatment? In part, it is necessary and good, especially in periods when migrant communities are under ferocious attack, for some political action to take the form of stirring up righteous moral fervor among the better protected to alleviate the suffering of those distinctly threatened by the deportation regime. Casa Latina and Voz both attempt in various ways to kindle that kind of activism, among their many other activities. At the same time, the analysis in this chapter points to the essential need for antiprecarity politics to encourage the growth of autonomous leadership by and within migrant worker communities. Such politicizing work is vital, both to spearhead efforts to address these workers' exceptional precarities and to coordinate migrant workers' involvement in bigger movements on thoroughly equal terms. This makes it especially important to carry out further critical development of the theme of desperate responsibility through popular-educational dialogues among day laborers and other similarly situated migrant workers, following procedures discussed in the preceding chapter and in the context of ongoing political action by those workers' organizations.

As I have noted in this chapter, additional ventures in critical-popular education also should investigate the gendered valences of migrant workers' encounters with the temporal predicaments thematized by day laborers in terms of desperate responsibility, further informing the transmission of such inquiries into new forms and phrasings of political commitment. In particular, research that illuminates the generative themes circulating most vigorously among women domestic workers, who are day laborers' closest comrades in migrant worker struggles and worker-center organizing, surely would bring to light distinctive thematics regarding aspects of precarity that apply in specific ways to women. Critical-popular researchers need to know, for instance, what new lines of vision toward precarity's constituent, politically salient features open up when migrant domestic workers discuss dimensions of desperation and responsibility that concern intimate partner violence, continental separation from one's children as a substantive qualification for work, and reproductive labor in workers' own households.

At the same time, more extensive inquiries of this sort with women migrant workers could further heighten the militancy of antiprecarity politics undertaken in response to the conceptual reorientations suggested by the theme of desperate responsibility. Women traditionally have experienced far more than men the blurring of lines between productive and reproductive work—or, to put it more confrontationally, the onslaught of temporal invasions, occupations, and thieveries—that has become more generalized with the ascendance of immaterial labor. If, as Weeks rightly insists, a truly radical refusal of the work ethic means taking into account *every* kind of work and the *full* working day, then people's resolve to take back *all* the time that has been stolen from them surely would deepen with the thematization of migrant women's exhausting navigations of their work's temporal corridors. Likewise, inasmuch as the psychopathological economy involves an aspect of guilt that stems from never satisfying structurally impossible but fervently embraced forms of work-related responsibility, listening to how domestic workers name their dilemmas in this regard likely would intensify the militancy of political action that repudiates precarity's psychosocial harms.

Finally, my foregoing exploration of the theme of desperate responsibility should prompt critical examination of how the persistence of precarity at large depends on the dichotomization of day laborers' experiences from those of nonmigrant working populations. In other words, counterprecarity organizing amid scenes of desperate responsibility involves more than balancing recognition of parallel experiences among different working groups with due appreciation for certain subgroups' exceptional forms of subordination. Such organizing also needs reflection on how the dominant working groups' subjection to capital significantly hinges on the splitting off of migrants' conditions of work and political priorities from more general struggles. When capitalist interests are permitted to execute such strategies of division through disciplining, terrorizing, and illegalizing migrant subjects, it is little wonder that unions in urban construction, for instance, increasingly find themselves losing power in the industry, as the structural bases for workers' leverage erode (i.e., through the growth of subcontracting) in step with accelerated financialization. As James Martel writes, building on Jodi Dean's exhortation that strategists of anticapitalist insurrection acknowledge and "seize" the situation that "division is common," capitalism historically has generated working populations that are rent with "internal tensions and divisions" rather than being "unitary and integrated."[90] The point is to thematize those distinctions *as* "the common," at least to some degree, and to use an awareness of the systematic creation of those differences as a basis for cultivating solidarity. It is thus vital to engage in this spirit, too, the simultaneous manifestation of day labor as both exception and synecdoche in relation to precarity's bedeviling temporalities.

The common and the exceptional have spatial coordinates, as well, and day laborers signal the special importance of one particular, temporally inflected space of everyday urban life where their circumstances both diverge from and brush up against those of other working populations. The next chapter thus focuses on this temporal-spatial context: the time-space of the day labor corner, where many migrants tend to gravitate when they first arrive in a new city, where they continue going at least occasionally even if they frequent worker centers, and where most day labor centers inaugurated their organizing campaigns. Further dimensions of precarious time and a promising politics of precarity emerge, as we shall see, when we attend to the themes day laborers articulate about these concretely spatialized expressions of acute desperation and unthinkably heavy burdens of responsibility amid the temporal flows and fluctuations of work-life in the city.

3

Fighting for the Job

THE CORNER—*LA ESQUINA*—IS a figure that looms large in the imaginations and bodily experiences of migrant day laborers in the United States. Uprooted, hungry, and looking for the basic means of sustenance, migrant workers arriving in any medium or large US city these days often wind up on street corners that have become informally designated as hiring spots for temporary laborers. On the corner, one's prospects for getting work are not especially bright. By contrast, the chances are quite good of having one's wages shorted by employers, being harassed by neighborhood cops or residents, or getting into bruising conflicts with fellow workers. Nonetheless, day laborers are driven and drawn to the corner by a complex mix of motives that include dire poverty, entrepreneurial optimism, loneliness, and a resolve to prove their toughness. Most day labor centers like Casa Latina and Voz's MLK Center originated with efforts to give workers on the corners safer and more orderly venues for seeking jobs. Yet even as day laborers have formed lively spaces for political solidarity, popular education, and interpersonal connection through their burgeoning network of worker centers, the more ruthlessly competitive and individualist milieu of the corner continues to thrive.

The field research for this book was performed at worker centers in Seattle and Portland rather than on day labor corners in those cities, and it was conceived in partnership with those centers' coordinators. In the final chapters, I emphasize the crucial role worker centers can and should play in combating precarity among acutely subjugated migrant workers and the general working population, alike. Nevertheless, when day laborers discuss their incessant searches for work and the ways they conceive of themselves and others in the midst of these efforts, it is clear that the corner retains vital significance for them even if they tend to frequent the centers rather than looking for jobs on the street. This means, in part, that a critical-popular investigation of precarity in dialogue with day laborers must include an exploration of the corner's specific temporal, spatial, and social dynamics. It also suggests that an antiprecarity politics should attend closely to the generative-thematic resources abiding in the distinctive time-space of the corner, not only to identify forms of subjugation to contest but also to discern sources of courage and stamina for mounting the fight against precaritization.

This chapter listens to day laborers' commentaries about seeking work on the corner with the aim of developing further the analysis of precarity initiated in my foregoing critique of the syndrome of desperate responsibility. Day laborers' reflections regarding the corner suggest dimensions of precaritized time that hinge on *bodily* practices of movement and immobility, which workers characterize through the central theme of "fighting for the job." Such practices and formations of body-time gain lucidity when we contemplate this theme in tandem with contemporary theories of corporeal mobility-governance in liberal societies and of the fantasy structures of social mobility in a precarious economy. Contrary physical impulses on the corner impel day laborers to stand wearied and inert for hours doing nothing, then suddenly to break into bursts of physical combat when an employer appears. In both cases, however, workers violate politically salient conventions of proper bodily comportment in these public urban spaces, as Hagar Kotef's cogent analysis of liberal regulation of subjects' bodily movements helps us see. In turn, day laborers' dreams of extricating themselves from the fight on the corner and finding less embattled forms of work-life imbue their bodily practices with the energy of personal and social fantasy, in ways that exacerbate their contradictory quality. These dreams, I argue, fall prey to the self-defeating dynamics of "cruel optimism" that Lauren Berlant identifies as a general malady of precaritized culture. If the bodily predicaments on the day labor corner subject these migrants to exceptional forms of precaritization, their labors of the imagination put them in company with precarious workers throughout the economy and manifest day labor as a synecdoche for precarity writ large.

As with our critical-popular probing of the theme of desperate responsibility, furthermore, the theme of fighting for the job not only exposes how marginalized and excluded migrant workers emblematize widespread circumstances of precarity even as they remain subject to targeted forms of domination—in addition, this exercise yields new and politically potent terms of transformative engagement with the engines of precaritization. Keeping critically alive a sense for the fight on the corner, albeit with the foes and prizes reconceived, is politically imperative even if one stresses the far-reaching implications of worker center activities for antiprecarity struggles. This is so, not only because it is difficult to imagine worker centers developing the capacity to handle the full demand for day labor among migrant workers.[1] Nor is it only because many worker centers and the National Day Labor Organizing Network often established themselves through defending workers' rights to solicit jobs in public spaces and have continued to cultivate mutually supportive relations with day labor corners rather than simply promoting centers as alternatives to the corners.[2] Nor is it just because efforts to organize corners, for instance through workers' pacts to demand certain minimum wage rates, have shown promise but remain limited to the minority of corners in US cities. In addition, and more importantly, the abiding pertinence of the corner to the political potentialities of day laborers and precaritized working people throughout society consists in its siting of the fighting: its symbolically rich em-place-ment of a militant spirit that can be turned in directions quite different from the individualist competition that prevails in these spaces today.

To explore these antiprecarity possibilities, I take a more elastic approach to critical-popular analysis than in the preceding chapter, moving beyond the interviews and field observations to scrutinize representations of the day labor corner in an astonishing documentary film called *Jornaleros* produced by Voz in 2009. Voz's documentary makes audibly and visually perceptible what the theme of fighting for the job indirectly suggests: that rather than straining to replace the fight with well-disciplined order, the better path, politically, would be to adapt the pugilistic attitude day laborers take on in the corner's milieu to a more ambitious and solidaristic fight against the combined potencies of the deportation regime and the neoliberal work culture. More specifically, political energies vibrating between the lines of workers' commentaries on the fight for the job and resonating more palpably in *Jornaleros* move toward a politics aimed at the *refusal of work*. I borrow this concept from autonomist Marxism and critically elaborate it through considering day laborers' intimations of such a refusal's temporal and spatial aspects. I locate an unlikely basis for the refusal of work in the tenuous, small, dispersed, shabby, and seemingly trivial patches of urban territory where hungry day laborers immerse themselves, body and soul, in desperate battles *for* work—and where they also foster a shared feeling of resolute struggle that can unexpectedly nourish antiprecarity politics.

Body-Time and the Fight on the Corner

When day laborers spoke about looking for work on street corners in Seattle and Portland, many used some version of the phrase "fighting for the job" (*peleándose por el trabajo*) to describe what it was like to frequent these time-spaces of precarity. On a general level, the workers wanted to convey that seeking jobs on the corner meant strenuously competing for the relatively few and precious opportunities that arose when employers cruised by these places. More specifically, their terms flagged the fierce physical combat that often broke out, making competition not just an abstract economic logic but also a matter of establishing bodily dominance while making one's body vulnerable. A bipolar temporality distinguished bodily practices on the corner. One pole was comprised by the mayhem that erupted when an employer arrived, in moments that were hard to predict but in which workers concentrated their hopes. With an employer's abrupt appearance, workers set off in a sudden sprint to be the first one at the car. Not simply a footrace, the dash to the vehicle was also a surly wrestling match in which workers tried to muscle each other out of the way, as José Ruiz explained with dismay: "The employer arrives and you run and run, and the one who reaches the door first is the one who gets in. . . . They all push against each other—there's no respect at all."[3] With men frantically chasing after cars and fending each other off, Juan Carlos Garza elaborated, the physical risks they posed to one another multiplied:

> I don't like to run or to fight for the job. . . . Usually there are about twenty to thirty guys on the corners. . . . And when an employer arrives and stops, well, we all want it, and the employer is coming for one or two [workers], and none of us want to let him go. . . . Up to ten or fifteen [men crowd] around the two doors, shoving and elbowing each other—and I don't like that. I don't like it because I could hit someone or they might hit me, and it will end badly.[4]

The severity of the physical conflicts on the corner could be quite severe and sometimes lasted beyond the employer's brief arrival, as Israel Campos stressed:

> The other day . . . I got to the corner and all the others came. Many of them were shoving me, just about killing me. The employers got scared and left because all the workers wanted to get inside the truck. That is bad. Not only do you risk your life—you also can end up fighting over nothing. The people fight over there. One time, someone said he was the first, and they fought.[5]

The threats to workers' bodies in these tense moments, furthermore, came not only from competitors but also from employers' moving vehicles. Pablo Maldonado recalled: "I've seen young guys who are there, and they fall down because they grab onto the car and then they can get run over."[6] In part, then, fighting for the job meant engaging in violent and unpredictable spurts of combat characterized by perilous exposure to bodily injury in an affective milieu of harrowing physical insecurity, bellicose animosity, and desperate urgency.

The bimodal temporality of everyday activity on the day labor corner also involved a contrasting temporal pattern defined by intolerable continuities rather than chaotic disruption. Each day on the corner, workers faced the grim task of living through long, drawn-out passages of time in which very little happened even as workers' anxieties never let up and hostilities simmered. Workers' bodies registered this temporal formation in the flesh. In part, sustained body-time on the corner involved the wearing and wearying embodied temporality of waiting. Going to these spots required inordinate "patience," as Mario Valdez emphasized when he described "waiting . . . in the street" for hours on end while hoping for jobs that might never materialize.[7] He and others also underscored how corrosive these circumstances were in physical and cumulative ways: "standing the whole day" with nowhere to sit down, no bathroom, and no shelter from the elements.[8] Stultification of the mind accompanied such insistent enervation of the body because, Steven Chung noted, doing this was simply "boring."[9] At the same time, the impossibility of knowing when an employer might show up made it difficult to relax while waiting, as did the certain prospect of an all-out fight for the job whenever an opportunity arose. "You have to be alert for when the cars come," said Pablo Villa.[10] Thus, workers kept their bodies constantly tensed and ready to lurch into combat. Meanwhile, their anxieties fed off one another and generated a toxic atmosphere of antagonism that sometimes boiled over into fights even when there was no employer in sight, as Campos noted: "The people are stressed, and they blow up over any little thing." Even if workers kept their fists lowered, another worker said, they often started "fighting verbally," bruising one another emotionally and keeping tensions inflamed.

Casual abuse by passers-by further stoked the climate of hostility, hypervigilance, and psychophysical tension on the corner. As Juan Ayala graphically explained, white people frequently hurled racist epithets at workers, who were easy targets as they stood for long hours in open city spaces waiting for jobs: "They come by yelling—American people come by in their car, [when you're] on the corner, [shouting] 'Fucking Mexicans!'—insulting you."[11] Echoed Isaac Ramírez: "There are Americans who go by there, and they snub us and treat us horribly. . . . They say, 'Fucking Latino—dirty drunks, drug-addicts!'"[12] Workers did not view such taunting as mere words or idle threats (and empirical studies confirm that day laborers endure routine exposure to violence, including rates of aggravated assault that dwarf those for the general population.)[13] Rather, they believed those who reviled them were seriously threatening physical violence, thereby adding to the panoply of "dangers on the corner" and forcing day laborers to brace themselves perpetually for yet another kind of a fight. Fearful of getting drawn into unwinnable conflicts with people who held advantages of racial privilege, however, workers constantly held their bodies in check as they guarded against such assaults, steeling themselves to stomach routine social and emotional wounding along with mundane menaces to their corporeal integrity.[14]

Everyday racist cruelties and denials of recognition by ordinary people in the street were matched by more gravely terrifying treatment by agents of the state, once more as a consequence and regular feature of the protracted stretches of immobility and inactivity that fighting for the job ironically entailed. Workers on the corner constantly prepared not only for a fight but also to take flight, hurriedly dispersing when police officers harassed them, or declared by fiat that job solicitation was only allowed during certain hours of the day, or searched their backpacks with no warrant. Such incidents happened frequently enough that Voz conducted a workshop on police brutality during the time we did our fieldwork at the MLK Center. Multiple workers told us that officers cracked down on the corners at arbitrary times, bullying the workers and warning that they might be arrested if they did not scatter at once. Arturo González described how one freakishly tall officer whom the workers called "Superman" sometimes came by without notice and chased workers from the corner.[15] Bobby Kalani elaborated on this vulnerability to police intimidation:

> Some days you go to the corner, they don't mess with you. Then one day you start going to the corner and they say, "Hey, you guys, get out of here!" . . . Some cops are really mean. . . . Sometimes you get, like—four cops come to intimidate you, and they tell you to get out of the corner. They threaten us, saying if we come back tomorrow they're gonna take us to jail.[16]

Several workers confirmed that after such encounters they had been locked up, or had barely escaped being taken into custody, or had witnessed the police carting other workers away and saying they would be heavily fined (for urinating in the street). Of course, the undocumented migrants among these day laborers—that is, the vast majority of them—knew that jail easily could become a way-station to deportation due to local law enforcement's broadening cooperation with federal immigration authorities, and several underscored this threat explicitly. This danger further reinforced the bipolarity of body-time on the corner, with its competing pulls between oppressive continuities and ruptural moments of chaos, as well as such corporeal time's heteronomous control by forces impervious to workers' agency.

Desperation and Aspiration on the Corner

We asked the workers why so many of them went to the corners at all, given that they had the option of going to Casa Latina or the MLK Center instead. As discussed in the last chapter, waiting for work at a center carried its own temporal conundrums, yet at least the centers provided places to rest, access to toilets, protection from bad weather, and insulation from harsh treatment by police officers, immigration agents, and people in the neighborhood. The lottery also made the process of seeking work much calmer, less rancorous, and less physically dangerous, and eliminated the tooth-and-nail competition that was the rule on the corner. Why, then, did so many workers still engage the fight for the job at least periodically?

My last chapter discussed the contradictory entwinement of day laborers' relentless sense of desperation with their ardent embrace of personal responsibility, accentuating that this thematic figure applied to workers' experiences with the lotteries as well as their general instability of employment and vulnerability to wage theft. This same conjunction of tropes emerged from workers' reflections on their struggles to find jobs on the corner. On the one hand, participants often stressed that sheer necessity impelled them out to the street to look for work despite the hardships, indignities, and perils they knew they would meet there, especially if the lottery failed them. As noted before, most interviewees averaged only two working days per week and too many workers participated in the lottery for it to yield jobs for everyone. The same urgent economic pressures and looming personal crises that drove the workers to distraction as they waited tensely for the lotteries' results—physical hunger, mounting utility invoices, unresolved debts, actual or imminent homelessness—also propelled them out to the corners. Speaking to this situation, José Álvarez said that on the corner, "everyone's going around really sad because they don't have a way to pay the rent or the bills. Lots of people are going through really difficult times."[17] Others mentioned the general economic crisis or undocumented workers' sorely limited job options as further factors forcing them out to the corner, despite the manifold hazards and deeply dispiriting conditions there.

On the other hand, even as day laborers underscored their desperate straits, they also frequently characterized their motivations for going to the corner in terms of staunch commitments to a vigorous work ethic. Temporal considerations again came to the fore, moreover, when workers discussed how fighting for the job meant more than just resigning themselves to ugly combat with their fellows and to terrorization by racist individuals and state authorities. Some workers saw going to the corner as a crucial component in a larger strategy to manage their time in efficient, street-smart, self-directed ways and thereby to fulfill entrepreneurial aspirations. Often, workers tried to maximize their chances to secure jobs by immediately heading to the corner if their number failed to come up in the lottery and by going to the corner when the centers were closed on Sundays or after their scheduled hours on weekdays. For many, going to the corner also involved a temporalized competitive challenge they were keen to take on, as Roberto Mendoza suggested:

> On the corner, you have to *move* and try to get that job. Everyone is there trying to do the same thing, and so you have to be more ready. . . . It has happened to me that I've come [to the MLK Center] for a month and I haven't gone out [to work] one single day, but I don't lose hope. On the corner there is more opportunity because every employer is an opportunity. . . . You go up to the car along with all the others. . . . But if you are the first one, you get in and you leave for work. There, it's the one who is most on the ball who goes to work. . . . On the corner every employer is a chance to go to work.[18]

Note how the tone of these remarks, with Mendoza's optimistic invocations of "opportunity" for people who are "on the ball" (or who "look sharp," or "act smart")[19] when an employer arrives, differs from those of other workers, like Juan Carlos Garza, who found the racing and shoving so distasteful. Similarly, José Álvarez remarked that on the corner, "you have to get your act together."[20] Both Garza and Álvarez intimated admiration for those who prevailed in these contests for jobs, suggesting that the victors were shrewdly self-disciplined individuals who pursued their interests in efficacious and time-conscious ways. Other participants stressed their entrepreneurialism by noting that workers often went to the corner knowing that previous employers tended to look for them there. Such workers thus used the corner as a means to build their employment networks, much as other workers took a similarly strategic attitude toward job searches at the centers.

Echoes of this more positively agentic and acquisitive approach to the fight for the job resounded in workers' comments about the abundant risks they faced in these time-spaces. Of course, many interviewees referred to "risk" negatively when they discussed the hazards of injury, abuse, arrest, and deportation that awaited them on the corners. For others, however, assuming risk signified rationally calculating and morally responsible action (once more, echoing the juxtaposition of desperation with responsibility examined in the preceding chapter). Carlos Hernández observed that many workers go to the corner "even though they know that they are risking themselves over there" because the corner attracted certain employers who preferred to avoid even modest oversight by the centers, such as requiring employers to provide contact information.[21] For Hernández and others who spoke in similar terms, a day laborer had to risk more, to earn more. Not just a matter of prudence, this attitude often featured invocations of the ready-and-willing ethical disposition we encountered in the last chapter: the worker's determination to "give it his best" (*echarle ganas*) every time he went on a job and thereby to demonstrate personal responsibility. Given the greater flexibility surrounding compensation and expectations when day laborers were hired on the corner rather than at the center, workers who accepted the risks out on the street occasionally made out quite handsomely, as in this episode related by Emanuel Ramos:

> If you don't give it your best, they don't pay you as much. But if you give it your best and do a nice job for him, they even give you extra. That has happened to me. One time, on the corner, around three in the afternoon, I got a moving job. The employer said he was going to pay us for four hours, but there were lots of things. Later he bought us lunch and he gave us $150 for five hours, to each one of us.[22]

Here, Ramos credited his own self-motivation with effecting an uncommonly favorable conversion of his work time into money (and a meal—as well as *time* to eat while on a job). Such initiative, in turn, hinged on careful stewardship of his everyday time: Ramos stressed that he had only gotten that job because he had gone to the corner after the MLK Center had closed for the day, having resolved to use every hour productively.

Still, many workers were far from sanguine about the negative aspects of such risk-taking and felt that these problems mostly prevented their ventures from paying off. Beyond the perils of running after cars and grappling with competitors, innumerable things could go wrong when workers offered their services to total strangers who knew that any day laborer who pried open the car door felt lucky to get any work at all. Occupational safety and health hazards, which the next chapter treats in detail, were especially prevalent in jobs acquired on the corner, as was wage theft. Indeed, the deranging temporal effects of wage theft were magnified because, according to numerous workers, getting hired there never involved any initial agreement on a wage rate. Luís Fernando Chávez told us: "When you go to the corner you have to jump in the cars—there is no formal way to talk with the employers. So you don't know how much they are going to pay you—you just get into the cars and then they take you."[23] Élmer Santamaría pointedly corrected me when I naively asked him how employers "decide" whom to hire on the corner: "Whoever opens the [car] door goes. There's no 'decision' of any kind there. . . . On the corner, you have to accept however much money he gives you because there is no decision."[24] Occasionally, a few workers noted, a kind of inverse auction took place in which workers tried "haggling" with employers and quickly bid each other down in a contest to win the job by offering the lowest rate.[25] In such cases, however, day laborers were effectively renouncing their ability to cut a favorable deal because their wage levels bottomed out at rates as low as three dollars an hour, and employers retained the discretion to modify the hastily set figure at will.[26]

Day laborers' hopeful variations on the theme of *echándole ganas* on the corner thus need to be heard in the context of their own testimonies to the violent, tense, and temporally contradictory formations of body-time in this fraught space as well as the dominant tendency of any temporal stabilizations they sought through entrepreneurial behavior to evaporate. Day laborers spoke and acted *as though* they were strategic agents on the corner even while it was obvious (to them) that others were mainly just taking advantage of them. In this respect, voicing the theme of fighting for the job was more a matter of *imagining* an abundance of opportunities and expressing a *wish* for forward progress than concretely improving one's situation. For these workers, the feeling of individually and correctly regulating their everyday time stood in for the actual establishment of stable and autonomously determined time-flows, both in the everyday sense of hours passed on the corner and in terms of any long-term trajectory toward easier economic circumstances.

Still a further set of equivocations regarding the optimistic belief in finding opportunity on the corner came through reinvocations of the "good/bad worker" dualism, which we encountered in the preceding chapter. Day laborers regularly relied on this trope to disparage workers who went more often to the corners than to the centers—even though most interviewees, by their own admission, ended up on the corners at least occasionally, whether enthusiastically or not. Many participants not only were skeptical that fighting for the job laudably demonstrated entrepreneurial virtue but also portrayed such combat as reprehensible conduct by shiftless people who lacked a proper regard for social order. According to numerous accounts, the profound "disorder" of men on the corner was a matter of mind, body, and affect. Disorderliness sprang from the individual's willful refusal to act in rationally rule-governed ways and predilection for ill-mannered speech and behavior. Workers on the corner had "no respect at all," disdainfully remarked José Ruiz, while Ricardo Vélez wryly noted there was "a different class of language" on the corner.[27] Disrespect toward women was reputed to be a particular problem. Female staff and volunteers at the worker centers frequently put up with catcalling by the male workers, even though coordinators made concerted efforts to encourage more appropriate behavior. On the corners, circumstances were much looser and the harassment of women who passed by, our interviewees lamented, was that much worse. Our participants also connected substance addiction to a more general bodily dissipation and lack of self-control among workers in these spaces, ascribing myriad antisocial tendencies to such dependencies. Said Oscar Morales:

> They don't behave normally, and it certainly doesn't look good. When this center wasn't here, of course I went out to the street. I saw a lot of

incidents, like people staggering around, all because they were on drugs or alcohol. . . . There were a lot of problems with the day laborers for the owner of the [nearby car] dealer because they did their necessities there between the cars and with the people passing by. . . . A lot of them have been deported for doing dirty business like selling drugs or prostitution. . . . A human being in his right mind doesn't act this way, but you are different when you are on drugs.[28]

Comments like these implied that fighting for the job meant habitually taking leave of one's rational faculties and incapacitating oneself bodily and mentally. In particular, it was argued, workers like these rendered themselves unable to use their *time* wisely. Guillermo Zelaya implied this when he contrasted his own time-conscious work ethic to the delinquencies of workers on the corner, saying: "If you go to work, you have to work. If they tell me I'm going for an hour, I work and I take advantage of that hour."[29] From this judgmental viewpoint, standing on the corner thus became mere loitering and looking for trouble, while getting hired meant simply gaining the chance to con gullible employers into wasting their time, too.

Day laborers described those on the corner as not only incapable of disciplining themselves but also in revolt against external rules and laws. This usually meant the modest regulations that day laborers imposed through democratic assemblies at the worker centers, for instance prohibiting smoking and drinking on the premises. Sometimes, however, it meant laws governing criminal acts, including drug-dealing, participating in the sex trade, and robbery, which our interviewees accused workers on the corner of perpetrating against neighborhood merchants. Workers on the corner were also disparaged for flouting public decency laws as well as common courtesy by indiscriminately soiling the environs with their trash and human waste. For Isaac Ramírez (a Mexican migrant), workers on the corner offended against a broader cultural and racial code: "the law of the Americans," which he said preserved social order by refusing to tolerate "drunken Mexicans" who acted like "pigs."[30] All these negative imputations congealed in the basic characterization of the corner as a scene of untrammeled violence and lawlessness, aptly summed up by Adán Trejo when he quipped: "There, it's the law of the strongest."[31]

In sum, through the theme of fighting for the job, day laborers expressed the contradictions and multiplicities of embodied time on the corner. Waging this battle, workers were caught between extremes of corporeal stasis and hypermobility, both of which entailed serious threats to their psychophysical integrity. Their bodies were alternately locked in a condition of anxious immobility for long stretches and then abruptly forced into hectic and violent movement. In

both temporal permutations, day laborers' body-time registered the brutally competitive dynamic among workers as well as pressures emanating from the racial
policing of the city by official and unofficial agents, alike. A different temporal
polarity characterized workers' comments on their motivations for enduring
the hardships of the corner. On the one hand, workers envisioned the corner as
a gateway to a more economically stable existence as well as a training ground
for the ethical and entrepreneurial aptitudes they often claimed would enable
them to progress toward that goal. Fighting for the job, in this conceptual frame,
instigated a temporal sequence of orderly forward movement toward a better
future while also instantiating the worker's discretion over his own time in the
here and now. On the other hand, workers openly acknowledged the desperation
that drove them to the corner as a last resort and their sense of powerlessness in
interacting with employers. This countertendency truncated the future-oriented
temporal vector and recoiled its affective energies back on the urgencies of an
all-absorbing present. Like workers' dreams that a steadily expanding series of
opportunities would radiate out from their humble beginnings on the corner,
their affectively charged ethical distinctions between diligent day laborers and
the disorderly mob on the corner seemed better suited to making stubbornly
precarious circumstances slightly less disagreeable than to extricating themselves
from the fight.

Bodily Mobility and Corporeal Excess: Day Labor as Exception

The complex and evocative meanings bound up with day laborers' theme of
fighting for the job suggest that efforts to build *conscientização* among these
workers should devote keen attention to their experiences on the corner. As with
the notion of desperate responsibility, so likewise this theme exudes prospects
for generating popular-educational dialogue among day laborers and other similarly situated migrant workers. The generative capacities of a theme identified
through critical-popular research, I have argued, stem in part from the theme's
sturdy anchors in mundane experience. In this respect, popular education with
day laborers cannot *not* talk about what happens on the corner because whether
a day laborer goes to this place frequently, occasionally, or rarely, it remains an indelible and formative component of most workers' personal histories and social
self-conceptions.

The concrete physicality of day laborers' remarks about the corner speaks
to the readiness with which they could elaborate this theme creatively and visually through popular-educational dialogue. One can imagine, for example, a
"body-mapping" exercise through which participants would depict and analyze

what happens to various body parts as interminable hours and pressure-packed minutes unfold—the legs that throb, the bladder that aches, the feet flattened under rolling tires, the elbow skinned in a tussle. The semiotically multivalent and sometimes poetic notion of "fighting" also lends itself to critical-popular examination in dialogical settings. As we have heard, day laborers speak the word in ways that range from the starkly physical to the highly metaphorical, including the belligerent "piling up" of bodies by an employer's vehicle, verbal jousting, and the internal struggle to keep their tongues and fists in check. Additionally, and in ways similar to those discussed in the preceding chapter, the good/bad worker dichotomy seems primed to spark critical investigation, in particular by asking who the workers on the corner are and whether they and center members are really two different groups.

The theme of fighting for the job also invites critical-popular reflection on its connections to broadly gauged, existing theoretical critiques of precarity, and tracing such linkages comprises my central task in the remainder of this chapter. In the corner's stark abnormality amid the regular distribution of activities and temporalities in the city's built environment, this social space seems to iconize the exceptional position of day laborers within the wider urban milieu. Yet as we shall see, the notion of fighting for the job also expresses pervasive dynamics of precaritization that apply to masses of working people who may never set foot near a day labor corner.

When day laborers discuss the dilemmas of bodily movement and immobility on the corners, along with the temporal conundrums they face in doing so, they evoke historically ingrained processes that have long marked racial and class Others as deviant within liberal societies. In such societies, as Hagar Kotef argues, norms regarding human bodies' motions and movements through social spaces bear on the fundamental question of who should be treated as a rational being capable of freedom. An extensive tradition in liberal political theory, she further contends, posits self-regulated movement as crucial to freedom, rationality, and individual autonomy. For classical liberal theorists such as Hobbes and Locke, movement served as "the privileged mode by which the liberal subject was corporealized" and provided "the corporeal condition for rationality itself."[32] To be still or unmoving was to fail to manifest oneself as a being in progress toward higher achievements of mind and property—as unable or unwilling to compete in the race of life and hence as undeserving of being considered an independent person. Only a specific kind of movement, however, could authorize autonomous subjectivity in classical liberal theory, according to Kotef: "The movement that is interlaced with rationality is not each and every movement but rather restrained movement that should always be given within certain bounds."[33] Both Locke and Hobbes associated excessive movement with violence and a refusal to contribute in stable and positive ways to the public good. Such conduct thus warranted efforts by the state "to slow movement down," to fix unruly movers within enclosed locations, and to compel them to perform socially productive activities.[34] As manifestly "irrational" beings, moreover, hypermobile populations were subjected to a longer-term and more abstract logic of temporal governance: paternalistic supervision based on the premise that these beings were mired in delayed maturation and thus should be dealt with as perpetual dependents.[35] The twin temporal deviances of subjects whose bodily movements manifested rational deficits thus involved both moving neither rapidly nor steadily enough, in developmental terms, and moving too quickly and erratically in everyday action.

Kotef further argues that historically and socially embedded legal regimes in liberal societies induce subaltern populations to move in certain ways, within distinctly governed social spaces, that seem to prove their incapacity for freedom. Hence, consequent to the settler colonization of indigenous North American lands enabled by public law, Locke and others classed Native others as "savages" because of their supposed "nomadic" tendencies and unwillingness to "settle" lands that were lying in "waste."[36] Kotef (with coauthor Merav Amir) sees a contemporary analogue of this process by which the law both prompts and punishes the violation of liberal temporal-spatial norms at checkpoints in the Occupied Territories of Palestine. According to Kotef and Amir, the routine piling up of people forced to go through checkpoints on foot simply to conduct their daily affairs, together with the sluggish pace of elaborate and degrading security checks, fosters a situation in which Palestinians end up moving (and not moving) in ways that bring down arbitrarily applied but legally authorized Israeli discipline:

> Everybody is pressed against one another so that the people at the front of the line are constantly being pushed forward by the crowd behind them, violating what the soldiers see as the appropriate distance between the head of the line and the security-check booths. Then the imaginary line makes a sudden appearance: "Irja La'wara!" (Go back!) the soldiers shout in what is most often the only phrase they know in Arabic. "Go back" behind the line—the line that cannot be seen, the line that is never marked, the imaginary line.[37]

Precisely the invisibility and perpetual mutability of the "imaginary line" ensures that some Palestinians will cross it, leading to "disciplinary punishments" and "violent" reprisals by the soldiers that leave the perpetrator "badly injured or even killed."[38] In short, "The imaginary line produces movements that can be presented and perceived as unrestrainable and thus threatening, thereby enabling their configuration as 'terror.' "[39] The political logic of domination is "built into the spatial configuration of the checkpoints" and works itself out by virtue of the temporally inflected movements this social space provokes.[40]

Bound up with this legal and spatial logic of domination is an ideological dynamic, such that together these processes yield the phenomenon Kotef and Amir characterize as "corporeal excess," defined as follows:

> *Corporeal excess* . . . is a function of two factors. The first is a seizing of one corporeal axis over others: if a body is a compound matrix, comprised of multiple axes (such as sexuality, reproduction, skin color, size, vulnerability, and so forth), a corporeal excess is produced when one of these axes gains disproportionate dominance over the others. Second, excess is a function of the context in which this seizing is made: it is produced when a particular bodily axis consolidates and emerges within a temporal and spatial field in forms and density that do not comply with a given norm (a norm that is often constructed particularly to constitute this corporeal presence as excessive).[41]

Checkpoints in the Occupied Territories, argue Kotef and Amir, exemplify this technique of domination by creating the "aberrant dominance" of "the axes of reproduction and volatility" in materializations of Palestinian bodies.[42] More specifically, these corporeal axes come to the fore through the intersection of "leftist Israeli discourse of the injustice of the checkpoints," which fixates on the predicament of Palestinian women giving birth at the checkpoints, and "the discourse of national security" in Israel, which suspects every male Palestinian of being a terrorist on the verge of exploding in a suicide attack.[43] In both cases, despite the acute political friction between these two discourses, the body is similarly imagined as bursting beyond its fleshly boundaries and violating social-spatial norms. In turn, the interaction between these gendered discourses ends up legitimating the occupying regime and entrenching its organization of social space in ways that both provoke and punish corporeal excess, by folding an "enlightened," compassionate response to pregnant women's needs (i.e., installing toilets) into the overall system of antiterrorist state terrorism.[44]

The social positions of Palestinians at checkpoints and day laborers on the corner are quite different, of course, and I do not mean to suggest any direct analogy between these groups' circumstances. However, Kotef and Amir offer an instructive critical language and theoretical orientation for conceiving of a general problematic within liberal societies that implicates day laborers and resonates with the theme of fighting for the job. This problematic concerns the ways that norms of bodily movement, with distinctive temporal and spatial facets as well as gendered aspects, enable these societies to designate populations for exceptional and illiberal regimes of control rather than liberal rights and freedoms.

Regardless of whether day laborers are watching the hours slip by on the corner or throwing themselves into physical combat over a job, they end up violating the norms of proper bodily movement that apply to the public areas where they congregate. Most immediately, these norms concern the informal social rules by which street corners are supposed to be conduits and intersections in the midst of purposeful, economically productive movement by residents, shoppers, or working people in the neighborhood. By just standing there rather than going somewhere, day laborers both interrupt these normative flows and locate themselves outside such patterns. Yet when they do move, day laborers' bodies disrupt temporal-spatial norms just as egregiously, if not more so. Employees', residents', and customers' movements might be hasty, but always in a calm and controlled manner, whereas the mayhem that erupts when day laborers fight for the job manifests their bodies as out-of-control and dangerous. In short, on the corner, day laborers invariably are moving entirely too little (and too slowly) or far too much (and too quickly). Their bodies encode menace as much with their suspicious inactivity as with their furious bursts of action, and their movements never follow a reassuringly predictable protocol.

As Kotef and Amir help us see, these abnormalities of bodily movement are artifacts of mobility-governance patterns on the corners where day laborers gather. The law and the state constitute these time-spaces of illiberal deviance both when they actively intervene and when they refrain from doing so. Everyday use by workers and employers alike gives the corner a quasi-legitimate presence in the urban landscape and a structural anchor in the local residential housing economy, and overall the police permit these job markets to persist. Yet local law enforcement reserves the discretion to declare when day laborers have crossed the "imaginary line," as it were, between allowable and proscribed public activity. Hence, as the workers explained, officers step in at will to chastise, roust, and punish the miscreants for violating ordinances prohibiting public indecency and disturbances of the peace. Of course, the legal condition of being unauthorized blocks migrants from most regular jobs and drives them out into these informal public spaces to seek work in the first place. Federal immigration agents, in turn, police the corner with just as much arbitrary discretion as local police officers. Immigration raids prompted early organizing efforts among day laborers in the 1990s and they remain a distinct and increasing threat, although as of this book's writing federal authorities were still largely holding back from such incursions. Nevertheless, federal immigration enforcement underwrites the schizoid protocol of mobility governance on the corner and helps make the law, to use Kotef's terms, "an obstacle over which" day laborers "are set to stumble."[45] Vigilante attacks and hateful shouts from ordinary passers-by on the street reinforce this regulatory matrix. Such assaults also further blur the boundaries between the various state and nonstate actors that govern mobility on the corner, as does the participation of local law enforcement in federal immigrant detention and deportation efforts.

The state's efforts to keep day labor corners under police surveillance also have become a matter of conscious planning and mundane bureaucratic procedure, as a remarkable 2006 US Department of Justice document "Disorder at Day Laborer Sites" demonstrates. Published by the Office of Community Oriented Policing Services (COPS), this self-styled "problem-oriented guide for police" purports to take a nonjudgmental approach toward "illegal immigrants," and it mentions that day laborers may be "routinely robbed" or otherwise "victimized" by "citizens" and others.[46] The report nonetheless treats day labor corners as crime-prevention challenges for local police because of their propensity to generate "parking and traffic problems" and "assaults" (by unspecified perpetrators) as well as unruly and illegal behaviors by workers: "loitering," vandalism, property defacement, public alcohol and drug use, harassment of pedestrians, public urinating, and "swarming" around employers' vehicles.[47] In ways that evoke a broader set of state-regulatory interests, the COPS guide also darkly notes "the link between day laborers and human smuggling," suggests that day laborers reduce job opportunities as well as "salary levels and employee benefits" for other workers, and effectively blames day labor corners for inciting "fear of crime among community members" and stoking "citizens' frustration and disdain for immigrants."[48] Rather than an aberration, the COPS guide belongs to a genre of government initiatives that target day labor corners as special sites of intervention during crackdowns on unauthorized migrants. Infamously, such initiatives have included H.R. 4437 in Congress and Arizona's S.B. 1070, which originally included a provision to "prohibit motorists from stopping traffic to solicit day laborers," although this was later nullified by the federal courts.[49]

As the COPS document illustrates, a peculiar form of corporeal excess that is ideologically attributed to day laborers reinforces the sociospatial and temporal strategies that fashion day labor corners as sites of exceptional precaritization. Dominant public discourses about immigration, endorsed by both major parties and recharged every time national policy debates return to the interminable question of which immigrants to punish and exclude in exchange for allowing others highly qualified leniency, typically distinguish between good and bad immigrant types. Day laborers' mobility deviances on the corner land them squarely in the latter category, notwithstanding their enthusiastic comments about working hard, providing for their families, and advancing economically, as dutiful immigrants are supposed to do. Their counternormative action and inaction convict them of a specific type of corporeal excess attributed to the undesirable sort of immigrant: *excessive bodily mobility*. This logic of corporeal excess casts unauthorized migrants who lack stable jobs and homes as vagrants whose mobile bodies trouble the borders between nation-states, incite international tensions and security risks, subvert the law, foment public disorder, invade legitimate workers' job markets, and threaten to violate women's bodily integrity through sexual predation.[50] This narrative of the immigrant threat has a distinctly masculine bent, opposed to that of the hard-working father-provider.[51] It is also allied with another ideological strand that associates such antisocial behaviors with irrational attachments to clannish loyalties and patriarchal traditions that prevent assimilation to "America's" supposed pluralism, modernity, and respect for women's equality. Unwanted immigrants' hypermobile bodies thus ironically manifest their inveterate *immobility* in temporal terms, in the sense of remaining stuck in the past and unable to progress, just like other subaltern subjects who historically have fallen afoul of liberal mobility governance.

Together, these ideological narratives and state officials' policing strategies constitute the corner as a time-space where day laborers' stigmata of corporeal excess perpetually surface. Day laborers reinforce this process when they advance their own ethical binary between good and bad workers, which corroborates the official dualism regarding immigrants in general. In a concrete-practical sense, in turn, day laborers propel the gears of liberal mobility governance on the corner by performing precisely the sorts of bodily deviations that seem to bear out their imputed traits of corporeal excess. Both by fighting for the job and by transposing the fight to an ethical-entrepreneurial register, they facilitate their own designation as nonnormative subjects who are ruled by excessive bodily mobility and who therefore warrant special state interventions—at the pleasure of the authorities—to immobilize, control, and expel them. This, then, is the complex form of precarity-as-exceptionality on the corner to which day laborers' thematic rendering of their experiences speaks: a form narrowly aimed at unauthorized migrants, articulated through temporal figurations of illiberal identity and movement in public space, and effected in part through the agency of the precaritized.

The theme of fighting for the job, however, also suggests that day laborers face a specifically *neoliberal* form of power on the corner that Kotef's theory of liberal mobility-governance does not entirely capture and that makes their exceptional precaritization even more acute. In this way, the generative theme does more than express the power formation theorized by Kotef: the theme also prompts a politically significant revision of this conception. For Lockean liberals, Kotef notes, the poor needed to be forced to abandon "the motion of vagrancy and begging" by being spatially enclosed within workhouses and compelled to undertake "the motion of labor—repetitive, confined, productive"; constitutionally lacking "the time to actualize rationality," they had to be subjected to a direct, intensive temporal discipline.[52] The corner does contain day laborers, which makes them more locatable and controllable by the governing authorities.[53] However, instead of being *required* to undergo rigorous *formal training* to develop work-oriented aptitudes and values they are presumed to *lack*, these migrants are *informally permitted* to cluster in places where the market-oriented and individualist inclinations they are *assumed to possess* can have free rein. The day labor corner thus seems to iconize the neoliberal condition in which market rationality becomes the sole criterion for right social conduct and self-realization, and in which expanded, more discretionary, and more police-oriented state power asserts itself through the dissembling guise of the withdrawal of direct regulation. It is precisely –and deeply ironically—by virtue of their unalloyed enthusiasm for participating in this milieu and showing themselves to be good neoliberal subjects, in turn, that day laborers violate the norms of properly controlled mobility and invite punishment. Manifesting a total, unequivocal, and uninterrupted dedication to self-advancement through economic competition, as they hurl themselves into the fray and devote hours upon hours to waiting for a chance to work, day laborers end up occupying urban time-space in ways that brand them as unfit for liberal autonomy.

A related neoliberal shift in the dynamic of exceptionalization through mobility governance becomes discernable when we consider what day laborers' theme of fighting for the job suggests about the peculiar disappearance of contracting on the corner. Neoliberalism esteems the contract within market exchange as the fundamental guarantor of human freedom, as exemplified by Milton Friedman's argument regarding the virtues of "competitive capitalism."[54] Notably, the notion of freedom through contracting carries temporal presuppositions: the individual invests time in seeking and comparatively evaluating the options available; also, contract negotiation with other market participants requires a certain duration. Neoliberal state and corporate policies have ignited a vast profusion of contracting activity, especially in low-wage labor markets, where workers increasingly find themselves negotiating contract after contract as permanent work arrangements recede into the past while part-time jobs proliferate. Yet in the midst of this general explosion of contractualism, day laborers and other severely marginalized migrant workers find themselves largely excluded from the culture of contracting. Precarity, for them, is not so much a matter of having to make do with more temporary, conditional, and fragmented employment agreements. Rather, precarity brings utter subjection to employers' capricious powers to command their labor and their time at will, at whatever terms employers wish and without employers necessarily even making those terms known. Day laborers ironically foster the growth of this form of precarity through their own activities. The contract as such evaporates in the labor pseudomarket on the corner, and along with the contract the practical basis of neoliberal freedom disappears. Workers, themselves, effect the contract's dematerialization through their body-time, as the time for sifting among choices recedes into the time of waiting in boredom for any chance to work at all, and as the interactive time of bargaining condenses into the desperate dive into an employer's back seat.[55]

These modifications of theory regarding schemas of exceptionalization through bodily mobility-governance, catalyzed by the theme of fighting for the job, have important political implications. They prod us to ask: if liberalism has always needed to engineer the hypermobile, too-speedy, menacingly unbounded actions of its *starkly illiberal* Others to legitimate the liberal state and its capitalist and imperialist projects, then what can it mean that liberalism in its neoliberal phase seems to thrive on more indirectly eliciting its Others' willing and enthusiastic performances of *all-too (neo)liberal* behaviors? One problem is that this new development pulls the rug out from under a conventional mode of critique: it no longer works so well to denounce departures from guiding liberal values as a basis for improving the situation of those populations subject to these dynamics of exceptionalizing precarity. This insight has direct relevance for day labor organizations. It means that worker centers should avoid assuming uncritically that, to escape social abjection and control, day laborers need only a safe, calm, well-regulated environment where they can look for work without violating the norms for proper conduct in public space. This framing of worker centers overlooks the problem that most workers who frequent the centers also go to the corners with some regularity. In addition, if worker centers do not actively question but rather simply reaffirm the sanctity of work as the activity to which the individual should assign priority over all others, then they will end up feeding the forces of precaritization they want to contest. Worker centers will likewise bolster these forces if they provide essential services that meet day laborers' bodily needs and ensure their physical capacity to work, but refrain from questioning the systemic organization of socially reproductive work that leaves day laborers' needs largely unmet.[56]

More generally, if the pursuit of work as not just the highest but the exclusive good is also precisely what condemns individuals caught up in these exceptionalizing matrices of precarity to social death, then the organizations of day laborers and other migrant workers should radicalize their critiques of work and approach workers' issues with the same militancy they have been devoting to immigrant rights. Immigration enforcement policies and practices crucially shape the processes by which migrant workers suffer extraordinary forms of precaritization today, as day laborers make bracingly clear. Thus, a counterprecarity politics by migrant justice organizations needs to sustain full-throated opposition to the deportation regime, as they are doing in ways I discuss in chapter 6. Yet as the critical convergence of theme and theory here suggests, the protocols of mobility governance that render migrant bodies public threats spring from the complex *interaction* of work-oriented norms and tactics geared toward deportation. Especially insofar as the neoliberal feedback loop on day labor corners may also exist in other time-spaces of migrant work, the warrant for a stepped-up critique of work in migrant justice organizing becomes all the more imperative.

To inform and inspire such efforts, further critical-popular research should elicit the generative themes other groups of migrant workers might articulate to characterize the prods and impediments that apply to their bodily movements in spheres of work other than day labor. For instance, an antiprecarity politics aimed at contesting the exceptionalizing forces mapped by considering Kotef and Amir's analysis requires critical-popular investigation of the different gendering of corporeal excess for women who earn wages as domestic workers, perhaps beginning with the one corner in the United States known to day labor organizers, as of this book's writing, as a corner for migrant women.[57] New research also should explore how workers thematize the distinct forms of mobility governance that apply in isolated, interior, nonpublic domains of migrant work such as restaurant kitchens, office buildings cleaned by night-shift janitors, and the homes of housecleaners' employers. In addition, day labor leaders have become increasingly concerned about a growing distinction between workers who gravitate toward the centers and those on the corners, such that the centers tend to attract older workers who are no longer physically able to fight for the job. Besides raising difficult questions for worker centers about how to assist day laborers in later life, this issue also signals the value of probing how age affects migrant workers' implication within (neo)liberal schemas of mobility governance. In combination, these critical-popular trajectories could help bring into view a radical antideportation *and antiwork* politics of precarity, in which women and men, the old and the young, and workers in hypervisible and highly sequestered work-realms, alike, could take on intellectual and strategic leadership.

The copresence of work-based regulations of mobility along with those that derive from immigration enforcement in the fight for the job also invites curiosity about how the situation day laborers face on the corner might have politically meaningful parallels with circumstances for working people beyond the larger population of migrant workers. In particular, consider how day laborers connect their impossible predicament with respect to *physical* movement and time to self-conflicted dreams of upward *social* mobility. The spread of precaritized conditions throughout society has damaged hopes of economic progress for working people generally. Likewise, although the consequences of manifesting counternormative movement in public spaces are much more severe

for unauthorized Latino migrants than white legal residents and citizens, the neoliberal casting of individual motivation and conduct that is so clearly distilled
on the corner pervades contemporary cities at large. How, then, might the
theme of fighting for the job generate further insight into these more widespread
economic-cultural phenomena?

Aspirational Normativity and the Refusal of Work: The Corner as Synecdoche

Whether lamented as an unsightly blot on a gentrifying cityscape, or grudgingly tolerated as an unfortunate but inevitable byproduct of a thriving real estate and home improvement economy, or simply ignored, the day labor corner
tends to be seen as an aberration. As a tiny and tenuous spatial-temporal zone
within the city, it seems to epitomize the social and cultural fringe-existence of
its denizens. Yet the corner also stands as a vivid synecdoche for syndromes of
precaritization that affect working populations in every quadrant of the metrop-
olis and throughout the class hierarchy. Juxtaposing day laborers' reflections on
the theme of fighting for the job with other theoretical accounts of widely distributed precarity-dynamics suggests that while it remains vital to recognize the
exceptionalizing forces at play on the corner, discerning the corner's encapsula-
tion of much broader tendencies is also politically and theoretically essential.

Resonances abound between day laborers' self-conflicting explanations of why
they fight for the job on the corner and Lauren Berlant's insightful critique of the
tangled webs of fantasy, bodily activity, and affect found in contemporary scenes
of precarity. For Berlant, precarious existence today is more than a set of economic
facts—more than tolerating contingent or part-time employment, experiencing a
dwindling connection between work and earnings, losing personal autonomy in
the workplace, or making do with more limited public welfare benefits. Although
precarity involves all these things, in Berlant's view, it is also a habitual structure
of corporeal, attitudinal, and emotional orientations that have distinctive political
valences. Moreover, precaritization not only applies to socially excluded groups
like migrant workers or the residents of impoverished black neighborhoods but
permeates society as a whole. "Precarity," writes Berlant, is a "pervasive life environment" and "an affective atmosphere penetrating all classes."[58]

According to Berlant, precarious individuals in the neoliberal world characteristically enact "the affects of aspirational normativity."[59] The accent here lies
on the qualifier "aspirational," in the sense that precaritized subjects increasingly
content themselves with harboring a fervent *wish* for achieving a normative social existence rather than actually attaining such a life. "They perform not the

achieved materiality of a better life but the approximate feeling of belonging to a world that doesn't yet exist reliably," Berlant writes acerbically.[60] In the affective milieu of precarity, Berlant thus detects "submission to necessity in the guise of desire. . . . The key here is *proximity;* ownership has been relinquished as the children's fantasy."[61] This desire has a markedly fraught temporality—a "visceral temporality" that shapes "a life dedicated to moving toward the good life's normative/utopian zone but actually stuck in what we might call survival time, the time of struggling, drowning, holding onto the ledge, treading water—the time of *not-stopping.*"[62] Perpetually in motion yet going nowhere, precaritized subjects hold yearnings that cut against one another: at once to find a foothold in a stable place and to stride forward to someplace new.

Berlant complicates our sense of what mobility means in liberal and neoliberal societies by drawing attention to the spatial and temporal inconsistencies that imbue subjects' desires. On the one hand, the subject embraces the teeth-gritting resolve simply to endure the onslaught of present life, such that just staying in place and avoiding further setbacks becomes this subject's ruling desire and the quest of her every living moment. On the other hand, this posture co-exists with a sense of futurity by which the subject imagines himself to be moving toward a better kind of life, although he has relinquished all hope of actually getting there. In her illustrative commentary about these dynamics in the Dardennes brothers' film *La Promesse*, the plotline of which concerns unauthorized migrants and those who exploit them in Belgium, Berlant notes that this awkward confluence of temporal-spatial orientations can be found among acutely marginalized social figures, such as African migrant workers, and members of more comfortably situated populations, like white Belgian citizens, alike:

> What's striking in the temporal imaginary of both the citizen and the migrant workers . . . is the ways they look forward to getting ahead, to making it, *and* to a condition of stasis, of being able to *be somewhere* and to make a life, exercising existence as a fact, not a project. In other words, in this version of transnational class fantasy, mobility is a dream and a nightmare. The end of mobility as a fantasy of endless upwardness, and the shift to the aspiration toward achieving an impasse and stop-loss, is a subtle redirection of the fantasy bribes transacted to effect the reproduction of life under the present economic conditions.[63]

Precaritized subjects thus both dread and crave mobility, wanting it as a release from their entrapment within an ever-extended moment of crisis yet also loathing it as the deprivation of the chance to "make a life" over time's duration in some definite place.

More than just an ambivalence, this affective posture amounts to a self-undermining stance, or what Berlant ironically calls a "cruel optimism." Attachment to the fantasy of achieving the good life motivates the down-shifting of hopes into the gear of stop-loss activity, thereby normalizing the individual's distance from a genuine change of life circumstances. Day laborers in Portland and Seattle speak to this self-unraveling affect of precarity writ large when they attempt to lend ethical coherence to the notion of fighting for the job. Their thematic current of seeing "every employer as an opportunity" and *echándole ganas* articulates a disposition of aspirational normativity. Redolent with the cheerful hope of getting somewhere (else) by seizing any chance to work and manifestly performing the work ethic, workers' comments simultaneously express a resigned contentment with the fight on the corner as something that at least resembles a competition in which one can imagine coming out meaningfully ahead. Worker-entrepreneurs who strive to "look sharp" and "get their act together" on the corner strain to *approximate* a work-life path where such strategic behavior would elevate their social position and diminish their exposure to wage theft and other indignities. In practice, the survival-focused temporality of "not stopping" while running in place (or "treading water") overtakes the cadence of forward movement in time.

The cruelly optimistic desire for proximal belonging animates not only the commentaries of those day laborers who sound like well-tutored neoliberal entrepreneurs but also the remarks of participants who moralize disapprovingly about the crowd on the corner. The latter similarly struggle to grasp a life that comes close to a normative existence without really having a chance of achieving it. For them, the wished-for validation of the individual's normatively approved status emerges through condemning the imputed socially and personally destructive habits of the despised type of worker, even though the individual's own actions undermine his attempt to distinguish himself from this contemptible foil. Self-satisfied moral rectitude comprises its own fervently desired fantasy, with its own logic of self-negation. It, too, becomes an unworkable substitute for achieving the higher social status that is supposed to accrue naturally to those who act respectfully to others, obey the law, avoid vice, and use time wisely.

In these multiple respects, the theme of fighting for the job bespeaks the persistent force of the broadly precaritizing dynamics that Berlant theorizes via the figures of cruel optimism and aspirational normativity. The theme thus reveals the day laborer on the corner as an unsuspected synecdoche for this widely inclusive social syndrome, albeit an inexact one inasmuch as, for these migrants, failing to stay afloat means not only experiencing declining economic fortunes but also being stigmatized as criminal and degenerate. Notwithstanding the potency of Berlant's observation regarding the society-wide pervasiveness of this precarious condition, in other words, it is important not to lose sight of the exceptional precarity to which day laborers and other similarly positioned migrants are subject. This situation pushes them to abandon not only their wishes to attain a materially abundant "good life" but also, at times, the more modest goal of staying fixed in place economically, and to cling to the hope of simply staying out of the authorities' punishing grip. Nevertheless, it is also easy to overplay the differences between precaritization as it applies to day laborers and more far-reaching social dynamics. The theme-theory resonance between the notion of fighting for the job and Berlant's analysis helps keep the symmetries between exceptional and general social experiences sharply in view.

Even more importantly, the theme makes it possible to understand the problem of aspirational normativity in a different and politically consequential way. Berlant's precarious subjects suffer, dream, yearn, love, and "live on," but they rarely *fight* for what they desire in their domains of work and attachment.[64] Fighting on the corner, in all the ways I have discussed, constitutes day laborers as targets for control and expulsion as well as subjects who thwart their own efforts through their self-conflicting aspirations. Yet despite its neoliberal entanglements, a germinally radical militancy is encoded in the theme of fighting for the job. Certainly, day laborers who engage in such combat strive to get what they want as individuals who compete brutally with one another. Nevertheless, they also come to the corner having mustered within themselves a fighting spirit and a resolve to survive that ends up becoming something profound and passionate that they *share* with one another. It is part of what they are saying when they claim the identity of the *jornalero* (day laborer) with defiant pride, in the face of those who harass and spit on them in the street, as every character does in the remarkable 2009 documentary *Jornaleros*, produced by Voz's workers, staff, and volunteers.[65] Such spirit was just as palpable and electric in the street protests outside the San Mateo County sheriff's office in the summer of 2017, when participants in NDLON's annual assembly dance-marched to a samba beat as Los Jornaleros del Norte, the day laborers' band, sang out *"¡Soy jornalero . . . voy jornalero!"* (I'm a *jornalero*—I'm going out looking for day labor jobs!). The worker centers that make up NDLON's national network, in turn, have nurtured this fighting spirit by cultivating ongoing contact with the corners rather than just offering alternatives to them and quelling the tenacious militancy of *los esquineros*. In short, day labor leaders and activists do not aim to abandon the fight but rather to reconceive it with reference to different methods, rogue temporalities, and an alternative animating vision.

Glimpses of such a fight were rare in our interviews, but they flourish in Voz's film *Jornaleros*, which transfigures the benighted time-space of the corner into a powerful staging ground for antiprecarity politics. This short documentary features a series of fragmented interviews with five day laborers in Portland who talk about and display what they do—not as day laborers, however, but as artists who paint murals, write and perform poetry, or sing while playing guitar. The film's central device is thus to startle the viewer into a shift of perspective away from the stock frames for depicting migrant workers sympathetically that emphasize individuals' stalwart dedication to wage-earning work and persecution by the immigration authorities. The artists in *Jornaleros* candidly acknowledge their intense needs for work and the hardships they have met as migrants. Yet they fold these concerns into a richer lead-narrative in which they declare outright that they are creative, imaginative persons who do more than just *work*. The film's audiovisual elements, in turn, let viewers experience on affective levels how this is true.

Several key sequences of *Jornaleros* take place on a day labor corner in Portland, and these moments of the film foster a sense of how the fight for the job could become, and indeed for some workers already has become, a strikingly different kind of fight, freed of the ballast that drags its protagonists into the self-defeating rituals I have discussed with reference to the theories of cruel optimism and liberal mobility governance. The main segment within this set initially provides close-ups of two Salvadoran migrant workers, Francisco Aguirre and another man who goes by the name Lolo, as they play guitars and sing a jaunty corrido about a day laborer's conflictual encounter with a racist employer. Aguirre's and Lolo's sly grins match the comical tone and lilt of the song, which wryly laments that "just because" the worker could not speak "fucking English," this "goddamn white guy" yelled at him: "You wetbacks don't understand what you are supposed to do!" Shrewdly, the lyric intimates that these workers who are accused of linguistic incompetence actually have subtle and tactical command of language because they switch easily back and forth between English and Spanish, as do the film's subtitles, which keep the movie consistently bilingual. The scene's most pronounced impact, however, comes toward its end. The camera suddenly pans out, away from Lolo and Aguirre, showing that they have been singing and playing on a street corner where other day laborers are avidly engaged in the all-out fight for the job, hailing cars that approach, shouting at the drivers, and breaking into sprints as the cars slow to a halt.

More than just a momentary break in the oppressive temporalities of precarity on the corner, this musical detour in *Jornaleros* throws these power dynamics deeply into question. Most immediately, the song intervenes audaciously into the given "distribution of the sensible" that aesthetically governs how day laborers are perceived on the corner—that is, that consigns them to perform the self-convicting pattern of temporalized and spatialized movement that combines protracted, inactive waiting with abrupt plunges into frantic physical combat.[66]

Suddenly, albeit fleetingly, the corner is transformed into a site of freedom. The form of freedom practiced by these street musicians pivotally involves artistic creation and performance in ways that remake aesthetic time-spaces and, in doing so, challenge the political power-relations that have constituted those fields. Freedom of this sort differs radically from that which animates the liberal norms that make individual autonomy contingent on properly regulated bodily movement and that ordinarily govern the physical-sensory milieu of the corner. Perhaps the most crucial difference lies in the *fighting affect* of this alternative freedom, which comprises a brisk undercurrent just beneath the more evident tonalities of sarcasm and pleasure-taking. Lolo and Aguirre make a directly transformative incursion into the prevailing temporalities and spatialities on the corner rather than issuing a call for change; they launch a practical assertion of power in lieu of asking for pity, respect, or rights.

Voz's film also situates Aguirre and Lolo's performance on the corner and its locally specific, immediate transmutational dynamics within a much more extensive political geography and long-range history of militant struggle, and this mitigates the ephemeral character of the gesture.[67] In an earlier segment, Lolo discusses his background as a "self-taught" and politically committed musician who sang "protest songs" with the Marxist-revolutionary "people's movement" in El Salvador. Sitting near a wall adorned with old posters from the Farabundo Martí National Liberation Front, Lolo weeps as he recalls being driven to flee the country by reactionary forces. Yet the movie also shows him carrying on his devotion to political song in the United States, playing at a festival and then in the sequence with Aguirre. Aguirre, likewise, shares his experience of political persecution in and flight from El Salvador due to his leftist involvements. The context provided by these other filmic elements, in other words, implies that the impromptu concert on the corner is no mere isolated event. Rather, it is just one salvo within a transcontinental and long-term popular mobilization against imperialist capitalism. The worker-artists' musical performance thus both instantiates freedom with a fighting affect in the here and now and carries forward a more ambitious collective fight for liberation. Aguirre then affirms this ongoing fight as the film concludes, explicitly connecting the battle for migrant worker justice in the United States to the revolutionary struggle in Central America, over the soundtrack of Lolo singing a well-known song from the Salvadoran left-popular movement, *"Casas de Cartón"* ("Cardboard Houses").

Just as day laborers' generative theme helps sensitize us to the kindling of *fighting* spirit that can occur in the very midst of aspirational normativity's confounding pressures, so likewise the theme suggests the need to develop a nuanced and radically critical approach to what the *job* signifies—that is, a politically generative critique of work in the face of precarity in both its society-wide and exceptional permutations. Especially considering the dilemma of neoliberal mobility governance I examined in the previous section, and also in light of the vicious circles activated by the social mobility-fantasies that Berlant analyzes, the theme-theory valences in this chapter urge nothing less than a politics committed to the *refusal of work.*

As Kathi Weeks discusses, the autonomist-Marxist conception of the "refusal of work" implies "a refusal of the ideology of work as highest calling and moral duty, a refusal of work as the necessary center of social life and means of access to the rights and claims of citizenship, and a refusal of the necessity of capitalist control of production."[68] Yet the concept indicates not only these aspects of negation but also positive, creative practices:

> The refusal of work comprises at once a movement of exit and a process of invention. The refusal can make time and open spaces—both physical and conceptual—within which to construct alternatives. Rather than a simple act of disengagement that one completes, the refusal is, in this sense, a process, a theoretical and practical movement that aims to effect a separation through which we can pursue alternative practices and relationships.[69]

To engage in the refusal of work, on this account, means to bring into being new time-spaces of daily activity where unheralded forms of freedom apart from those manacled to work can arise. Notably, in light of the encounter I have traced between day laborers' commentaries and Kotef's theory, the refusal of work also involves conceptualizing and experimenting with new configurations, temporalities, directionalities, and interactivities of bodily movement as part of the "theoretical and practical movement" suggested by Weeks. Thus, even as the refusal of work decisively rejects the hegemonic privileging of work in people's practices and imaginations, it also nourishes tendencies toward untried modes of freedom that emerge from within current circumstances.

Day laborers' commentaries about fighting for the job, along with the filmic revisioning and resounding of the corner in *Jornaleros*, raise the intriguing prospect of converting the spaces where work's imperatives reach their utmost intensity into springboards for the refusal of work. To be sure, it is important not to overstate the extent to which day laborers are inclined toward the renunciative aspect of the refusal of work. As my explorations of the workers' commentaries on fighting for the job, desperation, and *echándole ganas* (both here and in the preceding chapter) show, our participants usually told us without hesitation that what they wanted above all else was a job. They also wasted no time in declaring their staunch fidelity to the work ethic, as we have seen. Nor does *Jornaleros* endorse a wholesale rejection of wage labor. For instance, its main characters movingly recall their abundant joy upon first finding day labor jobs as newly arrived migrants. Nonetheless, the film resolutely displaces work from its central position as the axis of migrants' social-practical imaginaries. This opens up the possibility of reconstruing the fight for the job as a more political, radically popular, historically conscious, and geographically expansive fight that incorporates within itself, among other elements, poor people's struggles to survive through work without granting these strivings primary significance. Arguably, this approach challenges work's hegemony even more incisively than a dramatic refusal-as-negation would do: *Jornaleros* portrays waged work as an important aspect of life, but one that no more deserves rapt attention as that which must be passionately renounced than as the ultimate criterion of self-worth and social membership.

That said, moments of negation with respect to work *do* occur in Voz's film, and they strike blows against the problem Berlant exposes by which affectively secured desires strengthen the tenacious hold of the dominant work culture over workers' lives. In the scene where Lolo and Aguirre play their song on the day labor corner, the radicality of their activity exceeds the redistribution of the sensible I discussed previously in this section. Aguirre and Lolo, in effect, stage a refusal of work by sitting out the fight for the job that goes on behind them while they enjoy their jam session. A related scene in the film supplies more concrete ideational content to this gesture. In this segment, Jesús Kobe, a young visual artist and day laborer, flatly rejects the standard assumption that all people, especially immigrants, aspire to live the "American dream": "For a lot of people, the United States are not the place all the people yearn for. Not everyone has the privilege of enjoying the first world, and the first world is eating us up." Kobe thus roundly rejects the dominant white, imperial-capitalist culture's definition of "the good life" and calls out the self-destructive dynamics of migrant work-life in the "first world," especially the cruel reversal of migrants' common expectations of far greater consumption opportunities in *el norte*. He challenges viewers to imagine instead what they might "yearn for" if they gave up the reigning fantasy of success and the glorification of work it commands. His on-screen actions as a painter, moreover, mingled with the spoken-word poetry performances and song renditions of the other protagonists, offer images and soundings of the expanded sensory universe that could result from such a refusal of work.

Weeks stresses that the refusal of work must involve lively plays of affect that "make time and open spaces—both physical and conceptual—within which to construct alternatives." *Jornaleros* both documents and incites such affective currents, as much through the street-art ventures of its leading personalities as through its sensory impacts on viewers/listeners. The worker-leaders of Voz have also sought to multiply and extend these effects by designing a series of local community screenings of the film, which were continuing at the time of this book's writing (and which I helped coordinate on two occasions).[70] These events are meant to be political organizing opportunities in the mode of popular education. After showing the documentary, the conveners spark critical discussion among audience members about the film's content and political implications. Sometimes, organizers do live performances of songs in the film. Thus, the *Jornaleros* project complements the film's backward glances toward Central American revolutionary times by provoking the forward gaze, sustained temporality, and spatial inventiveness that organizing a mass-popular refusal of work would require.

Thinking about the embodied spatial-temporal dynamics that arise through community screenings of *Jornaleros* invites further consideration, finally, of the relation between the refusal of work and the patterns of (neo)liberal mobility governance. As we have seen, day laborers on the corner are not so much required to conform anew to a system of ethical-corporeal regulation presumed to be foreign to them as to give full-blown expression to the economic-rational subjectivity they are assumed to have already. They are supposed to do this all the more heartily, the more self-evident it is that acting in this way prevents them from adequately manifesting normative subjectivity and leads them into the state's clutches. This extreme penetration of twisted neoliberal logics into the liberal protocols that regulate mobile bodies, as I have argued, belongs to a set of power relations that distinguish day laborers and other low-wage, unauthorized migrant workers as an exceptionally precaritized population. Such extreme precarity requires the targeted response that I have proposed in my interpretation of *Jornaleros* in relation to Weeks's theory, with respect to migrant justice organizations' deepening of their critique of work. Yet various versions of this neoliberal conundrum surely apply to countless sites of work activity well beyond day labor corners.[71] Consider, in this regard, how the dynamic by which day laborers' work compulsions yield self-destructive effects on the corner parallels the problems with the postindustrial work ethic, as theorized by Weeks, and the psychopathological economy, in Berardi's sense, that I detailed in the preceding chapter. This symmetry highlights the urgency of making a truly radical break with prevailing norms regarding work. Antiprecarity politics on the mass plane should respond in kind to the totalizing neoliberal motif whereby the incessant and all-absorbing pursuit of work becomes not only the norm to which reluctantly liberal subjects must conform but also the means by which willing neoliberal subjects paradoxically display their deviancy and weaken their own functional abilities. The need right now is for a comparably grand-scale assault on the work society—a refusal of work and a fight for time, conceptualized in a manner informed by Weeks and prefigured in the filmic frames of *Jornaleros*.

Conclusion: Precarious Body-Time

The preceding chapter ended by underscoring that time for precarious workers is structured in contradiction and that the themes of day laborers offer resonant terms for politicizing and contesting the contradictory dynamics of everyday temporalities, in response to both the exceptional forms of migrant precarity and those that suffuse the economy writ large. In view of the foregoing contemplations regarding what day laborers say about their work searches on the corner, and concerning the critical animations these commentaries inspire with regard to theories of physical mobility governance and social-mobility fantasies in these precarious times, we can now specify further that antiprecarity action cannot do without a self-conscious, strategically eclectic, affectively inventive *politics of the body*. Not only is precarious time structured in contradiction but, in addition, temporal contradictions are enacted by the body and constitute bodies as precaritized entities. As the critical-popular explorations in this chapter have suggested, these contradictions are made palpable and socially effective through orderings and disorderings of body-time, like those in the figure of fighting for the job.

This means that the fight for time must be a struggle for new time-spaces where bodies can realize new, noncontradictory forms of freedom through movement. For day laborers and likely other unauthorized migrants, as we have seen, carving out such alternative temporal locations is an urgent matter of establishing new contexts for physical movement in city neighborhoods that no longer leave migrant workers trapped in the contradictory position of moving at once excessively and insufficiently. At stake is the migrant's ability to gain relief from constant and ironically self-induced vulnerability to corporeal harm, bodily confinement, and traumatic expulsion from the social body through the operation of the norms of (neo)liberal mobility governance in tandem with the deportation regime. Most working people in the wider economy are spared those specific dynamics of precaritization. In this sense, the political motivation for temporal-spatial innovation is bound to be most intense among the migrant (and other poor, nonwhite) communities for whom the contradictions of mobility-governance are fiercest.

Nevertheless, the territories where dire forms of precarity abound are expanding in US cities, bringing somewhat closer together the conditions of movement and thereby the political fates of hitherto more segregated populations. To riff on a theme by David Harvey, critical-popular analysis of day laborers' commentaries in light of this trend raises the prospect of transposing the fight for the job into not just the "right to the city" but a broadly collective *fight for the city* that takes special aim at spatialized, infrastructurally based protocols of body-time. As Jamie Peck shows, cities of all sizes throughout the

United States have entered an era of "austerity urbanism" marked by ongoing fiscal crisis and perpetual budget reduction.[72] Peck discerns a "cumulative incapacitation of the state" in cities, in the sense that relentless budget reductions threaten "basic, essential and skeletal services often deemed indispensable (even) to the neoliberal state, such as prisons, policing, and public safety."[73] Urban austerity schemes, moreover, are not only "resulting in default targeting of programs for the poor and marginalized, but also extending into middle class terrain."[74] By 2012, for example, 40 percent of Detroit had no streetlights and the great majority of such lights had been removed from Highland Park, Michigan.[75] Even Chicago, which had succeeded more than other cities in substituting public-private partnerships for government finance systems, had downsized its fire and police forces while raising fees for water and sewer services and privatizing parking meters.[76] As the physical infrastructure needed to support the correct performance of liberal norms of bodily movement decays or is withdrawn, the zones where people are liable to run afoul of these norms multiply and swell. An antiprecarity politics focused on liberating mobile bodies from the temporal constraints and contradictions thrust upon them by spatial incitements of corporeal excess thus seems likely to become increasingly imperative for growing numbers of people, in more class and racially variegated populations, in today's cities. Perhaps, too, as austerity urbanism spreads the effects of neoliberal public service cutbacks beyond the family support programs that have disproportionately impacted women by increasing the household care-work typically shouldered more often by women than men, the practical bases for gender-inclusive mobilizations to contest this regime of urban governance will grow.

Closer affinities exist between day laborers and masses of working people in more mainstream areas of the economy in the sphere of affective fantasy, where, as we have seen, contradictory attachments structured by aspirational normativity thrive. Here, as well, the intellectual and cultural work of day laborers casts light on strategies for an antiprecarity politics of time that politicizes the debilitating clash between desires for and aversions to mobility and wrangles from this contradiction a liberating exit. Body-time in the throes of precarity is keyed to fantasy rather than devoid of dreams, even for these most desperate of all low-wage, intermittently employed workers who would seem to have ample reason for discarding their hopes altogether. In defiance of the self-reversing temporality that immerses the wish for future fulfillment within the presentist ordeal of keeping one's head barely above water, day laborers unfold practices of dreaming through precarious body-time that brim with multidimensionality and creativity. Reviving a sense of historical precedents for struggles in the now, these workers foment a fighting spirit that refuses to forget or to be ashamed of revolutionary fantasies in the past even if they have fallen on hard times, and that revivifies these dreamworlds by connecting them to freedoms of the future.

The reflections in this chapter have focused on those aspects of embodied time for day laborers that prevail in the social ecology within which day labor is embedded: the time workers spend hustling and waiting for jobs on the corner; workers' visions of individual economic competence, praiseworthy personal diligence, and upward mobility, as they make ethical sense of the chances they take out on the street; the contradictions of precaritized body-time within these practical and imaginative endeavors, which dramatize the dual character of day labor as both exception and synecdoche in relation to pervasive social tendencies; the political ramifications of these contradictions, as suggested by workers' generative language. Having elaborated certain bodily permutations of precarious time by way of investigations aimed at these social fields surrounding the labor process, let us now turn our attention to the work processes day laborers engage, keeping the question of body-time in the foreground. As manual laborers who get paid to do physical tasks with very low-tech equipment, sometimes simply the muscles in their arms, day laborers might seem to work in ways quite at odds with characteristically post-Fordist work processes oriented toward affective labor in service industries and info-labor in digital communications. Yet just as day labor disconcertingly epitomizes core temporal contradictions of this economy with regard to the postindustrial work ethic and the fragmentation of production, as I discussed in chapter 2, so likewise, the viral spread of bodily risks in the *work* of day labor closely tracks the metastasis of corporeal hazards throughout much of today's working world, even though these migrant workers suffer distinctly grave forms of exposure to such problems. The next chapter takes up this issue of day laborers' risky body-time on the job, in search of further generative themes to spark popular counterthrusts against the forces of precarity.

4

Risk on All Sides, Eyes Wide Open

IN A WORLD of work where a great many people's jobs are getting more dangerous, day labor is among the most hazardous jobs one can do. A day laborer at Casa Latina once told my assistant bluntly: "We do the work that other people don't want to do, for the amount they want to pay."[1] Very often, that reluctance is there because the job at issue is physically risky. It might involve balancing on a roof, for instance, or hauling ponderously heavy objects, or tearing into decades-old fiberglass insulation. Yet the bodily risks of day labor derive not only from the nature of the tasks but also from social, economic, and political circumstances. The informal and temporary quality of day labor jobs breeds the abuse of workers because employers are under no official scrutiny to ensure that jobs are free of health and safety hazards, or that workers have adequate protective equipment, or that workers know how to use such devices. Add to this the well-founded fears of a largely undocumented and very poor migrant workforce that any non-compliance with employers' demands could lead to catastrophe, whether at the hands of immigration authorities or from dire economic need, and the likelihood multiplies that work, for day laborers, causes illness and injury, even death.

Empirical studies of occupational safety and health (OSH) in day labor have firmly established that job-related injuries and illnesses abound among these workers. Estimates of such problems' frequencies, severities, and defining characteristics vary, but the overall landscape is bleak. An oft-cited 2008 study of workers at Casa Latina and two other Seattle hiring sites found that day laborers have a 31 percent chance of being injured on the job.[2] The types of jobs most commonly done by day laborers—construction, moving, and landscaping—are known to be among the most dangerous occupations, but day laborers' rates of workplace injuries and illnesses surpass those for the general workforces in those jobs.[3] A slightly lower but still disturbingly high rate of job-related injuries—one in five workers—is reported in the one existing nationwide survey-based study of day laborers. These investigators add: "more than half of those who were injured in the past year did not receive medical care" and "more than two-thirds of injured day laborers have lost time from work."[4] Another analysis found that barely one-third of day laborers injured at work reported their injuries or health problems to employers, 50 percent received no breaks to rest, and just *3 percent* of day laborers doing roofing received safety harnesses.[5] Nor are isolated injuries the only, or necessarily the worst, forms of bodily damage that day laborers sustain as a result of their work. These workers' health impairments can extend for years, as long latency periods unwind for respiratory problems due to toxic metal exposures[6] or as cardiovascular disease develops in consequence to day laborers' high allostatic load.[7]

Changing the conditions of work that imperil day laborers' bodies and minds depends on further documenting and analyzing these problems, which fall out of the official data gathered about OSH problems that afflict the US working population.[8] Even more crucially, however, such change hinges on exploring with day laborers what it means to encounter such circumstances, why the problems arise, and what could be done to alleviate them. In other words, social research about OSH issues in day labor should also take a *politicized* and *politicizing* approach. It should explore how day laborers name the precaritizing forces that make work perilous for them, with the goal of inspiring collective action by these workers and others to contest these power relations. Following the critical-popular path elaborated in this book, this chapter thus delves into day laborers' commentaries about OSH dangers in search of thematic material that can invigorate both responses to the immediate threats day laborers face and wider mobilizations to transform the social power-relations underlying so many workers' mundane vulnerability to bodily harm through work.

I argue in this chapter that the theme of facing "risk on all sides," which stands out amid day laborers' reflections about their experiences with dangerous work, fosters insight into core features of precarity today. Building on the last chapter's discussion of embodied time on the corner, this critical-popular inquiry focuses on body-time in the midst of hazardous work. Time on the job, for these day laborers, proceeded according to a self-conflicting structure that should seem familiar to readers of the prior two chapters. On the one hand, day labor incessantly exposed workers to the looming prospect of bodily injury. On the other hand, at irregular intervals and according to no predictable rhythm, brief episodes of severe physical and emotional trauma punctuated this grim temporal continuity.

Confronted with this temporal conundrum, day laborers typically reached for visions and practices of individual agency to protect themselves from omnipresent risk. The theme of keeping their "eyes wide open" for encroaching OSH hazards aptly expressed this individualist disposition, in ways that connect with the workers' themes of personal responsibility in the fight for the job and in the midst of desperation. Grappling with shifting and constantly pressing threats to their bodily integrity that arose from their social and material circumstances of work, interviewees stressed their own ability, obligation, and resolve to shield themselves from harm. These claims of responsible individuality, however, frequently turned back on themselves through a self-undermining logic. Workers acknowledged that hierarchically superior social actors and forces beyond their own control made injury risks common in day labor, and they frankly admitted that they regularly violated their own codes of self-preservation. Their eyes-open approach to health and safety thus involved a profound tension between their professions of individual responsibility and their recognition that practical conditions made it nearly impossible to act appropriately with much consistency.

The latter parts of the chapter explore how this contradictory situation named by day laborers speaks not only to uniquely precarious circumstances endured by these and other low-wage migrant workers but also to forms of precarity based in OSH risks that working people throughout the economy suffer. In part, I argue that the unique confluence of drastically contingent and erratic employment with subjection to the deportation regime gives day laborers' predicament regarding OSH hazards an exceptional aspect, even in comparison to other large groups of nonwhite, working-class people. Such exceptionality is important to recognize even though endangered body-time as a basic condition of work comprises a norm for wider populations of Latinos and other nonwhite workers, in ways day laborers' commentaries express. Additionally, however, the theme of keeping eyes wide open while facing risk on all sides holds up a mirror to working people throughout society that makes visible startling reflections of pervasive forms of precarity. This looking glass manifests an image of a working world ever-more suffused with OSH risks and producing increasingly dysfunctional regimens of body-time for just about everyone. As a synecdoche for precarity writ large, day labor calls attention to the tremendous proliferation of OSH risks in all sectors, as hazards specific to the post-Fordist economy overtake those more characteristic of an earlier industrial era while public agencies' capacities for responding to the most urgent problems wane. The workers' thematic language propels a social-theoretical critique of risk made palpable in workers' bodily-temporal distress but originating in work's institutional disorganization, or what David Weil calls the "fissuring" of the workplace. Corporate reorganizations that involve subcontracting, outsourcing, and similar strategies aim at diminishing risk to investment capital and end by displacing that financial risk onto working people's vulnerable bodies.

Day laborers' themes about struggling to preserve their corporeal integrity on the job also reveal much about the moral discourses through which precarious subjects are constituted—and condemned—for their bodily practices in the context of increasingly killing work. Reading workers' commentaries in association with Lauren Berlant's conception of "slow death" not only suggests the operation of this form of precarious subjectivity among day laborers but also incites numerous critical adjustments to the construal of this power schema. Day laborers point to the ways working people help establish the hegemony of moralistic public discourses about bodily self-care along with the temporalities of everyday life they presuppose and provoke. Workers do this, furthermore, in ways that bind narratives of the slowly dying yet responsibilized self to mundane uses of commodities, onto which social power-conflicts can be displaced and thereby removed from political contestation. This portion of my critical-popular analysis thus elaborates multiple complexities of the syndrome of slow death, moving beyond Berlant's initial account. Contemplating day laborers' themes about protecting themselves from OSH risks also illuminates how slow death unfolds not only through the biopolitical differentiating of mass populations, on which Berlant concentrates, but also via narrowly targeted exceptionalizing components as well as through processes of precaritization that apply to the working population at large.

More than a venture in critical-popular theory, although it is importantly that, this discussion of day laborers' generative themes regarding risky work and the self-caring subject also lights up a politics of opposition to these alarming circumstances. Such a politics calls on working people to *take sides* in revolt against a situation where bodily risk is increasing on *all sides*, and at all times, for all but the very few. This antiprecarity politics also exits defiantly from the feedback loops of responsibilized labor under conditions of social irresponsibility by taking the risks of seeing work time and life time differently and cultivating new relations of solidarity among working people throughout the economy.

Risk on All Sides

In describing the tense meeting place between employers' demands and day laborers' work activities, day laborers at Casa Latina and the MLK Center cataloged corporeal risks too numerous to discuss here otherwise than through illustrative examples. No bodily part, sense, or function was exempt from these hazards. Working at heights, for instance, raised the prospect of falling and sustaining grave injuries. As Cristian Gutiérrez noted with an evocative metaphor: "So many times, we are just . . . juggling on top of a ladder trying to reach the highest points."[9] Breaking up concrete with loud machinery endangered workers' hearing and caused swollen and sore muscles and joints. Demolition involved a range of hazards, including the inhalation of fiberglass particles and skin problems, as César Torres explained:

> When you break down walls and the plaster has gotten old, it releases a lot of dust, and later when you take down the wall, in the middle of it, there is fiberglass.... You have to pull it out slowly because, since it's old, it releases the particles.... Fiberglass is really dangerous. And if it gets into your skin, welts start to come out on your skin because it's like little spikes.[10]

Víctor Estrada told us how his thick gloves—"of leather! Of hide"—would quickly "get all worn away" when he did roofing work and that his hands would get scraped to the point of bleeding.[11] Other workers had developed carpal tunnel syndrome from hammering, sustained puncture wounds while using a nail gun, become severely dizzy from inhaling paint fumes, injured their eyes using weed whackers, or been bitten by reptiles when clearing out brush.

Gerardo Mejía summed up workers' consensus view about OSH hazards in day labor in the following terms, in a way that yielded a generative theme:

> You can work in gardening: there can be pesticides, and if you don't protect yourself, you can have a problem with your lungs. You can work in construction and in roofing: if you don't tie yourself [with a harness], you can slip and fall. That is, the risk is on all sides, in any kind of job, no matter whether it's small or big.[12]

This notion of "risk on all sides" most directly connotes a spatial quandary, but the workers made it clear that this difficult aspect of everyday work-life involved distinctive formations of time. First, day labor was only the latest in a long series of work experiences in which the threat and reality of bodily harm had become commonplace. Day labor thus epitomized a *working life-time* characterized by endemic corporeal risk. Many workers emphasized that this pattern extended back to their years in their countries of origins, where heavier construction materials, grueling work norms, lax habits regarding the use of health and safety equipment, and such gear's scarcity combined to make their jobs even more dangerous than in the United States. Yet things had hardly improved for them after relocating north of the US-Mexico border. Tomás Otero, for example, had endured constant anxiety from never being sure whether, or how badly, toxic chemical exposures from his work in farm labor were compromising his health or even threatening his life.[13] Many others discussed stints of high-pressure, ultrafast meatpacking or fish-processing work, which yields shocking rates of musculoskeletal disorders, knife cuts, and back injuries from slipping on floors slick with blood, fat, and fish.[14] Such bouts of work, however, were often cut short and abruptly followed by periods of unemployment and heightened physical suffering when workers got hurt or could no longer tolerate the everyday pain of such jobs.[15] A second, defining temporality of these day laborers' working lives was thus the maddeningly constant *fluctuation* of time's rhythms stemming from the kaleidoscopically shifting array of OSH hazards they faced.[16] In sum, the individual's working life had taken shape as a protracted time-scape of bodily endangerment, and the experience of any given job was likely to involve constant vulnerability to bodily violation and relentless fear about when the moment of injury would occur;[17] yet day laborers' work-lives were also erratically modulated by temporal flux, unpredictability, and discontinuity.

Our interviewees were well aware that the social relations governing their work produced this complexly temporalized exposure to risk on all sides. By their accounts, day labor placed the social configuration of body-time at work in particularly stark relief. Day laborers stressed that they never knew when an employer might demand that they do an intrinsically dangerous job, or that they do an otherwise safe job at a hazardous speed or in another risky way. In this highly uncertain situation, employer prerogatives largely controlled the temporalized conditions of bodily endangerment. Juan Carlos Garza typified most day laborers' discomfited yet matter-of-fact acceptance of such routine unpredictability: "There are some . . . who want you to do the job in a hurry—fast. They don't want you to rest, they don't give you anything to eat. . . . There are others that want you to do the job slowly but well done. They don't want you to run risks."[18] The consensus was that there were more of the former type than the latter, but one seldom could be sure how the boss would act.

Employers' arbitrary control over work time, according to participants, not only generated excessive wear on workers' bodies and increased their likelihood of injury but also denied them basic personal autonomy. More than one worker analogized day laborers' situation to that of human bondage, as in this remark from Pablo Maldonado about one of his employers:

> He's always pushing you with the work—you can't concentrate because at every moment he is telling you something—it's like in those times of the slaves. He doesn't let you do things well, so you don't do them well and then he's not satisfied.[19]

Here, Maldonado pointed to the psychosocial maltreatment that corresponded to physical endangerment for these workers (and that, according to other research, tends to precipitate further physical health problems).[20] As he expressed, employers commonly refused to give workers social recognition as persons with their own conceptions of quality work and their own motivations for doing it. Here, too, workers were keenly sensitive to the temporal shaping of this predicament. Maldonado stressed the relentlessness of employer demands, while other workers, like Bobby Kalani, decried the way their jobs' temporal discontinuities exposed them to employers' willful command: "They treat you . . . like you're a slave to them because they hire you for the day."[21]

Employer prerogatives registered even more deeply in the flesh for day laborers during the processions of time that followed on-the-job injuries, as did the discretionary powers of other privileged social actors. Employers arbitrarily determined the temporalities of treatment—if the worker received any remedial care and assuming the employer even knew the worker had been hurt[22]—by deciding whether and how much to pay for medical services.[23] Juan Ayala had started doing day labor because he had lost his regular construction job after breaking a finger while working on a ladder:

> I went to get X-rays, and they sent me the hospital bill, telling me to pay it. I took it and brought it to the employer, and he told me he would give me just four hundred dollars [60 percent], and I had to leave it at that. I accepted it because I needed the money . . . and what he told me was that if I didn't accept it, I wouldn't keep working there with him.[24]

Despite a doctor's orders that Ayala not work for a month, Ayala went back to work after just two weeks because he could not afford to wait any longer. Ultimately, however, he was unable to continue because his injured finger had never sufficiently healed. In a similar story in which time's progression following an injury hinged on an employer's arbitrary choices, Juan Carlos Garza described how one employer had taken him to the hospital after he had fallen off a ladder and broken his hand. The employer had then given him "a few days of work with one hand"—"but just a few days," he added, "and now she doesn't give me work anymore." Garza's story also highlighted how other social actors held sway over the injured day laborer's fate. He had tried to obtain legal help, but, he said, "in the long run, not one lawyer would take my case." Fortunately, a hospital billing agent arranged for the employer's home insurance to cover Garza's hospital costs, but this still left Garza owing a substantial balance. Overall, the injured worker ended up adrift in currents of time that he was helpless to control and that he knew could be set in motion, interrupted, or recalibrated at will by more powerful individuals and institutions. The notable exception to this pattern was the worker's lack of such dependency on insurance companies, for the simple and grim reason that virtually none of these day laborers had health insurance, in line with tendencies found by other researchers.[25]

Amid these turbulent flows of bodily jeopardizing work time, day laborers frequently pinned their hopes for avoiding injury on the use of protective equipment. Most day labor centers have developed extensive and successful programs that teach workers to limit their risk exposures by consistently and correctly using personal protective devices (PPDs). Sometimes, centers provide simple gear, like mouth-masks, gloves, goggles, and earplugs, although many workers spend their own scarce funds to purchase such equipment; some workers lack such items and even those who possess them do not necessarily have equipment in the best condition. There is basic common sense in day laborers habitually using PPDs and receiving training to do so because of their shifting and unknown work environments. Workers' inclinations to use PPDs were growing when we did our interviews and had become fairly well established as group norms at Casa Latina and the MLK Center, at least in principle, by the time of this book's writing.

Uncertainties and conflicts regarding PPDs, however, introduced yet another category of temporal flux and indeterminacy into the bodily experience of day labor. Such problems arose when workers did not have even basic safety gear, or such equipment was not fully functional, or a job required more sophisticated kinds of protection. In these circumstances, employers forcefully asserted their power to determine the conditions of work, and this generated acute dilemmas for workers. Most interviewees said they could never be sure whether an employer would offer them sufficient protective equipment. The highly constricted time frame of the job also lowered employers' incentives to incur the trouble and expense of providing adequate safety gear while increasing workers' willingness to risk unprotected work. To be sure, according to our participants, many employers showed genuine regard for day laborers' safety and provided PPDs in some form. On balance, however, more employers did not offer such equipment and simply refused if a worker mounted the courage to request protection.[26] In addition, employers usually had not assessed the job's safety and health risks and lacked the practical experience to identify potential hazards.

Volunteer job dispatchers at the centers also typically spoke with employers very little, or not at all, about health and safety matters when setting up work orders over the phone. When I volunteered regularly at Casa Latina in 2016–17 fielding employer calls and arranging jobs, I was required to inform new employers that they would need to provide any safety equipment needed to do the job. However, I was not supposed to inquire what specific risks were involved, what equipment was needed, or whether the employer possessed such gear. Nor was there any procedure for following up on this issue with new employers or for mentioning health and safety to the many callers—a significant majority each day—who had hired from Casa Latina previously. The same circumstances maintained in 2008, when my research assistant spent a summer volunteering at

Casa Latina in the same capacity. Both in interviews and in comments we heard through participant observation, workers commonly expressed great reluctance about proposals for dispatchers to press employers further about health and safety because they worried this would scare employers away. To offer some telling context: Casa Latina is recognized as a leader if not *the* leader among day labor organizations nationwide in promoting sound OSH practices among workers.

Workers at both centers were divided on whether employers' general lack of regard for their employees' health and safety reflected inattentiveness or malice. Said Gerardo Mejía delicately: "It's not that they neglect you but rather that they let it happen. They omit what you really need; they leave out the risk that you have to run if you don't have the safety equipment." By contrast, Antonio Soto lashed out at employers for denying day laborers PPDs "the majority of the time" and added: "There's a lot of bad boys out there. A lot of people that don't care. They treat us like animals."[27] Ricardo Reyes recalled an unusual homeowner who always provided waterproof gloves and safety glasses for use with the weed-eater or chainsaw and even had taken Reyes to a doctor when he was feeling unwell. When my assistant asked Reyes why he thought the employer showed such attentiveness, he responded: "He had children, and that's why he protected all the people. He loved his children very much and that's the way he looked at us, because he was a fine gentleman. He called us [his] children."[28] This remark spoke volumes; it neatly encapsulated the fundamental power relation in the conflict over PPDs by expressing the worker's ultimate dependence on the employer's paternalistic benevolence.

Confronted with an employer's demand that a dangerous job be done without protection, the workers commonly shied away from asking employers to give them the gear they needed and performed the work anyway, although this was not always the case, as I shall discuss in the next section. Many workers simply could not raise the issue because they did not speak English and the employer spoke no Spanish. Rubén Contreras, in turn, emphasized how intensely these highly "insecure" workers felt their poverty at pivotal times of decision about health and safety:

> There are times when the people in that moment are really poor and what they want is to work, so, for example, if they ask for something and they don't give it to them, [they worry that] maybe the next time they won't invite them to work because [the worker] demands too much or talks too much.[29]

Diana Ortiz stressed that workers were generally reluctant to make requests or demands of employers regarding safety matters because of "fear—fear that the employer is going to fire you, leave you without a job, lay you off, or deport you."[30] Ortiz's comment that "the employer" could not only dismiss but also "deport" the worker was telling. It expressed how, for these workers, vulnerability to extreme economic hardship merged with the risk of capture and banishment by the immigration authorities. Her phrasing also indicated that for our interviewees, these twin perils converged in the power wielded and personified by the employer— power that posed continuous danger even while individual employers kept changing.

In sum, the workers' theme of facing risk on all sides expressed a temporal predicament in which risks broke out incessantly yet unforeseeably and in which actual bodily harms frequently followed from these hazards. The time of work was thus both the perilous time of "juggling on top of the ladder," ever on the verge of falling, and the helpless time of sustaining, recovering (somewhat) from, and learning to live with physical pain and trauma. As these day laborers perceived, the fluctuating temporalities of bodily vulnerability and hurt through work were sociopolitically constituted by the hierarchical employment relation, the discretionary interventions of institutionally privileged actors, and the workers' conditions of extreme poverty and illegality. Workers showed their attentiveness to these conditions in their abundant remarks about PPDs, although in another sense such comments occluded the social context by focusing on the immediate physical aspects of the job and the worker's individual action to stave off bodily harm.

Eyes Wide Open

Within this predicament where so many factors decapacitated workers physically, psychologically, and socially, workers not only lamented their powerlessness and expressed their fears—they also sought to see themselves as retaining significant forms of personal agency. They strove to modulate the fluidity, anxiety, and painfulness of day labor's body-time through temporalized discursive strategies that accentuated their own "responsibility" for the difficult situations they confronted. Day laborers thus again cited the keyword with which they frequently described their approach to seeking jobs through the centers and the corners, as prior chapters have discussed. Just as with those other invocations of personal responsibility, however, so likewise, with regard to health and safety, the theme featured acutely self-conflicting elements.

Our participants showed a pronounced tendency to develop the notion of self-reliance in OSH matters into a substantial ethos of individual responsibility that prescribed obligations to oneself and to others. In terms of the duty to self, workers typically described facing potentially hazardous work as an opportunity to demonstrate personal initiative, observational acuity, shrewd analytical thinking, and prudential stewardship of their own well-being. Jaime Ortega articulated this moral-practical stance in resonant terms:

> I'm going to tell you something: "Keep your eyes wide open" is one of the most important things you have to do. Many times, . . . when you go to work, laziness is one of the things that causes you a lot of accidents. Going around like nothing matters to you. You have to focus on what you're doing. Have your eyes open.

Notable here is Ortega's insistence that day laborers both can and should behave in such alert, cautious, and industrious ways. Furthermore, the idea of "being present in what you are doing," to translate more literally Ortega's line about staying focused on the task at hand, signals the temporal inflection of this ethos, as does his evocation of constant watchfulness.[31] Other workers further elaborated the temporal aspects of this responsibly vigilant orientation, for instance by underscoring the importance of "paying attention to what you're going to do without rushing," as Juan Carlos Garza did. Jesús Martínez invoked a more extensive and explicitly moralized temporal perspective, insisting that a worker had to "have the conscience necessary to say, 'I'm not going to do the job because I'm missing this and that—I need my equipment because my life is worth more than what you're going to pay me.'"[32] In these diverse ways, day laborers confirmed their duty of "conscience" to guard their own safety as well as their possession of the visual capacities, moral judgment, and temporal sensibilities needed to act accordingly.

As strenuously as the workers avowed their fidelity to this duty, however, they also acknowledged over and again how frequently they performed dangerous jobs even when they knew conditions were unsafe. In principle, these day laborers viewed their responsibility to protect themselves as paramount; in the moment, at the scene of work and when faced with an employers' demands, most routinely acquiesced and assumed risks, sometimes quite serious ones. César Torres, for instance, described various hazardous jobs he had done after unforeseen risks arose: breaking up concrete by hand when a jackhammer failed; stripping paint without eye protection after the cheap goggles provided by his employer fogged up; lugging sheetrock up multiple flights of stairs for an employer who had hired Torres to do "cleaning." Despite the blisters in his hands, burning pain in his eyes, and numbness in his knees from these ordeals, Torres stoutly professed his duty to protect himself and insisted, "I'm always one of the people for whom safety is really important." Torres represented not the exception but the rule in this respect: the common view that even when it was "not appropriate" for reasons of health or safety, as Víctor Estrada put it, "the person has to work."

Workers often sought to mitigate what they clearly sensed was an overstated emphasis on their own responsibility for preserving health and safety by assigning certain obligations to employers. Such qualifications reflected their more general awareness that the social context of employment relations largely determined the level of risk, but their comments typically fell into contradiction and left the worker effectively bearing the full weight of responsibility for ensuring job safety. Asked who was responsible for keeping day labor jobs healthy and safe, for example, Torres replied:

> I think it's the employer and the worker, like me, equally. The employer has the responsibility to provide me the equipment I need, the bigger things. And it's my responsibility [to protect] my integrity. The two of us have to share it. He has to provide me what's needed and I have to ask him for it.

Torres thus described a relation that both was, and was not, "equal." Both worker and employer were obliged in principle to make sure a job was safe, but the burden of raising the issue rested entirely with the worker—under circumstances in which, as we have seen, workers were quite hesitant to broach such tricky subjects with employers for multiple and intersecting reasons.

Our participants tried to mitigate this self-contradictory disposition toward safety and health through four practical-discursive, temporally keyed strategies. One, as we have seen, involved preparing for unpredictable eventualities on the job by bringing along basic safety items like gloves, earplugs, and mouth-masks. Workers thereby attempted to insert a small degree of self-governance into the configuration of day labor's body-time. They sought to extend time's duration voluntarily by adding a routine period of preparation, and to reduce the extent to which working life involved unforeseeable and constantly shifting hazards. A second strategy was to try to manipulate time by slowing down a hazardous task, as Estéban Avila suggested:

> If I have to run risks, I have to take my time to be safe. . . . One time we were installing insulation, but we didn't have protection for our mouths or anything. . . . Well you know, we're going to work anyway—we have to do the job. . . . But I have to give myself my time. . . . I have to take breaks a little more, because without protection you have to be blowing your nose every so often, or drinking water.[33]

Third, many workers redefined the criteria governing responsible behavior and thereby justified departures from risk-minimizing protocols, often drawing on masculine-gendered norms regarding physical toughness and the ability to support family members by earning income. More than a few workers said they found it inefficient, irritating, or "uncomfortable" to use protective gear.[34] Rubén Contreras, for instance, complained about wearing gloves, saying: "They cost me more work." Other workers articulated a more emphatic sense of masculine bravado. Torres, asked why he would risk injury on the job, responded flatly: "This is part of hard work" (and signaled a racial inflection of this notion by speaking the words "hard work" in English, recalling the canny code-switching associated with the theme of responsibility noted in chapter 2). Contreras similarly ridiculed day laborers who fretted about their safety as "too delicate." In temporal terms, this third strategy shifted the basis of moral achievement from the mission to care for one's bodily integrity on the job to the correct performance of normative masculinity. Such masculine virtue showed itself through efficiently executing wage-maximizing labor, manfully "bearing with" the pain any given job might produce because of the job's brief duration, or deriding as effeminate other workers who hesitated to do this.[35] Of course, there were distinctly masculine valences to the first two strategies as well, inasmuch as they expressed an individualistic resolve to exert technical control over one's immediate environment and thereby to take on enough risky work to yield self-sustaining (and, for many, family-sustaining) income while not overly imperiling one's physical capacities.

A fourth permutation of these day laborers' discourse of personal obligation regarding job safety and health involved invoking a "good/bad worker" dichotomy, repeating another tendency seen in their comments about fighting for the job and desperate responsibility. With respect to OSH matters, the speaker in this mode staunchly affirmed the duty to protect himself at work, soft-pedaled his own routine violations of this principle, and cast moral aspersions on fellow workers who disregarded this imperative. Jaime Ortega, for instance, proudly ticked off a list of safety techniques he had learned from Casa Latina's workshops and then lamented that "many times, the others don't listen" to the trainers out of "laziness." Voicing another familiar motif, Pablo Villa accused those who showed little regard for personal safety on the job of being drunks who deceived employers and endangered themselves:

> There are some who arrive [at a job] drunk or who come with beer or liquor, and the employers can't tell who they are among those who go out [for the job]. . . . You always have to arrive good and calm so an accident doesn't happen. Because if they make you cut [materials, e.g., with a saw], you can really injure yourself.[36]

Other participants voiced dismay over fellow workers who disingenuously claimed to have skills they lacked so an employer would hire them, thus jeopardizing both their coworkers' safety and their own long-range earning prospects. Once more, our participants' comments were temporally inflected: central to the responsible/ irresponsible worker dualism was the issue of *wasting time*, whether through alcoholic delinquency, imprudent use of the hours waiting for jobs at the worker center (when workshops were held), or inadequate long-term planning. Again, moreover, invocations of the good/bad worker binary wove these temporal characteristics together with masculine-gendered inflections: forms of manly virtue that renounced vices, demonstrated self-control, engaged in hard work, and embraced an efficiency-oriented pragmatism.

Our interviewees thus at least imagined, and sometimes enacted in small ways, strategies for pushing back against the moral and temporal double binds created when the imperative of autonomous moral conduct clashed with the heteronomy of practical circumstances. Yet in all these cases, workers' retemporalizing tactics scarcely altered the basic dynamics of the situation. Pointing fingers at the carelessly self-endangering worker may have furnished psychic relief from the sting of self-recrimination associated with holding oneself strictly responsible for safeguarding one's bodily integrity while routinely capitulating to the power-laden inducements, "on all sides," to put one's body at risk. It did not, however, change the terrain of pseudoequality on which exchanges with employers over health and safety occurred or were evaded. Indeed, the psychological effect of this stance was arguably damaging, inasmuch as these very workers also admitted to veering from their own standards and hence exposed themselves to their own moral missiles. Compared to the strategy of transferring moral blame to other workers, the first two approaches had the practical advantage of somewhat reducing the risk of harm through positive interventions to influence the work environment, which in turn could yield a certain sense of individual efficacy. These same strategies, however, further entrenched the presuppositions of worker obligation and employer discretion. In addition, all these approaches cut against efforts to build solidarity for collectively improving conditions of work-related health and safety. The first two did this by reinforcing individualistic framings of OSH problems, while the resort to moralistic binaries encouraged a culture of peer disparagement. Macho declarations of bodily invulnerability, in turn, had both these effects while also leaving the contradictory structure of action intact by failing to acknowledge the presence of any dilemma and embracing dangerous work as a positive good.

My point here is neither to criticize these day laborers for inaccurately appraising their risks at work nor to judge them for acting in ways inconsistent with their avowed principles. Rather, it is to use their theme of keeping eyes wide open to identify the temporal coordinates of their discursive efforts to salvage some measure of personal agency when faced with relentless yet unpredictable risk on all sides. What comes through vividly is just how dependent those imagined forms of agency are on a keen sense of individual responsibility, with the censorious visage of moral self-condemnation either lurking around the edges or in plain view. If, as we have seen, the physical pain and suffering wrought by day labor went along with injuries from being denied social recognition and interpersonal regard, then to these debilitations we now must also add a category of self-inflicted wounds. These abrasions of the spirit happened when the worker judged that job-related maladies were ultimately *his own fault* and sought to modify those maladies' temporalities, even while knowing that his parameters for moral decision were vanishingly narrow and fleeting.

There remained, nonetheless, a small but determined contingent of workers who insisted that if faced with the hard choice of either doing a job under hazardous conditions or losing that chance to work, they would *refuse the job*. In temporal terms, rather than either engaging in a low-grade struggle to control their time flows or conceding such control to employers, these individuals simply removed their body-time from the practical and discursive matrices of endangerment. Alberto Guerrero illustrated this approach when he insisted:

> Whenever a job is dangerous, I don't work. For example, if you would have to climb up and tie yourself up with a belt and all, I tell them no if they don't have a belt and a ladder—I don't go up. If it's very dangerous, I don't do it, because my health is worth more than anything.[37]

Antonio Soto suggested that refusing dangerous work required taking a more relaxed and enlarged temporal view of both the job itself and his own working lifetime: for instance, waiting to see if another worker would help him lift a load that was "too heavy to pick up," or simply not doing it because what he would lose if he "broke [his] back" would far outweigh the money he might forfeit in the short term. These workers and others credited Casa Latina's health and safety workshops with helping them learn how to make these kinds of judgments. Thus, even though the main thrust of the workers' ethos of responsibility for their own health and safety fostered vicious cycles of moralizing, dangerous work, and self-indictment, some day laborers escaped these dynamics in ways that suggested not only resolute self-preservation but also an aspect of solidarity. I discuss these activities and their political implications in detail in this book's final chapter.[38] For now, it is important simply to note the existence of this counterresponse to the predicament of facing risk on all sides, even though its defenders were relatively rare among our interviewees, especially at the MLK Center.

Notwithstanding some day laborers' unusual determination to prioritize bodily safety over wage-earning work when the two were at odds, our participants more commonly framed the problem of staving off ubiquitous risk as a highly individualized and moralized struggle to keep themselves perpetually on the lookout for hazards. Variable conceptions of the morally agentic self augmented the temporal complexity of workers' ethical-practical exertions in this regard, depending on whether the individual favored the pathway of assertive and competitive machismo, instrumentalist manipulations of time on the job or time preparing for work, or severe judgments of fellow workers for behaving irresponsibly. Especially by adopting the latter route, day laborers exposed themselves to the sting of their own moral condemnations of others. This self-undermining effect, in turn, arose in the context of a more generally contradictory clash of themes according to which unblinking vigilance and moral resolve were somehow supposed to compensate for the pervasiveness and unavoidability of serious corporeal endangerment as a structural component of day labor.

A Popular-Educational Interlude

In prior chapters, I have initiated the critical-popular turn toward exploring theoretically generative potentialities of day laborers' themes by first speculating about the prospects for popular-educational dialogue that the themes appear to pose. In the case of workers' commentaries about OSH risks and protective strategies, I had the good fortune to conduct actual workshops that invited responses to the themes by workers and volunteers in the Casa Latina community. The generative aspects I see in the themes of confronting risk on all sides and keeping eyes wide open thus are more than a matter of imaginative conjecture. They became manifest in live interactions with day laborers and others who have invested significant time and energy in helping worker centers thrive.

The goal of the workshop with day laborers was to provoke critical thought and discussion about where OSH hazards came from, who was responsible for preventing them, and what workers could do collectively to foster safer and healthier working conditions. We conducted the workshop as the main item on the agenda for a workers' assembly meeting in mid-December 2017. An assembly took place in the hiring hall every Thursday shortly after the 7:00 a.m. job lottery, and the scene for this event was fairly typical. Some workers chatted animatedly, creating a constant low-level hum near the coffee pots and around the room's edges. Others sat stoically in the rows of folding chairs, hoping for another chance at work if additional employers called. A few nodded off to sleep in the warmth of hall, no doubt in some cases after a cold and uncomfortable night on the street. The season being winter, only eight job assignments had been available, and a number of workers had been disgruntled to find that the free bus tickets Casa Latina often dispensed on Thursdays were unavailable that week. Rumors about the bus tickets had drawn an enormous crowd of nearly eighty hopeful raffle participants, many of whom were not usual attendees, but with the scarcity of jobs and disappointment over the tickets, around half had left by the time the assembly began. Still, a lively and even rowdy energy lingered in the hall as staffer Leo Ulate and I started off the workshop.

Hoping to stoke that energy, we began with a serious-comical theater exercise in which Leo played the role of a day laborer being told to use lawn-care machinery and do a painting job under various unsafe conditions, while I acted the part of an employer who trivialized the hazards, deflected the worker's halting requests for safety equipment, and made a show of being chummy but then got irritated that the worker was taking too long to start. This rather goofy skit led easily to an open and vigorous discussion about what the worker and the employer had done wrong. In tune with the theme of keeping eyes wide open, this conversation predictably gravitated toward what workers individually needed to do to remain safe. Those who spoke up seemed eager to show that they knew important things about job health and safety that they wanted to share with their peers. One insisted it was important to use safety equipment *all* the time, not just sometimes, because a worker never knew what dangers he might encounter. Another emphasized impassionedly that before commencing any job it was vital to inspect the worksite carefully, walking slowly all around it and identifying potential hazards. Sensing an entrée for the theme of keeping eyes wide open, I then projected and read the comment by Jaime Ortega that contained this phrase. The workers' responses were fascinating: they immediately criticized Ortega for believing he was keeping himself safe without really doing so. As one worker noted sarcastically, it hardly matters if your eyes are wide open as you are falling off a rooftop because you are not wearing a harness.

Proposing the theme of keeping eyes wide open thus stimulated critical conversation about the complexities of ensuring health and safety on the job in ways that validated workers' knowledge and that began with individual injury prevention techniques but gradually inched toward consideration of social power dynamics. "Decodifying" exercises based on the theme of facing risk on all sides moved the discussion further in these critical directions. I brought up the theme by projecting and reading the quotation from Gerardo Mejía discussed earlier in this chapter and by displaying a poster-sized graphic image—to use Freire's term, a "codification" of the theme—that depicted multiple day laborers doing different jobs, every one of which involved ominous dangers. (I had arranged for this and other images to be prepared by Salvadoran artist Alfredo Burgos, a long-time collaborator with Casa Latina and other US day labor organizations, and hence someone whose pictures were likely familiar to workers.) It was both exciting and instructive to witness the generative potency of this theme. The theme appeared to resonate immediately with workers' everyday experiences: heads nodded vigorously and voices murmured all over the room when I asked if they thought Mejía's words described the realities of day labor, which was an interesting contrast to their response to Ortega's eyes-open credo. Presenting the workers with Burgos's smaller graphic images of particular risks mentioned in the interviews then kindled numerous comments on the various hazards workers typically encountered. This fostered further opportunities for workers to demonstrate their knowledge in ways that seemed to build an atmosphere of analytical self-confidence, even as workers confirmed their frustration with the risks that popped up all the time and everywhere when they went out on jobs. For instance, an image of a stepladder quickly drew a sharp response from one day laborer who pointed out that this was the wrong kind of ladder to use for painting. Another worker, upon seeing Burgos's drawing of a menacing-looking spider, solemnly described how a coworker had once lost a leg after a poisonous spider bite. Then, in a more humorous and ironic vein, he discussed his difficulties with employers whose demands had exposed him to these insects. One employer had sent him down to clean out a basement infested with spiders after casually and disingenuously saying, "There might be a spider down there, so be careful." Another had sternly admonished him not to kill any spiders he came across because that would be "cruelty to animals." (This story, of course, elicited plenty of laughter and a few knowing grimaces. It also confirmed my sense from working the phones that exploring the attitudes of employers, many of whom obviously see themselves as good Seattle progressives but also seem clueless in some respects, would be a fertile area of further research on how to build solidarity for an antiprecarity politics.)

These moments in the workshop illustrate another crucial way in which our popular-education exercise proved generative: it provoked open consideration of the power relations at play in moments of tension and conflict over health and safety matters. In the relatively short space of an hour, and under conditions that were quite challenging at times (with disruptive conversations periodically breaking out, a loquacious worker in the front talking far more than his share, and a few interruptions to send workers out on jobs), those who attended zeroed in on most of the thematic features discussed earlier in this chapter regarding the social relations of employment. When I asked why there were risks on all sides in day labor, an older worker missing all his front teeth declared that it was because doing such work amounted to "slavery"—the boss arbitrarily controlled the conditions of work and workers' bodies essentially belonged to the *patrón*. The stress in the interviews on temporal factors likewise reappeared in the workshop: picking up on the slavery analogy, another worker cited the related concern about being unable to concentrate continuously on the tasks at hand because of employers' constant intrusions into the work process, which increased work hazards. In one especially compelling commentary, a young worker spoke gravely about how, as he put it, workers "have no voice" with which to confront employers who demand risky work, because they lack legally authorized status.

The workshop thus culminated in questions of politics and power, and more specifically by posing the difficult problems of how to educate employers about health and safety issues in day labor and how, in this way or otherwise, to change the ways employers act. To be sure, I do not mean to claim too much for what we accomplished. At the workshop's end, the idea of cooperative action by day laborers to improve job health and safety was on the table more as an abstract hypothetical than a concrete vision. The fatalistic echoes of remarks about workers being silenced by their unauthorized status and subjected to slavery still reverberated in the room, and the question of altering employers' understandings and modes of conduct had been raised but not even provisionally answered. Yet this was still a genuine accomplishment, as Freire's conception of popular-educational dialogue suggests, in the sense that the possibility of workers intervening to change the relations of power in their everyday worklives had been "posed as a problem." The workshop also helped motivate workers to participate in OSH training opportunities available to them through Casa Latina, which staff and visitors described upon our workshop's conclusion and which comprised an important avenue by which workers could become more actively involved in the organization apart from seeking jobs, as I discuss in chapter 5. In terms of the critical-popular enterprise that is central to this book, in turn, the workshop amply validated that the themes extracted from the interviews do, indeed, have generative potential to spark intellectual engagement by day laborers.

With Casa Latina's volunteers, my approach was different and produced distinct but equally provocative results. About twenty-five volunteers gathered in the spring of 2017 for a three-hour workshop to build community among these individuals, who often only knew a couple other volunteers in their activity area, such as teaching English or taking employer calls. The workshop also aimed to enable volunteers to learn more about day laborers' challenges as workers and unauthorized migrants. I spoke to the group about the issue of precarity, the theory and practice of popular education, and the basic dimensions of my research project. Then I introduced the generative themes, offered examples of specific hazards frequently discussed by workers, and asked the other volunteers how they imagined it felt, emotionally and physically, to encounter such dangers routinely. Ready responses from around the table suggested that the attendees grasped the ubiquity and relentlessness of the risks as well as the pressure workers felt to react by keeping ever alert for new hazards.

Even more interesting was what came next. When I inquired whether any workshop participants had ever had similar experiences in their own jobs, hands shot up around the room. A young nurse told us with audible distress that she had to brace herself for risks of injury when dealing with patients, whom she often had to move physically, using awkward positions and straining to lift heavy individuals. A middle-aged freelance writer talked about never knowing from week to week whether he would have enough work to get by and feeling his stress build up over time to the point that it had become seriously unhealthy. Others expressed fears about using machinery when it was unclear whether safety mechanisms were functional; still others shared stories of sustaining musculoskeletal injuries from repetitive motions. The energy in the room grew larger and more palpable with each new anecdote. Evidently, day laborers' thematic articulations of health and safety problems had struck a resounding chord with people whose jobs were significantly different but who nonetheless shared forebodings, fragilities, and risks that the workers had incisively named.

These experiments in popular education speak to the real generativity harbored by the themes of facing risk on all sides and keeping eyes wide open. Our workshop with day laborers demonstrated such generative potential in the sense of spurring theory from the ground up among precaritized working people whose critical-analytical capacities usually go unacknowledged. The session with volunteers, in turn, suggested the themes' power to foment political solidarities across lines of class and race through the startling recognition of experiential affinities. Moving into the critical-popular mode now gives us the chance to sketch in key aspects of the broader social background for these thematic generativities. In what ways do day laborers' dilemmas regarding job-related injuries and health problems expose them, along with other acutely oppressed and excluded migrants, to exceptional forms of precaritization? How, nonetheless, might the tortured unfolding of body-time at work for day laborers as expressed through the themes also reflect generally pervasive dynamics of precaritization among workers today?

OSH Risks, the Fissured Workplace, and the Fight for Time

Earlier in this chapter, I reviewed empirical findings that day laborers experience disturbingly high rates of exposure to OSH hazards and correspondingly elevated levels of work-related injuries and illnesses. Contextualizing these figures in relation to patterns for larger groups underscores how day laborers represent the most acute cases within an already exceptionalized population for whom OSH risks and harms decisively exceed the norm. Between 1992 and 2006, work-related deaths for Hispanics increased by 86 percent, while occupational fatalities dropped for non-Hispanics by 15 percent.[39] Hispanics number disproportionately among those fatally injured in construction, and they are "nearly twice as likely as non-Hispanic construction workers to be killed by occupational injuries."[40] In a study of urban-dwelling Mexican immigrants, 39 percent of construction workers had been injured on the job, compared to 5 percent of the general population; for factory workers the figures were 40 percent and 5 percent, respectively; for restaurant workers, the numbers were 16 percent and 4 percent.[41] Another author reports: "Mexicans hold 27.3% of the employment positions held by foreign-born workers in the United States, but account for 44% of recorded occupational fatalities that involved immigrant workers in the United States, the highest percentage of any immigrant group."[42] Not only are job-related injury and illness rates markedly higher for Latino migrant workers (and for all Latinos, and for all migrants) than for the US population at large—in addition, work-related injuries and health problems are distressingly elevated in absolute terms. This applies, for instance, with respect to depression among migrant farmworkers,[43] traumatic injuries among youth farmworkers,[44] musculoskeletal and neurological injuries among Latino poultry processors,[45] job-related injuries for migrant construction and service workers,[46] and headaches and eyesight problems for women garment workers—among whom a stunning 99 percent also report work-related musculoskeletal pain.[47] In short, day laborers and other Latin American migrants are extensively and unequally exposed to bodily debilitation through work, as are all Latinos. These tendencies hold even as official federal data have shown a "pattern of annual decline" in "nonfatal workplace injuries and illnesses reported by private industry employers" from 5.0 per one hundred workers in 2003 to 3.2 per hundred workers in 2014.[48]

Yet the picture is more complicated than one might think, notwithstanding the basic rule that work imperils brown people's bodies—especially migrants' bodies—more than white people's bodies. Disturbing trends in OSH matters increasingly plague the vast majority of US working people with heightened bodily risk at work. Any consideration of these tendencies must start by observing that the major public sources of information and analysis almost certainly vastly understate the actual frequencies of work-related injuries, illnesses, and deaths.[49] Independent analyses reveal incidence rates of job-related injuries and illnesses for the general population that far exceed official figures, are extremely costly, and generate expenses that workers and their families largely bear, with some contribution from the government but little from employers.[50] One widely cited study concludes that instead of just over three million work-related injuries and illnesses annually, as the Bureau of Labor Statistics reports, the actual rate is nearly nine million, at a total cost of $250 billion—"at least as large as the cost of cancer."[51]

Occupational safety and health problems not only occur on a more massive scale than official figures indicate—they also suffuse society at large, for reasons that concern the types of OSH hazards that are proliferating most actively in the current economy. The major risks facing workers today depart from the Occupational Safety and Health Administration's (OSHA's) traditional paradigm, which was developed in an era when manufacturing comprised the core of the US economy. This conventional approach associates OSH hazards with isolated threats and discrete remedial actions, such as eliminating particular toxins or requiring safety mechanisms for specific machines. In post-Fordist workplaces, however, the most rapidly growing risks stem from accelerating changes to the structure of businesses, the technical organization of work, and the physical and social environments where people work. Many of these ascendant risks derive from corporate restructuring, the job reductions that result, and the overall climate of uncertainty for workers about their employment futures. Abundant research in public health associates "major organizational restructuring and downsizing" with heart dysfunction, elevated blood pressure, high cholesterol, and "increases in body mass index."[52] Unhealthy and even lethal problems of these kinds stalk populations of US workers well beyond the most vulnerable migrant laborers.

Poor air quality is another major OSH hazard that increasingly affects broad swaths of the US working population. As the twenty-first century dawned, the proportion of the workforce employed in "artificially ventilated indoor spaces" rose above 75 percent for the first time.[53] Yet although OSHA obligates employers to ensure the absence of individual pollutants such as formaldehyde, the agency has never defined a comprehensive air quality standard that would address the "combined or synergistic effects of toxins in the environment."[54] The result has been mounting exposure to pervasive but invisible health hazards for janitors, factory workers, retail salespeople, and executives alike.

Still another mushrooming threat to workers' health and safety comes from employers' failure to apply ergonomic principles to work processes even as the forms of work liable to ergonomic problems and the proportions of the labor force engaged in such work have multiplied. Like air-quality hazards and risks stemming from corporate restructuring, OSH threats related to ergonomic factors pervade all quarters of the economy. The main health issues posed by these factors are work-related musculoskeletal disorders (WMSDs) due to "monotonous and repetitive tasks" and "speed-ups" that overtax workers' "muscles, tendons, joints, and nerves."[55] These problems are disproportionately concentrated in lower-status jobs but extend throughout the employment hierarchy. They affect "auto assemblers, meatpackers, construction workers, delivery workers, poultry cutters, workers doing manual lifting, and clerks using price scanners" as well as the legions of office workers who spend their working hours typing at computer terminals.[56] Despite the enormous increase in WMSD incidences since about 1980, however, OSHA has yet to promulgate an ergonomics standard, although one was developed during the Clinton years but then canceled shortly after George W. Bush's administration took office.[57] Hence, whether on the shop floors of deregulated factories or in the burgeoning world of online labor, more and more working people face the risk of WMSDs traceable to the temporal and physical organization of work processes.

From their tenuous position on the remote edges of the working world, day laborers resonantly articulate these distressing circumstances that confront workers throughout the economy. For working people at large, risk on the job is exploding on all sides and according to temporalities that discordantly mix relentless continuities with emergency outbreaks, reinstantiating the contradictory motif of precaritized time that I have discussed in relation to prior themes. Mortifying continuities of time that gradually wear down workers' bodies with no letup become perceptible in the gathering numbness and throbbing of body parts repeatedly abused in ergonomically dysfunctional activities as well as in the slow accumulation of health problems driven by the standardized cycles of indoor air-circulation systems. Risks associated with protracted immutabilities of body-time also spread through the drawn-out effects of corporate restructuring, which damage workers' bodies and brains no less through the higher workloads, diminished autonomy, heightened insecurity, and sped-up work endured by "survivors" than through the anxieties of the "anticipation phase."[58] Extended etiologies of respiratory, cardiac, and psychological diseases stemming from all these environmental causes mock the monitoring capacities of outdated OSH regulatory systems (which, themselves, further reflect the temporality of the unchanging). Now and then, however, but at unpredictable intervals, these continuities of body-time are violently disturbed by psychophysical crisis: the trauma of actual job loss due to a firm's restructuring, or a cardiac event after mounting artery damage passes a tipping point, or the sudden loss of a limb due to machinery malfunction, which is hardly a thing of the past despite the rising predominance of service and online work.

The theme of facing risk on all sides names this counterabrasion of distinct temporalities of bodily imperilment.[59] Along with its companion theme of unblinking vigilance, the notion of omnipresent risk also prompts a politically salient appraisal of the socioeconomic dynamics behind the accumulation and general spread of OSH problems. For political economist David Weil, "the fissured workplace" is a crucial driving force of increased job-related safety and health threats for US workers. According to Weil, employment relations have been restructured such that the largest companies no longer directly employ the individuals who conduct their basic operations, whether that means making chocolate for Hershey bars, serving up McDonalds' French fries, or connecting Verizon customers to cell service: "Employment has been actively shed by these market leaders and transferred to a complicated network of smaller business units."[60] Increasingly, Weil finds, the biggest firms boost their profits by concentrating on developing "core competencies that produce value for investors and consumers," for instance by "building brands, creating innovative products and services, capitalizing on economies of scale and scope, or coordinating complex supply chains."[61] These major businesses have correspondingly reduced their payrolls through subcontracting, franchising, outsourcing, and worker reclassifications.

These epochal and accelerating changes have sharply diminished employers' respect for basic labor standards such as fair pay, decent working conditions, and protection from OSH hazards, while reducing employers' accountability for the proliferating violations of these standards. Weil argues that these effects arise principally because the smaller, lower-tier businesses that now directly employ most workers operate in more highly competitive markets than the big companies. Greater competitive pressures translate into stronger incentives to cut costs by forgoing expenses that would enhance workers' health and safety and by maintaining work processes that trade off more frequent worker injuries and illnesses for higher profits. In addition, mid- and lower-level employers are far less vulnerable than leading firms to scrutiny by government officials and journalists, which further diminishes the likelihood that they will develop sound OSH practices.

The problems detailed by day laborers thus speak to trends that envelope the working population as a whole, notwithstanding the uniquely harsh situations low-wage migrant workers confront in this regard. Weil emphasizes that fissuring pervades the US employment economy. Not only low-wage service and manufacturing workers but also white-collar employees and even professionals face a new employment norm wrought by fissuring: "Although the occupations that fissuring affects are concentrated at the low-wage end of the labor market (janitors, warehousing, home health aides, fast food), the practice increasingly includes mid-level employees (machine operators, cell tower workers, customer service providers) and even highly skilled workers (journalists and lawyers)."[62] For all these workers and others, basic labor standards are being compromised, the most powerful economic actors cannot be held legally responsible for workplace injuries and health problems, and such firms see decreasing incentives for engaging in preventative measures.

Risk serves as an axial concept that clarifies the complex social dynamics of these processes, especially through its connection to logics of *commodification* under neoliberalism. The managers and owners of leading corporations have engaged in fissuring as a strategy to minimize a range of risks, and this strategy depends on hypercommodifying various kinds of social relations. On a basic level, companies pursue fissuring to reduce the risks inherent in any direct relation of employment, such as those stemming from uncertainty regarding workers' productivity. Those risks are offloaded onto subcontractors or franchisees, and in the process, the labor needed to perform productive tasks for the leading firms gets doubly commodified. Not only is the individual worker's effort commodified as wage labor; in addition, the work done by the collective body of workers is commodified as a whole through the contract relation between companies. For example, Walmart pays subcontracting companies to load and unload a certain number of trucks at distribution centers; these companies bear the risks of making sure their employees meet Walmart's expectations for speed and accuracy; Walmart thus can substitute a steady budget allocation for the comparatively riskier direct management of workers.[63] As Weil points out, moreover, the downward-shifting of employment-based risks and the hypercommodification of labor intensifies at the lower rungs of this economic hierarchy. Increasingly, subcontractors and franchisers reclassify their own workers, eliminating their status as employees and redefining them as independent contractors.[64]

Shedding responsibility for the direct employment of workers means that major corporations also gain relief from liability risks when workplace injuries, deaths, or illnesses occur (in the minority of cases when such problems are reported and employer liability costs even become possible). As Weil emphasizes, when a company does not employ most individuals in its production facilities, that firm need neither contribute to workers' compensation plans nor meet workers' compensation obligations for job-related accidents or health problems.[65] For instance, when an employee for a Hershey subcontractor lost his life in 2009 by falling into a vat of liquid chocolate, "Hershey, now at arm's length from the production of its own chocolates, was not cited by OSHA" and suffered no adverse consequences.[66] This also means that in terms of ongoing expenditures and budgetary planning, the largest companies now lack incentives to spend resources on innovations and activities aimed at reducing liability costs by preventing OSH problems.

For Weil, it is essential to understand how sea changes in the financial industry focused on maximizing capital returns and minimizing investor risks have driven the organizational transformations leading to the fissured workplace. Given the gigantic increase in the quantity of private financial assets invested by institutional entities, the concentration of finance capital management in a relatively small number of mutual fund companies, and the rise of private equity firms, corporations face overwhelming incentives to prioritize investors' interests above all other concerns.[67] These mounting pressures, which contribute to the overall financialization of the neoliberal economy, yield deleterious effects for workers' vulnerable bodies and minds.[68] *The practical correlate of investors' risk reduction is the wild proliferation of bodily risk for workers.* Here we also find another respect in which the displacement of risk from the dominant to the subordinate populations depends on a dynamic of hypercommodification, in the sense that the multiplication, diversification, and increased sales of financial commodities peddled by companies that are "too big to fail" help fuel the corporate organizational shifts that increasingly subject workers to psychophysical damage.

That infamous phrase from the 2008 crisis evokes a further aspect of this social economy of risk: the massive socialization of private-capital risk through the absorption of the largest and most predatory financial firms' business risks by public ledgers even as Congress begrudges OSHA fewer and fewer dollars. Again, the connection of risk-shifting with commodification asserts itself. A well-established trend in policy discourse reduces OSH hazards to commodified preferences in individualized market transactions and thereby rationalizes the steep slanting of public policy in favor of capital risk-reduction and against workers' protection. As legal analyst Sidney A. Shapiro notes, public discourse has increasingly framed issues regarding workplace injuries and illnesses as trade-offs between "marginal costs" and "marginal benefits," treating both "as commodities whose relative economic value determines the appropriate level of risk reduction.[69] The grand-scale *de*commodification of capital risk through monetary and fiscal policy thus proceeds hand in hand with the thorough *re*commodification of workers' bodily risk, not only in material fact but also in public ideology.

In sum, everywhere one looks in the current economy, except in those quarters where the greatest gambles are taken, one sees risk: there is risk on all sides, more densely packed into daily body-time, for just about everyone. Even as day laborers' theme of risk on all sides points to dangerous circumstances that apply *exceptionally* to migrant workers, this theme thus also denotes a situation in which day labor stands as a *synecdoche* for the general precaritization of embodied time through work. More precisely, the notion of risk on all sides characterizes a situation in which the guiding temporalities of capital accumulation for the very few are becoming more lethally entangled with the embodied temporalities of work for the vast majority of working people. On the side of capital, the key temporalities involve compression and intensification in response to financial risk, as Weil explains:

> The scale of assets managed by companies like BlackRock, Vanguard, and Fidelity, the fungibility of those assets, and the large number of alternative investments available to fund managers together breed little patience

for low performance for stocks of a given risk level. Institutional investors increase the volatility in ownership of companies and the sensitivity of managers to changes in company valuations. For example, mutual funds seldom buy and hold stocks, but rather buy and sell them frequently. . . . Money flowing into publicly traded companies from mutual funds is therefore "impatient" and moves frequently in search of better returns for a given level of risk.[70]

In response to these financial pressures, big firms prioritize technological investments that enhance time-sensitive logistical coordination of supply chains and real-time monitoring of subcontractors' activities; as Weil notes, such digital technologies have substantially reduced the financial risks of fissuring.[71] Meanwhile, in a virtuous circle, at least from the investor's point of view, the technology sector of equities offers some of the highest returns available. Impatient and risk-averse capital, however, also breeds impatient labor processes that magnify work's risks to human sinew, bone, and mind. The computer technologies and employment protocols that enable agile responses to investors' demands foster regimes of work time that are more comprehensively orchestrated by managers and machines, more saturated with production imperatives, and more physically and psychologically perilous than ever before. As Weil explains, for example, when cell tower workers are reclassified as independent contractors for Time-Warner's subcontractors, pressures mount for these operators to squeeze more work into less time. This happens both because workers get paid by the job rather than by the hour and because subcontractors' agreements with Time-Warner specify narrow time constraints for responding to service breakdowns. Furthermore, subcontractors control these supposedly "independent" workers' labor time *more* thoroughly than ever by determining clients, job schedules, and fee rates.[72] As such work time is increasingly subjected to heteronomous control, injuries, illnesses, and mortalities proliferate. Compelled by the fissured (dis)organization of employment to exert themselves at sped-up paces but also in increasingly unpredictable intervals punctuated by moments of crisis, cell tower workers now die on the job three times more frequently than coal miners and ten times as often as construction workers.[73]

Connecting the fissuring phenomenon to day laborers' themes helps us think through these interlacing temporalities of accelerated and streamlined capital growth, on the one hand, and chaotically fractured, increasingly hazardous work, on the other hand. In political terms, the theme of risk on all sides evokes a situation in which it has become urgent to *take sides* in a *fight for time* centered on and in the working body. This fight would be *for* those whose body-time on the job is dematerialized, for the purposes of public discourse and institutional decision-making, by the logics of hypercommodification that are making labor lethal in the era of the fissured workplace. The fight would be *against* corporate and financial interests' endeavors to overload everyday body-time at work with risk for the sake of insulating investment capital from any risks that might jeopardize its steady, rapid, and massive accumulation.

Fights need willing protagonists, however, and day laborers' preferred terms for discussing OSH hazards also suggest much about how people could be drawn into this fight for time and what obstacles to such mobilization exist. What might day laborers' companion theme of keeping eyes wide open imply about the kinds of subjective dispositions that take shape as financial risk is transfigured into bodily risk at work? What alternative modes of subject-formation within these conditions might the workers' themes encourage, and with what further implications for conceptualizing struggles to transform these circumstances? How might further reflections on body-centered and time-conscious theorizations of precarity and work, in conjunction with day laborers' commentaries, spring loose such political potencies?

Slow Death

Earlier in this chapter, we saw how many day laborers embrace an ethic of personal responsibility and a vision of individual agency regarding their preservation of bodily wellness on the job, despite the self-undermining dynamics these orientations involve. These features of the workers' commentaries suggest the value of returning to Lauren Berlant's ruminations on "cruel optimism" as a way of extending this critical-popular analysis of day laborers' themes regarding OSH issues. In the preceding chapter, I charted points of affiliation between Berlant's conception of aspirational normativity and the entrepreneurialist work ethics of day laborers caught in the dilemmas of bodily movement on the corner. Here, I shall consider the workers' theme of keeping eyes wide open during dangerous work in light of Berlant's critique of the social syndrome she calls "slow death," which connects bodily damaging work to temporal processes of subject-formation in relation to dominant public discourses about healthy bodies.

Berlant uses the concept of slow death to denote a deeply ironic situation in which "collective physical and psychic attenuation," or a process of dying, has become the basic mode of living for large swaths of the US low-wage working population.[74] For this population, "Life building and the attrition of human life are indistinguishable," in the sense that the very activities necessary to reproduce bodily existence and maintain corporeal capabilities bring about people's "deterioration" and "physical wearing out."[75] The characteristic temporality of slow death, according to Berlant, takes the form indicated by Foucault's notion of the "endemic," which signifies the ongoing and normalized character of a biopolitical structure of social life. Biopolitics, here, refers to schemas of power that systematically differentiate the life chances and exposures to bodily damage of different categorical populations, which materialize through the routine operations of major state, capitalist, and other social institutions.[76] Berlant observes that this endemic temporality of gradual mortification through activities central to the continuance of physical life exists paradigmatically in neoliberal "spaces of production," where sped-up labor causes irreparable "damage to bodies" for "working-class and subproletarian populations" even as these mostly nonwhite workers rely on these jobs to survive.[77]

Berlant delineates not only how the rhythms of slow death unfold but also how they intermingle with other temporalities by which precaritized individuals are induced to shoulder responsibility for their bodily debilitation, despite the socioeconomic origins of workers' misery. Intrigued by the recent surfeit of public concern over obesity among working-class people, especially African Americans and Latinos, Berlant sees this discursive phenomenon as deeply connected to these groups' bodily imperilment through work and thus as implicated in the syndrome of slow death. Two temporalities infuse social commentaries about the purportedly unhealthy eating habits of nonwhite working-class Americans, both of which dull popular sensibilities regarding the bodily impairments these populations suffer from OSH hazards. In part, the public outcry about obesity figures the ill health of working-class nonwhite people as a "crisis": an extraordinary event and a striking but temporary departure from the norm.[78] By retemporalizing as an emergency what is actually an "environmental phenomenon" calibrated to the time of the endemic, Berlant contends, this public discourse deploys "a redefinitional tactic, an inflationary, distorting, or misdirecting gesture," which deflects public attention from the ongoing bodily destructiveness of work in the neoliberal economy.[79] Yet the antiobesity discourse does not simply divert thoughts and desires away from temporally protracted experience—it also reoccupies that temporal zone by affirming long-term bodily stewardship as an ethical life-practice of individuals. Hence, this discourse combines a "melodramatic view of individual agency," which figures subjects as moral deciders who must make clear choices between right and wrong in crisis moments, with a vision of personal responsibility enacted through long-term regimens of proper bodily self-care as an ongoing "life-making" project.[80]

For Berlant, the dually temporalized subjectivity associated with obesity's conquest is also figured as confronting both personal and social obligation: ensuring the rescue and stabilization of the individual's physical wellness is essential to promoting the nation's economic productivity. To refuse this endeavor is thus to invite moral condemnation on both grounds along with doubt about whether one is capable of either self-government or ethical sociality: "A manifest lack of self-cultivating attention can easily become recast as irresponsibility, shallowness, resistance, refusal, or incapacity," in both senses.[81] In other words, the cultural-discursive dynamics of slow death not only render low-wage workers' endemic bodily vulnerabilities and debilitations invisible. They also refigure these workers' ill health as evidence of moral failure, antisocial proclivities, and grounds for disciplinary intervention.

Day laborers' determination to keep their eyes wide open when faced with ubiquitous and incessant OSH hazards at once confirms the operation of slow death among Latino migrant workers and indicates certain ways of critically stretching Berlant's interpretation of the situation. Above all, listening to day laborers suggests that working people, themselves, actively help bring about the ideological substitution by which the achievement of bodily health as an individualized test of moral character supplants collective concern over work-related bodily damage as a public welfare issue. This bait-and-switch, in other words, relies not only on public discourses disseminated by media and policy leaders but also on everyday forms of common sense articulated by the very workers who suffer the most. Melodrama supplies the predominant tonality for day laborers when they chastise the irresponsible behavior of fellow workers who refuse or neglect to protect themselves in key moments of decision on the job. The dichotomy between good and bad workers also implies excoriating the latter for abdicating the duty to engage in a "lifelong" endeavor of responsible "self-fashioning" through health-promoting bodily practices.[82] Day laborers thus join the larger chorus of disapproving voices in pronouncing the condemnations unleashed by this rubric of judgment, reinforcing the dynamics of precaritization that unfold through bodily debilitating work.

At the same time, when day laborers voice moral disapproval of those who show negligence regarding bodily health and well-being, their opprobrium redounds upon themselves. This masochistic aspect of the subject of slow death thus represents another elaboration of Berlant's theory that the workers' themes suggest. As we have seen, day laborers routinely expose their bodies to pain and disfigurement while assuming that *they* are the agents of such exposure and bear the guilt for this conduct, which they know to be misguided. Yet even as they rationalize their risk-taking by embracing masculine-inflected strategies to adjust or suppress the temporalities of dangerous work, they remain fully aware that their bodily vulnerabilities stem from employers' significant social power advantages. That is, their eyes are wide open to their own participation in the schema of endemic bodily debilitation *and* to the socially imposed nature of this schema. In a sense, then, slow death involves *split vision*: subjects' knowing and active participation in the contradiction of insisting on their duty to behave responsibly under conditions in which that behavior brings about the very bodily impairments that convict them of irresponsibility, in their own eyes as well as those of the authorities.[83]

The density of day laborers' affective, reflective, and practical investments with respect to PPDs also suggests that material dynamics centered on the commodity form contribute to the syndrome of slow death, further complementing the discursive interplays that Berlant emphasizes. Endemic processes that damage non-white working-class bodies elude recognition as urgent public problems not only because of "misdirecting" discursive tactics like the obesity panic but also through the transposition of workers' risk exposures into everyday protocols of self-care. Such practices, day laborers underscore, coalesce around material fetish-objects. The social relations that structure work as dangerous are displaced onto these objects and encrypted within them as workers develop routine habits of using these things and attach affective intensities to them. The logic of displacement here loosely resembles that which Marx associates with the commodity form: the notion that commodities are both ciphers that encode relations of social domination and ideological devices that reinforce such relations through these things' unremarkable deployment in everyday life. In these ways, fetishistically investing hopes for bodily safety in the routine use of PPDs habituates day laborers to the social structuring of day labor as dangerous work: the organization of residential construction and home improvement economies in ways that extract surplus value from day laborers' extreme contingency and illegality as well as employers' prerogatives over work processes.[84]

Day laborers' themes further suggest that the temporal aspects of slow death are more complex and more devastating than Berlant's conception indicates. As I have discussed, keeping eyes wide open while facing risk on all sides binds the worker to a predicament characterized by temporal cross-shearing, akin to that associated with desperate responsibility and fighting for the job. Day laborers highlight not just the accelerated time of neoliberal work, as Berlant does, but also the tension between time's obdurate immutability, such that the pressure to stay alert and brace for injury never subsides while the body steadily wears away, and time's wild fluctuation, shifting rhythms whenever an injury occurs or whenever new safety imperatives arise as jobs and employers change. This conundrum further complicates the constitution of slow death's temporalities through the fetishization of PPDs and the moralization of self-care.

Berlant frames the overall distribution of bodily mortifying, preserving, and strengthening circumstances as the effect of a biopolitical system, as I have noted. Thus, the critical modifications of her conception of slow death that I have drawn from day laborers' themes—workers' active contributions to the discourses that facilitate slow death, the self-incriminating dynamic that these moral discourses involve, attachments to commodities as talismans of safety, and everyday body-time that mingles absorption in present-moment exigencies with life commitments to wellness—can be seen as illuminating processes of precaritization that apply to the nonwhite low-wage working population writ large and even more ruthlessly distinguish its social and corporeal fates from those of class-dominant and racially privileged populations. Thinking in these terms raises the interesting question of how this biopolitical perspective relates to the schema of exception-and-synecdoche with which I have been characterizing day laborers' relation to the general population of working people (white and nonwhite; blue, pink, or white collar; in all forms of work, whether waged or unwaged).[85] To be sure, day laborers' themes probably signal certain genuinely exceptional aspects of their circumstances of precarity, even in relation to other migrant workers and other workers of color. The great majority of Latino migrants work in jobs where they must keep eyes wide open to routinely emerging hazards because their employers blithely disregard workers' health and safety—this was emphatically the case for the meatpacking workers on whom prior research of mine has focused, for instance, and it is also true for dairy workers, farm workers, hotel workers, and restaurant workers. Yet how much more steadily unblinking must day laborers remain when the types, frequencies, and sources of bodily perils mutate so dizzyingly often and so unpredictably because workers' job assignments and employer relations are so constantly and rapidly in flux? In addition, critical-popular research with other groups in the biopolitically subordinated population would doubtless yield modifications or alternatives to day laborers' themes and hence further critical extensions of the conception of slow death. Nevertheless, given the numerous overlaps between day laborers' working conditions and those of the larger biopolitically defined population for whom life's maintenance results in life's attrition, it makes sense to see the theme-theory generativities here as fleshing out forms of precaritization that permeate this greater population.

Nevertheless, the elaborations of Berlant's theory of slow death propelled by day laborers' themes also make it possible to see how the eyes-open mode of precaritization pervades the experiences of working people throughout the economy. Critical-popular investigation suggests how the biopolitical differentiation between distinct racial and class populations' conditions of life and exposures to death reaches a certain limit—how *all* are enveloped in circumstances of systematic corporeal endangerment that might seem only to apply to some, or to a very few. Think, for instance, of the Fitbit corporation's marketing of its devices as tools for corporate "wellness programs" that will "improve employee health status" and "increase employee productivity."[86] Consider, likewise, the legions of consumers who buy these gadgets voluntarily, thus assuming personal responsibility for continual body self-monitoring to battle the ever-present risk of losing bodily vigor, in ways that involve intense affective attachments to these commodity fetishes. Also, ponder how the ubiquitous proliferation of employee wellness programs fosters a culture that renders the protection and fortification of working bodies far less a question of employers' duties to provide safe and healthy workplaces and much more a matter of medical-bureaucratic surveillance, employees' individual moral will, and workers' consumer habits. Those employer duties still exist by law in the never well-enforced Occupational Safety and Health Act of 1970. Yet employer-sponsored wellness programs place the onus on employees to prove their commitment to a body-centered ethic of personal responsibility and productivity by affirming approved narratives of self-care, submitting to regular medical screenings (including weight monitoring), and spending money on purchase plans for gym memberships (or Fitbits).[87]

Perhaps most importantly, think of how the redistributions of *risk* associated with workplace fissuring throughout the economy devolve and individualize *responsibility* for keeping watch over workers' health and safety on the job. Day laborers' theme of responding to this neoliberal transfusion of financial risk into workers' bodies by doing whatever they can on their own to identify hazards at work speaks directly to the practical dilemma of millions who have little immediate alternative to this course of action, in workplaces governed by corporations who have shed most obligations to preserve safe working conditions. At the same time, the self-undermining character of the theme and its related everyday practices resonates with the futility of trying to prevent work-related injuries and illnesses through the eyes-open strategy in an era when the most pervasive sources of such problems are work-environmental hazards. Of what use is it to keep vigilant watch on one's physical surroundings when air quality deficits, episodes of corporate downsizing, and ergonomically unsound work processes do not yield the kinds of health and injury risks that can be recognized and avoided through simple visual observation? Or, to paraphrase a worker who spoke during our popular-education workshop at Casa Latina, what does it matter if your eyes are wide open as your arteries are calcifying from stress over possibly losing your job, your fingers are locking up from repetitive motions, and your lungs are becoming weakened by bad air?

Conclusion: From Lateral Agency to Worker Organizing

When it comes to envisioning political resistance to slow death, Berlant keeps her expectations restrained. She offers a provocative, if limited, alternative to the prevalent figure of intentional and melodramatic subjecthood that she describes as "lateral" or "interruptive agency."[88] Berlant urges us to imagine how "agency and personhood" could include "unconscious and explicit desires *not* to be an in-flated ego deploying power and manifesting intention," yielding a form of "prac-tical sovereignty" centered in the body's not-fully-conscious habits and wants.[89] She sees such counterintuitively noncommanding sovereignty as exemplified by the very same eating habits that diminish obese people's bodily capacities and provoke showers of public condemnation. These behaviors make such per-sons less easily exploitable by capital, and they also offer venues through which workers can recuperate slow time for themselves from the sped-up rhythms of production—not just private time but social, "convivial" time, as well.[90] Lateral agency, as conceptualized by Berlant, does not change debilitating processes of work, but it does subvert the power relations and temporal configurations that govern them. It achieves this as "a practice of ordinary inefficiency" that takes detours from the privileged model of subjectivity that emphasizes consistently cultivating a productive and maximally capable self.[91] In the process, such inter-ruptive agency also fosters power-disrupting forms of collective experience: times of togetherness that draw enjoyment from disallowed bodily practices amid suspensions of productivist temporalities.

By focusing our attention on the rhythms and rituals of day laborers' practices in the workplace as well as the meanings workers make of the dilemmas they face in the midst of body-killing work, the theme of keeping eyes wide open offers crit-ical leverage vis-à-vis Berlant's privileging of consumption activity as the locus of resistance. Critical-popular engagement with the theme shows that the transfer of risk and the shifting of responsibility onto working individuals depends on those persons' *consent* via their willing participation and affective investment in practical visions of personal bodily responsibility and agency. This in turn means that workers have the power to call a halt to the grinding on of slow death on the job by withdrawing that consent.

Drawing the consequences of this potential through collective action depends on gaining a further understanding of how various groups of workers apart from day laborers articulate the terms of their consent, and how the regimens and discontinuities of body-time on the job vary among different groups. Most im-mediately, in light of both women's growing participation in day labor centers and the masculine connotations of keeping eyes wide open, critical-popular investigations should be conducted with migrant domestic workers. Casa Latina staff told me that the most common work-related injuries and health problems among workers in the women's program are respiratory ailments and skin or eye irritations from toxic chemicals in cleaning fluids, as well as back and arm injuries from vacuuming and other tasks involving repetitive motions or awkward body positions.[92] Other research points to domestic workers' vulnerability to phys-ical abuse by employers,[93] contagious disease exposure, and injuries from heavy lifting,[94] along with emotional problems like depression and anxiety.[95] Not only must workers and activists understand the nuances of these issues if they aim to develop broad and inclusive popular bases for political action—in addition, the OSH hazards that plague migrant domestic workers hew more closely to the society-wide trend toward the increasing significance of work-environmental OSH risks. Critical-popular research among these women thus holds especially strong potential to yield formulations of critique and resistance that could provoke solidarity among many different groups of workers in the lopsided social economy of risk.

The likely value of such further research notwithstanding, the foregoing analysis sheds light on political strategies that would respond in crucial ways to both the exceptional and synecdochal—and biopolitical—aspects of those forms of precarity that advance through the embodied temporalities of dangerous work. In part, the themes generate the clear sense that for exceedingly marginalized and oppressed migrant workers such as day laborers (and also for the broader population of unauthorized migrants), OSH issues are always already matters of subjection to the homeland security state. Job safety and health risks, and the need to keep eyes wide open, increase in direction proportion to the hostile intensification of ICE's ever-alert and ever-more-penetrating gaze. Thus, a viewpoint oriented toward precaritization as exceptionalization, and as biopolitical management, sees that a politics to liberate body-time from the social economy of risk cannot but be a militantly antideportation politics.

Probing these themes in conjunction with Weil and Berlant also clarifies the terms of a much broader effort to build solidarity among working people aimed at combatting the structural sources of dangerous work. This critical-popular endeavor encourages a militant mass rebuke of the workplace's fissuring, the financialization that fuels that process, and the slow-death syndrome that normalizes its body-killing effects—a collective effort to *take sides* against the risk on *all sides*. The small set of day laborers who had committed to refusing dangerous jobs offers a glimpse of the affects and actions such an organizing venture would need. These remarkable workers verify the tangible possibility of refusing consent to this (dis)order of precaritizing body-time. They further show how this can be done through forms of resistance that are importantly individual but also arise in circles of interpersonal relations as well as deliberate organizing endeavors. Those day laborers who dispensed with the eyes-open approach to OSH hazards, opting for a less self-defeating and more promising vision, did not do so simply on their own but because they belonged to an organizational culture at Casa Latina that emboldened workers to think differently about these matters. Casa Latina had begun systematically encouraging workers to make this difficult choice shortly before our interviews, and this initiative gained further strength after our fieldwork, such that workers ultimately became much more likely to refuse dangerous jobs when insufficient protection was provided.[96] Certainly, workers who began consciously rejecting risk-laden work demands expressed the form of agency premised on moral decision that Berlant criticizes, but not in ways that merely enacted personal melodrama. Rather, arising in the midst of the organization's reorientation of affects, thinking, and practices, this OSH-cultural shift signals the real possibility of mustering forms of collective agency that interrupt flows of precaritizing power in ways that are *both* embodied and intentional and that openly contest the social power-relations that spawn work-related hazards.

As the next chapter shows, a robust culture of conviviality helped stimulate workers' resolve not to concede to bodily jeopardizing employer demands as well as to experiment with positive forms of political activity. Workers described this convivial pattern of relations as both taking advantage of mundane inefficiencies in day laborers' everyday lives and helping them meet embodied needs for food, shelter, and companionship. Berlant's notion of conviviality, as a semiconscious practice of shared pleasure in satisfying bodily desires that delays productive work, makes the idea of the convivial among day laborers somewhat counterintuitive. These impoverished workers tend to be food-deprived and hungry, which makes companionable overeating rarely possible for them. The main kind of convivial consumption they stressed in the interviews was drinking, but although getting drunk can pleasurably interrupt the protocols of liberal-capitalist subjectivity and work, it also can be much more incapacitating than a bad diet as well as destructive to relationships, as many workers told us regarding their own experiences. Voz's MLK Center and Casa Latina, however, fostered forms of conviviality that not only routinized laterally agentic customs of sharing but also connected these practices to organizing projects. Let us now turn our attention from the temporal contradictions and political implications of day laborers' themes regarding their work searches and work practices to day laborers' comments about their worker center communities, through which they developed lively political responses to the dilemmas of desperate responsibility, fighting for the job, and keeping eyes wide open while facing risk on all sides.

5

Visions of Community at Worker Centers

FROM PROTECTED WORKFORCE TO CONVIVIAL POLITICS

TALKING WITH DAY laborers about their difficult efforts to find work and then to grapple with the dangers, uncertainties, and indignities their jobs involved, I was frequently struck by the lonely character of their lives. Without a common or remotely stable workplace, they lacked a steady set of coworkers. Sometimes they went out on assignments with others but afterward ended up back on the street by themselves, trying to figure out where to catch the bus in an unfamiliar neighborhood. The foregoing critical-popular explorations, correspondingly, have highlighted the atomizing qualities of day laborers' circumstances. Alone as they faced withering forces of precarity in deceptively mundane guises like the job lottery, the fight on the corner, and the never-ending chain of bodily hazards on the job, these workers were correspondingly drawn to individualist practices to shield themselves from precarity's scorching heat. As we have seen, they strained to detect dangers at work with unblinking vigilance, clung to entrepreneurial aspirations on the corner, and asserted themselves as paragons of personal responsibility. In the preceding pages, I have traced both the auto-disabling implications of these strategies and the radical effluxes of critique and demand exuded by the terms with which workers characterized these impossible predicaments, in ways sharpened through interchanges between workers' themes and theories of precarity.

Day laborers' common activities and political undertakings, however, make up another core dimension of their precaritized worlds. These endeavors are more than just a matter of abstract potential—more than a dissonant hum that subtly modulates generative themes' vibrations with theoretical conceptions of affective

and digital labor's temporal contradictions, protocols of liberal mobility governance, syndromes of cruel optimism, and neoliberal financialization. Day laborers
have occasionally developed tenuous relations of solidarity on the corners by
organizing to set wage floors or to rein in the racing and wrestling for jobs. Yet
more impressively and durably, day laborers have evolved formal and informal
modes of cooperative action at worker centers like Casa Latina and Voz's MLK
Center. This chapter considers workers' comments about their experiences in
these communities as they navigated lives that otherwise so frequently left them
struggling on their own.

As I show in the first section below, workers' dispositions toward their shared
domain of action at the center often ironically reinforced the individualist and
myopically work-centered rubrics that governed so much of daily existence for
them. Many characterized these communities via themes that centered around
the all-absorbing drive and need to earn wages. Workers underlined the paramount value of protecting what few job chances they had, against threats they
mostly saw as arising among shiftless individuals from their own ranks whose dis-
solute conduct alienated employers. They demanded crackdowns by staff with
the authority to enforce the rules along with stricter regulations and expulsions
of recalcitrant offenders. Endorsing a notion of Latino or *mexicano* identity that
was defined by the eagerness to work but often attributed incorrigible laziness
and antisocial tendencies to Latinos or *mexicanos*, they discerned only one route
toward the community's survival: uniting as a disciplined workforce. Given
the temporal, spatial, and embodied double binds in day laborers' work-lives
that I have already explored, it is readily understandable why workers so often
characterized their common endeavors by referencing the themes of protection,
insider/outsider divisions, the need for social order under strong authority, and
work's precedence over all else. Who among working people would not yearn for
the stability promised by these values and boundary drawings, if faced with the
incessant tumult, the assaults on physical and emotional health, and the dogged
temporal contradictions that abound for day laborers?

Nevertheless, an alternative cluster of themes in workers' commentaries
yielded a vision of a self-opening and politicizing community that questioned all
these security-minded inclinations. This vision began, as we shall see, by candidly
recognizing the constancy of suffering for most day laborers. Instead of propelling
redoubled self-reliance as a strategy to relieve mundane hardships, however, in-
eluctable suffering prompted workers to offer one another convivial sustenance
and mutualist assistance. Through routine practices of reciprocity, workers became increasingly committed to helping the centers thrive, to cultivating diverse
social and educational activities, to participating in worker leadership and self-
government, and to raising their voices in public demands for migrant worker

justice. Workers' interpersonal and collective activities alike recalibrated everyday temporal rhythms and unhitched time from the intolerable pressures of desperate responsibility, fighting for the job, and evading the risk on all sides by keeping eyes wide open. In short, and counterintuitively, at their *worker* centers these day laborers inaugurated pathways toward *postwork* futures no longer bounded by the work society's cramped horizons.

While preceding chapters have elaborated dimensions and temporalities of precaritization by contemplating valences between workers' themes and theoretical concepts, this chapter navigates between workers' commentaries and critical theory in search of stimuli for reconceiving radical-democratic politics and transformative social action in the midst of precarity. Hence, rather than seeking to show how the day laborer exists as both exception and synecdoche within general syndromes of precarity, the section on "theorizing radical democracy in precarious times with day laborers" takes up several main political-theoretical issues that workers' themes signal as especially important. These are the role of informal mutualism in fueling democratic practices, the indeterminate but guided emergence of anticapitalist sociality from within capitalist conditions, the corporeal dimensions of radical-democratic politics, and the political complexities of the unity ideal within Latino communities. In dialogue with day laborers, by my critical-popular contrivance, are several theorists who address these issues in overlapping yet sometimes contentious ways. Raymond A. Rocco, Anna Lowenhaupt Tsing, and Romand Coles share a curiosity about micrological processes of Latino and migrant community self-fortification amid the wreckage of working-class existence in the neoliberal era. Day laborers underscore how deeply the instigation of an antiprecarity politics depends on grasping these micro-level community-building dynamics, especially in terms of the temporal and embodied aspects of informal mutualism, day-to-day organizing, and ready responses to small-scale but ever-erupting personal survival crises. At the same time, workers' accounts of community formation at Casa Latina and Voz's MLK Center highlight the need to complement such communal activity with the bodily invigorations and temporal insurgencies of shock-type political events such as direct action and mass marches, in ways emphasized by both Coles and Cristina Beltrán. Day laborers' thematizations of community life at worker centers also shed light on distinctly neoliberal permutations of the Latino unity ideal criticized by Beltrán, along with dynamics by which more pliable and anti-neoliberal rearticulations of Latino identity can arise within precaritized conditions of social and economic blight.

Readers should bear in mind that in keeping with my critical-popular approach, my comments in this chapter focus on what workers say about their experiences and how they say these things. Thus, I do not attempt to offer a thorough description of all the manifold activities going on at worker centers or the values and priorities that guide these organizations.[1] The final chapter examines day labor organizations more directly, looking for organizational activities and discursive priorities that address the contradictions of precarity discussed in chapters 2–4 and unfold the pathways of convivial politics considered in the chapter at hand. Here, the accent remains on reconceiving precaritized conditions in ways sparked by day laborers' themes and their resonances with extant social critiques, foregrounding the question of how to envision and foment the political activation needed to nurture *conscientização* among day laborers and precaritized workers more generally.

The Community as Workforce: Rules, Protection, Unity

When day laborers discussed the kinds of community they sought at Casa Latina or the MLK Center, they often highlighted several themes that revolved around the core issue of finding employment. In key ways, the drive for work thus defined the forms of community life that mattered most. This prioritization of work needs also tended to reduce community engagements to a set of instrumentalities for ensuring the preservation of scarce job opportunities and a minimal chance to improve individuals' economic circumstances. Both centers asked us to probe what being a "member" of their organizations meant to interviewees; leaders hoped these inquiries would suggest new ways to cultivate a stronger sense of belonging and commitment among workers. Many workers abruptly said that membership was simply a matter of showing up and entering the lottery, as a comment by Juan Carlos Garza illustrated: "To say you're a member, the only thing needed is to be here. Come and sign up and be here waiting."[2] Similarly, Roberto Mendoza, like others, denied that the MLK Center expected any further commitment apart from not causing trouble for fellow workers or employers: "There are no requirements. You don't have responsibilities here.... [Just] obey the rules and respect the place ... [and] be responsible and honest on the job."[3]

Comments in this vein left the content of group belonging fairly insubstantial while also conveying a sense of individuality that was both single-mindedly focused on attaining economic success, or at least lessening economic hardship, and keyed to distinctive temporalities. Christián Gutiérrez thought membership in Casa Latina was a "good investment" because it provided access to diverse kinds of construction jobs.[4] Diana Ortiz similarly evoked future-oriented hopes for eased financial difficulties and gradual economic progress:

I think it's one more step toward opportunity. . . . It's like saying you're going to go to whatever house and you're not going to rest. If you work just four days through Casa Latina, the way [employers] pay, it seems like an excellent wage to me, but set. To be a member of Casa Latina means not to be struggling so much looking for work. We have a little more opportunity to improve ourselves.

This disposition toward the future typically went along with a disciplined resolve to restrict one's use of precious time in the present to pursuing individualist economic goals. Estéban Avila, for instance, stated flatly that he came to Casa Latina simply to seek employment and had no use for the political events or other activities organized by the center:

I see myself as a worker. . . . I need money. I have to pay my bills. . . . The more work I have, the better off I am. I'm focused on what I have to do. I don't want to run around in circles. I have to take advantage of my time as much as I can. . . . I have the mentality of just coming to work. I don't plan on staying here indefinitely—just in passing. . . . I've got to keep searching.[5]

Pressed about whether he would attend a workers' assembly if an important issue were being discussed, Avila responded: "The simple truth is that it doesn't interest me much—I think many times it's just wasting time. If I have a job, I'd rather do my job." Comments like this echoed characteristic sentiments discussed in the preceding chapters. Such remarks introduced into workers' conceptions of their center communities an exclusive and deeply anxious preoccupation with finding and performing work, similar to the disposition expressed in the themes previously examined. Whatever time one spent at the center, it was only time *well* spent if it was put directly and efficiently in the service of earning wages.

Day laborers' harsh situations of exploitation, poverty, bodily constraint, and physical risk make it easy to see why many participants viewed the kinds of community life that were possible or even desirable through the centers in these constricted terms. These circumstances also render it readily comprehensible why the themes of "protection" and "security" figured so prominently in the workers' reflections on what they wanted from the centers. Day laborers tended to invoke their desire for protection, in particular, when they compared coming to the centers to the ordeal of looking for jobs on the corner. In part, Héctor Molina noted, going to the center was helpful because it diminished the risk of wage theft: "That's the risk you run on the corner, because they don't pay you well and then there are problems. . . . You're more protected from the employers [at the center] because here they leave their [contact] information and they pay us."[6]

Raul Castillo elaborated on such risks and the insulation Casa Latina provided from them:

> There is less security in the street because there you run risks with the authorities, and you also run risks in the jobs. Because you don't know who you're going to work for—there's absolutely no control over anything— you just jump into the car, and God alone knows where they're going to take you—you don't know anything. However, here at Casa Latina, if eve-rything goes right, you go out to work and the coordinators here already have [the information]—they already know where you'll go work, with what employer, and everything.[7]

Other workers underscored that the center offered protection from getting arrested by immigration agents or by police officers who might notify ICE about an arrest, jail or fine a worker for public indecency, or act abusively toward workers on the corner. Workers also credited the centers with shielding them from occupational safety and health (OSH) hazards, partly because dispatchers gathered basic information about the jobs before workers left on assignments but also due to the centers' OSH trainings, which had been particularly well devel-oped at Casa Latina. In addition, said Gerardo Mejía, Casa Latina maintained a running list of employers banned from hiring workers because they had acted in racist ways, endangered workers' safety, or disrespected workers or even treated them "like animals."[8]

Beyond protecting workers from abusive employers, harassment on the streets, and arrest and detention, the centers also bolstered day laborers against the poverty and indignities in their everyday lives. As discussed in chapter 2, half our interviewees were homeless and alternated between brief spells in shelters and nights on the pavement; the rest made do with substandard, overcrowded, highly impermanent housing. Many were often hungry and took meals at city soup kitchens. At the center, workers could get hot coffee and sometimes a bit of free food. Even if their number did not come up in the lottery, at least they were sheltered from the cold, wind, heat, or rain for up to half a day. A medical van came to the MLK Center every Thursday to serve the Portland workers, almost all of whom lacked health insurance and had little other access to healthcare. In Seattle, Diego Flores said that among the forms of "protection" for which he was most grateful to Casa Latina was the chance to see doctors, so that "if you're sick, they send you to a hospital."[9]

Often, however, workers spoke with particular intensity about the need for security against various damages fellow day laborers might inflict upon them, es-pecially economic costs from lost work opportunities and wasted time. A great many workers called for the centers to institute tougher rules, enforce them more energetically, and eject from the community any who refused to comply. The fear was widespread that irresponsible individuals in their midst would drive away employers and, with them, day laborers' only hope of scraping by economically. Multiple workers expressed these apprehensions with some variant of the phrase *Por uno pagan todos* (essentially, "Everyone pays for one person's bad behavior"). With biting clarity, Sean Garcia expounded (in English) on this theme's main contentions that the center should stick to the basic function of facilitating employment, impose stricter rules to guard this endeavor, and discipline or expel anyone who violated center policies:

> The big problem here is rules and regulations. . . . People need to see that this is not a playground, but a workforce. . . . We want to keep these employers happy . . . but you got to weed out the bad workers, those that are only looking for money but don't want to work. You could tell them a thousand times, but they won't listen. . . . You got to find out who really wants to work and who doesn't. . . . You have to put your foot down.[10]

Garcia thus suggested that day laborers fell into one of two essential character types depending on whether they genuinely cared about hard work, echoing other invocations of the "good/bad worker" dualism discussed in prior chapters. Notably, the "playground" versus "workforce" distinction not only differentiated between time-conscious, productive activity and mere diversion; it also marked a related temporal difference between some who were stuck in childlike irresponsibility and others who had matured into adulthood. Workers' recommendations for new rules and enforcement strategies displayed further temporal aspects, in turn, many of which reflected the anxious desire that lazy and uncooperative day laborers be subjected to strict authority. Some called for the center to monitor day laborers' job performance, as when Ricardo Reyes proposed that Casa Latina routinely "check to see if they are working hard and to see if the employer is left happy and content."[11] Without such interventions, Reyes warned, "Through one person's fault, we're all going to lose." Jaime Ortega similarly recommended that Casa Latina require day laborers to call in and report on jobs in progress, explaining: "It's like saying, 'Here we'll have a father of the family.' You send your son to go do something and you say, 'Just give me a call—make a little time to see how everything is going.'"[12] This comment might suggest a tension between a communal conception of the center and the individualism that so frequently characterized day laborers' demands for protections. Yet either way, workers prioritized boosting the center's effectiveness as a hiring venue and as a vehicle for accomplishing quality work, and the patriarchal-familial analogy amplified the call for strong authority by workers intent upon enhancing the quality of the workforce.

As in other permutations of the good/bad worker dichotomy, our participants tended to decry the alcoholic derelictions, violent tendencies, and temporal incapacities of the irresponsible types from whom, they said, centers needed to protect well-intentioned day laborers. Many participants at both centers voiced dismay at workers who covertly drank in the portable toilets and sullied the centers with their empty bottles. A significant majority wanted the centers to crack down on workers who disregarded the rules banning the use of alcohol and drugs on their premises, for the sake of the well-being of workers who were seeking honest jobs and behaving responsibly. Julián Márquez, for instance, found it disgraceful that some workers at the MLK Center would go out for jobs "dirty and smelling of alcohol," and he added pointedly: "Those are the reasons why the employer doesn't want to come to the center to look for people."[13] When workers proposed suitable responses to such delinquency, time-based strategies of discipline and control took precedence. Many workers blamed drinking for the fights that occasionally broke out at the centers, just as participants did with regard to the mundane conflicts that arose on the corners. José Álvarez attributed fighting to alcohol abuse and favored increasing the suspension time for workers who fought from one week to three months, with expulsion for any offense after that, because, as he put it, "This here is not a center for fighting, it's a center for work."[14] Others suggested identifying and disciplining substance abusers by intensifying the surveillance of all workers, such as through randomly timed drug tests, which César Torres wanted Casa Latina to adopt so employers would not be saddled with workers unable to do their jobs.[15]

The disorderly individuals whom many interviewees denounced as unfit for center membership also were depicted as the sorts of characters who lurked on the corners and the streets in search of trouble. A spatial dimension thus accompanied the temporal connotations of the theme that center rules and exercises of authority needed to be strengthened. Some workers were particularly upset that staff did not enforce regulations prohibiting workers from seeking jobs on the corner while their names were active in the lottery. Others, knowing the centers often pursued unpaid wage claims for workers who had gotten jobs via the corner, wanted to reserve services like this for members only. The delinquents from whom workers demanded protection by the centers also included drug dealers in the streets, which had been a genuine problem since Casa Latina's early days. Shortly before our interviews, the Seattle workers had decided to erect a metal gate barring entrance to individuals who did not have the bright orange vests and identification cards issued to workers by Casa Latina. Rafael Sandoval was relieved to have the gate because, he explained, it kept out people who were "involved in dirty business" and with whom day laborers who arrived "with the better intention of working decently" were liable to be confused.[16] Similarly, Alejandro Delgado approvingly connected both the visible markers of individual membership and the physical barrier of the gate to the themes of security and tightened regulations:

> Casa Latina changed the rules. Now, a person who doesn't go looking for work, who just is involved with selling drugs and doesn't wear a vest—out . . . ! [Now] you're more protected. You feel more secure. . . . If that isn't there, we end up around drug addicts or around people who sell drugs. Because lots of people want that—they want to use Casa Latina as a refuge to do their business.[17]

By emphasizing the visual and spatial features of their delinquent foils in these ways, our interviewees further elaborated their protection-minded and economistic account of what it meant to belong to Casa Latina. This is by no means to gainsay the legitimate concerns of workers, staff, and volunteers with shielding workers from being mistakenly linked to illegal activities in the vicinity, which was a major drug-selling corridor. Especially in a climate of growing antimigrant hostility fed by racist associations of Latinos with the drug trade, these concerns were quite reasonable.[18] Also, workers from Casa Latina occasionally wound up on the sidewalk dealing drugs (although one staff member made a point of exhorting any whom she knew to desist for the sake of their own futures). Nonetheless, it remains significant that so many participants so resoundingly emphasized the policing of insider/outsider divisions as the basis of community at the center, and that the fundamental value of work served as the main axis for this multifaceted distinction.

With this distinction between responsible and irresponsible workers came an accompanying investment in enhancing the "unity" of the community, which our interviewees frequently understood in terms of the single-minded, purposeful conduct of economic endeavors. Often, when we asked a participant how strong he thought the "community" was at the center or what "community" meant to him, the individual indicated that he saw "unity" and "community" as synonymous, as in this exchange with Jorge Medina:

RESEARCHER: What is your idea of what it means to be a "community"?
PARTICIPANT: A place where there should be unity. A united group.
RESEARCHER: What do you think the center can do so that we'd be more united?
PARTICIPANT: Well, everyone being in agreement.[19]

Workers who held such a view also tended to believe that in order to enhance the community's unity, the center needed a sobering infusion of sound business sense. As Luís Pérez declared: "The center should be managed differently and in a more professional manner."[20] By this he meant deploying better advertising (by more visibly posting the MLK Center's phone number), making the hiring process more disciplined (by prohibiting workers from calling out work offers to employers), and making the lottery more expeditious (by doing it all at once rather than at intervals). In a similar spirit, Bobby Kalani unfavorably compared the MLK Center to a local for-profit temporary employment agency that many workers had tried, saying: "Labor Ready is run in an orderly manner, and here it's like a free-for-all. . . . They don't know how to run a business like this. . . . They need to go put somebody in Labor Ready so they could learn the business and they can come back and then apply it here."[21] Workers who thought along these lines also tended to transpose ideals of political unity into economistic orientations, as Estéban Avila did:

> You do a job as a team. If everyone is working together, the job is easier and goes faster . . . and the employer will be satisfied. . . . There is a saying that goes like this: "Union makes you strong." The more united we are, the more strength we have, the more power. . . . Many times, we try to be individualists, and it's not about that. For the job to be done better, it has to be done by the group, the team.[22]

In short, whether imposed from above as a regimen of managerial discipline or spreading out from below as a culture of workers' team spirit, the vision of unity that captivated many of our participants focused on molding groups of migrant workers into a well-toned, reliable labor force. This, in turn, was premised on "uniting to guard ourselves" from the shady denizens of the street, as Alejandro Delgado put it.

Curiously overlaying this entrepreneurial and boundary-conscious vision of the united community was often a sense of the community as racially and ethnically *mexicano*[23] or Latino. For a great many interviewees, the centers promoted an effort to "get ahead" (*seguir adelante*) socially and economically that was specifically *mexicano* or Latino (the terms' different connotations tended to blur in workers' comments). Sometimes, workers invoked the Mexican-derived notion of *la raza*, while at other times they gestured toward a pan–Latin American sense of commonality. Said the MLK Center's Ivan Cruz, for instance: "What they are doing is really good for all my people and the Latino people, the people from Guatemala or Honduras or wherever."[24] Casa Latina in Seattle, of course, placed racial-ethnic identity (and ambiguity) in the foreground through its very name.

Voz signaled racial-ethnic associations through its organizational designation, while its center gestured toward interracial cooperation by referencing African American civil rights struggles, although very few black workers (migrant or US-born) came to the center.

For many day laborers, however, the idea of forging a "professional" work-force out of their ragged crew was dubious, no matter how avidly desired, because of supposedly ingrained negative racial-ethnic dispositions. Such attributions evinced two interconnecting temporalities: they depicted Latinos and *mexicanos* as both collectively trapped within a historical condition of stunted development and individually incapable of managing their time in daily matters. Oribe Lozano invoked *mexicano* indolence to explain why workers avoided the MLK Center's English classes and to demand rules compelling idle workers to attend for their own good: "*La raza* out there—order them into the classes, because there are many who don't want to do it."[25] Cristián Gutiérrez used more astringent language to revile his coethnics and to justify his view that Casa Latina should make OSH training sessions mandatory (in English):

> Most Mexicans do not learn. . . . You try to teach them, and they still don't get it . . . In my personal opinion, Mexicans have a very nice way to learn and that is with a real big stick with a nail at the end, OK? . . . Every time you try to give them opinions, you get a big old disconfirm—everybody talks, everybody fights, everybody argues, and that's it. You tell them, "Look, I'm the boss right here and you are going to that workshop or you don't go out to work"—then they will do it. . . . Unfortunately, that's how Mexicans have lived for five hundred to six hundred years, and that's the way that they're gonna live for another thousand years.

Such acid contempt for "Mexicans" was rare, and it was noteworthy that both Gutiérrez and Vargas spoke English, had resided for decades in the United States, and seemed eager to present themselves as savvier about American ways than more recently arrived workers. Yet the tendency to disparage *mexicanos* and Latinos for lacking personal discipline and cooperative sensibilities also emerged in comments by workers who spoke only Spanish and had not lived as long in the United States. Such participants often chose more charitable terms but reiterated the disparaging implications, as in this comment from José Ruiz: "As a *mexicano*, your head is all mixed up, because you want to learn English but you don't go [to class] and you're just here."[26] Submerged in a cultural history bereft of progress[27] and saddled with an irrational, personal aversion to pursuing his own self-interest, the Latino or *mexicano* day laborer stayed "just there" in muddled fixity and temporal suspension.

Finally, those who framed center membership in terms of economic success, security, rule obedience, and unity also frequently disparaged the many activities at the centers that were not immediately instrumental to individual employment quests. Many were especially cynical about the regular assembly meetings through which workers participated in governing the centers by discussing matters of common concern and making policy decisions through majority-rule voting. Carlos Hernández complained that "the same people" participated each time, while others "just go to listen and just to watch," and that no one followed new rules passed by the MLK Center assembly. Similarly, according to Antonio Soto, although Casa Latina's day laborers made a show of affirming new self-imposed protocols for safe work during meetings, workers rarely changed how they acted on the job.[28] Others said that many workers refrained from speaking in the assemblies because they knew their fellows would make fun of them or shun them if they raised unpopular ideas. Juan Carlos Garza complained that workers just "clowned around" in the meetings, and others were irritated that all the chatter never led to any action. Both centers also had workers' committees with elected representatives to discuss policy proposals and make recommendations to the general body of workers, and we heard similar remarks in the same tone about these committees.

Underlying negative comments about worker self-government was often a deep-seated pessimism about day laborers' very abilities to govern themselves wisely and the corresponding view that center staff should exercise greater authority. Said Moisés Burgos of Casa Latina, for instance: "The coordinators should be united—they should keep order. . . . Beginning with workshops, with organizing every single worker to be in a place where the coordinators tell you what you should do."[29] Burgos had never been to an assembly meeting and added that for him, being a member of Casa Latina meant "taking orders from the organization." Marco Jérez offered a curious definition of democracy that seemed to make the MLK Center's assemblies irrelevant, at least as forums for determining policies collectively: "Democracy—we wrongly think it means majority rule. Democracy is when there's an idea that is the right thing for all, even though it might not have 50 percent."[30] To Jérez, democracy in the center was thus perfectly compatible with the notion that "the staff should be the ones who decide." Striking a similar chord, Gabriela Moreno doubted day laborers' capacities to show any regard for the common good at Casa Latina: "I think it would not be good if the day laborer made decisions because in reality the day laborer only thinks about himself. He isn't thinking about all the people, and each one just wants to get what he wants, nothing more. . . . It's good that there's staff and there are rules, but from above."[31] From perspectives like these, the only positive purposes served by assemblies were to provide "useful" occasions for workers to be instructed about the center's rules—as Portland's Pedro Santiago put it, about "how we have to behave," particularly not "going around drunk"[32]—or to publicize metrics of the center's success in getting workers hired over the preceding month. The meetings were not to be seen, however, as chances for day laborers to exercise collective self-government through deliberation, contestation, and voting, much less to muster solidarity for more public forms of political action as a group.

In sum, when day laborers came to Casa Latina or the MLK Center, a great many chiefly sought protection against their poverty, their employers, the immigration authorities, and the threats they believed unscrupulous fellow workers posed to their economic survival. They identified security with the condensation of community-making into the ethics, affects, and temporalities that regimented an unruly swarm of day laborers into a disciplined workforce. Sternly invoking the warning that *por uno pagan todos*, they glimpsed a path forward—or at least a reprieve from downward descent—through forging group unity enforced by strong-willed staff who set firm limits and expelled workers who crossed those lines. For workers who favored this approach, a rhetoric of racial-ethnic unity ironically intensified the impulse toward division and expulsion by making outcasts symbolize all that was out of time and out of order with the imputed *mexicano* or Latino character. This orientation toward center membership also denigrated organizational democracy as a waste of time and preferred bolstering the center's efficiency as a "business" that enabled individuals to find employment and achieve a modicum of economic progress.

Work, Suffering, and Convivial Networks of Political Possibility

My prior analyses of day laborers' themes all demonstrated in various ways how passionate desires for work suffused the cultures of Casa Latina and Voz's MLK Center, just as these yearnings animated the powerful thematic current that reduced the center community to a workforce. Yet by no means did all workers subscribe—only—to this narrow conception of center membership. In fact, nearly as many interviewees began by voicing generally held anxieties and ambitions about work, preoccupations regarding security and order, and demands for unity—but then bonded these concerns with a range of alternative and expansively creative responses to them. Instead of clinging to the clear lines and tight boundaries of the protectionist model, they modulated their own work-focused trepidations and let themselves imagine forms of community life that were more mutually supportive and more critically politicized.[33]

Often, participants began by expressing desperation about work or an impatient demand that coworkers shape up and obey rules imposed from above, but then started to say things that relaxed the desire for order and dislodged work from its all-defining role in community life. For instance, when my assistant asked Julián Márquez if he considered himself a member of the MLK Center, he replied:

> No, just a day laborer. I feel that I need a lot from the center. It's become my routine—it's as if the center were a part of my job. I got used to it; I have good friendships. If I don't go out to work, I'm going to talk with the people—inform myself about what's going on. . . . Here, all who want to work are welcome. All who go to the center are welcome. If you don't know how to respect the laws of the center, you're not welcome.

Márquez's answer features multiple and intriguing ambivalences. He refuses the designation of "member" . . . but then describes coming to the center as integral to his work and as a thick thread in the fabric of his everyday life. He proposes the work ethic as the main criterion of membership . . . but also emphasizes his interpersonal relationships and educational efforts there. He affirms excluding those who break the rules and show no desire to work . . . but immediately troubles his own boundary-drawing by avowing simply that "all who go to the center are welcome." Is it just that his "head is all mixed up," to recall José Ruiz's phrase? Or is he is speaking in a vernacular that is not logically consistent precisely because he is actively thinking new possibilities that can only emerge in acute tension with the reigning social conditions?

Comments from other day laborers suggest that Márquez's remarks point toward the tentative emergence of new social and political possibilities from out of circumstances with which these potentialities are sharply at odds. Other workers more thoroughly developed these possibilities, although almost always with tenacious ambivalences. Reflecting on two additional generative themes suggested by the workers, *suffering* and *conviviality*, brings these curious patterns to light. The term "suffering" frequently came up and workers used it to name a wide range of hardships and painful experiences. Often, the word surfaced when an individual spoke about being socially isolated and living apart from family and friends for lengthy stretches of time. These predicaments usually stemmed from being unauthorized, as in the case of Héctor Molina, who wept when he told my assistant he had not seen his family for nearly five years:

PARTICIPANT: What happens is that it's my responsibility. I have to send my kids to school.

RESEARCHER: Would you like to see them more often?

PARTICIPANT: Yes, but it's really hard to go back. I spent a lot of time on the border because they caught me four times. . . . Everything is really hard here. Even though I've been here five years, I can't find a job because of that situation of not having papers. . . . [I wish] I could come and go from Mexico. I'd come on an airplane and it would be easier for us, but unfortunately we have to suffer so many things.

Here, the theme of suffering interlinks joblessness, vulnerability to the deportation regime, a staggering burden of personal responsibility, and the emotional distress of being so distant for so long from loved ones. Yet Molina also identified the center as a locus of relief from these hardships because of the social connectivity it fostered, saying he wanted to participate in more center activities, especially sports: "It would help me because it would be a coming together with people I know, so I wouldn't have to be alone." Molina used the term *convivencia*, which I have translated as "coming together" here but which has multiple other connotations, including sharing daily life with others, building team spirit, and participating in social gatherings. Thus, we might render the theme more adequately in English with the word *conviviality*.

Opportunities for conviviality at worker centers responded to acute needs among day laborers, one of which was simply the need for human contact to mitigate isolation. In this respect, convivial relations modulated the temporalities of precarity bound up with the theme of desperation: these connections eased the solitariness that exacerbated the painfulness of time's unpredictable fluctuation between the continuity of mounting dread at one's lack of work and discontinuous bursts of frantic work-effort. If a worker had no luck with the early morning lottery and wanted neither to stay at the center nor to go to the corner, often he wandered over to the library to sit by himself and "study," as several workers put it, for hours on end, although more often it seemed he ended up just sitting listlessly alone. Sometimes, workers who remained at the MLK Center after failing to get work appeared lost and imprisoned in their own traumatized minds, as Federico Rojas explained:

It happens when they don't succeed in the lottery; they come all excited to succeed in the lottery and sometimes they don't succeed, and that's when they get disoriented. . . . There are some who are so discouraged, it's like they shut themselves up in a world that has neither doors nor windows.[34]

Yet finding the sustenance of human connection was always possible at the center, according to numerous participants. Our field notes from both locations are replete with observations marveling at how many workers tended to stay at the centers, often just talking, although sometimes participating in more formal activities, even on days when there was very little work. Such experiences of relationality replaced the lonely posture of anxiously watching time go by, as a steady draining away of individual opportunities to work productively, with temporal orientations that were less fixated upon immediate urgencies and more substantively diverse. Roberto Fernández, for example, described the culture of interpersonal uplift at the MLK Center as follows:

> When I arrive here I feel like I'm supported, and it's that we talk with a friend, and I say, "Well, I worked yesterday," and [he says,] "I didn't work." And you talk over your problems—what happened and what didn't happen, your problems, going back to when we came here from Mexico. And we like to talk a lot about our life, about our family, about the problems we have. And when you talk about those things with them, you feel that your problems get lighter—when you pour your heart out to them.[35]

As these remarks illustrate, workers did not lay aside their intense concerns about work when they interacted as friends at the center. Rather, friendship grew in and around those concerns and was woven through them and vice versa. The conviviality nurtured by the center, in other words, was not a matter of *nonwork* activities or relations, pure and simple; nor was it ever removed from the temporalities of working and searching for work. Rather, conviviality was a current of energy that coursed through these day laborers' work pursuits and desires and began modifying them on a molecular level, so that they started to yield practical consequences that were not strictly limited to finding jobs and earning money.[36]

Along with their stories, worries, and compassion, workers also shared an abundance of material and practical things with one another, including job connections, money, food, living space, and information about services. Conviviality at the centers thus responded to sufferings of the body that were wholly bound up with those of the heart and mind, such as the privations workers experienced when, as Julián Márquez put it, "You go around suffering in the street" and "You have nothing for the rent." Whereas many workers looked to the center staff and volunteers to provide them with badly needed direct human services, as I have discussed, informal networks catalyzed by the workers, themselves, also served as key conduits for such aid. Some workers formed households together after meeting at the MLK Center. Juan Ayala[37] and Ángel López[38] both reported that Portland day laborers commonly lent each other money or gave each other food so those who had ill fortune in the lottery could get through particularly lean periods. Rafael Sandoval told us he hoped workers in Seattle would "get together, to create savings funds to help one another." Workers' informal networks also spread vital information about where to get help with housing and food, especially among homeless workers.[39] Occasionally, a day laborer at Casa Latina reversed the dynamic of care between center and workers by using his food stamps to buy orange juice for center staff and volunteers. Sometimes a Casa Latina worker gave others haircuts; workers also donated to a common fund through which they purchased a new coffee maker. At both centers, individuals with more years and experience living in the United States (or, more rarely, with legal status) helped others learn to navigate US society, for instance by going with them to public service agencies. In addition, a subculture of mutual support for alcoholism recovery was quite noticeable at the MLK Center and fed a broader sense of reciprocal commitment. Going sober had been a personal watershed for Francisco Herrarte, along with many others, and he stressed that an ethos of "responsibility of the group" on the part of each individual, which he had learned in his sobriety support group, shaped how he understood the worker center.[40]

In all these tangible ways, day laborers activated networks of mutuality that arose in conjunction with their pressing desires for and urgent pursuits of work, but that did not condense into a reductionist resolve to streamline the center into nothing but a workforce training and deployment operation. As these channels of conviviality unfolded, furthermore, they interrupted the chain of associations that made work opportunities seem contingent on rigid insider-outsider distinctions and that premised membership on having particular temporal orientations and social-spatial positions. For example, Pedro Santiago insisted that workers from the corner should be welcome to come to any fiestas or just drink coffee at the MLK Center, even if they did not "sign up" for the lottery or a special event. Santiago was one of many who acknowledged the significant overlap between the workers who tended to come to the center and those who more often went to the corner and who noted that many individuals did both as a matter of routine. Unlike most of these others, however, Santiago validated the fluid boundaries of the workers' community rather than decrying them. His remark thus posed a vivid alternative to the aspect of the protectionist theme that drew sharp distinctions between the types of workers on the corners and those suited for center membership.

Yet at the same time, countless comments expressed the open-ended and synergistic interimplication of conviviality and mutualism with economic needs and preoccupations. Over and again, participants wove together references to actions of care, sharing, and reciprocity with invocations of work-related hopes, anxieties, and practicalities. Virtually every interviewee had relied on networks of family and friends to learn about the day labor opportunities at the centers along with job prospects in other industries and places. Some had offered similar help to others; Ricardo Vélez noted: "If I see that someone is a good worker, I can tell my employer that I know someone who does good work. . . . I can use my leverage."[41] In words that cut against the grain of the competitive undercurrent of feelings regarding the daily announcements of "winners" and "losers" in the lottery, not to mention in the fight on the corner, Israel Campos said: "Sometimes it makes you glad when your *compañeros*[42] go out to work, because you say: 'Tomorrow, I'll go out—if the people keep on going out to work, it'll happen to me.'"[43] Even as these workers evoked mutualist practices, they neither renounced work desires nor rejected the language of self-interested economic negotiation. Campos maintained a clear focus on his own need to find work even as he wishes his *compañeros* well; Vélez adopted the lingo of "leverage." In a different but related way, Ángel López affirmed the themes of protection, center boundaries, and work's importance even while praising the communal ethos at the MLK Center:

> For those who are loyal here to the trailer, yes—we work in community; we have a connection, and we protect each other and help each other. For example, say I have an employer and if my employer needs another person, I tell someone from those who are here; I don't tell those who are out there [on the corner].

Francisco Herrarte, in turn, suggested a racial-ethnic form of community boundedness in describing how he sought to practice mutual aid at the MLK Center:

> If I don't get work, I go out with a *compañero* to look for work. . . . If I know about a job and I have no luck [in the lottery], I'm going to call him and take him with me. I know that years ago, my family needed help and wanted someone to lend them a helping hand. I don't do it so they'll give me ten or twenty dollars—I just do it because they're *mexicanos* and I'd like to help my own *raza*, not screw them over. Supposedly that's why you come here, right? To get ahead.

Herrarte thus reiterated the theme of *mexicano* migrant advancement through hard work, which as we have seen can also be linked with the primacy of work above all else, the insider/outsider distinction, and the desire for authoritarian regulation of the center community. Yet for him as for these others, actualizing the convivially mutualist community was not a matter of relinquishing the desires for strict lines, heightened security, and more plentiful work. Rather, it meant channeling those desires in mutualist directions, modulating them with other needs and aspirations, and breaking down their rigid structures.

Casa Latina's workers further developed this concatenation of economic matters with mutualist practices when they discussed their interactions regarding OSH issues. Some Seattle day laborers enthusiastically described occasions when they had educated one another about OSH techniques. For all his venom about "Mexicans" supposedly being unteachable, Jaime Ortega emphasized that he made a point of sharing knowledge about how to do hazardous jobs safely, especially with younger workers. Gerardo Mejía similarly noted that "over the years" he had picked up protective strategies from "*compañeros*" at the center and also credited Casa Latina's workshops with helping him "protect other people" who had less experience and training regarding OSH issues. He then underscored that day laborers, themselves, were the best instructors about occupational safety and health:

> The people they've brought from the university—they don't know how to hold a hammer. . . . I believe that if I'm a construction worker, I can teach someone else how to work in construction. . . . A student . . . can give you certain guidelines about how the worker should protect himself, but [a student] doesn't have the experience of doing the job. I've known . . . programs where they bring in a person who . . . works in construction, and he tells them: "I'm going to teach you how to work in construction." And the people learn more easily, and they like it, because it's . . . a live experience, not something he only studied.

In these comments, Mejía not only guided desires for work and protection toward mutualist practices—he also posed a distinctly egalitarian-popular alternative to the notion that day laborers needed to be ruled by strict authority figures and rigid codes of conduct. He thus expressed the thorough entanglement of actions to meet desperate economic and safety needs with the cultivation of a community in which workers exercised intellectual agency and leadership.[44]

While the conception of the center as workforce privileged the efficiency, uniformity, and intensification of everyday time-flows in the service of work, the temporalities associated with the workers' convivial and mutualist practices were inherently variegated, indeterminate, and undisciplined by any systematic set of goals. People shared with one another when urgent personal needs arose, which often happened without warning. When hazardous conditions emerged amid perpetually shifting work sites, tasks, and employers, these events furnished opportunities, either in the moment or later during casual chats or workshops, for workers to swap know-how regarding work techniques, injury risks, and safety practices. Prior chapters have explored how the chaotic fluctuation of everyday time-flows for day laborers created disconsolate and even excruciating affective experiences, especially in paradoxical combination with the oppressive temporal continuities of risk and anxiety. Yet at Casa Latina and the MLK Center, workers converted the precarious circumstances of temporal indeterminacy and flux into opportunities for convivial community-making. In particular, conviviality and mutualism in the centers' everyday cultures fostered novel enactments of *corporeal time* that met suffering with care and drew workers' bodies into exploratory and responsive rhythms. In doing so, these communal temporalities broke the hold of the contradictory rhythms of body-time associated with the fight on the corner, incessantly risky work, and the conundrums of desperate responsibility.[45] The more indeterminate form of embodied time also extended time's horizons in ways that countered the myopic presentism that characterized these syndromes of precarity. Convivial-mutualist time extended backward through processes of experiential learning, sideways through the sharing of knowledge, and forward toward the achievement of an intellectually and organizationally egalitarian community.

Peer-led OSH workshops at Casa Latina offered but one example of the cooperative dispositions that emerged from the convivially mutualist ethos at these day labor centers. For Luís Fernando Chávez, being a member of the MLK Center meant not only coming "to look for work" but also being willing to "pick up the trash," "attend the meetings," and "voluntarily" do anything needed to provide "help and a step forward" for the "organization." [46] Positive comments about such deceptively small and mundane contributions came from a multitude of other interviewees. Such remarks suggested a marked departure from the thematic frame of the community as workforce: an openness to more experimental social relations and configurations of time, an embrace of desires for daily activity that were not always regimented by the immediate mandate to maximize individual employment, and a notion of membership that emphasized bottom-up sources of organizational vitality. Once more, these innovative perspectives arose among workers not *despite* the imbrication of their mutualist ethos with work-oriented concerns and constraints but *by virtue of* that relation. For instance, workers often spoke enthusiastically about participating in group volunteer efforts to increase local awareness of the centers by distributing flyers in area neighborhoods that urged residents to hire day laborers. Such flyering directly responded to the issue of improving publicity that many participants saw as vital to building the centers as venues for workers' entrepreneurial aspirations. Yet giving up potential work time and going out for several hours with *compañeros* to hand out brochures also both tangibly expressed cooperative commitment and repulsed the pressure to devote every moment to the acquisition and performance of work.[47]

More ambitiously, many interviewees either held or gestured toward visions of a center governed by and for workers that *politicized* these energies of mutualist association—again, in ways that interfused temporally generative cooperativist sensibilities with expressions of economic individualism or desires for stricter rules. Jesús Martínez had been coordinating Casa Latina's flyering program, in return for which he received preference in the next day's job lottery, although he emphasized that this was not his only motivation:

PARTICIPANT: I started out as a volunteer without their giving me a job [as compensation], and now as the coordinator I take those people out and the next day I go out to work. In that way, I cooperate and they cooperate with me. . . .
RESEARCHER: So that's why you do it?
PARTICIPANT: No, that's not why I do it—I do it so that there's more work for everyone, for all the people, for all of us who go looking for jobs. . . . If my reward is a job the next day, well, that's magnificent.[48]

Disavowing neither his own nor his colleagues' job-oriented interests, Martínez thus modeled a cooperative spirit and actively engaged others in the project of forming a mutualist community. His leadership rationalized his own work schedule by making job opportunities slightly more predictable—*and* new temporalities of collective experience and popular-egalitarian power took root within the context of his practices. Alejandro Delgado, in turn, posited workers' direct experiences of overwhelming economic pressures as necessary qualifications for leadership at Casa Latina. A genuine leader, Delgado stressed, had "to have a heart"[49] and had to "have come from below, to have suffered what we suffer." He continued:

You feel it when he's speaking—you feel it. And when [another] person is talking about what he suffered . . . they're going to hold out a hand to them. . . . The worker who is with the workers . . . you see them right away. It doesn't take much time. . . . How are they going to take charge of this, if they don't know what things are like for us? It has to be one of the same people who comes around here, to know . . . where the problem is, how to help someone, everything.

Delgado certainly reiterated aspects of the protectionist conception of center membership by offering an image of leadership that exerts energetic authority, elicits ready obedience, and (elsewhere in the interview) imposes tougher rules. Still, he projected confidence in day laborers' capacities to direct their own affairs by insisting that power and knowledge had to come "from below." The culture of temporalized affects he associated with such leadership, with his evocation of stirrings of the "heart," moments of gut-level conviction, and a sense of common cause in the midst of shared suffering, also differed significantly from the apprehensive and defensive thrust of the desire to consolidate the center as a workforce.

Other workers drew attention to the ways their organizational vehicles for cooperative self-governance accomplished a similar feat of wringing transformative possibilities from circumstances structured by precarity, in all the ways prior chapters have shown, and prone to protectionist framing of community life. Luís Fernando Chávez suggested that even as interpersonal relations of conviviality spurred new motivations and opportunities for workers to govern the centers, the organization in turn catalyzed further mutual aid and connected such practices with expressions of political solidarity. Chávez voiced this thematic conception of the center as "opening pathways" to increased cooperation and heightened politicization when he reflected on Voz's worker leadership classes, which he had been attending enthusiastically:

> We always start by having the group choose a theme about which we want to talk—for example, rights in this country or free trade. We talk about how to do more publicity for the center. . . . We choose a theme and we ask questions about the ideas, and how we could improve the center. . . . I think the organization is a way to open a pathway for workers to help one another. For example, with the leadership classes—that's the way to teach how to get information about the laws, about your rights.

Notice the agility with which leadership dialogues, in this telling, darted between pragmatic matters regarding work and grand-scale political issues.[50] Precisely along these lines, and in a way I found somehow both jarring and fluid, workers at one Voz leadership class blended brainstorming about marketing innovations for the MLK Center with dialogical reflection on principles and strategies to guide a local pro-migrant-justice alternative to ICE's "Secure Communities" program, which Portland activists had christened "Safe Communities." Similarly, Casa Latina's day laborers often emphasized proudly that they had jointly instituted new rules on their own initiative through their assemblies, notwithstanding the chorus of cynicism discussed earlier. They particularly stressed raising wage levels, banning smoking, putting up the security gate, and requiring workers to wear the orange vests that distinguished them from drug vendors in the neighborhood.[51] These expressions of admiration for their group accomplishments usually still leaned on the good/bad worker distinction and retained the desire for security associated with the vision of the center as workforce. Yet the spirit of cooperation neither terminated in such wagon-circling nor gravitated toward authoritarianism. Rather, it took on a life of its own as a self-consciously political and democratic sensibility.[52]

Numerous participants also underscored that they had become more heavily involved in political mobilizations as their affiliations with the centers intensified and their participation these organizations' mutualist and convivial practices increased.[53] Apart from three individuals who had been active in union affairs or party politics in their countries of origin, no interviewees had had any political experience of note prior to coming to the United States, at least according to what they were willing to discuss in the interviews. Yet multiple participants in both cities eagerly said they had joined local marches that denounced Arizona's notorious anti-immigrant Senate Bill 1070 and copycat measures in other states, which were urgent topics in migrant communities at the time of our interviews. For Tomás Otero, participating in such actions as a member of Casa Latina and in partnership with allied groups went to the heart of what belonging to the center meant: "To be a member of Casa Latina is coming to mean including different organizations, and to go to talks not just here at Casa Latina but in other places in the state or in nearby places. There are some who even go as far as New York to be representatives of Casa Latina." In this view, center membership, far from locking the individual into a strict protocol of action and aspiration narrowly focused on employment, freed the worker to move into new political territories, to take precious time away from work's all-consuming exigencies, and to engage in collective projects of migrant self-assertion. To be sure, most workers who took part in these activities acknowledged they would nearly always decline to participate if a job conflicted with doing so (and many said the same about assembly meetings, classes, and workshops). Still, public advocacy endeavors exposed new corridors and unfolded novel temporalities of politicized experience that counteracted the centrifugal force of compulsions to consolidate the centers as rule-bound business operations.

Miguel Vargas had engaged in such exploration of unfamiliar time zones of political action: he had crossed the country in the 2003 Immigrant Workers' Freedom Ride (IWFR), in which migrant workers took bus rides originating in ten cities across the United States, including Portland and Seattle, and converged on Washington, DC, and New York City for mass rallies and lobbying efforts, having paused along the way to hold public events demanding justice for migrants. Vargas explained (in English) the connection between his participation in the IWFR and his relationship with Casa Latina:

RESEARCHER: Do you consider yourself a member of Casa Latina?
PARTICIPANT: Yes, of course. And I love Casa Latina, because I'm part of Casa Latina.

RESEARCHER: What does it mean when you think of yourself as a member of
  Casa Latina?
PARTICIPANT: For me, it means it's my second home, because they offer a chance
  to me to have a training and rise, or the English classes, not only to earn
  money.... And being a member of Casa Latina for me means you are engaged
  in political activism and to fight for all rights, not for individual but for general rights, like for the community.... For me, being part of Casa Latina, it
  means a place to stay, talking with my partners and doing a social life. Because
  it's different in the streets.[54]

Stressing how profoundly moved he had been by the experience of the IWFR,
Vargas then startled and moved *me* by singing a song called *"Peregrinos de la
Libertad"* ("Freedom Riders") that another rider had written on the bus. Vargas's
impromptu singing affected me because I had organized local events for an IWFR
stop in eastern Washington state, in association with the migrant meatpackers'
union with which I was conducting research. Vargas's reflections, in turn, resoundingly conveyed how day laborers' yearnings for basic bodily, emotional,
and economic security could move along markedly different pathways than those
that culminated in a self-protective and self-enclosed workforce. By calling Casa
Latina his "second home" and invoking the isolation and physical duress that
came with living on the street even as he reminisced about the IWFR, Vargas
welded psychological and corporeal suffering to audacious collective action—in
a way that actually heightened his personal insecurity as an unauthorized migrant who risked speaking out in public. Likewise, by intermixing work-oriented
concerns, such as getting job training and seeking upward mobility, with his affirmation of direct action, Vargas suggested how politicizing energies emerged
from within the most devastating conditions of poverty and desperation while
pressing beyond these circumstances' horizons.

  Vargas's invocation of "general rights for the community" and Otero's reference to engaging "different organizations" in "other places" also point to the
implications of convivially rooted politicization with respect to the issue of
"unity" in the center community. Notwithstanding the essentialist and con-
formist connotations of racial-ethnic identity claims discussed in the preceding
section, many workers who saw forging Latino or *mexicano* unity as central to
their center's mission allowed for degrees of flexibility and mutability in these
identity constructs. Interviewees typically acknowledged they enjoyed special
intimacy and understanding with day laborers from their own places of origin.
However, more than a few also stressed the value of learning to interact with
workers from different backgrounds through the center communities.[55] More
than just expressing a politically innocuous multiculturalism, such remarks usually

rearticulated notions of racial-ethnic identity in relation to *concrete experiences of precarity*. The latter especially included migration-related predicaments of family separation, invisibilization, and illegality, in addition to the economic struggles of *la raza* to "get ahead." Workers also integrated these identity conceptions into affirmations of political resolve, as when Pablo Maldonado explained why he attended migrant rights marches in Portland:

> It's good to participate and see new faces, fellow countrymen who want to give it their best, and that's why I'm here with them—because the same need that they have is what I say and I feel. . . . It's for my children and for my family. It's what we ourselves do to try to make things better for ourselves. You're mentally and emotionally incomplete, because your mind is here—and it's there.[56]

Maldonado perhaps assumed a questionable uniformity among the marchers in the sense of feeling the "same need." Yet more significantly, instead of grounding commonality in any transhistorical and essential cultural unity, he based it in a concrete account of migrants' politicization through enduring devastating distance from those who mean the most to them. This "mind" (and heart) that was split between two places was neither debilitated nor "mixed up"—it was an uncommonly capacious mind, living in two faraway spaces at once and inhabiting a dynamic temporality that connected sustained periods of sorrowful waiting to performative disruptions of the standard time-flows that normalize the terrorization of migrants.[57] Ángel López similarly suggested that day laborers who took political action through Voz converted the oppressions of being legally unauthorized, which were formative for racial-ethnic identity, into sources of collective resolve to demand fundamental change. He walked in migrant rights marches, he said, "because I want to support my *raza*. I want the organizations that don't want us to hear us, to look at us more, to take us more into account." In other words, López found in racializing pressures for migrants to make themselves silent and invisible a wellspring of motivation to make himself and others audibly seen.

Redefining Latino or *mexicano* identity in these ways contested widespread tendencies to reduce these identity constructs to sets of economistic desires and practices even as such modifications took shape on the social terrain plowed by precarity. By boldly affirming the collective political efficacy of Latinos or *la raza*, workers also countered the frequent flipping of such economism into racial-ethnic self-disparagement. These thematic moves might seem likely to have posed obstacles to full center membership by non-Latinos, of whom there were admittedly few but still some in both locations. Nevertheless, non-Latino interviewees consistently told us they "always felt welcomed," as Jeff Roberts put it in reference to the MLK Center.[58] Particularly fascinating in this regard were comments by Bobby Kalani, a US citizen who strongly identified with his native Hawaiian origins. Kalani said that "to the people," Hawaii was not "America" but their "own country" even though it was "part of America now," and he described his anger at being denied the chance to learn and speak indigenous languages while growing up. Regarding the MLK Center, Kalani reflected:

> Here it's like one big family, you know? We get together and it's like where I grew up, it's what I'm used to. That's why I like it here; I feel more freedom. . . . We're foreigns [sic], and in this case I feel like them, 'cause I come from a different country and I come to America . . . I feel just like them because I feel like I'm a foreign guy, too. . . . The ones who talk English, they're the ones who help me. . . . They know I speak English and that I don't understand [Spanish]. . . . They tell me what's happening, so I know what's going on.

As fervent as invocations of loyalty to Latino or *mexicano* identity could be at the MLK Center, this evidently did not prevent the community from opening itself to those with different racial, ethnic, and linguistic backgrounds, including someone like Kalani who had legal status and linguistic privileges the Latino workers largely lacked. The community did this by both mitigating its own tendencies toward linguistic exclusion and fostering an ethos of "family" that was not limited by conventional *mexicano* or Latino understandings of that notion. At least in Kalani's eyes, the center's familial sensibility derived from affinities between different colonized populations' sociohistorical subjections to domination, especially from similar experiences of being treated as perpetually "foreign" in one's "own country."[59] Perhaps, as Kalani intimated, this commonality also stemmed from a joint desire for a kind of "freedom" that involved exploring the novel relationships and creative forms of group power that mutuality among different sets of "foreigns" made possible.

In sum, day laborers offered a highly nuanced and complex account of an alternative approach to community-making at these centers that resisted the gravitational pull toward constricting and policing the community's borders for the sake of protecting precious work opportunities. Crucially, however, workers thematized a mode of community cultivation that did not merely reject the desires that all these *compañeros* shared for reliable security, sound rules, and group unity grounded in Latino or *mexicano* identity, all of which were entwined with their passionate focus on work. Rather, they gradually forged a spirited, caring, and increasingly politicized collectivity from within and from out of the dire situation of precarity that provoked these shared desires by generating intense and ongoing suffering. In the wake of preceding chapters, furthermore, we can see that the granular processes of composing community life and laying down politicized pathways responded to the various hardships of precarity named by the themes of desperate responsibility, fighting for the job, and facing risk on all sides. Perhaps most significantly, as day laborers generated distinctive communities of *place* at the centers through organizational innovation and informal networks, they likewise coaxed into daily existence new modes of *temporal* experience. Amid the excruciating temporal double binds that characterized so many facets of their lives, from waiting for the lottery to racing on the corner and struggling with hazardous jobs, day laborers explored improvisational routes and rhythms of interaction that expanded their community boundaries, relational densities, and commitments to autonomously collective forms of politics.

Theorizing Radical Democracy in Precarious Times with Day Laborers

Workers' commentaries on the themes considered in this chapter supply a wealth of material for popular-educational dialogues through which day laborers and others could develop these conceptions of center community life further and elaborate their political implications. Such dialogues could spur further theoretical exertions among the day laborers at Casa Latina and Voz's MLK Center, in ways that would complement the popular-educational exercises I have outlined in preceding chapters, whether speculatively or in light of actual experiments. The core notion of conviviality lends itself to visual representations that might spur discussion about the kinds of support workers find and give one another at the centers. One can easily imagine such representations depicting workers engaged in practices of mutual aid, objects around which such interactions cluster, and political activities both within and outside the centers that could be linked to the convivially mutualist culture with the help of visual aids. Organizers at Casa Latina and Voz constantly strive to find new and different ways to broaden the circles of workers who are more avidly involved in the centers. Dialogues focused on the themes of conviviality and pathways to politicization hold rich potential to enable workers who are already aware of the connections between conviviality, mutualism, and the centers' political ambitions both to deepen their own ideas about these ties and to encourage fellow workers to consider how these activities reciprocally feed one another.

As such theory on the ground gathers momentum through popular education, critical-popular reflection can furnish additional insights into the valences between day laborers' community-making efforts through worker centers and the challenges of activating social transformation and democratic politicization amid conditions of precarity that increasingly apply throughout society. Not just acutely marginalized and excluded populations like day laborers but working people more generally find themselves entangled in precaritized circumstances today as the hypertrophic vines of neoliberalization—the loss and destabilization of jobs, the withering of state social supports, the emboldening of racism, the decay of urban infrastructure—choke the sources of basic survival for many and the sense of economic and political futurity for virtually all. In response, critical and political theorists have sought to envision how radically transformative dynamics could still arise in the midst of such precarity. How might day laborers' themes help us gauge the moments of promise in such accounts and extend theorists' sight lines in still more visionary directions?

Informal Mutualism and Democratic Innovation

The practices of conviviality and mutualism emphasized by day laborers manifest forms of community action very much like those Raymond A. Rocco identifies as characteristic of working-class US Latinos in the neoliberal era. Through field research in East Los Angeles during the 1990s, when job loss and countless other social difficulties spawned by deindustrialization, deunionization, and social welfare retrenchment were pummeling these neighborhoods, Rocco discerns the lively prevalence among local residents of "associational networks characterized by relations of reciprocity, mutuality, and trust."[60] Rocco stresses that these complex relations include but go well beyond "utilitarian" acts of "exchange" for "mutual advantage."[61] The transactions that comprise associational networks more precisely involve "situations . . . in which an individual has faith, confidence, or the expectation to be treated in a particular way," as well as a shared experience of "trust" that stems "from being extended recognition, respect, or care."[62] Such associational affects and practices spring to life "across a variety of distinct mediating sites in civil society" ranging from "informal economy networks" to "soccer associations," "social clubs," and "swap meets."[63] In other words, through ethnographic study among working-class Latinos, Rocco conceptualizes how mutualist relations arise from within the dense interchanges between production, reproduction, distribution, and even finance that constitute lived experiences of capitalist domination.

Rocco also finds that within the community's self-composed and self-constituting associational practices, potent forms of resistance against neoliberal pressures emerge. Rocco views this resistance as enacted not only through barrio residents' mutualist networks as such but also through organized ventures of local political action promoted by those channels of connection. As he examines the transmission of informal associational energies into spheres of formal political activity, Rocco underscores how political mobilizations and unprecedented claims to "rights" and "citizenship" sprang up among East LA community residents who had found some basic security amid increasingly insecure circumstances through thickly spun webs of mutuality. Among the research subjects who testify to this process is a day laborer, who discusses how conversations with people in his personal circles had led him toward a more critical perception of Latinos' racial position, a belief that his and his neighbors' rights were being violated, and a resolve to "fight for fairness and justice."[64] For Rocco, such political sensitization powerfully challenges the core structure of anti-Latino racism in the United States: the historically embedded situation of "exclusionary inclusion," by which Latinos are allowed to be present but not to participate audibly or visibly in US public and social life.[65]

In a spirit that resonates profoundly with my own critical-popular orientation, furthermore, Rocco discerns in grassroots community-making processes among working-class Latinos not only evidence of potent anti-neoliberal counterthrusts from below but also a basis for reconceptualizing what democracy, itself, means in theoretical terms. By taking stock of the inventive forms of community action and politics that have fermented in neoliberal East LA, Rocco gains a foundation for re-envisioning democracy in a way that sees it as structurally dependent on informal associational activity. Such an understanding, because of its grounded quality, powerfully refutes political theorists' traditional privileging of formal and institutionally sanctioned avenues of legal citizenship as the activities that make democratic action real. Rocco's alternative vision also decouples democratic action from the territorially sovereign nation-state and resituates it in cosmopolitan spheres that are at once local and transnational. In short, from Latinos' everyday actions and reflections within their ambivalent positioning as perpetual foreigners in an America that paradoxically includes them via racist norms of exclusion, Rocco draws conceptual nourishment for a theorization of democracy that has a much sharper antiracist edge, a more complex political-geographic orientation, and an intrinsic connection to anticapitalist struggle.

Day laborers' themes regarding the unfolding of convivial mutualism into pathways toward politicization give ringing expression to the culturally grounded political dynamics Rocco formulates while also suggesting further specifications of this complex model of democracy. To begin with, accounts of these dynamics at Casa Latina and Voz's MLK Center show how such processes can take shape in the provisional spaces of the most exceedingly transient and severely displaced Latino workers, not just among people who have relatively more stably situated lives in the barrio. Day laborers thus highlight even further the improvisational aspects of convivial mutualism that *create new spaces* of community and politicization, in ways that are often makeshift but still tenuously enduring. Appreciating this dynamic is vital given how precaritization has recently rendered migrant populations even more violently "out of place," to recall a thesis from this book's introduction, than during the 1990s when Rocco conducted his fieldwork. Such innovative space-making also involves important *optical and aural* dimensions, which Ángel López signaled by emphasizing that the Portland migrant rights marchers sought to make themselves seen and heard in defiance of the sense-governing mechanisms that effect Latinos' exclusionary inclusion. Beyond this, day laborers suggest that novel space creation through the politics of conviviality at worker centers stimulates a *decolonizing political-geographical* dynamic, such that distinct groups cast as "foreigns" within America learn to associate on the basis of varying but sometimes similar histories of colonization.

A further turn of the radical-democratic theoretical screw that day laborers exert concerns the *temporalities* of political activation through convivial community formation. Day laborers bring sharply into relief how much a focus on time and temporality matters for radical-democratic politics in the associational mode favored by Rocco. A distinctly gradualist temporality is associated with Rocco's account of "quotidian spaces of everyday life" among working class Latinos and of the "relations of reciprocity" in these spaces that help trust accumulate over time and steadily intensify political desires.[66] His critique provokes a sense that time must move slowly for local associational networks to extend, person by person and family by family, in new directions, gently converting urgent necessity-driven preoccupations into unprecedented future-oriented aspirations.[67] Day laborers' generative themes, in turn, suggest that this temporal structure of affect bears political fruit because it interrupts, redirects, and supplants—at least briefly and occasionally—the dominant time-flows of precaritized work-life. In this regard, I mean not only the temporal condensation and regimentation that go with the workers' protectionist/economistic model of center membership but also the contradictory constructs of time that shape day laborers' tortured searches for jobs and perilous working conditions, as analyzed in prior chapters. Crucially, however, attention to the temporalities of community formation among day laborers also underscores that new temporal possibilities in everyday life can unfurl from within and by virtue of the time structures of precarity, eroding work's primacy and other neoliberal conditions by dint of inventive responses to the practical exigencies forced upon migrant workers by neoliberalism.

In addition, day laborers foster an appreciation for how the dynamics of convivial politicization can kindle a critical sense of historical time, upsetting the imperialist narratives that secure the processes of racialization Rocco unpacks and exerting a longitudinal temporal effect that complements the creative retemporalization of everyday experience. At Casa Latina and Voz's MLK Center, workers suggest, an orientation toward historical time takes hold that reframes history as open to ordinary migrants' political interventions to create a dramatically different future fueled by an awakened sense of historical injustice in the past. This historical-temporal disposition affirms the desire for racial-ethnic group affiliation but does not allow itself to be too tightly gripped by it, and thus remains open to solidarity with other colonized populations who understand their past experiences in somewhat parallel ways.

Indeterminate Possibility amid the Wreckage of Neoliberal Capitalism

Anna Lowenhaupt Tsing offers another provocative theoretical conception of how transformative processes can materialize amid scenes of precarity, and her work resonates with day laborers' themes in ways that enrich an account of conviviality's microdynamics while also bringing more sharply into relief the politically instigative character of these relational processes for day laborers. Tsing explores how symbiotic relations between precaritized subjects can call forth unforeseen and paradoxical possibilities of rejuvenation on the basis of social devastations wrought by neoliberalism. Precarious existence, for Tsing, unfurls among the "ruins" that are left when capitalist forces abandon places that have been tapped of all resources and lack other conditions necessary to fuel further accumulation:

> Global landscapes today are strewn with this kind of ruin. Still, these places can be lively despite announcements of their death; abandoned asset fields sometimes yield new multispecies and multicultural life. In a global state of precarity, we don't have choices other than looking for life in this ruin.[68]

Tsing finds in the Matsutake mushroom a fitting image of such emergence from within "blasted landscapes."[69] These mushrooms are avidly sought-after commodities in globe-spanning specialty food markets. They also thrive in ecologies that develop in the aftermath of forest devastation. In the Pacific Northwest, furthermore, unauthorized migrant workers comprise the chief labor force in a relatively informal economy of mushroom gathering and distribution. The fungi these workers hunt and sell, Tsing argues, grow as organisms through processes of self-extension and ecological interrelationality that furnish apt metaphors for the coming forth of new forms of sustaining life in migrant communities.

For Tsing, the notion of "indeterminacy" is crucial to both the temporal and the spatial features of the social growth dynamic that symbolically references the Matsutake mushroom and responds to the surrounding predicament of precarity.

In temporal terms, precarity appears as a loss of futurity, both in the sense that people no longer have the potential to develop alternate possibilities and in the sense that what lies ahead can only be conceived of as wholly bleak, with incessant vulnerability to sudden upheaval being one ironic aspect of this unbroken bleakness. To live in precarity, Tsing writes, signaling a temporal contradiction we have encountered often in this book, is to "confront the condition of trouble without end" and "life without the promise of stability."[70] Yet it is also to inhabit "patches" of not-fully-organized and incompletely capitalized activities: social spaces wherein one finds "open-ended assemblages of entangled ways of life, with each further opening into a mosaic of temporal rhythms and spatial arcs."[71] In other words, the very "unpredictability" of events in these patches can foster the creation of alternative time-spaces of life activity, even as such zones produce labor power and material commodities that can be "appropriated by capital."[72] On the historical-temporal plane, in turn, Tsing discerns a new promise of freedom in the nonteleological character of the "precarious world" inasmuch as the temporalities of indeterminate relations introduce alternatives to the commonly assumed "time line of progress."[73] She writes: "Progress is a forward march, drawing other kinds of time into its rhythms. Without that driving beat, we might notice other temporal patterns."[74]

Tsing proposes that open-ended relations of interdependence in a mobile process of articulation and enhancement enable the materialization of indeterminate possibilities that elude total capitalist control even while arising within scenes of capitalist activity. She names such relations "mycorrhizal," noting that this term is etymologically "assembled from Greek words for 'fungus' and 'root'; fungi and plant roots become intimately entangled in mycorrhizal relations. Neither the fungus nor the plant can flourish without the activity of the other."[75] Tsing discerns analogous patterns of mutual sustenance within communities of fellowship that have sprung up among Southeast Asian mushroom pickers in the Oregon forests. She marvels at how these migrants have created fragile yet lively circles of reciprocal assistance and conviviality as they search for an economic foothold in an era when neoliberal reforms have stripped away public resources and private opportunities for working-class people, especially migrants. Tsing also shows how inescapably interfused these migrants' innovative community-forging activities are with their exertions to navigate capitalist circuitries and wrangle a livelihood from their work.

On a general level, Tsing's theory of indeterminate emergence has useful affinities with Rocco's conception of informal mutualism, and both accord with the vision of convivial community thematized by day laborers. As I have argued, the transformative potency of this vision springs from its capacity to arise amid work-preoccupied imperatives of security but to escape finalistic determination by these exigencies; its generative potential is actualized in the *open-ended* quality of the pathways that unfold through workers' everyday interactions. Workers' testimonies to the ongoing suffering they endure, in the context of the dilemmas of precarity explored in prior chapters, map the social coordinates of the "blasted landscape" they inhabit. Adapting Tsing's image of the logged-out pine forest where Matsutake mushrooms grow, we might say that workers who held the protectionist conception of center membership aspired to learn the arts of clear-cutting, while knowing they would never be the ones wielding the chainsaws and contenting themselves with the "business" of scavenging wood scraps. Yet as the workers' other thematic strand demonstrates, it is also within and by virtue of the elements of life remaining in this burned-over terrain that day laborers recom-pose communities of promise, through processes that are frequently knotty and unsystematic. As we have seen, like the Southeast Asian migrants in Tsing's ac-count, day laborers do so through autonomously evolved patterns of conviviality that evoke a sense of freedom as mutual care and creative sociality.

Especially when read alongside Rocco's theory, however, the workers' gener-ative themes suggest that Tsing's focus on survival and living on in the midst of neoliberal destruction (like Berlant's) unnecessarily restricts our sense of the so-cially transformative effects these patterns of relationality can foster. Seattle and Portland day laborers, like the East LA barrio dwellers in Rocco's study, did more than just extend new fungi-like shoots of life and potentiality as they developed habitual practices of mutual aid and convivial sharing—through these activities, they also cleared pathways toward ambitious forms of political self-organization, migrant leadership development, and public advocacy for institutional changes. Acknowledging this distinction highlights a pitfall into which these workers did *not* stumble: cultivating local-level forms of sustaining communal life that ensure workers' social reproduction as an exploitable workforce without taking mean-ingful steps to challenge these capitalist processes. If convivial mutualism, as such, had comprised the full gamut of workers' interrelations at Casa Latina and Voz's MLK Center, then these activities' main *social* significance would have been to complement the centers' humanitarian services, such as providing shelter referrals and basic medical care, to keep workers functioning at the minimal level required by the home improvement and residential construction economies. [76] As the gen-erative themes and their critical-popular juxtaposition with Rocco's critique dem-onstrate, however, day laborers' indeterminate relations cannot be reduced to a simple and formalistic structure of mere contingency. Rather, these associational endeavors, open-ended though they were, yielded a trajectory of politicization by eliciting emboldened practices of collective autonomy and public action.

Tsing artfully coaxes readers to marvel at the instantiations of new life potential that arise *paradoxically* from neoliberalism's burned-over social territories and time-scapes. Her logic of paradox, however, obscures both the intentional organizing that makes such newfound vitality matter politically and the historically distilled situations of opposition that give workers' organizations opportunities to mobilize for change. Day laborers do not paradoxically kindle new life from out of devastation. Rather, their practices of conviviality and associational democracy lay out pathways for drawing political consequences from the temporal and spatial *contradictions* that structure their precaritized worlds. Day laborers also *name* this developmental but nonteleological process in ways that heighten its galvanizing potential *for migrants*, as people who not only ignite convivial interchanges that expand along experimental and indeterminate social-spatial routes but also can do so with a self-conscious theoretical sensibility and political intention. These considerations, in turn, point to the stronger resonance of the workers' themes with Rocco's much more politically focused and specific theory, notwithstanding the value of Tsing's thought in further elaborating the elements of indeterminacy, conviviality, and mutualism in the workers' vision.

Attending to the political limitations of Tsing's perspective also suggests the need to avoid certain problems with using biological metaphors to represent social relations, even while drawing critical energy from the valences between her theory and workers' themes. Ideological implications of such rhetoric have repeatedly materialized in the vast and appalling histories of imperialist, colonizing, patriarchal, racist, heteronormative, and capitalist systems of domination, which typically have enlisted naturalizing language to legitimate their power. Especially insofar as political innovation at worker centers depends on moments of affiliation among differently colonized groups, as Bobby Kalani's sense of empathy with other "foreigns" indicates, the vernacular of community life should help workers negotiate racial and cultural differences in nonessentializing ways. In this sense, day laborers' theory-on-the-ground offers a salutary corrective to Tsing: instead of describing their communities via naturalistic notions of organic growth, they emphasize historical and material social processes. Similarly, whereas Tsing sometimes characterizes migrants' convivial work practices as "noncapitalist" and invests hope for altered social relations in a realm somehow set apart from capitalist processes, day laborers oppose this form of naturalism, too.[77] As we have seen, they consistently situate convivial habits *inside* matrices of capitalist power, in ways that open pathways and portals *beyond* such power formations and that challenge the contradictions of time and space in precaritized work-life.

In parallel fashion, the workers' orientation toward historical time cannot be reduced to the simple mode of temporal open-endedness that Tsing associates with indeterminate processes of social innovation within settings of precarity, although it includes this disposition. Rather, as Luís Fernando Chávez's enthusiasm for learning his legal rights through Voz's leadership workshops illustrates, the politics of conviviality decelerates the teleological momentum of the progressive temporality even as it may begin with and, to a degree, maintain an attachment to progress's timeline. The theme of opening pathways references the forward trajectory that leads from rightlessness and statelessness toward rights-bearing citizenship. It confirms workers' desires for such progress over time toward national membership, echoing long-standing imperialist and colonialist narratives that cast the process of becoming a citizen in a modern country as a gradual maturation into political adulthood. Yet the theme and the everyday community-making practices it expresses also invite colonized groups to imagine futures unrestrained by the temporal presuppositions of normative national belonging, among people who plainly acknowledge the tenacity of their exclusionary inclusion in the nation-state—their abiding "foreignness"—and who make that condition the basis of new solidarities rather than seeking inclusion on the terms laid out by the dominant institutions.[78]

Resonant Body-Time and Convivial Politics

Both the convivial practices of mutual care and the collective forms of politicized activity thematized by day laborers evoke specifically *embodied* temporalities of alternative action in the context of ongoing bodily suffering and endangerment. Such novel configurations of body-time both comprise further aspects of the temporal innovation in worker center communities signaled by day laborers' themes and enact creative responses to the contradictory permutations of precariously embodied time explored in the last two chapters. Paying close attention to the thorough interpenetration of convivial political activities and everyday imperatives of economic need, in day laborers' accounts suggests a provocative theme-theory encounter with Romand Coles's theory of "visionary pragmatism."

For Coles, the pursuit of radical-democratic politics crucially involves eliciting new temporalities of visceral experience. Coles underscores the expanded possibilities for radical receptivity to the unfamiliar that, he argues, proceed from enhanced and diversified forms of *bodily movement*, in the sense of both how human bodies physically move and the social spaces into which people move. He focuses especially on interactive affects that arise between bodies. Although political temporality is not a leitmotif for Coles, he does suggest certain kinds of embodied time associated with the receptivity-spurring dynamics of movement. Cultivating "the difficult arts of moving with responsive creativity in the face of entrenched and blinding challenges and unfamiliar opportunities" means, in part, "learning to pay full-bodied attention" and to "dwell with patience" with these challenges and one another.[79] Precisely this making time for patiently and corporeally being present, in turn, can awaken a sense of the transformations people could generate in opposition to political regimes that regiment and restrict bodily affective experience for the sake of perpetuating capitalist domination.[80] Coles thus defines intercorporeal "democratic resonance" as "a set of body practices through which futurity—the *not yet*, time's *possibility*—can be acknowledged and tarried with, emerge more intensely, and move powerfully into political becoming."[81]

As I argued in chapter 1, popular education practices involve affective dimensions that lend themselves to these jointly nourishing temporalities of present and future. Now, taking into account what workers say about the centers' wider gamut of mutualist activities and adopting a visionary-pragmatist angle, we can further see how the prospects for democratic resonance proliferate as day laborers *move* their bodies into the distinctive affect-spheres of worker assemblies, training workshops, and leadership classes. Art classes, theater exercises, and soccer matches at the centers, which were particularly strong elements of the MLK Center's culture, further multiply and diversify such instigations of interbodily vibration. Through such activities, workers corporeally inhabit the centers in ways that break from the body-time of taut and anxious waiting for a job to materialize. A more creatively indeterminate, politically fruitful, and socially cooperative disposition of *waiting* characterizes these other activities. This posture is more like "dwelling with patience" than sitting on edge as job lottery names and numbers are announced. It also involves dimensions of interbodily resonance that work against the profoundly isolated character of desperately responsible body-time. Likewise, when workers *move outward* into local neighborhoods as *compañeros* who put work on hold and graciously volunteer time for one another and the center as their collective project, or as protestors in the streets, they contest the norms of neoliberal mobility governance and counteract the whipsawed body-time of fighting for the job. They do this by performing alternative ways for migrants to move and to be perceived as moving in public spaces, thereby releasing further intercorporeal resonances.

Day laborers' accounts of embodied practices of politically inclined mutualism also illustrate the self-accelerating quality of body-to-body resonances, which comprises another component of Coles's conception of visionary pragmatism. When workers like Miguel Vargas and Tomás Otero discussed their ventures into political activism through Casa Latina, they expressed with palpable conviction how their actions featured a self-fortifying dynamic that resembled the process of "autocatalysis" Coles attributes to (bodily) movement-based democratic resonance.[82] As Coles would lead us to expect, for these day laborers, moving into more expansive and diverse contexts of political action kindled desires for *more* of these experiences. Such movements also heightened affects of care for the fabric of conviviality at the center that supported workers' activism. I myself felt these dynamics' spontaneously intensifying vigor during my interview with Vargas because of my own prior work with the IWFR, which he evoked through singing the *peregrinos*' ballad. What transpired between us in that musical moment was a reciprocal amplification of radical democratic resonances. More than just shared nostalgia, this felt like a spur to renew my own commitment to seeking justice for migrants, and it seemed to affect Vargas in a similar way.

Thinking about the workers' themes in league with Coles's theory helps elaborate the temporalities of convivial politics in still another respect: there is a theme-theory congruence here regarding the need to set a temporally diverse assortment of activities in interaction with one another. In a way that puts both Rocco's and Tsing's privileging of gradualist temporalities in critical perspective, Coles proposes that for radical democrats, the core temporal challenge involves "interweaving and oscillating between evanescent shock politics and quotidian practices of radical democracy to generate something like an alternating current that vivifies the demos."[83] Coles construes his notion of fleeting but high-voltage political events in dialogue with Naomi Klein's appeal for a more temporally adroit and eventful left politics in response to "disaster capitalism"[84] as well as with Cristina Beltrán's argument for the profoundly democratizing significance of the 2006 immigrant rights marches, condensed though their duration was. Coles contends that such "evanescent political events can send shocks that transfigure senses and tastes, and engender energetic aspirations for possibilities far beyond the limits of the dominant order."[85] Such transfigurative and generative effects bolster the spirit and critical acumen of "quotidian practices" of community organizing even as these practices extend the effects of shock events over time, thereby yielding the "alternating current" of temporal ventures Coles proposes. In turn, by making subtle connections between ordinary habits of mutual aid and worker self-government, on the one hand, and public actions that dramatically upset norms of migrant invisibility and inaudibility, on the other hand, day laborers demonstrate how the alternating currents of radically democratic politics can arise. They show how the shock-political temporality of a singular event like the IWFR, which so deeply affected Vargas, can be intercirculated with the patiently dwelling temporalities of local community activism, which come through vividly in Otero's and Chávez's remarks.

Just as day laborers' commentaries incite critical responses to the other theoretical interventions I have been considering, however, so likewise the workers' remarks suggest a modification of Coles's proposition regarding radical-democratic temporalities of struggle. In reflecting on their daily encounters with suffering at the centers and when voicing the themes discussed in prior chapters, day laborers draw attention to the suffusion of time in everyday life with never-predictable but always-threatening and sometimes-occurring jolts of crisis. In other words, for these workers, time *already* oscillates between shock events and steady continuity within the temporality of the everyday—and this is a key facet of precaritization. Thus, elegant though Coles's notion of the alternating temporal current is, a more complex thought-model is needed to take into account this contradictory structure of time in mundane experience. We might instead imagine the time of radical-democratic politics as *triangulating* among three modes. In addition to those temporal formations that Coles highlights— densely charged moments of collective upsurge and the slow grind of grassroots organizing—the time of radical democracy should also involve the creative conversion of the everyday temporal irregularities precipitated by personal crisis events into moments when ready responses of mutualist aid kick into action. Day laborers pose the intriguing prospect, in other words, that deeply precaritized people might turn their debilitating exposure to daily temporal contradictions into an adeptness for navigating such temporal minefields and extracting from them sources of communal and political fortitude.

Neoliberal Latinidad, Gender, and the Unity Ideal

Day laborers' thematic rendering of their community lives at worker centers also speaks in a critically sympathetic manner to Beltrán's influential critique of unity as a common ideal in Latino politics. For Beltrán, "advocates and adversaries of Latino power" alike tend to presuppose—erroneously, yet with profound political consequence—that all Latinos "share a common collective consciousness."[86] Correspondingly, the view prevails that "this pan-ethnic collective *ought* to behave politically" by acting only in ways that both reflect and foster "a united community" that understands itself as such.[87] Beltrán traces repeated manifestations of this preoccupation with unity in a historical sequence of Latino political and intellectual movements, including the Chicano and Puerto Rican movements, the subsequent Latino electoralist push, the flowering of Chicano studies and Chicana feminist criticism, and the 2006 immigrant rights marches. Taking issue with this "limited vision of Latino empowerment" and its "homogenizing logic," Beltrán argues for reconceptualizing *Latinidad* "as a site of permanent political contestation" and thus "as a site of ongoing resignifiability—as a *political* rather than merely *descriptive* category."[88]

My own critical-popular analysis responds to Beltrán's provocation by introducing the resignifying creativity of some of the most class-subordinated members of the Latino population into a discursive field typically dominated by Latino professionals, whether in law, business, or politics. Listening to day laborers both confirms the potency of Beltrán's critique and suggests another iteration of the appeal for unity that has emerged in the neoliberal age. Recall how central the demand for unity was to many day laborers' conception of the center community as an efficient and dutiful workforce. Recall, as well, how participants coupled this urgent desire for unity with a narrow notion of Latino or *mexicano* identity defined through the pursuit of work and by culturally ordained failure in such endeavors. This thematic dynamic suggests that in day laborers' present social situation, and likely in that of many other Latino working people today, the unity ideal fosters a relation of mutual reinforcement between a dehistoricized notion of Latino identity and an acquiescence to work's total rule over daily life. Interviewees who favored protectionist understandings of the center community connected the call for Latino unity not only with an individualist regard for economic self-advancement but also with the affirmation of commitment to working as the one and only worthwhile activity and the exclusive measure of group loyalty.[89] In addition, their racially and ethnically self-denigrating remarks oddly reinforced the common neoliberal injunction that individuals should hold themselves at fault for their socially determined failures, even as it pinned the blame for economic failure on entrenched cultural dysfunctions.

Day laborers' convivial politics generate countercurrents against this specifically *neoliberal* Latino identity ideal, which finds expression in the thematic cluster of desires for work, security, boundaries separating insiders from outsiders, and unity. Importantly, however, the racial-ethnic sensibilities of workers' politics of conviviality loosen, stretch, and rework attachments to a united *Latinidad* rather than simply abandoning such routes of desire. In this sense, day laborers' convivial politics can be seen as representing one concrete process by which Latino *solidarity* can be developed as a critical alternative to Latino unity as a fixed essence. Rocco proposes using the notion of solidarity in this way as a response to Beltrán, whose emphasis on the negotiation of differences he endorses but whom he also criticizes for insufficiently acknowledging that calls to unity are often indispensable means to vitalize Latinos' collective action efforts.[90] Rocco suggests that developing Latino solidarity requires not only the embodied acts of political "performance and the claiming of public space" that Beltrán sees as constitutive of identity, and not just the agonistic interventions needed to contest artificially foreclosed constructions of *Latinidad*, but also processes that enable Latino collectivities to develop a sense of "connectedness" and "mutual understanding."[91] Day laborers' politics of conviviality offers a concrete demonstration of how such Latino solidarity could arise. As day laborers confirm, appeals to unity can be voiced in ways that undo their own lacing up of identities and differences and give rise to everyday practices of inclusive mutualism and open-ended dialogue. These workers also show that this form of solidarity is capable of transformatively engaging the specifically neoliberal permutation of the wish for Latino unity that has gained force today.

Beltrán's incisive critique of the ways the Latino unity ideal has enabled historically reiterated patterns of gender domination, nevertheless, should prompt efforts to intensify the radical-democratic implications of day laborers' convivial politics by deepening its gender-critical sensibilities. Visions of unity at worker centers and in the broader day labor network have often been premised on masculine-inflected notions of what it means to be a *jornalero*. Although this is unsurprising, given that most day labor centers were founded by men and have drawn many more male than female participants, it also reflects and reinforces the masculinist tendencies of prior formations of *Latinidad*. These historical echoes resounded, for instance, when some men resisted the development of Casa Latina's women's program (even though a woman had founded the organization and women occupied many key staff positions). Such reverberations also could be heard in the easy banter among the men and their voluble commentaries in assemblies while women kept quietly to themselves along the edges, as we did our field research during the period when this program was in its infancy. Even at the time of this book's writing, and even though by then the women's leadership group had outdone the men's projects in generating momentum and women were central, numerous, and equal participants in the activist and staff core, women workers still seemed to display reticence in general membership activities, and a masculine atmosphere continued to be palpable in the hiring hall. Voz's MLK Center, for its part, has continued to operate as a facility entirely for men.

These considerations, especially as illuminated through the theme-theory juxtaposition with Beltrán's work, should motivate critical-popular researchers to explore how migrant workers' visions of convivial politics could be expanded and adjusted through inquiries with women workers. Such research could intensify the radical democratic thrust of the politics of conviviality by opening up critical perspectives on gendered aspects of the themes discussed in this chapter and the ways such gendering might close off certain political and intellectual generativities. In particular, critical-popular inquiry should investigate what different forms of informal mutual aid and convivial interaction migrant domestic workers would highlight if they were asked about the meaning of membership at worker centers. Almost certainly, women's interactions would reflect the tendency for women to shoulder more responsibility than men to care for young, elderly, and ill or vulnerable family members. The interrelational practices emphasized by domestic workers also might reflect historically based cultural patterns of cooperative family care among *mexicana* and other Latin American–origin women.[92] Additionally, critical-popular research with domestic workers might reveal important things about migrant women's (unpaid) work to meet male day laborers' social-reproductive needs. Even though we observed that most male day laborers either lived alone or shared housing with other men and that these workers relied on the centers and local service providers, along with their mutual networks, to help them address their generally underprovisioned basic needs (e.g., for meals), women's contributions to meeting these needs might well have existed while going unspoken in the interviews. Critical-popular investigators also should ask: how might the temporalities, effects, and affective features of workers' volunteer activities, participation in assemblies and workshops, and center-enabled involvements in public actions differ, and how might convivial practices connect differently with politicized endeavors, from the perspectives of women at day labor centers?

Notwithstanding the vital need for such further critical-popular research to illuminate additional pathways a bold and capacious politics of precarity should pursue, this chapter's discussion of community-making at worker centers has brought into view a range of luminosities that day laborers kindle with respect to key issues in radical-democratic theory. These workers attest to the lively prospects for cultivating renegade bodily interactivities and skilled combinations of distinctly temporalized modes of struggle within apparently deathly social and economic landscapes. Day laborers' evocations of conviviality, mutualism, and the politicizing pathways they plow also help sharpen a theoretical sensitivity to the practices radical democracy involves as well as the kinds of attachments to nation, race, and ethnicity that democratic subjects might hold, with a relatively tighter or looser grip.

Conclusion: Mutualism and Militancy

Day laborers fashion communities of promise at worker centers in ways that ingeniously and subtly, yet with increasing boldness, draw upon small everyday acts of fellowship and reciprocal aid to fuel courageous advocacy for migrant justice and other collective endeavors. This process contests workers' authoritarian, economistic, and exclusionary inclinations through a logic of granular transmutation rather than via stark confrontation, abrupt renunciation, and a decisive change of course. A curious tension thus arises between this dynamic of transformation and the political trajectories that have emerged from prior critical-popular investigations in this book. Each of these earlier explorations yielded distinctly militant political implications, whether in terms of redirecting and intensifying the combative spirit that imbues fighting for the job, or renouncing the desperation that defines the temporal and ethical governance of post-Fordist work, or recasting antiwage theft advocacy as a battle to reclaim the people's stolen time, or *taking* sides against the outbreak of risk on *all* sides—except for the hyperwealthy—driven by rampant financialization. Friction exists between the ways politicization typically takes shape for day laborers through processes that titrate convivial and mutualist wellsprings, drop by drop, with political incitements and the push toward militancy that day laborers' themes generate, especially when brushed up against theories of precarity.

Noticing this tension, in turn, raises a more fundamental question regarding day labor organizations: to what degree and through what strategies have these groups been addressing the specific predicaments of precarity disclosed through this book's critical-popular investigations? How extensively and in what ways, additionally, have day labor leaders and organizations actively promoted the forms of convivial politics that have proven so supportive and energizing for ordinary day laborers? In fomenting politicization among these migrant workers, moreover, what mix of militancy and gradually transmutational provocation have day labor groups deployed, and with what effects? The next chapter concludes this book with a parting look at these intriguing organizations and seeks to answer these questions at least provisionally. It also draws together the threads unfurled in preceding chapters into a composite vision for an antiprecarity politics that melds insurgencies against exceptional forms of precaritization with opposition to precarity on a general social scale, and that wages a fight for time on multiple fronts.

6

Organizing the Fight against Precarity

IN AUGUST 2017, the National Day Labor Organizing Network (NDLON) convened its annual assembly of day labor groups from across the United States. Contingents of workers, staff, and volunteers from Casa Latina and Voz drove through the night to gather in Santa Clara, California, with worker center delegations from places as diverse as Alabama, Massachusetts, Colorado, and Pasadena. Throughout the conference, a popular-educational elan fused ebullient outbreaks of conviviality with methodical deliberations on strategy, social-structural power analysis, and defiant public protest. From the opening roll call of delegations through four days of panels, plenary discussions, workshops, and lectures, and also in a march outside the San Mateo County sheriff's office, events moved with an electric fluidity from verbal exchanges to outpourings of music, dancing, and other kinetic exercises. The assembly focused the intense emotional and embodied interactions it sparked on the core task of *organizing* to change the conditions that loaded such relentless pressure, pain, and anxiety on the shoulders of day laborers. "Courage > Fear" read the chief slogan on the posters and program, acknowledging both that this first NDLON assembly under Trump's administration was a time of heightened trepidation and that migrant workers knew how to be courageous in such times. *"De la indignación—¡a la acción!"* ("From indignation—to action!") rang out as the call-and-response cry from the speakers' lectern and the convention floor.

The foregoing chapters have shown that by attuning our ears to day laborers' words, we can more sharply perceive the temporal rhythms of precarity that course through today's society. Especially by listening for moments of affinity between workers' commentaries and self-consciously theoretical accounts of precarity, we have recognized cadences specific to the most deeply marginalized and excluded migrant workers as well as beats that resonate through the working world at large.

These exercises have enabled us to formulate a critical theory of precarity defined by characteristic temporalities of work, patterns of ethical responsibilization, matrices of space and time that govern bodily movement, and syndromes of exposure to bodily torment and death. They also have crystalized a series of militant demands twinned with a vision of slow-paced transformation in the molecular activities of workers' organizations.

What might a concluding glance at day labor organizations' primary activities suggest about the initiatives needed to pursue these demands and to foster the politics of conviviality? In their concrete organizing ventures, how dynamically are these groups responding to the specific features of precarity this sojourn among day laborers has brought to light, both in terms of day laborers' exceptional circumstances and with respect to the general social conditions for which day labor stands as a synecdoche? What lessons can be gleaned from day labor groups' endeavors that might help orient a broad-based and autonomous-collective movement to prosecute the fight for time envisioned in these pages?

Antideportation Action as Antiprecarity Politics

Day labor organizations have engaged many of the central forces undergirding the exceptionalizing dynamics of precarity through their frontal attacks on, and tactical maneuvers to wear down, the deportation regime. Chief among these efforts has been the #NOT1MORE antideportation campaign founded in 2013 by NDLON and now an independent operation that brings together a host of migrant justice organizations. To an extent, the project frames its goals in negative terms: "Together we say: not one more family destroyed, not one more person left behind, not one more indifferent reaction to suffering, not one more deportation."[1] The campaign also voices more constructive goals, however, including efforts to "build migrant power" and "build community" through "cultural creations that illustrate the ugliness of criminalization and the beauty of our communities."[2] More generally, day labor organizations' political engagements of the deportation regime display an impressive mix of approaches that include protests in the streets, lobbying in legislative corridors, and vigorous online activism. Examining these efforts can shed light on the kinds of challenges day labor groups are posing to the precaritizing forces of migrant surveillance, detention, and deportation while also illuminating how these organizations are mingling urgently militant with gradually emergent modes of struggle.

As Kathryn Abrams argues, with the genesis of #NOT1MORE, the day labor movement has taken a significant turn toward militancy and direct action, notwithstanding the network's continued and even heightened investments in mainstream public policy advocacy.[3] On the one hand, as NDLON executive director

Pablo Alvarado emphasized in our 2014 interview, during the Obama administration NDLON participated in high-stakes negotiations over comprehensive immigration reform in Congress, before bipartisan Senate efforts foundered on the shoals of House GOP intransigence.[4] Alvarado clearly felt satisfied about his success in gaining the removal of little-publicized measures from the original bill that had directly targeted day laborers. On the other hand, through #NOT1MORE, NDLON, its associated worker centers, and other coalition partners unleashed a feverish and resolute array of direct action protests upon the federal deportation apparatus. Activists staged a cascading series of sit-ins in major cities, blocking the roadways in front of ICE vehicles that were attempting to transport unauthorized migrants to and from detention facilities. These actions lasted over a year, and NDLON multiplied its effects exponentially by sending out an email blast each time that urged supporters to watch the protest unfold via streaming video. In temporal terms, these events thus deftly interspersed shock temporalities within a longer trajectory of patient movement-building and sustained elite-level policy advocacy. I attended a 2014 march from ICE headquarters in Washington, DC, to the White House, where about thirty activists with the Casa de Maryland day labor and migrant justice organization staged civil disobedience and were arrested, spurred on by a cheering crowd of hundreds that included many unauthorized migrants. Hunger strikers at NDLON's affiliated worker centers across the country foreswore food for weeks to pressure the president to grant immediate deportation relief, rebuffing pleas from moderate Democrats to withhold criticism of Obama and bolster his resistance to extreme Republican nativists. Due in no small part to such tenacious and forceful direct action by #NOT1MORE participants, Obama ultimately relented and handed down the Deferred Action for Childhood Arrivals executive order.

Such determined pushback against the deportation regime has not succeeded in the formidable task of stopping migrants' arrests, detentions, and expulsions. Yet it strikes at motor forces of the exceptionalizing precaritization to which unauthorized migrant workers are exposed today. Ever-present fear of deportation, as I have argued, contours the peculiar form of desperate responsibility experienced by day laborers. It layers intense anxieties about lack of work with added pressure to make the absolute most of each moment when one might find a job, because one never knows when ICE might arrive. Such fear also redoubles the contradictory temporal formation associated with day laborers' experiences of work-related desperation: time's unpredictable vacillation between continuities of dread and insecurity, on the one hand, and tumultuous shifts of circumstances and action paces, on the other hand. Terror of *la migra* further prods day laborers to voice their commitments to personal responsibility according to tropes that mimic the authorities' discursive binary between good and bad immigrants, and to strive to make such dedication visible to those better positioned in the racial hierarchy. Day labor groups' militant antideportation activism, in shrewd combination with their inside-the-Beltway strategizing, aims to defuse each of these dynamics.

Day labor organizations' opposition to deportation is thus more than a politics of migrant justice and rights—it is also a potent and essential form of antiprecarity politics. As such, it involves further dimensions that address the other domains of precaritized experience brought to light by day laborers' generative themes. The double binds of bodily movement on the corner, which contort workers between the equally counternormative alternatives of protracted immobility and sudden physical outbursts, carry weighty consequences because of the never-predictable but always possible interventions of immigration agents (and police officers deputized as immigration enforcers). Additionally, antimigrant discourses that figure migrant workers' "corporeal excess" as either a surfeit of uncontrolled movement or a recalcitrant resistance to forward progress help generate the disciplinary and punitive effects of transgressing liberal mobility norms. Meanwhile, immigration policy and procedure bar millions from accessing a wider range of jobs and relegate them to public spaces like day labor corners where their vulnerability to these dynamics of neoliberal mobility governance spikes upward. The corner is thus in crucial respects a creature of the deportation regime, and to combat that regime is also to thwart the form of precarity that workers name *fighting for the job*. In turn, to oppose the homeland security apparatus is also to contest major impediments that block day laborers from refusing to do dangerous jobs while multiplying the bodily risks and temporal dilemmas of their work. Less obviously, #NOT1MORE strikes a blow at the condition of illegality that fosters motifs of subjectivity associated with slow death, especially masculine-gendered claims of individual mastery over one's work time and moralistic professions of devotion to a life path of bodily self-care.

Day labor organizations have combined these struggles to disrupt the deportation apparatus's operations with efforts to foster novel spaces and temporalities of action in which alternative forms of sociality can emerge among migrant workers. In this respect, day labor groups' antideportation organizing repertoire harmonizes with affirmations by numerous theorists considered in this book, especially Kathi Weeks, of the need for antiprecarity politics to meld negative with constructive impulses. Such elements also indicate how these organizations complement militant thrusts toward taking sides in plain recognition of intolerable outrages with efforts to instigate the gradual transmutation of desires, perceptions, and conceptions. Casa Latina, Voz, and other worker centers host myriad activities of this latter form, which engage community members in learning about current events, historical precedents, and action opportunities with regard to immigration enforcement and migrant rights. Operating in the mode of convivial politics discussed in the preceding chapter, Voz has carried out ingenious cultural events that stimulate intercorporeal affect-exchanges keyed to immense suffering, supportive kinship, and full-bodied celebrations of political possibility. Thus, for instance, a "salsa solidarity party" for day laborers and community supporters in 2011 mingled dancing with phone-banking to build opposition to Congress's proposed extension of the E-Verify immigration control initiative. Annual Day of the Dead celebrations observe this familiar Mexican tradition by publicly remembering migrants who have died making the brutal trek across the US-Mexico border. Ceremonies honoring the Virgin of Guadalupe involved exhortations to sign a petition demanding that the sheriff of Multnomah County, Oregon, cease assisting ICE in apprehending undocumented migrants.

A "popular assembly" convened by Casa Latina shortly before Trump's inauguration, in which I volunteered, showed vividly how local community events generated by day labor centers convert personal pathos into politically vitalizing affective currents that flow outward into wider political-geographic territory. This gathering of some 150 people on a frigid January evening focused on how unauthorized migrants could protect themselves under the hostile incoming administration. The general discussion and breakout sessions elicited tearful testimonies of fright, offers of interpersonal aid, expressions of collective determination to resist racism, and pragmatic plans of action. (One example of the latter that I will not soon forget was the sheet of butcher paper with matter-of-fact yet heartrending advice to fellow parents: "What will happen to my son or daughter if they detain me?—Letter granting power of attorney, if possible to a citizen or legal resident. Put those people's names in children's school records. No notary required.") In the time-space of the church social hall where the assembly took place, conviviality fostered gestures of mutualism and kindled political spirit among participants with an electric immediacy. Nor did these energies remain contained within this hall on that night—they spread beyond it and swelled Casa Latina's large and defiant contingent in Seattle's record-smashing Women's March one week later.

Worker centers' responses to deportation pressures have shown a particularly impressive capacity to undermine the good/bad worker dichotomy that resurfaces in each of our interviewees' three main thematizations of their precarious circumstances. Alvarado told me a revealing story about one Pasadena day laborer named Martín who had been detained by ICE and slated for deportation in connection with four charges of driving under the influence of alcohol. After much debate, and bucking their own impulses to condemn this fellow worker for reinforcing negative stereotypes about migrants, workers at the Pasadena Community Job Center ultimately rose up to support him. According to Alvarado, Martín's *compañeros* decided that encouraging public perceptions of day laborers as full and complex human beings—in his case, not just a reckless driver and substance abuser but also a dedicated worker, valued community member, and devoted father—was worth risking disfavor in the wider locale. Alvarado then underscored what he saw as his and other leaders' obligation to involve and assist all day laborers rather than reserving their efforts for the putatively deserving, saying: "I have to be accountable to Martín because my organization is made up of people like that."[5] In other words, both on the level of molecular community-building at worker centers and in the stated priorities of national leadership, the day labor movement is exerting counterpressure against the deportation regime's self-legitimating reliance on schemas that dichotomize between responsible and irresponsible migrants. Day laborer organizations are also fighting the ways workers reproduce these patterns through their own thematic terms and practical dispositions.

A distinctive confluence also exists between local worker centers' convivially politicizing responses to suffering and national day labor leaders' rhetoric. In a 2014 *Democracy Now!* interview about #NOT1MORE, Alvarado excoriated then-president Obama for having "built an incredible deportation machine" and added:

> This is changing. And the reason why it's changing is because suffering is speaking. Last Saturday, there were a hundred events where affected communities came out and said, "This is enough. This is my story." They have protested. They have marched. They have engaged in direct civil disobedience. And as a consequence, they have made sure that the end of deportation becomes Plan A.[6]

Thus, while our interviewees depicted the minute and faltering steps that led from simple companionship to more organized forms of mutual support and public advocacy in the local milieu promoted by worker centers, Alvarado drew broader-scale political consequences of the determination to "let suffering speak." The wave of #NOT1MORE hunger strikes in 2015 further exemplified such catalytic conversion of everyday bodily and emotional distress into multiscalar political emergences.

In sum, day labor organizations' courageous and heated struggle against the deportation regime is a fight against precarity—and a fight for time. Perhaps this battle would be fortified even more, in turn, if day labor groups openly recognized its significance vis-à-vis oppressive temporalities of precarious work-life and explicitly affirmed that seeking justice for migrants means, in part, developing alternative modes of social time. What if NDLON and its member groups were to acknowledge outright that part of what makes the deportation apparatus so devastating for migrants is its contradictory rule over time in everyday life? What if an explicit point of antideportation strategy were to *politicize the contradiction* between time's anxiety-burdened, ever-vigilant, body-bracing immutability in the face of always-incipient catastrophe, and such time's randomly occurring ruptures through immigration agents' sudden incursions and migrants' abrupt separations from friends and family members? Furthermore, what if worker centers sought to draw political consequences from the attendant contradiction, which similarly runs throughout the workers' generative themes about precarious work-life, between a moralistically imagined life-trajectory of steadily upward mobility and responsible self-stewardship, on the one hand, and a sense of unavoidable immersion in urgent present-moment imperatives—to win the lottery, to prevail in the fight for the job, to stay vigilant amid erratically erupting safety hazards? Suppose day labor organizations took stock of the alternative temporalities of solidarity and individuality percolating within worker centers' antideportation activities and traversing diverse political-geographic scales, and consciously sought to invigorate such dynamics further? All these possibilities for strategic development stem directly from critical-popular reflection on the articulated frustrations and desires of workers who comprise the movement's base and whose political activation, on terms they help formulate, is the decisive sign that the movement is thriving. Reframing the struggle against deportation as, in part, a fight for time would be one way to nourish the movement with the sustenance of popular generativity.

Re-placing the Corner, Retemporalizing Public Spaces

The preceding chapter discussed how day laborers' participation in marches and other demonstrations for migrant justice brought them into urban public spaces in ways that forged alternative pathways beyond the vexed protocols of movement and immobility on the corner. Other activities sponsored by NDLON and pursued by worker centers contest neoliberal mobility governance in further ways and thus comprise additional avenues by which day labor organizations are challenging the exceptionalizing dynamics of precarity. We have seen how day laborers associated with worker centers tend to disparage those who frequent the corners as violent and indolent drunkards, menaces to public order, wastrels with no regard for proper bodily self-care, and troublemakers who resist internal discipline and external rules alike. Spatially associating the irresponsible worker type with the corner thus informs each permutation by which day laborers thematize their situations of precarity while also shaping their desires with respect to worker center communities. In important ways, worker centers were created to give day laborers alternatives to the corner—to move them off the corners into the centers—and the centers offer tangible advantages over the corners.[7]

Yet from the outset, day labor organizing has involved efforts on the corner and on behalf of workers on the corners, even when a major goal has been to found a worker center. Casa Latina, Voz, and other day labor groups typically began organizing on street corners where day laborers congregated. Casa Latina had its genesis under the viaduct in Seattle's Belltown neighborhood; Voz's founders launched their efforts near an interstate highway overpass on Portland's east side; worker centers in many other major cities have arisen in similar pockets of urban street life. Day labor leaders still speak proudly about their successful defeats of local ordinances banning work solicitation on the street in Los Angeles, Chicago, and elsewhere during the movement's early stages in the 1990s.[8] These victories solidified the existence of day labor corners rather than routing workers to the centers, and leaders consider such triumphs pivotal moments in their long-term push to build power among day laborers in whatever spatial zones they inhabit. Moreover, the contemporary revisioning of the corner as a time-space for freedom and the refusal of work through manifestations of workers' artistic creativity there, as Voz's documentary *Jornaleros* illustrates, reprises parallel experiments in prior phases of day labor organizing. Such ventures include, for instance, a 1990s project to paint murals on the cement undergirding of the viaduct near Casa Latina's old quarters. Early Seattle day labor activists also used "theater of the oppressed" methods on the corners, drawing on a street-thespian tradition linked to popular education, to spark enthusiasm for Casa Latina in its infancy.[9]

These transits between center and corner continue today, and if anything were becoming more lively and innovative as I finished this book. Eric Rodriguez, director of the Latino Union worker center in Chicago, informed me that a newly instituted policy provided voting rights to workers on the corner in elections for the workers' committee at the center.[10] Following Casa Latina's exemplary success in developing OSH training programs, the organization developed an endeavor in 2016–17 to conduct similar training modules on the corners. Like many other day labor centers, furthermore, when Casa Latina pursues wage claims against employers who cheat workers of their due pay, staff members and volunteer attorneys mostly address problems stemming from employment on the corners. The annual list of priorities announced at NDLON's 2017 national assembly prominently included an initiative for every worker center to "adopt a corner" (which revived a slogan from the earliest days of day labor organizing in Los Angeles)[11] and to increase organizational capacities for supporting day laborers in those nearby spots. Also, although attendance at the assembly had been mustered largely through centers in the network, when an NDLON organizer asked representatives of corners to raise their hands, nearly 10 percent of those in the room did so.

In these diverse ways, day labor organizations have been defusing the moralistic denigration of the corner that feeds self-undermining thematics of personal responsibility among workers. These groups are seeking, instead, to foster a sense of autonomous collectivity among day laborers that bridges center and corner, and that through this spatial expansiveness materializes the same kinds of inclusiveness and solidarity that the Pasadena workers demonstrated in sticking up for their *compañero*, Martín. More tangibly, by introducing into the corners mechanisms of political self-government, OSH education, and other aspects of the center-based practical culture, day labor activists are interrupting and reordering the dissonant rhythms of body-time in these spaces. They are thereby undermining and supplanting the patterns of neoliberal mobility-governance, buttressed by the deportation regime, that consign workers on the corner to such acute conditions of precarity. Again: what might a more *self-aware* pursuit of such alternative figures of bodily mobility and stasis on the corner contribute to the strength of these efforts in the future? What further realizations of the promise depicted in *Jornaleros* could be achieved, in the sense of corporeally keyed interventions that refuse the corner's space-time contradictions and make the corner a more convivial place?

Other initiatives by NDLON and local worker centers have called neoliberal mobility-governance into question more obliquely by fostering alternative ways for migrant bodies to move, and to be perceived as moving, in public spaces. These modes of movement emphasize mutual aid and social responsibility, and they thus counter both poles of the mobility dilemma on the corner: that of listless, body-wearing stasis and that of violently excessive motion. From NDLON organizers in New York City and Los Angeles, I learned about remarkable events through which day laborers have claimed the role of urban and global "citizens," despite lacking national legal authorization, in response to environmental catastrophe and degradation.

Day laborers vividly illustrated such efforts through their astonishing mobilization, effected by worker centers, immediately after Hurricane Sandy pummeled New York City in 2012. According to Long Island–based NDLON organizers Nadia Marin and Omar Henríquez, day laborers speedily stepped forward as underappreciated but effective "first responders" to emergency conditions caused by the hurricane:

MARIN: The workers were at the scene in Staten Island helping homeowners before the Red Cross, before churches, before—

HENRÍQUEZ: As volunteers, not for any money but out of the goodness of their heart[12]—

MARIN: From the Center [sic] de Inmigrantes, because I heard it on the radio. There's this lady who called in to the *Brian Lehrer Show* [saying]: "I'm here on Staten Island . . . there's nobody here from the city, there's nobody here from FEMA, there's nobody here from the American Red Cross. The only people are a group of immigrants!"

HENRÍQUEZ: You have to realize that a lot of immigrants come from places where they have been exposed to disaster—in Central America, Hurricane Mitch, earthquakes. When that happens, there's a sense of solidarity. You help each other. And they know that the disaster was bad, but not as bad as they probably had seen back home.[13]

Under emergency conditions, these migrants subjected themselves to personal danger by working "with no protective equipment" and "no training" in flood-inundated areas where the water contained infectious bacteria and toxic chemicals—"just a sludge full of stuff," as Henríquez wincingly put it. Hazards abounded, from contracting trench foot, to being hit by falling trees, to suffering electrocution from downed power lines. Yet working amid such perils did more than simply reaffirm these day laborers' ordinary subjection to the predicament of facing risk on all sides. Instead, the workers enacted what we might call an alternative version of desperate responsibility that also overturned the protocols of neoliberal mobility governance. In the midst of an urgent *social* situation, day laborers acted in ways that were dynamically cooperative rather than atomistically individual and that manifested their bodies in ways quite other than those linked to the morphology of movement-based corporeal excess. In a time of desperation, they modeled a temporality of public action that was improvisational yet directional, speedy yet controlled. Such action in time clearly differed from the self-conflicting temporality—the vacillation between noxious continuities and disorienting fluctuations of time—that is typical for migrant workers in public spaces and that the deportation regime helps constitute. Furthermore, the temporality of day laborers' first-response activities departed from the work-obsessed neoliberal norms that mandate market participation as the individual's sole duty for every waking minute, and hence from this norm's ironic effect of self-criminalization for day laborers. Crucially, the local worker center enabled these actions, as Marin stressed, although the astonished radio caller seemed to miss this.

As first responders to Hurricane Sandy, the Staten Island day laborers also recomposed public space as a cosmopolitan domain of mutual social regard and action in solidarity across lines of nationality, language, and legality. Their political-spatial disposition contested national territorial boundaries as well as the nationalist temporalities tied to aspirational normativity. The social histories of the migrants *mattered* as sources of ingenuity and experience in the face of climate disaster, rather than being effaced by the stiffly forward-looking timeline associated with the normative view of immigrant integration into American society. Day laborers from El Centro del Inmigrante, in other words, performed in real time the wry repudiation of American dream mythology by the worker-artists in *Jornaleros*. They also posed a positive and creative alternative to this nationalist fantasy through their cosmopolitan practices of sociality, thereby importing into the broader local culture the cosmopolitan incitements found within worker center communities.

During nonemergency periods, day labor organizations have catalyzed temporal-practical innovation in further ways that strike back at the deportation regime, reclaim time in public from neoliberal mobility governance, and connect the short-duration time of the event to the protracted time-frames of community organizing and environmental deterioration. Pablo Alvarado told me about a project carried out by Los Angeles day labor organizations in 2015 through which workers volunteered en masse to clean up the heavily polluted Los Angeles River:

> We are bringing together two hundred day laborers to clean the LA River, together with the Office of Immigrant Affairs in the city.... But we are not doing it just because we want to increase the visibility of day laborers.... This is about us caring about the place that we live, caring about the environment, caring about relations in the community.

Like the first response to Sandy, the LA River cleanup project featured a related but distinctly temporalized form of what we might call *unauthorized citizenship* for day laborers. This deployment of day laborers for community service reinstantiated the cosmopolitan implications of the episode on Staten Island by drawing day laborers out of the migrant-exceptionalizing temporalities of mobility governance and fostering a sense of common cause between migrants and other area residents and workers. In contrast to the Sandy response, however, the LA River cleanup combined the highly charged and condensed temporality of the (publicly staged) event with the temporal rhythm of step-by-step organizing and gradually intensifying mutualist ties. Day labor organizations thus enabled a performance of community belonging and responsibility—of "citizenship" in the practical sense—that audaciously broke from the standard temporalities for gaining legal national membership. Workers demanded through their actions in the moment that other Angelenos recognize them as fellow "citizens" immediately rather than only after state authorization; workers also demanded acknowledgment of their long-term and continuing participation in local community life.[14]

It is worth underscoring that day labor organizations undertook both the LA River cleanup and the Sandy first response in the context of environmental problems. It is fairly well known that climate change is fueling mass migration flows in all parts of the globe, as changing climates and climate-related disasters foster intolerable living conditions for poor populations who see no alternative but to move elsewhere. It is less frequently appreciated that migrant workers have become crucial participants in localized responses to climate-related problems, whether as emergency volunteers or paid laborers. This means that climate change has a complex relation to precarity: the former not only generates the latter but also spawns opportunities for combining environmental action with antiprecarity politics in mutually bolstering ways. Day labor groups show how ecological devastation, whether occurring as a crisis event or as an imperceptibly gradual mutation, can furnish concrete points of departure for migrants to challenge the power structures that create and govern time-spaces of precarity. In turn, as active responders, migrant workers help increase the general political salience of environmental destruction through interventions that lend a similar temporal complexity to climate change, at once declaring it to be a crisis that requires immediate intervention and acknowledging its sustained duration over time.

Engaging the Collective Fight for Time

Through their advocacy and direct action against the deportation regime, their cultivation of center-corner connections, and their performances of unauthorized citizenship, day labor organizations have boldly confronted forces that expose migrant workers to distinctly acute forms of precaritization. Yet have they also instigated or joined efforts to foment widespread popular opposition to the more encompassing dynamics of precarity illuminated by the critical-popular explorations in this book? Insofar as day labor is a synecdoche for precaritization writ large, what signals do day labor groups emit that they perceive this correspondence and plan to help organize broad-based, autonomous collectivities to combat precarity on the grand scale?

For the most part today, engaging a general fight for time remains a matter of inchoate potential encoded in the generative themes of ordinary day laborers rather than a conscious plan of day labor organizations and leaders, as is the case for most labor, migrant justice, and other progressive groups. Nonetheless, the foregoing critical-popular sojourns allow the elaboration of a specific, nuanced, and multifaceted conception of an antiprecarity politics in which the day labor movement is in key ways already invested, consciously or not, and which this network could take up more explicitly in association with other organizations. Pulling together the politically elucidating implications of the investigations in this book, the following composite image of such a politics—a politics *of precarity*, in the sense that it can arise among subjectivities and collectivities constituted within scenes of precaritized work-life, and *against precaritization*, as the array of social dynamics that structure these settings—comes into view:

- A politics that goes beyond seeking marginal relief from overwork and instead demands fundamental alternatives to a pervasively debilitating condition of desperation driven by the contradictory temporal culture of work
- A repudiation of the work ethic that prescribes personal responsibility in the face of desperation, not only because it embraces a too-limited vision of freedom but also because it consigns responsibilized subjects to rituals of self-destruction that leave them socially isolated and psychologically damaged
- A politics that calls employers to account not just for stealing workers' wages but for robbing the people of their time, and that demands the restoration of this time to the people
- A refusal of work as the axial concept that constricts working people's social and political imaginaries and the fetishized practice that constrains people's mundane affective experiences
- A fight for the city that inaugurates a plenitude of urban time-spaces for the performative enactment of bodily movements that elude and incapacitate neoliberal mobility-governance
- A militant resolve to take sides against the capitalist forces that insulate themselves from financial risk by effecting wild proliferations of bodily risk for working people—against the big financial firms, the private equity companies, the corporate giants that fissure workplaces, and the employee wellness industry
- A withdrawal of popular consent to the (dis)order of endangered body-time on the job, inspiring collective refusals to do hazardous jobs by mass groups of workers
- The conquest of slow death through organizing rather than just the interruption of slow death through lateral agency
- The development of antiprecarity strategies keyed to the limits of biopolitical differentiation, in dynamic relation with political contestations of both the biopolitical sorting of racialized populations and sub-biopolitical regimes of exceptionalization

In dispersed moments within the preceding chapters, we have seen how day labor organizations take initial steps along these ambitious political trajectories. We have also glimpsed scattered signs that these groups perceive the broad-scale struggles at stake in their day-to-day activities with and on behalf of the poorest migrant workers—even broader than legalization and citizenship for millions of unauthorized migrants. Some indications are pre-figurative, as in the aesthetic experiences through which *Jornaleros* evokes an anticipatory aural, visual, and palpable sense of urban space liberated from neoliberal mobility-governance, and of the refusal of work. Through film screenings in community settings amid dialogical interactions, however, Voz also evinces a restlessly practical desire to expand the political ambit of the *Jornaleros* project beyond its prodding of individual viewers' imaginations and senses. What if similar impulses to draw wider circles of people into day labor groups' activities, and to induce more people to see day laborers' struggles as their own fight, too, could be activated by migrant workers' gambits of un-authorized citizenship or their protests against the homeland security state? What if day labor organizations, in league with other workers' groups, were to generate such impulses intentionally and explicitly?

Occupational safety and health presents a particularly fruitful field of ac-tivity for fostering the popular-theoretical and strategic linkages that could connect day labor organizing to much more broadly encompassing polit-ical initiatives in the face of precarity. To a limited but encouraging degree, day labor groups have already begun exploring such connections. In 2015, NDLON's then-director of OSH programs, Loyda Alvarado, told me enthusi-astically that NDLON had begun participating in the National Coalition for Occupational Safety and Health (COSH).[15] She described the waxing sense of common purpose and shared vulnerability that had arisen at the coalition's meetings, where groups representing many different constituencies of workers had gathered:

We get to sit down at the table and put those issues of day laborers on the table and also get that feedback and the issues from other workers and see, like, "Hey, we're all in the same boat. This is basically happening to everyone, and it has nothing to do with whether you're a union worker or not, or whether you're a temporary worker or a permanent worker. The fact is we're all getting screwed by all these corporations, by the system. So how can we work together to be able to make a change?"

In opening up for scrutiny the grand-scale capitalist mechanisms that are making work increasingly hazardous not only for day laborers but for working people at all levels of the employment hierarchy, NDLON's representatives[16] and other labor-affiliated participants in the coalition are thus opening pathways to new political solidarities between migrant workers and nonmigrants, and among workers involved in variously temporalized labor-processes. With a network of local COSH groups spanning the country and resources published in fourteen different languages, the coalition provides an organizational structure that enables workers throughout the economy to see how there is risk on *all* sides, and that is motivating them to *take sides* against the private companies propelling this situation.[17]

Other elements of day labor organizations' responses to hazardous work show unrealized but striking potential to inspire more expansive visions of social struggle among diverse cadres of workers. Such promise can be seen in an intriguing popular education exercise developed by NDLON to cultivate critical awareness and altered practices among day laborers with regard to OSH problems. When I interviewed Alvarado, she showed me a floor puzzle that depicted day laborers and domestic workers encountering typical hazards on the job: here a woman scoured a toilet and held a bottle of toxic cleaning fluid, with stars circling her kerchiefed head; there a man jackhammered a slab of concrete, his body shaking with the machine's vibrations. In the exercise, a coordinator divided workers into two groups, gave each squad half the puzzle pieces, and directed them to put the pieces together but without speaking for the first five minutes. The workers were not informed that the fragments made up a single puzzle; nor were they told *not* to talk to members of the other team after they could speak. Yet invariably the teams assumed they were competing against one another until, at some point, the players discovered they were all working on the same task and realized they could complete it better by collaborating.

Alvarado emphasized that the ensuing discussion not only led participants to identify dangers illustrated in the puzzle and to debate strategies for handling them individually—it also prompted workers to consider their real-time experience, via the puzzle exercise, of interacting with an authority figure and deciding, consciously or not, whether to challenge that person's power. Explained Alvarado, with a mischievous smile:

We reflect on the process and then I ask them about my instructions as a facilitator, or as the person in charge—like, "What about my instructions, were they good or were they bad?" They always tell me they were good! And . . . I'm like, "Really? So, if I was your employer and I told you, 'Solve the puzzle, don't talk,' would that be good for you . . . ?" And then I would start using that to let them know: you have to communicate, you have to talk to your employer.

In other words, the exercise induced day laborers to confront their own reluctance to stand up to employers who endangered workers' bodies and encouraged a work environment of silent obedience, which, as we saw in chapter 4, workers recognize as a key social cause of overabundant risk. Through the activity, participants also experienced how they could move beyond the double binds of individualist responses to these social-power dynamics through peer-to-peer cooperation. No doubt, the physically mobile and interactive character of the exercise boosted its capacity to generate a sense of time in the moment that felt palpably different from the temporal conundrums of hazardous work, in ways heightened by the intercorporeal resonances fostered in that temporal zone, as Coles's visionary pragmatism would suggest.

NDLON's puzzle game also precipitated critical reflection that contextualized immediate sense experiences, temporal shifts, and practical insights within broader arenas of political power. After completing the puzzle, Alvarado said, coordinators urged the players to ponder: "Why are we going out to work, exposing ourselves to all these hazards? Why do we [need to] protect ourselves?" She continued: "And then people usually talk about the *actores sociales* [social actors], which is just basically: 'Who is part of this whole community of health and safety?'" Not just the human agents behind OSH dangers received attention but also the logic of commodification through which OSH risks spread, she noted:

> One thing that I tell them is, "If I told you to sell me your hand right now, how much would you sell me your hand for? Or a finger? Do you need that finger? What do you need it for?" And then from that, for them to value themselves, to have some self-worth, of like, "Yeah, I cannot sell you my hand because I need it." Or basically what you're doing when you go to work and you're using that saw that could potentially cut your hand, you're basically telling them: "Here, I'm selling you my body."

Alvarado added that she undertook such interventions to counteract day laborers' tendencies to naturalize their physical pain and debilitation, failing to see these problems' relation to work processes even when it was patently obvious, such as in the case of one worker who had crushed his hand with a hammer and yet did not "think of it as a workplace accident." Beyond simply revealing *that* this connection between work and bodily damage existed, however, the exercise also exposed to critical scrutiny the *commodifying means* by which this lethal relation came to seem so unremarkable.

Beyond providing a deceptively sophisticated means for catalyzing collectively and individually fortifying processes of *conscientizaçao* among exceptionally precaritized day laborers, NDLON's OSH puzzle exercise furnishes a final synecdoche for a widely encompassing social situation—and for a general political opportunity. In multiple ways, the puzzle game encodes the vital features of a prospective broad-based fight by working people throughout the precaritized world to refuse dangerous work and to demand new social power-arrangements that anchor bodily thriving in the people's radically free disposition of their own time. The exercise does this through inciting the questioning of authority and by beckoning vocal expression under conditions that breed silence. It prefigures a broader collective uprising when it stirs cooperation where competition is the common-sense order of things, when it stimulates interbodily exchanges of enlivening affects, and when it problematizes who the *actores sociales* are. It indicts the capitalist practical ideology that desensitizes workers to their own suffering and their vital relations to others when it identifies commodification as the primary source of risk. It invites active and collaborative discovery of ways to compose a new social order of time from out of the temporal fragments that (dis) organize precaritized workers' lives.

Loyda Alvarado noted that her job mostly involved "training the trainers"— workers, staff, and volunteers at NDLON's affiliated worker centers whom she equipped to stage the OSH puzzle exercise and to conduct other kinds of OSH education with workers locally. Casa Latina, Voz, and their allied organizations are thus encouraging day laborers to interrogate precaritizing power more generally as workers wrestle with the dilemmas of risky jobs. Apart from the COSH network, what other organizational innovations, backed by what political demands, could engage more far-ranging collectivities of workers in similar processes of *conscientizaçao?* What are the more fundamental organizational prerequisites of a broad-based fight for time that could mobilize disciplined, long-lasting, intentional forms of political struggle on the full repertoire of antiprecarity initiatives I have outlined in this section, including but going beyond matters of job safety and health?

Worker Centers for All Workers

Critical-popular investigation of day laborers' themes regarding community life at worker centers has demonstrated that these organizations open up new temporal and spatial contexts within which interpersonal conviviality, everyday mutualism, autonomously collective self-government, and political mobilizations can flourish and fortify one another. In turn, the selective scan of the day labor network's activities in the preceding sections of this chapter suggests how powerfully worker centers can challenge structural generators of precarity when they operate in solidarity with each other. In view of these achievements, one crucial demand that working people at large today should voice is the demand for *worker centers for all workers.* We need to demand of our major social and political institutions and of ourselves that the conditions be furnished—that physical quarters be provided, that budgets be amassed, that time be freed from the exigencies of work, that leadership be developed and equipped—for community organizations that generalize to working people of all sorts the dynamics of politicization in the midst of neoliberal devastation that are at once so lively and so fragile at Casa Latina and Voz. We also should demand the capacities to affiliate these centers through a solidarity network that not only seeks power on the national stage but also, and crucially for our planetary future, trespasses the borders dividing nation-states and forges transnational ties among workers.

If day labor supplies a synecdoche for precarity on the grand social scale, then analogues to the organizational forms that have invigorated day laborers' politicization likely can help ignite collective challenges to forces of precaritization on that level. The rationale for this organizational innovation can be further elaborated, however, through a series of more concrete considerations. First, through generalized cultures of popular education, worker centers for all would proliferate experiences of *conscientizaçao* as the awakening of critical consciousness in the context of ongoing and mounting political struggle by people subjected to social domination. *All* workers need such education. Working people in the knowledge and high-tech industries that are today's leading engines of capitalist growth may hold degrees from prestigious universities, but the vast majority have never faced the political-pedagogical incitements that popular education sets loose. This book shows that such workers *need* those prods, just as day laborers do, to understand more critically their own conditions of precarity and the problems they unexpectedly share with other working populations.

Second: worker centers for all would furnish continuous but flexible organizational contexts for negotiating interchanges between *demand*-politics and *dialogically* oriented popular education processes. Such demands, of course, would include those aiming to secure the ongoing material conditions for worker centers to thrive, as well as demands springing from the antiprecarity agenda outlined in the previous section. Yet not only would universal worker centers allow working people to formulate and organize on behalf of such demands— these facilities also would set demand-politics into a mutually critical and reciprocally strengthening relation with popular-educational dialogue. As I argued in chapter 1, in ways inspired by Kathi Weeks and Paulo Freire, dialogue and demand represent different subject-constituting processes, each of which involves distinctive components of affective animation and circulation, on the one hand, and the prompting of critical-reflective thought, on the other hand. Likewise, each mode of action fosters dispositions of generous receptivity along with temperaments of militant resolve. With worker centers for all, vital organizational fields would open up for workers from all reaches of society to engage in this dynamically open-ended dialectic of practices.

Third, worker centers for all would enable associational and political activity tuned to the indispensable task of reconstituting the flows, fluctuations, and ruptures of *time* in our precaritized worlds of work, in all the ways highlighted by critical-popular reflection on day laborers' themes regarding their politics of conviviality. In this respect, the demand for worker centers for everyone complements the other major proposal for a politics of time that has been gaining attention in left and progressive circles: the demand for a universal basic income. As Weeks argues, demanding a basic income not only expresses the utopian desire to transcend the work society and claim freedom as "time for what we will."[18] It also has an expanding material basis in the growing disconnects between wages and income, and between compensated time and work time.[19] Even so, this demand can only emerge as a genuine political force if it is grounded in concrete organizing efforts.[20] Founding worker centers for all would complement Weeks's vision for the universal distribution of the money needed for people to temporalize their activities for themselves rather than having these time formations straitjacketed by work imperatives and related family norms. People need these fungible assets, but they also need organizational frameworks in which to imagine and realize new forms of freedom that lead beyond the work society and past precarity.

Fourth, through a universal network of worker centers, working people could unfurl further trajectories of an antiprecarity politics about which this book has mostly just speculated because of its focus on men and their gendered themes. Day labor organizations have recently planted signposts to guide more gender-critical and differently gendered responses to precaritization. Of model significance in this regard has been Casa Latina's full-bored development of its women's program. As discussed in the last chapter, along with a hiring operation for domestic workers, the program includes a women's leadership group linked to the National Domestic Workers Alliance and a vigorous worker-volunteer component.[21] Meanwhile, at the 2017 national assembly, NDLON took the unprecedented step of equalizing representation for women on its governing board. In addition, around the same time NDLON stepped up its militant opposition to the deportation regime, it initiated a vibrant publicity campaign to support LGBTQ rights and to recognize nonstraight individuals as fellow workers and targets of *la migra*, often in particularly humiliating and brutal ways.[22] In 2016, Casa Latina also hired as its new executive director Marcos Martinez, who had directed the main Latinx LGBTQ organization in Seattle, Entre Hermanos. Thus, the day labor movement has been moving toward a more broadly cast antiprecarity politics that responds to the experiences and ideas of women and nonstraight workers and that questions the family norms that historically have been deeply entangled with capitalist cultures of work.[23] Mustering a fight for time that incorporates a full-fledged struggle to transform precarity's gendered structures, in turn, would comprise a sine qua non for a universal network of worker centers. Such a network would enable the pursuit of a refusal of work capacious enough to subject *all* forms of work—whether paid or unpaid, productive or reproductive (or both), performed in households or in more public spaces, done mainly by women or more by men—to critical scrutiny and repudiation in their present forms.[24]

Fifth, with worker centers for all, the organizational milieu would exist for cultivating the *political-intellectual* exertions the fight for time needs, in the sense of continually generative, situationally rooted, self-reflexive, and fully participatory programs of critical-popular research. A worker center movement that extends its scope over the working population at large needs inquiries that follow out the linkages and divergences between particular groups' themes and self-consciously theoretical accounts of structural power-dynamics. Politically active solidarities among very different worker collectivities require the sharp-eyed recognition and subtle negotiation of moments when exceptionalizing forms of precarity dominate workers' experiences and concerns, fostering tensions with efforts to address commonly shared predicaments. Conversely, a lively critical-popular culture in the centers would encourage participants to stay mindful of widely shared social dilemmas during periods when pressures of exceptionalization become overwhelming. Such a culture, furthermore, would enable engagement in two intensifications of popular education mentioned briefly in chapter 1 but not pursued in this book: routine re-evaluation of critical-popular research processes and the popular-educational programs in which they are embedded (in other words, metatheoretical reflection aimed at revising investigative and pedagogical methods); and participatory action research that involves ordinary workers as the researchers and analysts from the inception of research projects through their culmination.

It could be argued with some validity that this notion of worker centers for all exceeds the bounds of what should properly be called a demand, in the sense specified by Weeks and discussed in the first chapter. Distributing income in the abstract form of unconditional cash payments is one thing; it is potentially quite another to engage in the planning that a network of worker centers might require, such as determining locations for worker centers, equipping them with concrete facilities, and defining expectations for how they must function to merit support. In this sense, the vision seems to lack the simplicity and singular focus that Weeks associates with viable demands. This is not the same as merely saying the demand is "unrealistic"—it *is* unrealistic, and that is partly the point. One mission of a utopian demand, as Weeks contends, is to enact a significant break with the status quo even as it draws on continuities with what exists—"to think the relationship between present and future both as tendency and as rupture."[25] It is not realistic to think that cities in perpetual financial crisis because of urban austerity, which at the time of this book's writing had become even bleaker because of Republican budget cuts and tax reform (abetted by the bipartisan commitment to gargantuan military spending), would eagerly or even possibly fund worker centers for all. It is just as unrealistic to demand a universal basic income in the current political climate, and yet this, too, is vitally needed to reclaim the people's time from the powers that precaritize. Furthermore, there may well be ways to streamline the vision of worker centers for all that consolidate it more neatly as a demand. For instance, just as the basic income could be paid without conditions for the money's use, as Weeks advocates, so likewise, worker center space and operating funds could be provided without restrictions or requirements regarding the kinds of activities undertaken beyond the sorts of minimal rules that govern other open public facilities such as parks and playgrounds.

Perhaps the more cogent objection to what I am proposing is that the demand appears to overlook the densely community-rooted character of day labor centers and other actually existing worker centers today, and thus to prescribe an innovation that is dubiously artificial. As scholars who study worker centers commonly note, and as was the case with both Casa Latina and Voz's MLK Center, worker centers typically have sprung up within tangible communities of marginalized workers, especially migrant communities. They draw on deep wells of local resources that include patterns of trust, relational habits, shared perspectives on valid needs and the meaning of justice, common historical sensibilities, linguistic commonality, and various material capacities. Yet the worker centers that occupy center stage in this book also rely significantly on public funding, as do most worker centers, and this means that a sense that such organizations serve important *public purposes* already exists among urban leaders and residents. Moreover, the making available to all workers of space and time for worker center activities need not, and should not, come with strings attached that specify standard operating procedures, which inevitably would devalue prodigious capacities and meaningful particularities in working-class communities of color. There would be daunting challenges involved in finding ways for particular communities of workers to make publicly available worker centers their own *and* to have centers remain open enough to supply organizational connective tissue within the larger population of working people. Given the mounting desperation of these precarious times, however, it is well past time to face challenges like these.

Here, a parting reminder is in order about the very real prospects for radically transformative forms of sociality to emerge from within and by virtue of circumstances that are ruled and rent by the contradictions of precarity—when workers' organizations provide animated contexts for people to call forth these innovations. Just like the individual workers who nested their conceptions of politicized, mutualist, convivial community life within ongoing but pliable attachments to work, security, and rule-bound unity, day labor organizations have pursued visionary and militant projects even as they have struggled to make day labor jobs more generously paid, more reliably compensated, more plentiful, and more stable components of local urban economies. Working with "marketing specialists," NDLON has developed "branding" strategies for its affiliated worker centers that standardize color palettes, messages, and logos—even while laying bodies on the line in front of ICE vehicles.[26] Casa Latina has come to function more "professionally" and more like a "business"—just as it has fostered political and critical practices that fundamentally question these values and defy the deportation regime. As discussed in chapter 5, in the interim between our interviews and this book's completion, Casa Latina developed a robust and savvy fundraising operation, moved into bright new permanent buildings, tightened membership requirements, and streamlined operations—while also inaugurating the day labor network's most advanced OSH trainings, activating a stand-out women's leadership initiative, and, beginning in 2017, coordinating a local rapid-response and resistance effort as Seattle braced for stepped-up ICE raids under Trump.

Pursuing a demand for worker centers for all analogously requires mingling militancy with the patiently dwelling elicitation of transformative possibilities from the murky detritus in neoliberalism's waste waters. The key is to recognize that virtually all working people are caught up in swiftly moving currents and mired in brackish pools of time, as it flows and festers in today's landscapes of precarity. As critically illuminating and politically generative figures of precarity, day laborers reveal to other workers who live very different lives the contorted shapes of the latter's own suffering as well as the dim outlines of community forms where affliction gets transmuted into power. Out of time, on the move, and on their own, day laborers are taking the time, making the moves, and banding together to fight back. In a world saturated by risk and deformed by risk's warring temporalities, they risk devoting time to desist from the all-pervasive imperative of work, to spread conviviality, and to organize. These workers thereby both bravely multiply the risks they endure and orient such risk assumption toward precarity's transformation. In negative terms, they risk aggravated poverty, uncomfortable feelings of moral irresponsibility, the unmooring of fixed identities, and the loss of freedom as captives in ICE jails. In positive terms, they risk attachment to one another and the hope for political futurity. What might other working people be willing to risk, were they to find in day laborers' struggles a fight of their own?

Notes

INTRODUCTION

1. Dean, "Communicative Capitalism."
2. Berardi, *Soul at Work*, 86–90.
3. Neilson, "Five Theses," 332.
4. Benjamin, *Illuminations*, 253–64; *Reflections*, 61–94.
5. Yardley, "Report on Deadly Factory Collapse."
6. Greenhouse, "Some Retailers Rethink Role"; Agence France-Presse, "Bangladesh Packaging Factory Fire."
7. McVeigh, "Cambodian Female Workers."
8. Merchant, "Life and Death in Apple's Forbidden City."
9. Charles, "EPA Announces New Rules"; Padilla and Bacon, "Protect Female Farmworkers"; Hoang, "Lawsuit Seeks to Extend Overtime Pay"; NBC, "Cow Palace Settles"; Grabel, "Cut to the Bone."
10. Berlant, *Cruel Optimism*, 19.
11. Kantor and Streitfeld, "Inside Amazon."
12. Scheiber, "How Uber Uses Psychological Tricks."
13. Heller, "Gig Is Up."
14. Petroff, "U.S. Workers Face Higher Risk"; Bowcott, "Rise of Robotics."
15. As chapter 3 discusses, Lauren Berlant calls this tendency "aspirational normativity," according to which the popular fantasy of achieving upward mobility and stable family relationships is displaced by the attenuated wish for mere "approximations of the normative good life" and the effort to gain compensatory pleasure from simply fantasizing about this not-quite-good life (*Cruel Optimism*, 166).
16. Gorz, *Critique of Economic Reason*, 196.
17. Gorz, *Critique of Economic Reason*, 65–67, 196.

18. On the major institutional and ideological components of the "work society," in an analysis that focuses on South Africa but yields a more general theory of this social formation, see Barchiesi, *Precarious Liberation*.

19. Gorz only considers these issues regarding women's domestic labor to a limited extent, as Nichole Marie Shippen shows in her sympathetically critical account of Gorz, which informs her own theorization of precarious work-time (*Decolonizing Time*, 139–56).

20. Harvey, *Ways of the World*, 116.

21. Harvey, *Ways of the World*, 120.

22. Berardi, *Soul at Work*, 89–90.

23. Weeks, *Problem with Work*, 38, 69–75.

24. Weeks, *Problem with Work*, 70.

25. Marazzi, *Violence of Financial Capitalism*.

26. Burawoy, *Manufacturing Consent*.

27. Apostolidis, *Breaks in the Chain*, 111–60.

28. Hondagneu-Sotelo, *Doméstica*; Parreñas and Silvey, "Precarity of Migrant Domestic Work."

29. Apostolidis, *Breaks in the Chain*, 85–86.

30. Dean, "Communicative Capitalism," 6.

31. Dean, "Communicative Capitalism," 6–7.

32. Dean, "Communicative Capitalism," 6–7.

33. For Dean, the "competition, division and inequality" that permeate the "social field" of networked identity construction further aggravate this segregation of one from others, and from all ("Communicative Capitalism," 7–8).

34. Brown, *Undoing the Demos*, 84.

35. Brown, *Undoing the Demos*, 32–35, 84.

36. Lazzarato, *Making of the Indebted Man*, 9, 38–42.

37. "Global Migration Trends Factsheet," International Organization for Migration, http://gmdac.iom.int/global-migration-trends-factsheet.

38. International Organization for Migration, "Global Migration Trends," 5.

39. International Organization for Migration, "Global Migration Trends," 7.

40. International Organization for Migration, "Global Migration Trends," 7.

41. International Organization for Migration, "Global Migration Trends," 8.

42. Dehghan, "At Least 55 People."

43. ILO News, "Informally Employed Syrian Refugees."

44. ILO News, "Informally Employed Syrian Refugees."

45. ILO News, "Informally Employed Syrian Refugees."

46. Hernández-León, "Conceptualizing the Migration Industry."

47. Berlant, *Cruel Optimism*, 172.

48. Wacjman, *Pressed for Time*, 57.

49. Kalyvas, "An Anomaly?," 356.

50. Kalyvas, "An Anomaly?," 357–58.
51. Ouziel, "Vamos Lentos."
52. Regarding these demonstrations, see LaVaque-Manty, "Finding Theoretical Concepts," 106–9; Standing, *The Precariat*, 1–4.
53. Dean, *Crowds and Party*, 28–29.
54. Hardt and Negri, *Assembly*, 8–14.
55. Aslam, *Ordinary Democracy*, 8.
56. Aslam, *Ordinary Democracy*, 9.
57. Coles, *Visionary Pragmatism*, 49, 122–23.
58. Guy Standing unfortunately avoids crucial questions of organization in his writings on "the precariat" and the social and political reforms that would counter precarity. Nevertheless, his provocative and widely read discussion of precaritization has its virtues. Standing recognizes the manifold forms of precarity faced by varied mass-scale populations even as he acknowledges migrants' special place within the ranks of the precaritized. As in my analysis, moreover, he attributes a defining significance to temporal matters in the constitution of precarity. See Standing, *The Precariat; A Precariat Charter*.
59. "sojourn, *v.*," Oxford English Dictionary.
60. "sojourn, *n.*," Oxford English Dictionary.
61. Apostolidis, *Breaks in the Chain*.
62. Fine, "Worker Centers," 47.
63. Fine notes that from 2006 to 2011, "worker centers and their networks . . . significantly evolved and matured, institutionalizing themselves and substantially expanding their strategic capacities" ("Worker Centers," 46).
64. See Apostolidis and Valenzuela, "Cosmopolitan Politics"; Abrams, "Contentious Citizenship."
65. Coles, *Visionary Pragmatism*, 1–20.
66. Rocco, *Transforming Citizenship*.
67. Gonzales, *Reform without Justice*. Gonzales borrows the concept of the homeland security state from Nicholas De Genova, who proposes this notion to denote a modification of the Cold War–origin US "national security state" in the aftermath of the 9/11 attacks. For De Genova, the concept signals the historically unprecedented focusing of security concerns on migrants and the normalization of "indefinite" migrant detention with no pretense of due process as a primary mode of state action ("Production of Culprits," 425). Gonzales develops this conception further and more deeply politicizes it by exploring the growth of a multifaceted cultural apparatus that endows antimigrant policies and ideologies with not only state authority but also broad social hegemony, in the Gramscian sense of eliciting mass consent through the normal operations of dominant cultural institutions.
68. I am grateful to Lia Haro for our conversations regarding the relation of my work to ethnography, which inform my comments here.

69. Forrest, "Engaging and Disrupting Power"; Kang, "What the Documents Can't Tell You"; Majic, "Participating, Observing, Publishing"; Schwartz-Shea and Majic, "Ethnography and Participant Observation."

70. Tully, *Public Philosophy*, 3.

71. Tully understands a "citizen" to be anyone who is implicated in a "relationship of governance" (*Public Philosophy*, 3).

72. Although Tully's work focuses more than mine on intersections between historical theoretical trajectories and state institutional designs, readers may discern affinities between my recrafting of conceptions of precarity in conversation with day laborers and his interrogation of liberal notions of democratic constitutionalism in dialogue with indigenous cultures. See also Tully, *Strange Multiplicity*.

73. We conducted twenty-seven interviews at Casa Latina and fifty-one interviews at the MLK Center.

74. Casa Latina had a formal process for evaluating research proposals, which the organization had developed after prior engagements with researchers had sometimes yielded little of value to the center. At the time I submitted my plan for research, Casa Latina was approving roughly one-quarter of such proposals. The process of developing a research agenda was more ad hoc with Voz, but in both cases, this happened through a series of meetings and emails to propose and revise an initial plan, including general topics and specific interview questions. We also jointly developed procedures for recruiting participants by lottery at each center and determined that we would pay each worker twenty dollars for an hour to ninety minutes of conversation with us.

75. We also conducted the interview in whatever language the participant preferred. In the great majority of cases, this was Spanish, but some interviews were done either in English or in a mix of English and Spanish.

76. Garelli and Tazzioli, "Challenging the Discipline," 245–46.

77. Garelli and Tazzioli, "Challenging the Discipline," 246.

78. Choudry, *Learning Activism*, 1.

79. Doussard, *Degraded Work*, 164–67.

80. See Doussard, *Degraded Work*, 159–67.

81. Valenzuela et al., "On the Corner." Day labor wages can vary significantly by location. A more recent study of Tucson day laborers found substantially lower earnings among these workers, who averaged only $400 per month and among whom over 80 percent were homeless (Trautner, "What Workers Want," 325–26). By contrast, although workers at Casa Latina were earning just ten dollars per hour in 2008 when we did field research there, they subsequently increased their wage rates and by 2016 were earning nineteen to twenty-two dollars per hour, depending on the type of job.

82. Valenzuela et al., "On the Corner"; "Employment Projections," US Department of Labor, Bureau of Labor Statistics, https://www.bls.gov/emp/ep_table_201.htm.

83. Valenzuela et al., "On the Corner." This study also found that 80 percent of day laborers sought jobs through informal hiring sites, mostly in or near residential neighborhoods, and that day laborers were concentrated in the western and eastern regions (40 percent and 23 percent, respectively), with a sizable contingent (18 percent) in the Southwest and smaller numbers in the South and Midwest.

84. Trautner, "What Workers Want."

85. Pablo Alvarado, interview on *Democracy Now!*, April 10, 2014.

86. Fine, *Worker Centers*, 81, 88–89, 100–19, 157–79; Cummings, "Litigation at Work"; Apostolidis and Valenzuela, "Cosmopolitan Politics"; Theodore, "Ballad of Industry."

87. Bloom, "Ally to Win"; Stuart, "From the Shop to the Streets"; Milkman, *L.A. Story*, 114–86; Milkman, "Immigrant Workers."

88. "About Us," National Domestic Workers Alliance, https://www.domesticworkers.org/about-us. See also Parreñas and Silvey, "Precarity of Domestic Workers."

89. Shah and Seville, "Domestic Worker Organizing," 443–45.

90. De Lara et al., "Organizing Temporary, Subcontracted, and Immigrant Workers." Migrant workers have also made noteworthy organizational innovations through the New York–based Taxi Drivers Alliance and Restaurant Opportunities Center (Fine, "Worker Centers," 48–49). Like day laborers and domestic workers, furthermore, taxi drivers in the Alliance have formed a national network of organizations (Fine, "How Innovative Worker Centers Help").

91. Fine, "Worker Centers," 46.

92. According to Fine: "Most centers focus their work geographically, operating in a particular metropolitan area, city, or neighborhood" (*Worker Centers*, 13).

93. Eric Rodriguez, interview by author, November 8, 2013, Chicago, IL.

94. Kwon, "Koreatown Immigrant Workers' Alliance"; Ghandnoosh, "Organizing Workers."

95. Apostolidis and Valenzuela, "Cosmopolitan Politics."

96. Fine, *Worker Centers*, 13. Although not exclusively for migrants, the "vast majority" of worker centers mainly serve migrant populations, and many, including the major centers in Seattle, Los Angeles, and Long Island, had origins in 1990s efforts to shield migrant workers from federal immigration raids (Fine, *Worker Centers*, 112–13).

97. Fine, "Worker Centers," 51; Goldberg and Jackson, "Excluded Workers Congress." Fine notes that even though most worker centers concentrate on workers in specific areas of the labor market (e.g., day labor or restaurant work), these organizations also invariably set their sights beyond industry-specific organizing, and they commonly seek political transformations and structural economic changes that include but go beyond securing legal protection for workers' rights ("Worker Centers," 52–53; see also Cordero-Guzmán et al., "The Development of Sectoral Worker Center Networks").

98. Paret, "Precarious Labor Politics," 767.
99. Paret, "Precarious Labor Politics," 768; Fine, "Worker Centers," 49.
100. Narro et al., "Building a Movement Together." For more extensive accounts of day labor centers' and other worker centers' historical relations with unions, see Fine, *Worker Centers*, 120–56; Fine, "A Marriage Made in Heaven?"; Fine, "Building a Future Together"; Fine, "Worker Centers"; Fine and Gordon, "Strengthening Labor Standards Enforcement"; Milkman, "Immigrant Workers"; Theodore, "Realigning Labor"; Avendaño and Hiatt, "Worker Self-Organization"; Apostolidis and Valenzuela, "Cosmopolitan Politics," 238–40. The increasing cooperation between unions and worker centers notwithstanding, obstacles to such coordination exist. Fine notes: "There is a dramatic culture clash between many unions and worker centers. Worker centers experience many local unions as top-down, undemocratic, and disconnected from the community; unions view many worker centers as undisciplined and unrealistic about what it takes to win" (*Worker Centers*, 124). Such cultural friction exacerbates structural barriers to joint action stemming from competition over jobs in overlapping labor markets, especially construction, and many unions' historical patterns of racism and nativism. Nonetheless, as Fine and others document, the tendencies toward ever-greater mutual support between unions and worker centers have been marked and encouraging since the turn of the millennium. At the time of our interviews and other fieldwork at Casa Latina in 2008, for instance, the organization was experimenting with a program to encourage day laborers to seek membership in a local laborers' union, in the context of a broader partnership negotiated that year by NDLON with the Laborers International Union of North America (Fine, "Worker Centers," 49–50). On Casa Latina's successful navigation of conflict with local construction unions, see Avendaño and Hiatt, "Worker Self-Organization," 91.

CHAPTER 1

1. Dziembowska, "NDLON and the History," 28–29; Theodore, "Generative Work," 2040–43.
2. Freire, *Education for Critical Consciousness*, 15.
3. Weeks, *Problem with Work*, 128–36, 175–225.
4. Freire, *Pedagogy of the Oppressed*, 48.
5. Freire, *Education for Critical Consciousness*, 15.
6. Freire, *Pedagogy of the Oppressed*, 49.
7. Freire, *Pedagogy of the Oppressed*, 54.
8. Freire, *Pedagogy of the Oppressed*, 62–65.
9. Freire, *Pedagogy of the Oppressed*, 46–47, 81.
10. Freire, *Pedagogy of the Oppressed*, 82–83.
11. Freire, *Pedagogy of the Oppressed*, 88.

12. On the concept of narrativity, see White, *Content of Form*; Disch, "Impartiality, Storytelling."
13. Disch, "Impartiality, Storytelling."
14. See Apostolidis, *Breaks in the Chain*.
15. Berardi, *Soul at Work*, 88–90.
16. Dean, "Communicative Capitalism," 6–8.
17. Ross, "In Search of the Lost Paycheck," 28–30.
18. See Hondagneu-Sotelo, *Doméstica*.
19. See Adorno, "Cultural Criticism and Society"; Apostolidis, *Stations of the Cross*.
20. See Marazzi, *Violence of Financial Capitalism*; Lazzarato, *Making of the Indebted Man*.
21. My argument for focusing on generative themes rather than narratives relies on an understanding of the politics of narrative that differs sharply from Freire's take on narrative. Freire typically condemns the narrative mode of expression *tout court* as the characteristic tool of traditional education that treats students as passive receptacles for the teacher's supposedly expert knowledge. In "narrative education," Freire writes, there is "a narrating subject (the teacher) and patient, listening objects (the students). . . . [The educator's] task is to 'fill' the students with the contents of his narration—contents which are detached from reality, disconnected from the totality that engendered them" (*Pedagogy of the Oppressed*, 71). As I discuss in this chapter's section on "theme and theory," however, other passages in Freire's texts suggest a more nuanced understanding of narrative's potential place in the political-pedagogical relationship, which is more in tune with my own critical-popular approach.
22. Freire, *Education for Critical Consciousness*, 44.
23. Freire, *Education for Critical Consciousness*, 140.
24. Freire, *Education for Critical Consciousness*, 132–33.
25. Freire, *Education for Critical Consciousness*, 43.
26. Freire, *Politics of Education*, 32.
27. Theodore, "Generative Work."
28. Freire, *Education for Critical Consciousness*, 43.
29. Freire, *Politics of Education*, 13.
30. Freire, *Politics of Education*, 56.
31. Freire, *Education for Critical Consciousness*, 38.
32. Freire, *Education for Critical Consciousness*, 43.
33. Freire, *Education for Critical Consciousness*, 4–5.
34. Freire and Faundez, *Learning to Question*, 52.
35. See Lewis, "Teaching with Pensive Images." Cath Lambert is closer to the mark when she compares Freire to Jacques Rancière and notes that the following principles characterize both theorists' conceptions of radical pedagogy: "To assert that all intelligences are equal, that all have equal rights and capacities to see, hear, feel,

to speak and to be heard, presents a re/distribution of the sensory organization of society and a concomitant re/configuration of time and space. This attention to the sensory is what places aesthetics at the core of politics and offers generative resources for addressing educational concerns" ("Redistributing the Sensory," 215). Darren Webb confirms: "Freire refuses to recognise a separation between the cognitive and affective domains of human existence" ("Paulo Freire," 328–29).

36. Freire, *Politics of Education*, 61–62.

37. Theodore, "Generative Work," 2042.

38. Freire, *Education for Critical Consciousness*, 41–44.

39. Freire, *Education for Critical Consciousness*, 44.

40. Freire, *Education for Critical Consciousness*, 45–46.

41. Freire, *Education for Critical Consciousness*, 44.

42. Freire, *Politics of Education*, 60.

43. Freire, *Politics of Education*, 141.

44. Freire, *Politics of Education*, 141.

45. See Freire, *Pedagogy of the Oppressed*, 71–72.

46. Freire, *Politics of Education*, 61–62.

47. Freire explicitly aspires for popular education to yield some version of "theory," in a sense that implies a close relation to "research." Popular educational practices, he asserts, become "theoretical" by maintaining a "bent toward substantiation, toward invention, toward research"; by "substantiation," Freire means "intervention in reality, the analytical contact with existence which enables one to substantiate and to experience that existence fully and completely" (*Politics of Education*, 33). Here, Freire again invokes the principle of intellectual egalitarianism: just as all people can do "research," so likewise all are capable of producing "theory."

48. Freire, *Politics of Education*, 52. Similarly, Freire declares elsewhere: "When people lack a critical understanding of their reality, apprehending it in fragments which they do not perceive as interacting constituent elements of the whole, they cannot truly know that reality. To truly know it . . . they would need to have a total vision" (*Pedagogy of the Oppressed*, 104).

49. Freire seems to presuppose a fundamentally human inclination and capacity to perceive phenomena as totalized wholes. Through dialogue, he contends, popular-education participants conceptualize the historical features of the social whole into which codified images fit. Yet Freire pinpoints a wordless instant before dialogue begins in which the basic orientation toward thinking in terms of wholes comes alive for each individual participant. He writes that the "moment in time which precedes" the verbal analysis of a codification is "the moment when the consciousness directed towards the codification apprehends it as a whole. In general it is in a person's silence that this occurs" (Freire, *Education for Critical Consciousness*, 142). Freire's reference to "silence" is telling: he seems to be uncritically naturalizing the effort to conceptualize totalities as a fundamental human faculty or desire, rather

than acknowledging how such thinking results from historically specific, normative practices.

50. Freire, *Pedagogy of the Oppressed*, 102n.

51. Freire, *Education for Critical Consciousness*, 140.

52. I spent approximately eighty hours over sixteen months doing this dispatch work in 2016–17.

53. Apart from the NDLON assembly events, these additional activities added about thirty-five hours to my total participant observation time with Casa Latina.

54. Schoenfelder did this work by volunteering several days a week over two months in 2008, totaling approximately ninety hours of participant observation. Thus, her work in this regard crucially informed our design and conduct of the interviews that year; my own regular volunteering and participant observation with Casa Latina, in turn, mostly occurred during the final two years of this book project and furnished essential practical touchstones for the most intensive phases of writing and analysis.

55. I spent about thirty-three hours doing these activities over two months in 2010; my assistant contributed about fifty-four hours of such work, over one month in 2010. We performed the MLK Center interviews during that same time-period.

56. Coordinating *Jornaleros* screenings in 2014 and 2017 represented about twenty hours of additional time working with leaders and workers from Voz's MLK Center.

57. Here, also, is another respect in which this project performs immanent critique: by adopting a theoretical archive that is intentionally discontinuous, I aim to make the analysis as a whole more responsive to transformative impulses in the jagged-edged fragments of ruptured social experience in our precaritized times. Within the distinct slices of social life highlighted by different theorists, day laborers' situations and those of other social groups are likely to converge and diverge in varying ways. Under prevalent social conditions, an immanent approach to reconceptualizing precaritization thus involves initially abandoning ourselves to this multiplicity and then drawing fragmentary analyses loosely and provisionally together.

58. Freire also notes that the process of research into potential generative themes should be reiterative, with new stages periodically being undertaken in response to the outcomes of dialogues regarding whatever themes and codifications are initially explored: "The 'research groups' are prolonged into 'cultural discussion groups.' These in turn require new educational contents of different standards which demand further thematic research" (*Education and Critical Consciousness*, 140). In principle, therefore, dialogical sessions on the themes furnished by this study should also provoke new rounds of exploratory research aimed at bringing additional themes to light. For example, it is almost certain that dialogue on the themes drawn from our interviews, which involved an almost exclusively male population of workers, would provoke calls for new investigations of themes voiced by women

in these migrant communities, especially the domestic workers who now have a strong contingent at Casa Latina.

59. Freire, *Pedagogy of the Oppressed*, 48, 65, 66.
60. Weeks, *Problem with Work*, 103.
61. Weeks, *Problem with Work*, 121.
62. Weeks, *Problem with Work*, 131.
63. Weeks, *Problem with Work*, 131–32.
64. Weeks, *Problem with Work*, 131–32.
65. Weeks, *Problem with Work*, 132–33.
66. Weeks, *Problem with Work*, 134.
67. Weeks, *Problem with Work*, 149.
68. Weeks, *Problem with Work*, 219.
69. Weeks, *Problem with Work*, 131.
70. Weeks speculates that those who wage demand-politics might find it useful to construct "broader political visions" by connecting "points of common interest" among "different constituencies," ultimately producing "an assemblage of political desires and imaginaries out of which alternatives might be constructed" (*Problem with Work*, 224). Yet although Weeks notes the possible value of combining focused critical views into larger figures of social critique, she provides no account of the processes by which this would happen.
71. The disposition needed in Freirean dialogical endeavors is akin to the intellectual-affective orientation that Romand Coles describes as "receptive generosity" (see *Beyond Gated Politics*). I thank Coles for encouraging me to explore potential tensions between demand-politics militancy and the receptive affects on which popular-educational dialogue depends.
72. Furthermore, although it might seem that taking a militant political stance would dampen participants' "experimental curiosity" (Coles, correspondence with author, December 6, 2014), the experience of demand-politics also might kindle certain kinds of experimentally inquisitive thinking rather than tamping it down (e.g., "We are actually sticking together for this little local demonstration—maybe we should aim for a grander stage next time").
73. Freire uses theologically laden language to write about how those who are not the oppressed but nevertheless seek to join with them would make this commitment: "This conversion is so radical as not to allow of ambiguous behavior. . . . Conversion to the people requires a profound rebirth. Those who undergo it must take on a new form of existence; they can no longer remain as they were" (*Pedagogy of the Oppressed*, 61). Correspondingly, Freire urges the oppressed to enact a similarly momentous self-consolidation and break from their oppressors by "ejecting the oppressor within" (*Pedagogy of the Oppressed*, 48).
74. For a trenchant critique of this antiutopian tendency among radical thinkers since the 1960s, see Bosteels, *Marx and Freud*. Citing Bourdieu and pointing to Margaret

Thatcher's illustrative and infamous quip that "there is no alternative" to the Right's "free market" program, Weeks also discerns a "neoliberal anti-utopianism" defined by "a new kind of economic fatalism 'that wants us to believe the world cannot be any different from the way it is'" (*Problem with Work*, 180). Freire, especially in later writings, similarly warns that neoliberal conditions conspire to extinguish all provocations of utopian yearning (*Pedagogy of Hope*, 83).

75. Weeks, *Problem with Work*, 197.
76. Weeks, *Problem with Work*, 197, 202.
77. Freire, *Pedagogy of the Oppressed*, 85.
78. Freire, *Pedagogy of Hope*, 100.
79. Weeks, *Problem with Work*, 208.
80. Weeks, *Problem with Work*, 213, 215.
81. Weeks, *Problem with Work*, 220–21.

CHAPTER 2

1. Weeks, *Problem with Work*, 166.
2. Other researchers translate day laborers' term *la desesperación* as "despair"; Quesada et al. translate it this way, and also find a similar pairing of despair or desperation with a keen sense of personal responsibility among day laborers, as I do ("As Good as It Gets," 31–33). It is important to recognize the dimension of hopelessness the notion of *la desesperación* conveys, which the idea of despair more immediately connotes. Translating the term as "desperation," however, evokes more readily the constant counterbalancing of despondency among the workers in our study with expressions of hope for positive changes in their circumstances, including simply participating in the lottery as well as their extensive comments about individual responsibility that I discuss later in this chapter.
3. The atmosphere for the job lottery changed somewhat at Casa Latina after the opening of new buildings in 2011, at which point the process moved entirely indoors.
4. Jorge Medina, interview by Ariel Ruiz, Portland, OR, June 2010 (all further quotations from and comments on Medina refer to this interview). The term *el azar* that Medina used can mean "chance," but it can also mean "fate," which implies that an inscrutable necessity drives a process that individual is powerless to influence.
5. Fernando Sánchez, interview by author, Seattle, WA, August 2008 (all further quotations from and comments on Sánchez refer to this interview). In a variation on such invocations of blind fate, workers sometimes ascribed control over their unpredictable fortunes in the lottery to the mysterious purposes of the Supreme Being. One day laborer at the MLK Center, who was talking animatedly with another worker about theological matters, expressed this by saying that when it came to whether or not a worker got a job: "Man proposes, but God disposes" (*Tú propones, pero Dios dispone*).

6. Alberto Guerrero, interview by author, Seattle, WA, August 2008.

7. Luís Pérez, interview by Ariel Ruiz, Portland, OR, June 2010. All further quotations from and comments on Pérez refer to this interview. Interview quotations are my English translations of workers' comments in Spanish, unless I indicate otherwise. Sometimes, workers shift between these languages in ways that affect what I take to be their meaning. I discuss these dynamics when this occurs, although such shifts do not always comprise significant code-switching, as with Pérez's remark.

8. Juan Carlos Garza, interview by Ariel Ruiz, Portland, OR, June 2010. All further quotations from and comments on Garza refer to this interview. We asked what kinds of work the workers preferred to do, and most either named such a wide range of jobs that there was little distinctive about the list or said plainly they were just willing to take whatever opportunities arose. Tellingly, one worker mentioned that he had a certain skill training but in the next breath said he had worked multiple jobs that had nothing to do with the trade he had mastered: "I am a bricklayer, and have been for almost all my life over there. I was in the military and I've worked as a police officer" (Eduardo Salazar, interview by Ariel Ruiz, Portland, OR, June 2010; all further quotations from and comments on Salazar refer to this interview).

9. Daniel Rodríguez, interview by Ariel Ruiz, Portland, OR, June 2010.

10. Between the time of our interviews and this book's final writing, Casa Latina took steps to classify workers by skill and to channel workers with particular abilities into appropriate jobs. Even so, day laborers rarely can limit themselves to one kind of work unless they have special skills at times when the job market places those qualifications in high demand. This occurred, for instance, for carpenters in Seattle in the summer of 2017 amid a construction boom.

11. We met individuals who had been bakers, flower sellers, hairstylists, secretaries, taxi drivers, security guards, waiters, and workers in countless other occupations, sometimes with licensing credentials (usually inapplicable in the United States), before migrating north. In the United States, day laborers had worked in an enormous range of occupations and places: picking fruit in Washington's orchards; washing dishes in Portland restaurants; processing salmon on ships off Alaska; sewing clothing in Los Angeles garment shops—and the list went on. Sometimes workers migrated according to a rough regularity that characterized seasonal jobs, but more commonly their peregrinations had little pattern.

12. Two telling measures of this tendency were that only seven of the twenty-seven individuals we interviewed at Casa Latina had attended the center for over two years, and the great majority had been associated with Casa Latina for less than a year.

13. Edgar Medina, interview by author, Portland, OR, June 2010. All further quotations from and comments on Medina refer to this interview.

14. Valenzuela et al., "On the Corner"; Theodore et al., "La Esquina."

15. Víctor Estrada, interview by Ariel Ruiz, Portland, OR, June 2010. Sometimes workers lost substantial sums because they had worked for a lengthy period of time,

even up to a week, trusting in vain that an employer would pay them at the end of these jobs, although extended hires were fairly rare.

16. Cristian Gutiérrez, interview by author, Seattle, WA, August 2008.

17. César Torres, interview by author, Seattle, WA, August 2008 (all further quotations from and comments on Torres refer to this interview); Aguilar, 2010. Likewise, Edgar Medina had been hired to "clean the stable" only to have the employer demand that he "break concrete."

18. In another incident, Eduardo Salazar had worked all day until ten o'clock at night, laying bricks by himself in the steady rain, only to have the contractor refuse to pay him until the owner inspected the job. This never happened, so Salazar never got paid.

19. Some workers also noted they typically took prudent measures individually to prevent wage theft: asking employers for names and contact information, writing down employers' license plate numbers, refusing to take checks, and asking an employer to take them to an ATM if the boss claimed to be out of cash.

20. The centers did not send workers out on jobs without getting contact information and license plate numbers from employers. The centers also recruited volunteer attorneys to help workers pursue wage claims, and workers mobilized direct action efforts through the centers aimed at publicly shaming employers who withheld pay, usually by picketing their houses.

21. Gabriela Moreno, for example, recalled working in a Los Angeles garment shop where her manager frequently neglected to write down her hours and shorted her paychecks accordingly (interview by Caitlin Schoenfelder, Seattle, WA, August 2008). Diana Ortiz had her wages stolen routinely while working in a chocolate factory, where she often worked overtime with no overtime pay (Diana Ortiz, interview by Caitlin Schoenfelder, Seattle, WA, August 2008. All further quotations from and comments on Ortiz refer to this interview). As noted earlier in this section, a number of interviewees had done meatpacking work, and my prior research revealed that for meatpacking workers, wage theft was discouragingly common. At the plant I studied, as in other meatpacking facilities, managers often either arbitrarily reduced the hours listed on employees' pay statements or pressured workers into working overtime and into their breaks without added compensation (see Apostolidis, *Breaks in the Chain*; Compa, *Blood, Sweat, and Fear*).

22. Diego Flores, interview by Ariel Ruiz, Portland, OR, June 2010. All further quotations from and comments on Flores refer to this interview.

23. Estéban Avila, interview by author, Seattle, WA, August 2008.

24. Ricardo Reyes, interview by Caitlin Schoenfelder, Seattle, WA, August 2008.

25. Javier Castillo, interview by Caitlin Schoenfelder, Seattle, WA, August 2008. All further quotations from and comments on J. Castillo refer to this interview.

26. Raúl Castillo, interview by Caitlin Schoenfelder, Seattle, WA, August 2008. All further quotations from and comments on R. Castillo refer to this interview.

27. Ernesto Durán, interview by author, Portland, OR, June 2010; all further quotations from and comments on Durán refer to this interview.

28. José Álvarez, interview by Ariel Ruiz, Portland, OR, June 2010.

29. In addition, workers who held relatively more continuous jobs, either while also pursuing day labor gigs or before turning to day labor, abruptly lost these jobs and entered indeterminate stretches of unemployment not only when they were detained or deported but also when employers bowed to federal pressures and began checking the validity of their employees' Social Security numbers.

30. As noted in this book's introduction, Voz's MLK Center did not operate any programs for women when we did our field research there and still had not initiated any such efforts by the time of this book's writing.

31. Diana Ortiz, interview by Caitlin Schoenfelder, Seattle, WA, August, 2008. All further quotations from and comments on Ortiz refer to this interview.

32. Wagner, "Migration und Gewalt gegen Frauen"; Reina et al., "Undocumented Latina Networks"; Sampaio, *Terrorizing Latina/o Immigrants*; Kim et al., "Somos Hermanas."

33. Roberto Fernández, interview by Ariel Ruiz, Portland, OR, June 2010.

34. Pedro Santiago, interview by Ariel Ruiz, Portland, OR, June 2010.

35. Héctor Molina, interview by Ariel Ruiz, Portland, OR, June 2010.

36. R. Castillo; Rafael Sandoval, interview by Caitlin Schoenfelder, Seattle, WA, August, 2008 (all further quotations from and comments on Sandoval refer to this interview); Emanuel Ramos, interview by Ariel Ruiz, Portland, OR, June 2010 (all further quotations from and comments on Ramos refer to this interview).

37. Antonio Soto, interview by author, Seattle, WA, August 2008. All further quotations from and comments on Soto refer to this interview.

38. Roberto Mendoza, interview by Ariel Ruiz, Portland, OR, June 2010. All further quotations from and comments on Mendoza refer to this interview.

39. Sean Garcia, interview by Ariel Ruiz, Portland, OR, June 2010. All further quotations from and comments on S. Garcia refer to this interview.

40. Alejandro Delgado, interview by Caitlin Schoenfelder, Seattle, WA, August, 2008. All further quotations from and comments on Delgado refer to this interview.

41. Arturo González, interview by author, Portland, OR, June 2010. All further quotations from and comments on González refer to this interview.

42. Edgar Medina manifested a similar sensibility, saying: "I put the most effort and the most determination into the job that I can, and I try to make them satisfied. . . . So that when I finish, they tell me, "You did a good job—[switching to English] Good job, [switching to Spanish] I feel satisfied, thank you very much." And they tell me, "I promised you this much money but here, you get this much [more] because I like the excellent work you did."

43. Other workers, such as Emanuel Ramos, suggested that they had sought to *echarle ganas* as a way of appealing to an employer's shared Mexican values of hard work

and personal integrity: "Yesterday I went to move things for a Mexican woman—we worked three hours and she gave us fifty dollars [each]. . . . The employer knows—if you don't give it your best [*si no le echas ganas*] they won't pay you as much. But if you give it your best and you do a nice job, they might even give you extra."

44. Akalin, "Affective Precarity," 422–23.

45. Akalin, "Affective Precarity," 421. See also Hondagneu-Sotelo, *Doméstica*, 68–69.

46. Hondagneu-Sotelo, *Doméstica*, 122–25.

47. Hondagneu-Sotelo, *Doméstica*, 30–37. Hondagneu-Sotelo's analysis further suggests that the specific form of desperation associated with live-in domestic work also involves physical hunger arising from the sense that taking breaks to eat would be improper, isolation from feeling the need to be "unobtrusive" in the employers' family domain, and workers having "no space and no time they can claim as their own" (*Doméstica*, 31–34).

48. As noted in the preceding chapter, the principles of popular education led us to ask workers not only to describe their difficulties but also to say why they thought those problems exist. The point was to address workers as critical intellectuals and thereby to recognize their abilities in this regard, as well as to help the centers motivate them to exercise those capacities more strenuously.

49. In the uncommonly sunny summer of 2017 in Seattle, for instance, Casa Latina emptied out daily and early in the morning, many jobs were scheduled well in advance, and the center often turned away employers who sought workers with special skills like carpentry or masonry. This was a drastic change from the rainy winter and early spring, when I often sat for hours by phones that stayed silent.

50. Oscar Morales, interview by Ariel Ruiz, Portland, OR, June 2010. All further quotations from and comments on Morales refer to this interview.

51. Enrique Jiménez, interview by author, Portland, OR, June 2010. All further quotations from and comments on Jiménez refer to this interview.

52. Freire, *Pedagogy of the Oppressed*, 62–63.

53. Harvey, *Limits to Capital*, 238.

54. Duménil and Lévy, *Crisis of Neoliberalism*, 150–51.

55. Duménil and Lévy, *Crisis of Neoliberalism*, 28, 63, 84–85, 167–69.

56. Duménil and Lévy, *Crisis of Neoliberalism*, 150–51, 178–80.

57. Harvey, *Limits to Capital*, 395.

58. Harvey elaborates: "Periodic episodes of localized growth have been interspersed with intense phases of localized creative destruction, usually registered as severe (and often socially devastating) financial crises in particular places at particular times" (*Cosmopolitanism and the Geographies of Freedom*, 65–66).

59. Harvey, *Limits to Capital*, 434.

60. Harvey, *Limits to Capital*, 438.

61. Duménil and Lévy, *Crisis of Neoliberalism*, 137–40.

62. For a critical elucidation of Marx's concept of abstract labor and a discussion of the advancing prevalence of such labor as capitalism matures, see Postone, *Time, Labor, and Social Domination*. Notwithstanding the ever-nearer approximation of day laborers' work to abstract labor in the classical Marxian sense, distinctive cultural relations still help shape day laborers' work experiences in ways the concept cannot capture, as a number of Marx's critics have argued (see especially Chakrabarty, *Rethinking Working-Class History*). Marc Doussard's account of the sociocultural relations among day laborers, contractors, and homeowners in Chicago probes this more complicated texture of workers' everyday lives and underlines the potentialities for resistance that such interactions can foster (*Degraded Work*).

63. De Genova, "Legal Production of Mexican/Migrant 'Illegality,'" 161.

64. See De Genova, "Deportation Regime."

65. Mezzadra and Neilson, *Border as Method*.

66. De Genova, "Production of Culprits."

67. On the extensive historical roots of this hegemonic trope regarding immigrants in US political culture and its legitimation of capitalist and state authority, see Honig, *Democracy and the Foreigner*; Behdad, *Forgetful Nation*; Ferguson, "Is It an Anarchist Act."

68. Weeks, *Problem with Work*, 46.

69. To some extent, Weeks is describing changes in business cultures and labor relations that Harvey identifies with the rise of the "flex-spec" ideology, in which "flexible specialization in labor processes" and "flexi-time arrangements" supposedly opened up a new world of self-determination, meaningful collaboration, and creative expression through work for employees. Harvey observes, however, that "all the benefits accruing from increasing flexibility in labor allocations in both space and time go to capital" rather than to workers themselves (Harvey, *Brief History of Neoliberalism*, 53).

70. Weeks, *Problem with Work*, 69–70.

71. Weeks, *Problem with Work*, 70.

72. Weeks, *Problem with Work*, 70.

73. Weeks, *Problem with Work*, 71.

74. Rosenblat et al., "Workplace Surveillance"; Goldstein, "To Increase Productivity"; Bernton and Kelleher, "Amazon Warehouse Jobs."

75. Weeks, *Problem with Work*, 72.

76. Weeks, *Problem with Work*, 142.

77. Weeks, *Problem with Work*, 50–51.

78. Bobo, *Wage Theft in America*.

79. Berardi writes: "The cognitariat is the semiotic labor flow, socially spread and fragmented, as seen from the standpoint of its social corporeality" (*Soul at Work*, 105).

80. Ross, "In Search of the Lost Paycheck," 20.

81. Ross, "In Search of the Lost Paycheck," 20.
82. Berardi, *Soul at Work*, 90.
83. Berardi, *Soul at Work*, 183.
84. Berardi, *Soul at Work*, 100–102.
85. Duménil and Lévy, *Crisis of Neoliberalism*, 150–51, 168–70.
86. Duménil and Lévy, *Crisis of Neoliberalism*, 104–12.
87. Berardi, *Uprising*, 114.
88. Berardi, *Uprising*, 147, 158–59.
89. Berardi, *Uprising*, 127.
90. Martel, "Division Is Common," 701, 704.

CHAPTER 3

1. Two National Day Labor Organizing Network (NDLON) staff members whom I interviewed confirmed that for this reason, and because centers have limited outreach capacities, there always would be "a parallel corner" in neighborhoods where a worker center is situated, along with corners in other city localities (Omar Henríquez and Nadia Marín, interview by author, Hempstead, NY, March 24, 2015; further quoted comments by or references to Henríquez or Marin in this chapter refer to this interview). See also Fine, *Worker Centers*, 114.
2. See my discussion of these matters in chapter 6. Chicago's Latino Union, for instance, allows day laborers on the corners to vote in worker center elections.
3. José Ruiz, interview by author, Portland, OR, June 2010. All further quoted comments by or references to Ruiz in this chapter refer to this interview.
4. Juan Carlos Garza, interview by author, Portland, OR, June 2010. All further quoted comments by or references to Garza in this chapter refer to this interview.
5. Israel Campos, interview by author, Portland, OR, June 2010. All further quoted comments by or references to Campos in this chapter refer to this interview.
6. Pablo Maldonado, interview by author, Portland, OR, June 2010.
7. Mario Valdez, interview by author, Portland, OR, June 2010.
8. In another study, a Bay Area day laborer described the bodily consequences of standing on the corner for long hours of the day in more graphic and specific terms: "We get lower-back pain, body aches, pain in the shins from standing all day"; for this worker, getting a job was a relief because it meant that he would "get to move" (quoted in Quesada et al., "As Good as It Gets," 41).
9. Steven Chung, interview by author, Portland, OR, June 2010.
10. Pablo Villa, interview by author, Portland, OR, June 2010.
11. Juan Ayala, interview by author, Portland, OR, June 2010.
12. Isaac Ramírez, interview by author, Portland, OR, June 2010. All further quoted comments by or references to Ramírez in this chapter refer to this interview.

13. Valenzuela, "New Immigrants"; Valenzuela et al., *On the Corner*; Kennedy, "Invisible Corner." Violence against migrant workers on day labor corners also sparked formative efforts to organize day laborers in the 1990s, most dramatically on Long Island. At that time, as NDLON's Omar Henríquez told me, "It was open season on immigrants"; his fellow organizer Nadia Marin then recalled common incidents of migrant workers on bicycles being run off the road and beaten with baseball bats in the notorious small town of Farmingville. See also Fine, *Worker Centers*, 182–88.

14. In a study of Bay Area day labor hiring sites, James Quesada et al. locate such abuses within a broader continuum of racial mistreatment aimed at day laborers: "Daily instances of discrimination occur from insults being hurled at them from passing cars to the reduction of scarce public resources (i.e., homeless shelter beds allocated for Latinos)" ("As Good as It Gets," 39).

15. Arturo González, interview by author, Portland, OR, June 2010.

16. Bobby Kalani, interview by author, Portland, OR, June 2010.

17. José Álvarez, interview by author, Portland, OR, June 2010. All further quoted comments by or references to Álvarez in this chapter refer to this interview.

18. Roberto Mendoza, interview by author, Portland, OR, June 2010.

19. The phrase in Spanish was *él que se ponga más abusado*.

20. In Spanish: *tenías que ponerte las pilas*.

21. Carlos Hernández, interview by author, Portland, OR, June 2010.

22. Emanuel Ramos, interview by Ariel Ruiz, Portland, OR, June 2010. All further quoted comments by or references to Ramos in this chapter refer to this interview.

23. Luís Fernando Chávez, interview by author, Portland, OR, June 2010.

24. Élmer Santamaría, interview by author, Portland, OR, June 2010.

25. Leonel Romero, interview by author, Portland, OR, June 2010.

26. Other research finds that employers further augment their dominant position in the day labor hiring market when workers bargain with them for wages on the corner because through such activity, workers undercut the wage rates demanded by worker centers (Fine, *Worker Centers*, 114; Crotty and Bosco, "Racial Geographies"). Sometimes racial segmentation of the day labor workforce facilitates these wage differentials, as in the case of a San Diego County day labor center with a predominantly Latino membership located near a corner where mostly African American day laborers tried to attract employers by offering cheaper rates (Crotty and Bosco, "Racial Geographies").

27. Ricardo Vélez, interview by Ariel Ruiz, Portland, OR, June 2010.

28. Oscar Morales, interview by author, Portland, OR, June 2010.

29. Guillermo Zelaya, interview by Ariel Ruiz, Portland, OR, June 2010.

30. Quesada et al. found similar sorts of "perverse internalized racism" among the Bay Area day laborers they studied, such as one individual who explained a recent uptick in deportations by saying: "We Latinos are not very clean, we come and leave the places dirty" ("As Good as It Gets," 42). Like day laborers in this other study,

our interviewees also were concerned that workers who went to the corner just "to get a bottle or a drink" gave others a bad impression of Mexican migrants in general ("As Good as It Gets," 39). To be sure, racial denigration was not the norm when our participants voiced dismay over the proclivities of workers on the corners. Yet it was a notable variation on the theme of fighting for the job, and it connected with some workers' (self-blaming) racial disparagement of "Mexicans" and "Latinos" in worker-center communities as lazy, vice-ridden, and ungovernable, a thematic current I discuss in chapter 5.

31. Adán Trejo, interview by Ariel Ruiz, Portland, OR, June 2010.

32. Kotef, *Movement and the Ordering of Freedom*, 74.

33. Kotef, *Movement and the Ordering of Freedom*, 76.

34. Kotef, *Movement and the Ordering of Freedom*, 94.

35. Kotef, *Movement and the Ordering of Freedom*, 109.

36. Kotef, *Movement and the Ordering of Freedom*, 101–6.

37. Kotef, *Movement and the Ordering of Freedom*, 30–31.

38. Kotef, *Movement and the Ordering of Freedom*, 31.

39. Kotef, *Movement and the Ordering of Freedom*, 34.

40. Kotef, *Movement and the Ordering of Freedom*, 34.

41. Kotef and Amir, "(En)Gendering Checkpoints," 975–76.

42. Kotef and Amir, "(En)Gendering Checkpoints," 978–79.

43. Kotef and Amir, "(En)Gendering Checkpoints," 978.

44. Kotef and Amir, "(En)Gendering Checkpoints," 978.

45. Kotef, *Movement and the Ordering of Freedom*, 106.

46. Guerette, "Disorder at Day Laborer Sites," 2–3, 12. By 2017, this document was no longer available from the department, although both the Obama and Trump administrations continued and intensified efforts begun during George W. Bush's presidency to involve local police more actively in federal immigration enforcement. The publication of this guide under Bush exemplified this trend.

47. Guerette, "Disorder at Day Laborer Sites," 3.

48. Guerette, "Disorder at Day Laborer Sites," 3–4.

49. Carcamo, "Arizona Loses Appeal."

50. See also Chavez, *Latino Threat*.

51. On the masculine coding of Mexican migrant men's entrepreneurial aspirations for upward mobility, see Ramirez and Hondagneu-Sotelo, "Mexican Immigrant Gardeners." In an argument that coheres with my interpretation of day laborers' double bind on the corner while further exploring the gendered dimension of this problem, Thomas Ordoñez argues that distant relocation from family members and *macho* forms of identity manifestation on the corner diminish day laborers' prospects for coherently occupying the "provider" role ("Boots for My Sancho," 695–96).

52. Kotef, *Movement and the Ordering of Freedom*, 109.

53. Quesada et al. explain: "Because undocumented Latino day laborers are visible and associated with certain spaces, the manner in which they are treated by local police and officials operates to socially isolate. The containment of undocumented Latinos to specific sites functions to corral them in ways that maximizes [*sic*] social control" ("As Good as It Gets," 37).

54. Friedman, *Capitalism and Freedom*, 14.

55. This notion of the contract's evaporation stands in tension with other analysts' claims that day laborers' everyday lives are defined by constant negotiation. Quesada et al. contend: "They must make instant decisions about whether the person in the car soliciting work is a good employer or not. . . . They carefully measure who to trust and not trust" (Quesada et al., "As Good as It Gets," 34). Such habitual and perpetual negotiation may indeed present itself to day laborers as necessary in principle, but our participants' commentaries point to a powerful counterdynamic by which negotiation is repeatedly pre-empted.

56. Chapter 5 revisits this issue regarding the political-economic effects of worker centers' provisioning for day laborers' basic needs. Kotef and Amir discern the operation of a similar self-undermining dynamic in activists' successes in pushing the Israeli authorities to make humanitarian modifications to the checkpoints such as setting up shelters, installing toilets, and providing drinking water. Through these enhancements, the theorists conclude, "The terminals create the illusion of the occupation's end, while maximizing and stabilizing its techniques and effects" (Kotef, *Movement and the Ordering of Freedom*, 48). Similarly, inasmuch as they provide infrastructure to meet day laborers' basic needs and protect them from physical harm, worker centers may be seen as enlisting humanitarianism in the consolidation of both the deportation regime and the abusive system of casual, low-wage migrant day labor—unless these services are rendered in an organizational context that politicizes the social conditions of work, productive and reproductive alike.

57. Scholars and day labor/domestic worker activists have conducted several studies of this unusual women's corner located in Brooklyn, New York, which have interesting intersections with my project. Regarding this corner, for instance, Elizabeth J. Kennedy writes: "Unlike the experiences of their brothers, fathers, cousins and sons, whose presence on similar street corners is met with hostility, arrests, epithets and violence, this group of workers attracts little attention from passersby" ("Invisible Corner," 127–28).

58. Berlant, *Cruel Optimism*, 201.

59. Berlant, *Cruel Optimism*, 164.

60. Berlant, *Cruel Optimism*, 166.

61. Berlant, *Cruel Optimism*, 177.

62. Berlant, *Cruel Optimism*, 169.

63. Berlant, *Cruel Optimism*, 179.

64. Berlant also offers little sense of how it might be possible to contest or alter the precaritizing dynamics she insightfully dissects, including perhaps through sensory or cognitive dissonances provoked by the films she analyzes, such as representations of migrant cultures in *La Promesse*. Day laborers' thematic and filmic renderings of the corner, however, suggest that cultural practices transported from migrants' home territory to the global North may yield significant transformational possibilities.

65. Fine notes that the "nascent day labor movement reappropriated the term, transforming its connotation" from the "pejorative" insinuation of being "the lowest you can be," as NDLON's executive director Pablo Alvarado put it, to expressing "pride in one's work" and "one's occupational community" (*Worker Centers*, 202).

66. Jacques Rancière's concept of the "distribution of the sensible" illuminates provocative political implications of *Jornaleros* (Rancière, *Disagreement*). Elsewhere, however, I argue that the film's and day labor groups' commitments to popular education provoke critical perspectives on visions of radical democracy and critical theory that lean too heavily on Rancière's excessively individualist and ruptural approach to cultural transformation (Apostolidis, "Lessons of *Jornaleros*").

67. In this respect, the film moves beyond the acts of "politics" that are of greatest importance to Rancière, which overprivilege momentary breaks in orders of the sensible and fleeting repudiations of social-intellectual hierarchies (see Apostolidis, "Lessons of *Jornaleros*"). This aspect of Voz's film has more in common with the evocative notion of occupying and performatively reconstituting public urban spaces that Judith Butler and Athena Athanasiou advocate (*Dispossession*, 177–80, 194–95). Nevertheless, day laborers' commentaries, especially when considered alongside Kotef's critique, also suggest that these theorists overemphasize the political significance of stopping movement and standing in place when they conceptualize the spatial groundings of antiprecarity body politics. Such a politics, this critical-popular exercise indicates, should seek to open up spheres of bodily stasis *and movement* that depart from precaritizing routines.

68. Weeks, *Problem with Work*, 99.

69. Weeks, *Problem with Work*, 100.

70. In 2017 and 2014, I organized screenings of *Jornaleros* followed by dialogue sessions for combined campus and local community audiences at Whitman College in Walla Walla, Washington, where I am on the faculty.

71. The same can be said for the contract's ironic disappearance in the midst of market scenes where contractualism would seem to attain its purest expression. As companies contract out more jobs, labor markets become more saturated than ever with contracts. Yet the contracts that abound involve scantier and hazier mutual promises, while their temporal horizons have become narrower and more evanescent. Meanwhile, work activities are subjected to more extensive monitoring keyed to performance goals, which induces workers to utilize the limited time available

during any given contract to maximize the probability of subsequent contract offers. The social-distributional function of contracts in determining the allocation of future employment thus begins to overtake contracts' significance as agreements focused on present tasks. The ironic dematerialization of the contract on the day labor corner, among workers who must enter into new employment arrangements with dizzying frequency and who constantly struggle to wring further employment chances out of any job they do at present, provides a fitting image of this broader socioeconomic tendency.

72. Peck attributes these conditions primarily to the proliferation of state laws that prohibit municipal deficits and mandate spending cuts within a broader environment of ever-diminishing federal spending and constantly rising needs for services that are concentrated in urban areas ("Austerity Urbanism").

73. Peck, "Austerity Urbanism," 630.

74. Peck, "Austerity Urbanism," 631.

75. Peck, "Austerity Urbanism," 635–37.

76. Peck, "Austerity Urbanism," 641–47.

CHAPTER 4

1. Daniel Rodríguez, interview by Ariel Ruiz, Portland, OR, June 2010.

2. Seixas et al., "Occupational Health," 399. These figures are conservative because researchers asked respondents to report only injuries occurring within the past year and only injuries "that occurred at work that forced [the respondent] to stop working and required first aid and/or medical treatment" (Seixas et al., "Occupational Health," 400).

3. Seixas et al., "Occupational Health," 405.

4. Valenzuela et al., "On the Corner," ii.

5. Burgel et al., "Work-Related Health Complaints." This study pegs the rate of "serious health complaints or injuries which prevented the day laborer from working" at 26 percent, on par with the grim numbers for the worst facilities in another occupation largely staffed by migrant workers and notorious for damaging workers' bodies: meatpacking (Apostolidis and Brenner, "Evaluation of Worker Health and Safety").

6. Rabito et al., "Longitudinal Assessment."

7. Illness due to "allostatic load" refers to the phenomenon by which deleterious physiological responses, especially cardiovascular problems, result from protracted and high-level psychological stress. For day laborers, key stressors are "chronic employment insecurity," "having difficulties paying bills and buying food," fearing deportation, and (with a circular logic) fear of being injured or killed at work. See de Castro et al., "Stressors among Latino Day Laborers." University of Washington researchers conducted this study at Casa Latina. A similar study finds that Latino

day laborers suffer negative mental health impacts from discrimination and social isolation; see Negi, "Battling Discrimination and Social Isolation."

8. Leigh, "Economic Burden of Occupational Injury"; Lowry et al., "Possibilities and Challenges"; Rosenman et al., "How Much Work-Related Injury."

9. Cristian Gutiérrez, interview by author, Seattle, WA, August 2008.

10. César Torres, interview by author, Seattle, WA, August 2008. All further quotations from and comments on Torres in this chapter refer to this interview.

11. Víctor Estrada, interview by author, Seattle, WA, August 2008. All further quotations from and comments on Estrada refer to this interview.

12. Gerardo Mejía, interview by Caitlin Schoenfelder, Seattle, WA, August 2008. All further quotations from and comments on Mejía in this chapter refer to this interview.

13. Tomás Otero, interview by author, Seattle, WA, August 2008. All further quotations from and comments on Otero refer to this interview.

14. In my previous research, I had heard grisly stories from migrant workers about such hazards in meatpacking (Apostolidis, *Breaks in the Chain*, 111–47). From day laborers, I learned that things could be even more perilous for workers processing fish in factory ships at sea that pitched with the waves and storms while individuals worked twelve- to fourteen-hour shifts, seven days a week, during some seasons.

15. Workers also had suffered diverse injuries and health problems in a wide range of jobs apart from day labor: lacerations in machine shops and restaurant kitchens; needle stabs in garment factories; chronic back pain from sewing or building furniture; having a foot crushed by an object falling from a warehouse forklift; chemical burns to the eyes while working with printing presses; temporarily losing the ability to walk after inhaling toxic fumes at a dry-cleaning facility.

16. Exacerbating this temporal predicament were the freakishly unpredictable ways events often unfolded in the various informal jobs our participants typically had done. One worker, for instance, recalled being attacked on the street while vending ice cream in Los Angeles (Jaime Ortega, interview by author, Seattle, WA, August 2008; all further quotations from and comments on Ortega in this chapter refer to this interview). Another had been forced to ride with a drunk driver while delivering newspapers (Gabriela Moreno, interview by Caitlin Schoenfelder, Seattle, WA, August 2008).

17. Other empirical scholarship confirms that day laborers experience incessant anxiety when they work about the possibility of getting injured (Walter et al., "Social Context of Work Injury").

18. Juan Carlos Garza, interview by Ariel Ruiz, Portland, OR, June 2010. All further quotations from and comments on Garza in this chapter refer to this interview.

19. Pablo Maldonado, interview by author, Portland, OR, June 2010.

20. De Castro et al., "Stressors among Latino Day Laborers." Other researchers find that well over 50 percent of day laborers experience "high rates of work-related

stress" (Duke et al., "Day Laborers and Occupational Stress"). Also, higher levels of migration-related "acculturative stress," to which tense interactions with employers such as the one discussed here by Maldonado surely contribute, have been found to correlate with lower levels of physical health (Salgado et al., "Role of Social Support").

21. Bobby Kalani, interview by author, Portland, OR, June 2010.

22. According to Loyda Alvarado, who was directing OSH programs for NDLON when I interviewed her, day laborers often did not inform employers they had been injured on the job, especially out of fear of losing the job along with further chances to work and in particular when working for a Latino contractor with whom they had a culturally rooted relationship of trust (*confianza*) (Loyda Alvarado, interview by author, April 21, 2016, Los Angeles, CA).

23. Some research suggests that day laborers' employers rarely help pay for medical treatment when a worker gets injured (Worby, "Occupational Health").

24. Juan Ayala, interview by author, Portland, OR, June 2010. All further quotations from and comments on Ayala in this chapter refer to this interview.

25. See Burgel et al., "Work-Related Health Complaints," 354; Leclere and López, "The Jornalero," 693. In a study of San Francisco day laborers, Nelson et al. found that only 14 percent of the workers in their study had health insurance; correspondingly, more than half the workers in their study "self-reported their health status as fair or poor" ("Sociodemographic Characteristics," 803).

26. In one story that departed somewhat from this pattern, César Torres recalled that an employer once had rebuffed workers' pleas that he provide safety goggles for a sheet-rocking job—until the employer tried doing the work himself without protection and a shard of sheetrock flew into his eye. Ultimately, he gave workers goggles, but the anecdote still reflects employers' tendency to provide safety equipment reluctantly if at all.

27. Antonio Soto, interview by author, Seattle, WA, August 2008 (all further quotations from and comments on Soto in this chapter refer to this interview). Reinforcing this view was the problem many noted (also discussed in chapter 2) that employers sometimes initially misrepresented the job, which further diminished the worker's ability to prepare himself for potential dangers and exacerbated communication difficulties with the employer.

28. Ricardo Reyes, interview by Caitlin Schoenfelder, Seattle, WA, August 2008.

29. Rubén Contreras, interview by Caitlin Schoenfelder, Seattle, WA, August 2008. All further quotations from and comments on Contreras in this chapter refer to this interview.

30. Diana Ortiz, interview by Caitlin Schoenfelder, Seattle, WA, August 2008.

31. In Spanish, the phrase I render as "you have to focus on what you're doing" was *tienes que estar en lo que estás.*

32. Jésus Martínez, interview by Caitlin Schoenfelder, Seattle, WA, August 2008.

33. Estéban Avila, interview by author, Seattle, WA, August 2008.
34. Roberto Mendoza, interview by Ariel Ruiz, Portland, OR, June 2010.
35. A similar sense of machismo seemed present when workers discussed how it had been customary in their places of origin to run serious safety risks on the job, suggesting the deeper ethnocultural roots of the gender-identity norms expressed in this thematic permutation regarding job safety and health risks. At the same time, other research finds that getting injured damages day laborers' sense of masculinity and patriarchal authority because they interpret injury as a personal failure, and we noticed this tendency as well in our participant observation (Walter et al., "Social Context of Work Injury"). In short, masculinity norms appear to set up an emotionally and physically painful double bind for day laborers by encouraging them to take abundant risks but punishing them when these risks lead to injuries.
36. Pablo Villa, interview by Ariel Ruiz, Portland, OR, June 2010.
37. Alberto Guerrero, interview by author, Seattle, WA, August 2008.
38. For additional comments on this issue within a focused consideration of violence in day laborers' work-lives, see Apostolidis, "Migrant Day Laborers."
39. Dávila et al., "English-Language Proficiency," 263–64.
40. Dong and Platner, "Occupational Fatalities."
41. Gany et al., "Mexican Urban Occupational Health," 177–78.
42. Gany et al., "Mexican Urban Occupational Health," 175. For research on job-related safety and health risk disparities between Latino migrant workers and the general population in other occupations in which the former largely constitute the workforce, see Smith, "Pitfalls of Home"; Mujeres Unidas y Activas et al., "Behind Closed Doors"; Wilmsen et al., "Working in the Shadows"; Liebman et al., "Occupational Health Policy."
43. Ramos et al., "Stress Factors Contributing to Depression."
44. Arcury et al., "Safety and Injury Characteristics," 354–55.
45. Arcury et al., "*You Earn Money by Suffering Pain*," 468.
46. Panikkar et al., "Occupational Health Outcomes," 882, 884.
47. Burgel et al., "Garment Workers in California."
48. US Department of Labor, "Employer-Reported Workplace Injuries," 1. A 2015 OSHA report adds: "Over the past several decades, the US has made great strides in reducing the incidence of workplace injuries, illnesses, and fatalities," in part by lowering the job-related death rate from 18.0 per 100,000 workers in 1970 to 3.4 per 100,000 workers in 2015 (US Department of Labor, "Adding Inequality to Injury," 12). As the report's title indicates, this publication frames the problem of persistent OSH risks as concentrated in low-wage occupations.
49. Scholars have widely criticized public data collection techniques and analytical methodologies in this regard. Obstacles to government tracking of OSH problems include reliance on employer reporting (with employers facing incentives not to report), numerous factors that inhibit employees from notifying employers about

OSH problems, the long latencies of common work-related illnesses, and the exclusion from Bureau of Labor Statistics data of large categories of workers, including the growing ranks of the "self-employed" (Rosenman et al., "How Much Work-Related Injury," 361–62).

50. Groenewold and Baron, "Proportion of Work-Related Emergency Department Visits," 1939; Leigh, "Economic Burden of Occupational Injury."

51. Leigh, "Economic Burden of Occupational Injury," 728–29. Another study of work-related injuries and illnesses in Michigan in 1999–2001 finds that "the current national surveillance system did not include . . . up to 68% of the work-related injuries and illnesses that occurred annually in Michigan" (Rosenman et al., "How Much Work-Related Injury," 357).

52. Benach et al., "Precarious Employment," 235.

53. Greenbaum and Kotelchuck, "Got Air?," 98.

54. Greenbaum and Kotelchuck, "Got Air?," 99.

55. Mogensen, "State or Society?," 111. These disorders are defined as "musculoskeletal ailments of the lower back, shoulders, neck, arms, wrists, fingers, hands, and nervous system" (Mogensen, "State or Society?," 111).

56. Mogensen, "State or Society?," 112.

57. Mogensen, "State or Society?," 112.

58. Benach et al., "Precarious Employment," 235. All told, the detriments to workers' health and the increase in their mortality rates from work environment problems connected with insecure employment are comparable to those from secondhand tobacco smoke (Goh et al., "Workplace Stressors and Health Outcomes," 44).

59. In addition, this theme-theory combination highlights the dimension of vulnerable bone and flesh that marks the physical side of the "psychopathologic economy" decried by Bifo Berardi, which I discussed in chapter 2 (*Soul at Work*, 98–103). This exercise also supplements Berardi's account of the emotional impairments fostered by this system and further elaborates the complicated temporalities associated with these problems.

60. Weil, *Fissured Workplace*, 8.

61. Weil, *Fissured Workplace*, 8.

62. Weil, *Fissured Workplace*, 94. Regarding the latter category, Weil points to the explosive growth since 2004 of "legal process outsourcing (LPO) firms," which provide "legal research, analysis, and brief writing" and fuel the "growing bifurcation of the earnings distribution among lawyers" (275–76). News corporations likewise have adopted various "forms of subcontracting to replace in-house reporting, particularly in areas like local reporting," including (ironically) the use of offshore "content farms" that furnish local news material by trawling the internet for location-specific data on crime, school performance, and other matters (277–78).

63. Weil, *Fissured Workplace*, 163–66.

64. Weil, *Fissured Workplace*, 9.

65. Weil, *Fissured Workplace*, 77–78.
66. Weil, *Fissured Workplace*, 117.
67. Weil, *Fissured Workplace*, 46–47.
68. As noted in chapter 2, Gérard Duménil and Dominique Lévy provide a particularly informative analysis of capital's financialization under neoliberalism, which emphasizes the trend toward reallocating company expenditures away from developing new productive capacities and toward increasing the values of investors' short-term returns and managers' compensation packages (*Crisis of Neoliberalism*, 28, 63, 84–85, 167–69).
69. Shapiro, "Dying at Work," 832. A telling example of the epistemological inclination supporting this policy-discursive tendency arises in a study by neoclassical economists who attribute Latino migrant workers' disproportionate OSH risk exposure to individual, utility-maximizing, cash-translatable choices. For these analysts, such "preferences" can be logically inferred from migrants' prior demonstration of their willingness to trade personal safety risks for expected wages, as expressed by their ostensibly utility-maximizing decisions to undertake physically hazardous unauthorized crossings of the US-Mexico border (Dávila et al., "English-Language Proficiency). A larger economics literature examines factors that increase or decrease "risk premiums" for immigrant workers on the basis of similar epistemological assumptions; see Orrenius and Zavodny, "Immigrants in Risky Occupations"; Hersch and Viscusi, "Immigrant Status"; Berger and Gabriel, "Risk Aversion."
70. Weil, *Fissured Workplace*, 46.
71. Weil, *Fissured Workplace*, 61–64.
72. Weil, *Fissured Workplace*, 119.
73. Weil, *Fissured Workplace*, 108.
74. Berlant, *Cruel Optimism*, 95.
75. Berlant, *Cruel Optimism*, 95–96.
76. Berlant, *Cruel Optimism*, 97. See also Foucault, *Society Must Be Defended*. For my earlier critique of Foucault's conception of biopolitics based on the self-narrated experiences of undocumented border crossings and hazardous labor in the meatpacking industry, see Apostolidis, *Breaks in the Chain*.
77. Berlant, *Cruel Optimism*, 104, 106.
78. Berlant, *Cruel Optimism*, 101.
79. Berlant, *Cruel Optimism*, 101.
80. Berlant, *Cruel Optimism*, 96, 99.
81. Berlant, *Cruel Optimism*, 99.
82. Berlant, *Cruel Optimism*, 99.
83. This motif by which individuals absorb guilt-laden responsibility for socially generated problems resonates with other theorists' conceptions of "responsibilization" under neoliberalism. In a dialogue with Judith Butler, for

example, Athena Athanasiou defines responsibilization as "the appeal to personal responsibility as a flight from social responsibility in the discourses of neoliberal corporate privatization: there are no social forces, no common purposes, struggles, and responsibilities, only individual risks, private concerns, and self-interests" (Butler and Athanasiou, *Dispossession*, 105).

84. As the next two chapters discuss, worker centers have countered this dynamic by inventively incorporating PPDs into OSH trainings and other solidarity-oriented efforts to improve OSH conditions in day labor. Workers' comments on OSH-related themes, however, illuminate the obstacles such measures confront and the ways material-object fetishes foster these impediments.

85. I am grateful to Chandan Reddy for his encouragement to address this question and to frame it this way.

86. Fitbit, "Group Health."

87. See Elliott et al., "Wellness as a Worldwide Phenomenon?"; Madison et al., "Using Reporting Requirements"; Rosenblat et al., "Workplace Surveillance." As these analysts observe, employer-sponsored workplace wellness programs spawn temporally significant modes of worker discipline, especially through regularly required medical tests and through mandatory or incentivized use of Fitbit devices.

88. Berlant, *Cruel Optimism*, 100.

89. Berlant, *Cruel Optimism*, 98.

90. Berlant, *Cruel Optimism*, 115.

91. Berlant, *Cruel Optimism*, 115.

92. Araceli Hernandez, email to author, October 28, 2017.

93. Nieves, "Domestic Workers Sue."

94. Mujeres Unidas y Activas et al., "Behind Closed Doors." This study places job-related injury rates for domestic workers on par with those for day laborers and notes that domestic workers share day laborers' difficulties obtaining safety equipment from employers.

95. Hondagneu-Sotelo, *Doméstica*, 32, 116–22. Domestic workers are also explicitly excluded from protection under the federal Occupational Safety and Health Act (Kennedy, "Hidden Corner," 140), and before 2011 received little attention in international labor law (Shah and Seville, "Domestic Worker Organizing," 442–44).

96. In the early phases of Casa Latina's OSH push, around the time we did interviews there, it was rare to hear workers say they valued their long-term health and wellbeing over a desperately sought opportunity to earn wages. Yet just two years later, when my assistant and I conducted a 2010 workshop with day laborers on our OSH-related research material, the culture of regard for health and safety had markedly improved. Most attendees readily criticized and even laughed out loud at day laborers whom we quoted as saying they had no choice but to work even if it involved serious risks. This workshop occurred before I thoroughly analyzed the field research material, but it furnished an early indication of generative resonances

in workers' commentaries, of the kinds I later explored through the 2017 popular education workshop.

CHAPTER 5

1. For such an account, see Janice Fine's comprehensive study of these organizations (*Worker Centers*) and subsequent updating of that research ("Worker Centers: Entering a New Stage").

2. Juan Carlos Garza, interview by Ariel Ruiz, Portland, OR, June 2010. All further quotations by and comments about Garza in this chapter refer to this interview.

3. Roberto Mendoza, interview by Ariel Ruiz, Portland, OR, June 2010. Putting such comments in context, Fine notes: "The majority of worker centers treat membership as a privilege that workers attain through participation and is attached to specific responsibilities and duties" (*Worker Centers*, 210). Typical requirements include completing training on workers' rights and other issues and regular volunteer service. Casa Latina and Voz's MLK Center thus evidently had less formalized membership rules than other worker centers, although as discussed below these circumstances changed at Casa Latina shortly after our interviews (see note 21 for this chapter).

4. Cristián Gutiérrez, interview by author, Seattle, WA, August 2008. All further quotations by and comments about Gutiérrez in this chapter refer to this interview.

5. Estéban Avila, interview by author, Seattle, WA, August 2008. All further quotations by and comments about Avila in this chapter refer to this interview.

6. Héctor Molina, interview by Ariel Ruiz, Portland, OR, June 2010. All further quotations by and comments about Molina in this chapter refer to this interview.

7. Raul Castillo, interview by Caitlin Schoenfelder, Seattle, WA, August 2008.

8. Gerardo Mejía, interview by Caitlin Schoenfelder, Seattle, WA, August 2008.

9. Diego Flores, interview by Caitlin Schoenfelder, Seattle, WA, August 2008.

10. Sean Garcia, interview by Ariel Ruiz, Portland, OR, June 2010.

11. Ricardo Reyes, interview by Caitlin Schoenfelder, Seattle, WA, 2008. All further quotations by and comments about Reyes in this chapter refer to this interview. As a Casa Latina volunteer in 2016–17, I learned that such monitoring of workers' performances had recently expanded through employers' use of an app.

12. Jaime Ortega, interview by author, Seattle, WA, August 2008. All further quotations by and comments about Ortega in this chapter refer to this interview. Rosario Mendoza similarly used the patriarchally inflected term *patrón* to emphasize that she saw Casa Latina as "like an employer [*patrón*] who protects us" (Rosario Mendoza, interview by Caitlin Schoenfelder, Seattle, WA, August 2008). Mendoza also called for Casa Latina to start issuing disciplinary warnings to workers who behaved improperly on the job.

13. Julián Márquez, interview by Ariel Ruiz, Portland, OR, June 2010. All further quotations by and comments about Márquez in this chapter refer to this interview.

14. José Álvarez, interview by Ariel Ruiz, Portland, OR, June 2010.

15. Especially at the MLK Center, workers offered many testimonies about alcoholism recovery. These stories fleshed out the virtues of deserving members in ways that connected self-discipline, bodily health, and positive relationships to the temporal experience of having made a life-changing break from past dissolution into a rejuvenated present and toward a promising future. Day laborers frequently engage in substance abuse; researchers associate this problem with high stress rates (Duke et al., "Day Laborers and Occupational Stress"; Valdez et al., "Fumando la Piedra"); poverty, unauthorized status, and other "structural vulnerabilities" (Worby et al., "Structural Vulnerability"); and drinking at home due to fears of encountering the police in public (Worby and Organista, "Contextual Influences").

16. Rafael Sandoval, interview by Caitlin Schoenfelder, Seattle, WA, August 2008. All further quotations by and comments about Sandoval in this chapter refer to this interview.

17. Alejandro Delgado, interview by Caitlin Schoenfelder, Seattle, WA, August 2008. All further quotations by and comments about Delgado in this chapter refer to this interview.

18. In 2008, the police also unfairly pressured a Casa Latina coordinator to report drug-dealing in the neighborhood more frequently; this individual told police that dealers had threatened to harm him and his family in Mexico if he reported them. These circumstances made the center's security measures even more understandable and offer context for the refrain *por uno pagan todos*, which the coordinator reiterated in speaking to workers after the police visited.

19. Jorge Medina, interview by Ariel Ruiz, Portland, OR, June 2010.

20. Luís Pérez, interview by Ariel Ruiz, Portland, OR, June 2010.

21. Bobby Kalani, interview by author, Portland, OR, June 2010. All further quotations by and comments about Kalani in this chapter refer to this interview. Workers' comments here reflect the somewhat less formalized operations at Voz's MLK Center compared to Casa Latina at the time of our 2008–10 fieldwork. Casa Latina had a basic skill-based organizational schema, and English education seemed to function better there than at the MLK Center, where my assistant and I taught classes and observed that the program was fairly disorganized. Nevertheless, Casa Latina's procedures were significantly more fluid during our 2008 fieldwork than when I volunteered there in 2016–17, and more efficient practices began during the intervening years. New membership protocols mandated a formal orientation that allocated skill-based job qualifications more carefully and that ensured workers understood center rules. Wage payment and job assignment procedures also became more formalized: in 2008, an individual who showed up for the first time could get a job that day if he had the *confianza* of others who frequented the center, whereas the new membership protocol precluded this; my assistant had greater discretion to negotiate wages when she did job dispatch in 2008 than when I did this in 2016–17;

workers also more frequently got lost traveling to job sites in 2008, whereas by 2016–17 a well-functioning system provided directions and specified logistics.

22. Tomás Otero similarly saw enhancing group "unity" as an important goal for Casa Latina's OSH trainings, which he said would be more effective if workers dutifully attended and just "listened" rather than disrupting them (interview by author, Seattle, WA, August 2008; all further quotations by and comments about Otero in this chapter refer to this interview).

23. I leave the term *mexicano* untranslated because workers used it to signify people born in Mexico and US-born Mexican Americans alike; the term also encompassed people who identified as "Mexican" and those who claimed "Mexican American" identity.

24. Ivan Cruz, interview by author, Portland, OR, June 2010. All further quotations by and comments about Cruz in this chapter refer to this interview.

25. Oribe Lozano, interview by author, Portland, OR, July 2010.

26. José Ruiz, interview by Ariel Ruiz, Portland, OR, June 2010.

27. Occasionally, participants also derived models of strict authority from experiences in their places of origin. Alberto Guerrero, for instance, believed Casa Latina should enforce its regulations as his union had done in Mexico: "Whoever violated the rules got punished. . . . If we didn't go to the meeting, they charged us a fine. So it's because of that, that everyone went. . . . If you didn't go to the meeting, you'd be suspended for a week" (Alberto Guerrero, interview by author, Seattle, WA, August 2008). Here, in contrast to other workers' racially self-disparaging remarks, *mexicanos* seem capable of discipline, but only under the command of strong-armed leadership.

28. Antonio Soto, interview by author, Seattle, WA, August 2008.

29. Moisés Burgos, interview by author, Seattle, WA, August 2008. All further quotations by and comments about Burgos in this chapter refer to this interview.

30. Marco Jérez, interview by Ariel Ruiz, Portland, OR, June 2010. All further quotations by and comments about Jérez in this chapter refer to this interview.

31. Gabriela Moreno, interview by Caitlin Schoenfelder, Seattle, WA, August 2008. In turn, Cristián Gutiérrez connected workers' supposed incapacity for reasonable deliberation to their irrational economic behavior in setting wage levels for skilled labor far below market rates. Hence, although workers frequently conceptualized worker center communities in individualist and economistic terms, they sometimes doubted whether individuals understood their own best interests and called for strong authority to *make* workers attain their goals.

32. Pedro Santiago, interview by Ariel Ruiz, Portland, OR, 2010. All further quotations by and comments about Santiago in this chapter refer to this interview.

33. Camou identifies a common tension between day laborers and center coordinators regarding the meaning and purpose of worker centers, with workers focusing on individual "material" rewards and organizers taking a more "collectivist" orientation

("Synchronizing Meanings"). My analysis questions this dichotomy and traces how cooperative inclinations and political motivations extend outward from workers' economic preoccupations, reshaping those concerns and drawing solidaristic impulses from them.

34. Federico Rojas, interview by Ariel Ruiz, Portland, OR, June 2010. Walter et al. confirm that day laborers in general experience extensive isolation, often in ways exacerbated by emotional difficulties stemming from job-related injuries and illnesses; the latter aggravate the pain of family separation by provoking feelings of failure to be a masculine provider, when injuries cause loss of work ("Social Context of Work Injury").

35. Roberto Fernández, interview by Ariel Ruiz, Portland, OR, June 2010. To be sure, workers sometimes behaved in petty or unkind ways toward one another, but this did not substantially mar the overall atmosphere of mutual support. Salgado et al. confirm, in turn, that "social support," in the form of actions and communicative expressions that lead "the subject to believe that he is cared for and loved, esteemed and a member of a network of mutual obligation," helps ameliorate accumulated stresses related from the disruptions of migration ("Role of Social Support," 380).

36. Cheung et al. discern analogous patterns by which day laborers find emotional support at worker centers in ways that mitigate their emotional pain and loneliness and that are intermingled with gaining personal security and enhanced job prospects ("Practical Insights").

37. Juan Ayala, interview by author, Portland, OR, June 2010.

38. Ángel López, interview by author, Portland, OR, June 2010. All further quotations by and comments about López in this chapter refer to this interview.

39. Bhimji finds patterns of mutual support in material and personal matters on day labor corners, particularly during economic crises, that resemble the practices at worker centers I discuss here ("Undocumented Immigrant Day Laborers"). Worker centers, of course, provide more resources for day laborers to develop these relational patterns and channel them toward political action.

40. Francisco Herrarte, interview by Ariel Ruiz, Portland, OR, June 2010. All further quotations by and comments about Herrarte in this chapter refer to this interview.

41. Ricardo Vélez, interview by Ariel Ruiz, Portland, OR, June 2010.

42. Workers typically invoked the term *compañero* to characterize an agent of such mutual regard; *compañerismo* thus offers another fitting name for their mutualist practices. The term carries a sense of being loyal companions in a joint effort, perhaps but not necessarily a political cause. Neither "companion" nor "comrade" nor "friend" is adequate to all possible uses of the term, although each captures an aspect of what *compañero* may indicate; hence I render the word in Spanish.

43. Israel Campos, interview by Ariel Ruiz, Portland, OR, June 2010.

44. Workers at Casa Latina also materialized such mutualist connections, as alternative responses to desires for protection, by sharing safety equipment and by alerting one another about abusive employers.

45. Importantly, these creative retemporalizations of everyday experience emerged synergistically with certain standardizations of time aimed at enhancing the stability and frequency of work. At Casa Latina, in particular, the convivially mutualist culture fostered more pliable temporalities of daily life even as the organization tightened membership requirements and formalized job dispatch procedures in ways noted above (see note 21 for this chapter).

46. Luís Fernando Chávez, interview by Ariel Ruiz, Portland, OR, June 2010; all further quotations by and comments about Chávez in this chapter refer to this interview. Several interviewees had just begun attending one of the centers, and these individuals typically observed that workers shared a willingness to keep the facilities clean and tidy. Multiple long-termers and our field observations confirmed this to be, generally, the common attitude.

47. A similar dynamic applied when a worker at Casa Latina cut the grass without being asked to do so or offered anything in return, after which the coordinator nonetheless recognized his contribution by giving him temporary priority for job assignments.

48. Jesús Martínez, interview by Caitlin Schoenfelder, Seattle, WA, August 2008.

49. This individual's expression *tener corazón* can variously mean to have courage, to have compassion, and to have a fighting spirit.

50. Chávez's telling reference to "themes" selected by workers reflects how Voz's leadership classes were organized as exercises in popular education that recognized workers' abilities for critically assessing social problems and taking action to address them.

51. For example, the 2008 police visit precipitated a particularly active and highly participatory assembly where workers debated ideas for increasing the center's security and distinguishing its activities from illegal dealings in the neighborhood. In general, we observed that worker assemblies, leadership committee meetings, and training workshops at both centers tended to spark abundant and vigorous participation and accomplished important objectives, despite the numerous negative comments about these events associated with the theme of protecting the threatened workforce.

52. Workers thus followed a common pattern noted by Fine: "Many worker centers strive to create a culture of democratic governance and decision-making. In place of just making decisions themselves, staff works not only to put deliberative processes in place but to foster expectations on the part of workers that decisions will be made consultatively and collectively" (*Worker Centers*, 202).

53. This study thus confirms Fine's general observations regarding the prodigious politicizing effects of worker center participation. She associates these effects with

the popular-education commitments of these organizations and emphasizes: "A major activity of worker centers is identifying and developing activists and organizational leaders from within the ranks of low-wage immigrant workers" (*Worker Centers*, 202).

54. Miguel Vargas, interview by author, Seattle, WA, August 2008. All further quotations by and comments about Vargas in this chapter refer to this interview.

55. Jaime Ortega, for example, praised Casa Latina for promoting a convivial community of "Latinos" in which it did not matter "what color or from where you are," especially through sponsoring social "get-togethers" (*convivíos*) including "little parties, meetings, [and] . . . soccer."

56. Pablo Maldonado, interview by author, Portland, OR, June 2010.

57. López also told a gripping story about how day laborers had repulsed a Minute Man group that had tried to shut down a Los Angeles worker center he had previously attended: "The community won. . . . the Minute Men were left with nothing. . . . [They threatened us] with words and they wanted to beat the people up, but *la raza* was clever and there wasn't any of that." López thus refigured *la raza* as quick-witted rather than wooden-headed, self-controlled instead of impulsively driven, and a politicized antiracist force rather than a congeries of individuals aspiring to economic self-advancement.

58. Jeff Roberts, interview by Ariel Ruiz, Portland, OR, 2010. Even though racial conflicts can harden boundaries between center communities and workers on nearby corners, the spatial dynamics of worker centers actively counter these effects. Hence, for instance, when tensions between Latino and African American workers aggravated a split between a San Diego County day labor center and workers on a neighborhood corner, the center offered a setting for mitigating these problems, according to Crotty and Bosco ("Racial Geographies"). More generally, at worker centers, "Workers develop interracial social networks through their shared struggle for employment, as well as through their time spent at the center" (Crotty and Bosco, "Racial Geographies," 239).

59. Another MLK Center day laborer who came from a Honduran indigenous background had a custom of teaching indigenous phrases to fellow workers and volunteers, especially just after English classes. His spontaneous lessons, which he undertook with pride and good humor, further encouraged a positive atmosphere for exploring decolonizing affinities among participants.

60. Rocco, *Transforming Citizenship*, xxxi. As Rocco notes, research on Latino communities from various ethnic-national backgrounds and in multiple cities has consistently found that such networks of informal mutualism operate vigorously and motivate collective action (*Transforming Citizenship*, 125).

61. Rocco, *Transforming Citizenship*, 125.

62. Rocco, *Transforming Citizenship*, 125.

63. Rocco, *Transforming Citizenship*, 146.

64. Rocco, *Transforming Citizenship*, 166.
65. Rocco, *Transforming Citizenship*, 1–5, 150–61.
66. Rocco, *Transforming Citizenship*, 179, 187, 189.
67. Rocco, *Transforming Citizenship*, 165.
68. Tsing, *Mushroom at the End of the World*, 6. In this respect, Tsing offers a complementary angle on the political-economic process that David Harvey theorizes as capital's repeated search for "spatial fixes" to its crisis tendencies. Harvey, *Cosmopolitanism and the Geographies of Freedom*, 65–66; *Limits to Capital*, 434.
69. Tsing, *Mushroom at the End of the World*, 3.
70. Tsing, *Mushroom at the End of the World*, 2.
71. Tsing, *Mushroom at the End of the World*, 4.
72. Tsing, *Mushroom at the End of the World*, 5.
73. Tsing, *Mushroom at the End of the World*, 20–21.
74. Tsing, *Mushroom at the End of the World*, 20–21.
75. Tsing, *Mushroom at the End of the World*, 138.
76. In that counterfactual case, furthermore, workers' practices at Casa Latina and the MLK Center would have offered no basis for questioning the notion that a simple, either-or choice results from the tension worker centers commonly experience between meeting workers' urgent needs through service provision and encouraging workers to exercise autonomously collective power (Fine, *Worker Centers*, 72–73, 82). In fact, this chapter demonstrates day laborers' capacities to think beyond this false dichotomy, just as their organizations do on a collective level.
77. Tsing wanders into dubious conceptual territory when she describes migrants' Matsutake gathering and quality appraisals as "noncapitalist" and urges readers to see "capitalist" action as only commencing with the mushrooms' preparation for shipping, and as ceasing when mushrooms are given as personal gifts after being purchased (*Mushroom at the End of the World*, 66, 121–28). These unconvincing attempts to delineate "noncapitalist" activities overlook the dense entanglements of production processes, cultural practices, and socially reproductive activities with capitalist systems of labor exploitation and surplus-value generation. This is ironic, because, to my reading, the underlying strength of Tsing's analysis lies precisely in showing how thoroughly intermeshed migrant community formation is with economic action in response to precarity's exigencies.
78. As noted in chapter 3, Voz's documentary *Jornaleros* suggests a similar critical posture with respect to traditional ideals of national sovereignty.
79. Coles, *Visionary Pragmatism*, 34.
80. Coles, *Visionary Pragmatism*, 37–40, 74–84.
81. Coles, *Visionary Pragmatism*, 62.
82. At times, there is a questionably speculative quality to Coles's argument that self-catalyzing patterns of expansion characterize radical democratic scenes where bodily affects interresonate. Further empirical study would strengthen this argument while

also offering a basis for evaluating some critics' arguments that Coles's reliance on complexity theory puts visionary pragmatism in danger of complicity with neoliberal ideologies about self-organizing systems that naturalize historically specific processes. For a sympathetically critical consideration of these issues, see Connolly, "Visionary Responsiveness."

83. Coles, *Visionary Pragmatism*, 169.
84. See Klein, *Shock Doctrine*; Coles, *Visionary Pragmatism*, 164–67.
85. Coles, *Visionary Pragmatism*, 168.
86. Beltrán, *Trouble with Unity*, 5.
87. Beltrán, *Trouble with Unity*, 5.
88. Beltrán, *Trouble with Unity*, 8–9.
89. This individualist absorption in work contrasts with the distinctly *working-class* identity that proved fundamental to cultivating militant enthusiasm in the Chicano movement (see García, *Chicanismo*).
90. Rocco, *Transforming Citizenship*, 185–86.
91. Beltrán, *Trouble with Unity*, 17; Rocco, *Transforming Citizenship*, 196–97.
92. Regarding such cooperative practices and the impacts of maternal responsibilities on Latinas' goals and roles as labor activists and community organizers, see Ruiz, *Cannery Women*; Zavella, *Women's Work*; Ruiz, *From Out of the Shadows*; Pardo, *Mexican American Women Activists*.

CHAPTER 6

1. "About," #NOT1MORE, www.notonemoredeportation.com/about/.
2. "About," #NOT1MORE, www.notonemoredeportation.com/about/.
3. Abrams, "Contentious Citizenship."
4. Pablo Alvarado, interview by author, April 15, 2014, Walla Walla, WA. All further quotations by and comments about P. Alvarado in this chapter refer to this interview, unless otherwise noted.
5. Correspondingly, Alvarado stressed that when NDLON promulgated suggested rules for worker centers, NDLON advised centers not to present rules to members as prescriptions for "punishment" or means for excluding unworthy workers but rather as tools for "keeping peace."
6. Pablo Alvarado, interview on *Democracy Now!*, April 10, 2014.
7. Beyond providing basic safety and physical comfort, worker centers also enable day laborers to earn higher wages and gain more employment opportunities, as a 2016 comparative study of work experiences for day laborers at Casa Latina and Seattle day labor corners demonstrates (Theodore, "Day Labor in Seattle").
8. P. Alvarado, interview by author; Nadia Marin, interview by author, March 15, 2015, Hempstead, NY (all further quotations by and comments about Marin in this chapter refer to this interview, unless otherwise noted). For discussions of day

labor organizations' efforts to counter municipal ordinance proposals to ban public solicitation of work, see Fine, *Worker Centers*, 88–89; Apostolidis and Valenzuela, "Cosmopolitan Politics," 232. Fine also notes that early worker center organizing directly countered the deportation regime by advocating for local ordinances to ban local police cooperation with federal immigration authorities (*Worker Centers*, 190).

9. Paul Zilly, interview by author, December 15, 2014, Seattle, WA. See Boal, *Theatre of the Oppressed*.

10. Eric Rodriguez, interview by author, November 8, 2013, Chicago, IL.

11. Dziembowska, "NDLON and the History," 29.

12. These organizers noted that besides volunteering as first responders just after the hurricane hit, day laborers quickly sought jobs and were eagerly hired by homeowners hoping to repair damaged property. Still, Omar Henríquez emphasized, many day laborers worked on a voluntary basis, sometimes through organizing "volunteer brigades on weekends" (interview by author, March 15, 2015, Hempstead, NY; all further quotations by and comments about Henríquez in this chapter refer to this interview). He also said that despite their brave interventions, day laborers ironically were ineligible for temporary municipal relief jobs because the workers were unauthorized. In any case, the transformative significance of workers' first-responder actions does not depend on their acting in purely altruistic ways, as chapter 5's analysis of communal impulses' imbrications with work imperatives suggests. On Houston day laborers' roles as "second responders" to Hurricane Harvey through their hired work, with an emphasis on their vulnerability to wage theft, OSH hazards, and immigrant detention, see Theodore, "After the Storm."

13. Marin and Henríquez claimed that day laborers had also assumed first-responder roles after Hurricane Katrina in New Orleans and the 9/11 attacks in New York City.

14. My conception of unauthorized citizenship parallels Rocco's conception of practically rather than legally oriented democratic action, as discussed in chapter 5. See also Theodore and Martin's account of a related phenomenon they call "migrant civil society," exemplified by Chicago day laborers' cultivation of a community-support network, with NDLON's help, to rebuild the Albany Park worker center after the city initially destroyed it ("Migrant Civil Society"). Torres et al. characterize as "social citizenship" those activities that constitute "immigrant civil society," illustrated through a worker center's partnership with academic researchers to evaluate construction working conditions in Austin, Texas ("Building Austin").

15. Loyda Alvarado, interview by author, April 21, 2016, Los Angeles, CA. All further quotations by and comments about L. Alvarado in this chapter refer to this interview.

16. At this book's completion, Nadia Marin, who had been a Long Island–based NDLON organizer when I interviewed her, was serving on COSH's national board of directors and had become associate director of the New York Committee for Occupational Safety and Health.

17. Day labor organizations have also moved toward such an expansive politics through OSH-focused alliances with labor unions, such as a national initiative Marin and Henríquez described in which the United Steel Workers trained OSH trainers for day labor centers. Efforts like this advance the coalition-building between worker centers and unions discussed in this book's introduction, and include other endeavors to ensure fair labor standards such as a New York State experiment in "tripartite" enforcement of wage and hour laws for informal migrant workers that involved worker centers, unions, and state officials (Fine and Gordon, "Strengthening Labor Standards Enforcement").

18. Weeks, *Problem with Work*, 167–74.

19. Weeks, *Problem with Work*, 140–43.

20. Apostolidis, "We Want More, Now."

21. In 2016 and 2017, Casa Latina also spotlighted women leaders at its annual gala events.

22. In 2016, Casa Latina also welcomed its first transgender worker to the "Household Helpers" women's program. Organizers worked with determination and sensitivity to defuse resistance among some cisgender workers to this individual's participation, as I observed in a meeting of the women's group.

23. Weeks, *Problem with Work*, 155–74.

24. Weeks, *Problem with Work*, 123–26, 162–63, 172–74.

25. Weeks, *Problem with Work*, 197.

26. Omar León, interview by author, April 21, 2016, Los Angeles, CA.

Bibliography

"About." #NOT1MORE. www.notonemoredeportation.com/about/.

"About Us." National Domestic Workers Alliance. https://www.domesticworkers.org/about-us.

Abrams, Kathryn. "Contentious Citizenship: Undocumented Activism in the Not1More Deportation Campaign." *Berkeley La Raza Law Journal* 26 (2016): 46–92.

Adorno, Theodor. "Cultural Criticism and Society." In *Prisms*, translated by Samuel Weber and Shierry Weber, 19–34. Cambridge, MA: MIT Press, 1983.

Agence France-Presse. "Bangladesh Packaging Factory Fire Kills 15 and Injures Many More." *The Guardian*, September 10, 2016. https://www.theguardian.com/world/2016/sep/10/bangladesh-garment-factory-fire-kills-injures.

Akalin, Ayse. "Affective Precarity: The Migrant Domestic Worker." *South Atlantic Quarterly* 117, no. 2 (April 2018): 420–29.

Alvarado, Pablo. Interview on *Democracy Now!* April 10, 2014.

Apostolidis, Paul. *Breaks in the Chain: What Immigrant Workers Can Teach America about Democracy.* Minneapolis: University of Minnesota Press, 2010.

Apostolidis, Paul. "The Lessons of *Jornaleros:* Rancière's Emancipatory Education, Migrant Artists, and the Aims of Critical Theory." *Philosophy & Rhetoric* 49, no. 4 (2016): 368–91.

Apostolidis, Paul. "Migrant Day Laborers, Neoliberalism, and the Politics of Time." In *Time, Temporality and Violence in International Relations: (De)Fatalizing the Present, Forging Radical Alternatives*, edited by Anna Agathangelou and Kyle Killian, 159–71. New York: Routledge, 2016.

Apostolidis, Paul. *Stations of the Cross: Adorno and Christian Right Radio.* Durham, NC: Duke University Press, 2000.

Apostolidis, Paul. "We Want More, Now—A Utopian Challenge to the Neoliberal Work Ethic: Weeks' *The Problem with Work.*" *Theory & Event* 15, no. 2 (2012).

Apostolidis, Paul, and Mark Brenner. "An Evaluation of Worker Health and Safety at the Tyson Fresh Meats Plant in Pasco, Washington." Amherst, MA: Political Economy Research Institute, University of Massachusetts, 2005.

Apostolidis, Paul, and Abel Valenzuela Jr. "Cosmopolitan Politics and the Migrant Day Labor Movement." *Politics, Groups & Identities* 2, no. 2 (June 2014): 222–44.

Arcury, Thomas A., Dana C. Mora, and Sara A. Quandt. "You Earn Money by Suffering Pain: Beliefs About Carpal Tunnel Syndrome Among Latino Poultry Processing Workers." *Journal of Immigrant and Minority Health* 17, no. 3 (June 2015): 791–801.

Arcury, Thomas A., Guadalupe Rodriguez, Gregory D. Kearney, Justin T. Arcury, and Sara A. Quandt. "Safety and Injury Characteristics of Youth Farmworkers in North Carolina: A Pilot Study." *Journal of Agromedicine* 19, no. 4 (October 2014): 354–63.

Aslam, Ali. *Ordinary Democracy: Sovereignty and Citizenship beyond the Neoliberal Impasse.* New York: Oxford University Press, 2016.

Avendaño, Ana, and Jonathan Hiatt. "Worker Self-Organization in the New Economy: The AFL-CIO's Experience in Movement Building with Community-Labor Partnerships." *Labour, Capital and Society* 45, no. 1 (2012): 66–95.

Barchiesi, Franco. *Precarious Liberation: Workers, the State, and Contested Social Citizenship in Postapartheid South Africa.* Albany: State University of New York Press, 2011.

Behdad, Ali. *A Forgetful Nation: On Immigration and Cultural Identity in the United States.* Durham, NC: Duke University Press, 2005.

Beltrán, Cristina. *The Trouble with Unity: Latino Politics and the Creation of Identity.* New York: Oxford University Press, 2010.

Benach, Joan, Alejandra Vives, Marcelo Amable, Christophe Vanroelen, Gemma Tarafa, and Carles Muntaner. "Precarious Employment: Understanding an Emergent Social Determinant of Health." *Annual Review of Public Health* 35 (2014): 229–53.

Benjamin, Walter. *Illuminations: Essays and Reflections.* Edited by Hannah Arendt. Translated by Harry Zohn. New York: Schocken, 1969.

Benjamin, Walter. Reflecctions: Essays, Aphorisms, Autobiographical Writings. Translated by Edmund Jephcott. New York: Schocken, 1986.

Berardi, Franco "Bifo." *The Soul at Work: From Alienation to Autonomy*. Translated by Francesca Cadel and Giuseppina Mecchia. Los Angeles: Semiotext(e), 2009.

Berardi, Franco "Bifo." *The Uprising: On Poetry and Finance.* Los Angeles: Semiotext(e), 2012.

Berger, Mark C., and Paul E. Gabriel. "Risk Aversion and the Earnings of US Immigrants and Natives." *Applied Economics* 23, no. 2 (February 1991): 311–18.

Berlant, Lauren. *Cruel Optimism.* Durham, NC: Duke University Press, 2011.

Bernton, Hal, and Susan Kelleher. "Amazon Warehouse Jobs Push Workers to Physical Limit." *Seattle Times*, August 17, 2015. https://www.seattletimes.com/business/amazon-warehouse-jobs-push-workers-to-physical-limit/.

Bhimji, Fazila. "Undocumented Immigrant Day Laborers Coping with the Economic Meltdown in Los Angeles." *Cultural Dynamics* 22, no. 3 (2010): 157–78.

Bloom, Joshua. "Ally to Win: Black Community Leaders and SEIU's L.A. Security Unionization Campaign." In *Working for Justice: The L.A. Model of Organizing and Advocacy*, edited by Ruth Milkman, Joshua Bloom, and Victor Narro, 167–90. Ithaca, NY: Cornell University Press, 2010.

Boal, Augusto. *Theatre of the Oppressed*. Translated by Charles A. McBride. New York: Theatre Communications Group, 1993.

Bobo, Kimberley A. *Wage Theft in America: Why Millions of Working Americans Are Not Getting Paid—and What We Can Do about It*. New York: New Press, 2009.

Bosteels, Bruno. *Marx and Freud in Latin America: Politics, Psychoanalysis, and Religion in Times of Terror*. London: Verso, 2012.

Bowcott, Owen. "Rise of Robotics Will Upend Laws and Lead to Human Job Quotas, Study Says." *The Guardian*, April 3, 2017. https://www.theguardian.com/technology/2017/apr/04/innovation-in-ai-could-see-governments-introduce-human-quotas-study-says.

Brown, Wendy. *Undoing the Demos: Neoliberalism's Stealth Revolution*. New York: Zone Books, 2015.

Burawoy, Michael. *Manufacturing Consent: Changes in the Labor Process under Monopoly Capitalism*. Chicago: University of Chicago Press, 1979.

Burgel, Barbara J., Nan Lashuay, Leslie Israel, and Robert Harrison. "Garment Workers in California: Health Outcomes of the Asian Immigrant Women Workers' Clinic." *Workplace Health & Safety* 52, no. 11 (2004): 465–75.

Burgel, Barbara J., Ronald W. Nelson, and Mary C. White. "Work-Related Complaints and Injuries, and Safety and Health Perceptions of Latino Day Laborers." *Workplace Health & Safety* 63, no. 8 (2015): 350–61.

Butler, Judith, and Athena Athanasiou. *Dispossession: The Performative in the Political*. Cambridge: Polity Press, 2013.

Calderon, José Z., Suzanne F. Foster, and Silvia L. Rodriguez. "Organizing Immigrant Workers: Action Research and Strategies in the Pomona Day Labor Center." In *Latino Los Angeles: Transformations, Communities, and Activism*, edited by Enrique Ochoa and Gilda L. Ochoa, 279–97. Tucson: University of Arizona Press, 2005.

Camou, Michelle. "Synchronizing Meanings and Other Day Laborer Organizing Strategies." *Labor Studies Journal* 34, no. 1 (2009): 39–64.

Carcamo, Cindy. "Arizona Loses Appeal over Part of Law Aimed at Day Laborers." *Los Angeles Times*, March 4, 2013. http://articles.latimes.com/2013/mar/04/nation/la-na-nn-ff-arizona-sb1070-day-laborer-ruling-20130304.

Chakrabarty, Dipesh. *Rethinking Working-Class History: Bengal, 1890–1940*. Princeton, NJ: Princeton University Press, 1989.

Chang, Charlotte, Alicia L. Salvatore, Pam Tau Lee, Shaw San Liu, Alex T. Tom, Alvaro Morales, Robin Baker, and Meredith Minkler. "Adapting to Context in Community-Based Participatory Research: 'Participatory Starting Points' in a Chinese Immigrant Worker Community." *American Journal of Community Psychology* 51, nos. 3–4 (2013): 480–91.

Charles, Dan. "EPA Announces New Rules to Protect Farmworkers from Pesticides." NPR/KUOW, September 28, 2015. http://www.npr.org/sections/thesalt/2015/09/28/444220963/epa-announces-new-rules-to-protect-farmworkers-from-pesticides.

Chavez, Leo R. *The Latino Threat: Constructing Immigrants, Citizens, and the Nation.* Stanford, CA: Stanford University Press, 2008.

Cheung, Monit, Elena Delavega, Irma Castillo, and Corrinne Walijaryi. "Practical Insights from Interviews with Day Laborers." *Journal of Ethnic & Cultural Diversity in Social Work* 20, no. 1 (2011): 77–92.

Choudry, Aziz. *Learning Activism: The Intellectual Life of Contemporary Social Movements.* Toronto: University of Toronto Press, 2015.

Coles, Romand. *Beyond Gated Politics: Reflections for the Possibility of Democracy.* Minneapolis: University of Minnesota Press, 2005.

Coles, Romand. *Visionary Pragmatism: Radical and Ecological Democracy in Neoliberal Times.* Durham, NC: Duke University Press, 2016.

Compa, Lance A. 2005. *Blood, Sweat, and Fear: Workers' Rights in U.S. Meat and Poultry Plants.* New York: Human Rights Watch, 2005.

Cordero-Guzmán, Héctor, Pamela A. Izvanariu, and Victor Narro. "The Development of Sectoral Worker Center Networks." *Annals of the American Academy of Political and Social Science* 647 (May 2013): 102–23.

Crotty, Sean M., and Fernando J. Bosco. "Racial Geographies and the Challenges of Day Labor Formalization: A Case Study from San Diego County." *Journal of Cultural Geography* 25, no 3 (2008): 223–44.

Cummings, Scott L. "Litigation at Work: Defending Day Labor in Los Angeles." *UCLA Law Review* 28 (August 2011): 1617–703.

Dávila, Marie T. Mora, and Rebecca González. "English-Language Proficiency and Occupational Risk among Hispanic Immigrant Men in the United States." *Industrial Relations* 50, no. 2 (April 2011): 263–96.

de Castro, A. B., Joachim G. Voss, Ayelet Ruppin, Carlos F. Dominguez, and Noah S. Seixas. "Stressors among Latino Day Laborers: A Pilot Study Examining Allostatic Load." *AAOHN Journal* 58, no. 5 (May 2010): 185–96.

De Genova, Nicholas. "The Deportation Regime: Sovereignty, Space, and the Freedom of Movement." In *The Deportation Regime: Sovereignty, Space, and the Freedom of Movement*, edited by Nathalie Peutz and Nicholas De Genova, 33–67. Durham, NC: Duke University Press, 2010.

De Genova, Nicholas. "The Legal Production of Mexican/Migrant 'Illegality.'" *Latino Studies* 2 (2004): 160–85.

De Genova, Nicholas. "The Production of Culprits: From Deportability to Detainability in the Aftermath of 'Homeland Security.'" *Citizenship Studies* 11, no. 5 (November 2007): 421–48.

De Lara, Juan D., Ellen R. Reese, and Jason Struna. "Organizing Temporary, Subcontracted, and Immigrant Workers: Lessons from Change to Win's Workers United Campaign." *Labor Studies Journal* 41, no. 4 (2016): 309–32.

Dean, Jodi. "Communicative Capitalism and Class Struggle." *Spheres: Journal for Digital Cultures* 1 (2014): 1–16.

Dean, Jodi. *Crowds and Party*. New York: Verso, 2016.

Dehghan, Saeed Kamali. "At Least 55 People Feared Drowned Off Yemen after Being Forced from Boat." *The Guardian*, August 10, 2017. https://www.theguardian.com/world/2017/aug/10/yemen-55-people-feared-drowned-after-being-forced-from-boat.

Disch, Lisa. "Impartiality, Storytelling, and the Seductions of Narrativity: An Essay at an Impasse." *Alternatives: Global, Local, Political* 20, no. 2 (March–May 2003): 253–66.

Dong, Xiuwen, and James W. Platner. "Occupational Fatalities of Hispanic Construction Workers from 1992 to 2000." *American Journal of Industrial Medicine* 45, no. 1 (2004): 45–54.

Doussard, Marc. *Degraded Work: The Struggle at the Bottom of the Labor Market*. Minneapolis: University of Minnesota Press, 2013.

Duke, Michael R., Beth Bourdeau, and Joseph D. Hovey. "Day Laborers and Occupational Stress: Testing the Migrant Stress Inventory with a Latino Day Laborer Population." *Cultural Diversity and Ethnic Minority Psychology* 16, no. 2 (2010): 116–22.

Duménil, Gérard, and Dominique Lévy. *The Crisis of Neoliberalism*. Cambridge, MA: Harvard University Press, 2011.

Dziembowska, Maria. "NDLON and the History of Day Labor Organizing in Los Angeles." *Social Policy* 40, no. 3 (October 2010): 27–33.

Elliott, Heather, Jennifer Bernstein, and Diana M. Bowman. "Wellness as a Worldwide Phenomenon?" *Journal of Health Politics, Policy and Law* 39, no. 5 (October 2014): 1067–88.

"Employment Projections." US Department of Labor. Bureau of Labor Statistics. https://www.bls.gov/emp/ep_table_201.htm.

Ferguson, Kathy E. "Is it an Anarchist Act to Call Oneself an Anarchist? Judith Butler, John Turner and Insurrectionary Speech." *Contemporary Political Theory* 13, no. 4 (November 2014): 339–57.

Fine, Janice. "A Marriage Made in Heaven? Mismatches and Misunderstandings between Worker Centers and Unions." *British Journal of Industrial Relations* 45, no. 2 (June 2007): 335–60.

Fine, Janice. "Worker Centers: Entering a New Stage of Growth and Development." *New Labor Forum* 20, no. 3 (Fall 2011): 44–53.

Fine, Janice. *Worker Centers: Organizing Communities at the Edge of the Dream*. Ithaca, NY: Cornell University Press, 2006.

Fine, Janice, and Jennifer Gordon. "Strengthening Workplace Standards Enforcement through Partnerships with Workers' Organizations." *Politics & Society* 38, no. 4 (2010): 552–85.

Fine, Janice, Jeff Grabelsky, and Victor Narro. "Building a Future Together: Worker Centers and Construction Unions." *Labor Studies Journal* 33, no. 1 (January 2008): 27–47.

Forrest, M. David. "Engaging and Disrupting Power: The Public Value of Political Ethnography." *PS: Political Science and Politics* 50, no. 1 (January 2017): 109–13.

Foucault, Michel. *"Society Must Be Defended": Lectures at the Collége de France, 1975–76*. Edited by Mauro Bertani and Alessandro Fontana. Translated by David Macey. New York: Picador, 2003.

Freire, Paulo. *Education for Critical Consciousness*. New York: Continuum, 2008.

Freire, Paulo. *Pedagogy of Hope: Reliving "Pedagogy of the Oppressed."* Translated by Robert R. Barr. New York: Continuum, 1994.

Freire, Paulo. 2000. *Pedagogy of the Oppressed*. Translated by Myra Bergman Ramos. New York: Continuum.

Freire, Paulo. 1985. *The Politics of Education: Culture, Power, and Liberation*. Translated by Donald Macedo. Westport, CT: Bergin & Garvey.

Freire, Paulo, and Antonio Faundez. *Learning to Question: A Pedagogy of Liberation*. New York: Continuum, 1989.

Friedman, Milton. *Capitalism and Freedom*. Chicago: University of Chicago Press, 1962.

Gany, Francesca, Rebecca Dobslaw, Julia Ramirez, Josana Tonda, Iryna Lobach, and Jennifer Leng. "Mexican Urban Occupational Health in the US: A Population at Risk." *Journal of Community Health* 36, no. 2 (April 2011): 175–79.

García, Ignacio M. *Chicanismo: The Forging of a Militant Ethos among Mexican Americans*. Tucson: University of Arizona Press, 1997.

Garelli, Glenda, and Martina Tazzioli. "Challenging the Discipline of Migration: Militant Research in Migration Studies, an Introduction." *Postcolonial Studies* 16, no. 3 (September 2013): 245–49.

Ghandnoosh, Nazgol. "Organizing Workers along Ethnic Lines: The Pilipino Workers' Center." In *Working for Justice: The L.A. Model of Organizing and Advocacy*, edited by Ruth Milkman, Joshua Bloom, and Victor Narro, 49–70. Ithaca, NY: Cornell University Press, 2010.

Gibson-Graham, J. K. *A Postcapitalist Politics*. Minneapolis: University of Minnesota Press, 2006.

"Global Migration Trends Factsheet." International Organization for Migration. http://gmdac.iom.int/global-migration-trends-factsheet.

Goh, Joel, Jeffrey Pfeffer, and Stefanos A. Zenios. "Workplace Stressors and Health Outcomes: Health Policy for the Workplace." *Behavioral Science & Policy* 1, no. 1 (2015): 43–52.

Goldberg, Harmony, and Randy Jackson. "The Excluded Workers Congress: Reimagining the Right to Organize." *New Labor Forum* 20, no. 3 (Fall 2011): 54–59.

Goldstein, Jacob. "To Increase Productivity, UPS Monitors Drivers' Every Move." National Public Radio, April 17, 2014. https://www.npr.org/sections/money/2014/04/17/303770907/to-increase-productivity-ups-monitors-drivers-every-move.

Gonzales, Alfonso. *Reform without Justice: Latino Migrant Politics and the Homeland Security State*. Oxford: Oxford University Press, 2014.

Gorz, André. *Critique of Economic Reason*. Translated by Gillian Handyside and Chris Turner. New York: Verso, 1989.

Grabel, Michael. "Cut to the Bone: How a Poultry Company Exploits Immigration Laws." *New Yorker*, May 8, 2017, 46–53.

Greenbaum, Joan, and David Kotelchuk. "Got Air? The Campaign to Improve Indoor Air Quality at the City University of New York." In *Worker Safety under Siege: Labor, Capital, and the Politics of Workplace Safety in a Deregulated World*, edited by Vernon Mogensen, 97–107. Armonk, NY: M. E. Sharpe, 2006.

Greenhouse, Steven. 2013. "Some Retailers Rethink Role in Bangladesh." *The Guardian*, May 1, 2013. http://www.nytimes.com/2013/05/02/business/some-retailers-rethink-their-role-in-bangladesh.html?_r=0.

Groenewold, Matthew R., and Sherry L. Baron. "The Proportion of Work-Related Emergency Department Visits Not Expected to Be Paid by Workers' Compensation: Implications for Occupational Health Surveillance, Research, Policy, and Health Equity." *Health Services Research* 48, no. 6 (December 2013): 1939–59.

"Group Health." Fitbit. https://www.fitbit.com/group-health.

Guerette, Rob T. "Disorder at Day Labor Hiring Sites." U.S. Department of Justice, Office of Community Oriented Policing Services, October 2006.

Hardt, Michael, and Antonio Negri. *Assembly*. New York: Oxford University Press, 2017.

Harvey, David. *A Brief History of Neoliberalism*. New York: Oxford University Press, 2007.

Harvey, David. *Cosmopolitanism and the Geographies of Freedom*. New York: Columbia University Press, 2009.

Harvey, David. *The Limits to Capital*. New York: Verso, 1999.

Harvey, David. *The Ways of the World*. New York: Oxford University Press, 2017.

Heller, Nathan. "The Gig Is Up." *New Yorker*, May 15, 2017, 52–63.

Hernández-León, Rubén. "Conceptualizing the Migration Industry." In *The Migration Industry and the Commercialization of International Migration*, edited by Thomas Gammeltoft-Hansen and Ninna Nyberg Sørensen, 24–44. New York: Routledge, 2013.

Hersch, Joni, and W. Kip Viscusi. "Immigrant Status and the Value of Statistical Life." *Journal of Human Resources* 45, no. 3 (2010): 749–71.

Hoang, Mai. "Lawsuit Seeks to Extend Overtime Pay for Washington Farm Workers." *Yakima Herald*, December 9, 2016. http://www.yakimaherald.com/news/business/local/lawsuit-seeks-to-extend-overtime-pay-for-washington-farm-workers/article_dc485aaa-be2f-11e6-8534-83245e06321c.html.

Hondagneu-Sotelo, Pierrette. *Doméstica: Immigrant Workers Cleaning and Caring in the Shadows of Affluence*. Berkeley: University of California Press, 2007.

Honig, Bonnie. *Democracy and the Foreigner*. Princeton, NJ: Princeton University Press, 2001.

International Organization for Migration. "Global Migration Trends: 2015 Fact Sheet." Berlin: International Organization for Migration, 2015.

Kantor, Jodi, and David Streitfeld. "Inside Amazon: Wrestling Big Ideas in a Bruising Workplace." *New York Times*, August 15, 2015. https://www.nytimes.com/2015/08/16/technology/inside-amazon-wrestling-big-ideas-in-a-bruising-workplace.html.

"Informally Employed Syrian Refugees, Working under Harsh Conditions, Further Strain Jordanian Labour Market." International Labour Organization. http://www.ilo.org/beirut/media-centre/news/WCMS_369592/lang--en/index.htm.

Kalyvas, Andreas. "An Anomaly? Some Reflections on the Greek December 2008." *Constellations* 17, no. 2 (2010): 351–65.

Kang, Susan. "What the Documents Can't Tell You: Participant Observation in International Relations." *PS: Political Science and Politics* 50, no. 1 (January 2017): 121–25.

Kennedy, Elizabeth J. "The Invisible Corner: Expanding Workplace Rights for Female Day Laborers." *Berkeley Journal of Employment and Labor Law* 31 (2010): 126–59.

Kim, Tiffany, Claire B. Draucker, Christine Bradway, Jeanne Ann Grisso, and Marilyn S. Sommers. "Somos Hermanas Del Mismo Dolor (We Are Sisters of the Same Pain): Intimate Partner Sexual Violence Narratives Among Immigrant Women in the United States." *Violence Against Women* 23, no. 5 (April 2017): 623–42.

Klein, Naomi. *The Shock Doctrine: The Rise of Disaster Capitalism.* New York: Metropolitan Books / Henry Holt, 2007.

Kotef, Hagar. *Movement and the Ordering of Freedom: On Liberal Governances of Mobility.* Durham, NC: Duke University Press, 2015.

Kotef, Hagar, and Merav Amir. "(En)Gendering Checkpoints: Checkpoint Watch and the Repercussions of Intervention." *Signs* 32, no. 4 (Summer 2007): 973–96.

Kwon, Jong Bum. "The Koreatown Immigrant Workers Alliance: Spatializing Justice in an Immigrant 'Enclave.' In *Working for Justice: The L.A. Model of Organizing and Advocacy*, edited by Ruth Milkman, Joshua Bloom, and Victor Narro, 23–48. Ithaca, NY: Cornell University Press, 2010.

Lambert, Cath. "Redistributing the Sensory: The Critical Pedagogy of Jacques Ranciere." *Critical Studies in Education* 53, no. 2 (April 2012): 211–27.

LaVaque-Manty, Mika. "Finding Theoretical Concepts in the Real World: The Case of the Precariat." In *New Waves in Political Philosophy*, edited by Boudewijn de Bruin and Christopher F. Zurn, 105–24. London: Palgrave Macmillan, 2009.

Lazzarato, Maurizio. *The Making of the Indebted Man: An Essay on the Neoliberal Condition.* Translated by Joshua David Jordan. Los Angeles: Semiotext(e), 2012.

Leclere, Oscar and Rebecca López. "The Jornalero: Perceptions of Health Care Resources of Immigrant Day Laborers." *Journal of Immigrant & Minority Health* 14, no. 4 (2012): 691–97.

Leigh, J. Paul. "The Economic Burden of Occupational Injury and Illness in the United States." *Milbank Quarterly* 89, no. 4 (2011): 728–72.

Lewis, Tyson E. "Thinking with Pensive Images: Rethinking Curiosity in Paulo Freire's *Pedagogy of the Oppressed.*" *Journal of Aesthetic Education* 46, no. 1 (Spring 2012): 27–45.

Liebman, Amy K., Melinda F. Wiggins, Clermont Fraser, Jeffrey Levin, Jill Sidebottom, and Thomas A. Arcury. "Occupational Health Policy and Immigrant Workers in the Agriculture, Forestry, and Fishing Sector." *American Journal of Industrial Medicine* 56, no. 8 (August 2013): 975–84.

Lowry, Sarah J., Hillary Blecker, Janice Camp, Butch De Castro, Steven Hecker, Saman Arbabi, Neal Traven, Noah S. Seixas, Sherry Baron, James Cone, and Barry Souza. "Possibilities and Challenges in Occupational Injury Surveillance of Day Laborers." *American Journal of Industrial Medicine* 53, no. 2 (February 2010): 126–34.

Madison, Kristin, Harald Schmidt, and Kevin G. Volpp. "Using Reporting Requirements to Improve Employer Wellness Incentives and Their Regulation." *Journal of Health Politics, Policy and Law* 39, no. 5 (October 2014): 1013–34.

Majic, Samantha. "Participating, Observing, Publishing: Lessons from the Field." *PS: Political Science and Politics* 50, no. 1 (January 2017): 103–8.

Marazzi, Christian. *The Violence of Financial Capitalism.* Translated by Kristina Lebedeva and Jason Francis Mc Gimsey. Los Angeles: Semiotext(e), 2011.

Martel, James. "Division Is Common." *South Atlantic Quarterly* 113, no. 4 (Fall 2014): 701–11.

McVeigh, Karen. "Cambodian Female Workers in Nike, Asics and Puma Factories Suffer Mass Faintings." *The Guardian*, June 24, 2017. https://www.theguardian.com/business/2017/jun/25/female-cambodian-garment-workers-mass-fainting.

Merchant, Brian. "Life and Death in Apple's Forbidden City." *The Guardian*, June 18, 2017. https://www.theguardian.com/technology/2017/jun/18/foxconn-life-death-forbidden-city-longhua-suicide-apple-iphone-brian-merchant-one-device-extract.

Mezzadra, Sandro, and Brett Neilson. *Border as Method, or, the Multiplication of Labor.* Durham, NC: Duke University Press, 2013.

Milkman, Ruth. *L.A. Story: Immigrant Workers and the Future of the U.S. Labor Movement.* New York: Russell Sage Foundation, 2006.

Milkman, Ruth. "Immigrant Workers, Precarious Work, and the US Labor Movement." *Globalizations* 8, no. 3 (2011): 361–72.

Mogensen, Vernon. "State or Society? The Rise and Repeal of OSHA's Ergonomics Standard." In *Worker Safety under Siege: Labor, Capital, and the Politics of Workplace Safety in a Deregulated World*, edited by Vernon Mogensen, 108–39. Armonk, NY: M. E. Sharpe, 2006.

Mujeres Unidas y Activas, Day Labor Program Women's Collective of La Raza Centro Legal, and Data Center. "Working Conditions of California Household Workers." March 2007. http://www.datacenter.org/wp-content/uploads/behindcloseddoors.pdf.

Narro, Victor, Saba Waheed, and Jassmin Poyaoan. "Building a Movement Together: Worker Centers and Labor Union Affiliations." Los Angeles: UCLA Labor Center, 2016. https://www.labor.ucla.edu/building-a-movement-together/.

NBC Right Now. "Cow Palace Settles with Former Employees over Disability Discrimination." NBC, April 18, 2017. http://www.nbcrightnow.com/story/35179436/cow-palace-settles-with-former-employees-over-disability-discrimination.

Negi, Nalini Junko. "Battling Discrimination and Social Isolation: Psychological Distress among Latino Day Laborers." *American Journal of Community Psychology* 51, nos. 1–2 (March 2013): 164–74.

Neilson, Brett. "Five Theses on Understanding Logistics as Power." *Distinktion: Scandinavian Journal of Social Theory* 13, no. 3 (December 2012): 323–40.

Nelson, Ronald W., Jr., Geri Schmotzer, Barbara J. Burgel, Rachel Crothers, and Marcy C. White. "Sociodemographic Characteristics, Health, and Success Obtaining Work among Latino Urban Day Laborers." *Journal of Health Care for the Poor and Underserved* 23, no. 2 (2012): 797–810.

Nieves, Evelyn. "Domestic Workers Sue, Lobby, Organize for Workplace Rights." Associated Press, June 4, 2008. https://www.commondreams.org/news/2008/06/04/domestic-workers-sue-lobby-organize-workplace-rights.

Ordoñez, Juan Thomas. "'Boots for My Sancho': Structural Vulnerability among Latin American Day Labourers in Berkeley, California." *Culture, Health & Sexuality* 14, no. 6 (2012): 691–703.

Orrenius, Pia M., and Madeline Zavodny. "Immigrants in Risky Occupations." Bonn, Germany: Institute for the Study of Labor, June 2012.

Ouziel, Pablo. "'Vamos Lentos Porque Vamos Lejos': Towards a Dialogical Understanding of Spain's 15Ms." PhD diss., University of Victoria, 2015.

Padilla, José R., and David Bacon. "Protect Female Farmworkers." *New York Times*, January 19, 2016. https://www.nytimes.com/2016/01/19/opinion/how-to-protect-female-farmworkers.html.

Panikkar, Bindu, Mark A. Woodin, Doug Brugge, Anne Marie Desmarais, Raymond Hyatt, Community Partners of the SomervilleCommunity Immigrant Worker Project, and David M. Gute. "Occupational Health Outcomes among Self-Identified Immigrant Workers Living and Working in Somerville, Massachusetts 2006–2009." *Journal of Immigrant and Minority Health* 15, no. 5 (October 2013): 882–89.

Pardo, Mary S. *Mexican American Women Activists: Identity and Resistance in Two Los Angeles Communities*. Philadelphia: Temple University Press, 1998.

Paret, Marcel. "Precarious Labor Politics: Unions and the Struggles of the Insecure Working Class in the United States and South Africa." *Critical Sociology* 41, nos. 4–5 (April 2013): 757–84.

Parreñas, Rhacel, and Rachel Silvey. "The Precarity of Migrant Domestic Work." *South Atlantic Quarterly* 117, no. 2 (April 2018): 430–38.

Parsanoglou, Dimitris. "Trojan Horses, Black Holes and the Impossibility of Labour Struggles." *Logistical Worlds* (blog). December 15, 2015. http://logisticalworlds. org/blogs/trojan-horses-black-holes.

Peck, Jamie. "Austerity Urbanism." *City* 16, no. 6 (2012): 626–55.

Petroff, Alanna. "U.S. Workers Face Higher Risk of Being Replaced by Robots. Here's Why." CNN, March 24, 2017. http://money.cnn.com/2017/03/24/technology/ robots-jobs-us-workers-uk/index.html.

Postone, Moishe. *Time, Labor, and Social Domination: A Reinterpretation of Marx's Critical Theory.* New York: Cambridge University Press, 1993.

Quesada, James, Sonya Arreola, Alex Kral, Sahar Khoury, Kurt C. Organista, and Paula Worby. "'As Good as It Gets': Undocumented Latino Day Laborers Negotiating Discrimination in San Francisco and Berkeley, California, USA." *City & Society* 26, no. 1 (April 2014): 29–50.

Rabito, Felicia A., Sara Perry, Oscar Salinas, John Hembling, Norine Schmidt, Patrick J. Parsons, and Patricia Kissinger. "A Longitudinal Assessment of Occupation, Respiratory Symptoms, and Blood Levels among Latino Day Laborers in a Non-agricultural Setting." *American Journal of Industrial Medicine* 54, no. 5 (2011): 366–74.

Ramirez, Hernan, and Pierrette Hondagneu-Sotelo. "Mexican Immigrant Gardeners: Entrepreneurs or Exploited Workers?" *Social Problems* 56, no. 1 (February 2009): 70–80.

Ramos, Athena K., Dejun Su, Lina Lander, and Roy Rivera. "Stress Factors Contributing to Depression among Latino Migrant Farmworkers in Nebraska." *Journal of Immigrant and Minority Health* 17, no. 6 (December 2015): 1627–34.

Rancière, Jacques. *Disagreement: Politics and Philosophy.* Translated by Julie Rose. Minneapolis: University of Minnesota Press, 1999.

Reina, Angelica S., Marta María Maldonado, and Brenda J. Lohman. "Undocumented Latina Networks and Responses to Domestic Violence in a New Immigrant Gateway: Toward a Place-Specific Analysis." *Violence Against Women* 19, no. 12 (December 2013): 1472–97.

Rocco, Raymond A. *Transforming Citizenship: Democracy, Membership, and Belonging in Latino Communities.* East Lansing: Michigan State University Press, 2014.

Rosenblat, Alex, Tamara Kneese, and danah boyd. "Workplace Surveillance." Data & Society Working Paper, October 8, 2014. https://www.datasociety.net/pubs/fow/ WorkplaceSurveillance.pdf.

Rosenman, Kenneth D., Alice Kalush, Mary Jo Reilly, Joseph C. Gardiner, Matthew Reeves, and Zhewui Luo. "How Much Work-Related Injury and Illness Is Missed by the Current National Surveillance System?" *Journal of Occupational and Environmental Medicine* 48, no. 4 (April 2006): 357–65.

Ross, Andrew. "In Search of the Lost Paycheck." In *Digital Labor: The Internet as Playground and Factory,* edited by Andreas Wittel, 13–32. New York: Routledge, 2013.

Ruiz, Vicki L. *Cannery Women, Cannery Lives: Mexican Women, Unionization, and the California Food Processing Industry, 1930–1950*. Albuquerque: University of New Mexico Press, 1987.

Ruiz, Vicki L. *From Out of the Shadows: Mexican Women in Twentieth-Century America*. New York: Oxford University Press, 1998.

Salgado, Hugo, Sheila Castañeda, Gregory Talavera, and Suzanne Lindsay. "The Role of Social Support and Acculturative Stress in Health-Related Quality of Life among Day Laborers in Northern San Diego." *Journal of Immigrant & Minority Health* 14, no. 3 (2012): 379–85.

Sampaio, Anna. *Terrorizing Latina/o Immigrants: Race, Gender, and Immigration Politics in the Age of Security*. Philadelphia: Temple University Press, 2015.

Scheiber, Noam. "How Uber Uses Psychological Tricks to Push Its Drivers' Buttons." *New York Times*, April 2, 2017. https://www.nytimes.com/interactive/2017/04/02/technology/uber-drivers-psychological-tricks.html.

Schwarz-Shea, Peregrine and Samantha Majic. "Ethnography and Participant Observation: Political Science Research in This 'Late Methodological Moment.'" *PS: Political Science and Politics* 50, no. 1 (January 2017): 97–102.

Seixas, Noah S., Hillary Blecker, Janice Camp, and Rick Neitzel. "Occupational Health and Safety Experience of Day Laborers in Seattle, WA." *American Journal of Industrial Medicine* 51, no. 6 (June 2008): 399–406.

Shah, Hina, and Marci Seville. "Domestic Worker Organizing: Building a Community Movement for Dignity and Power." *Albany Law Review* 75, no. 1 (2011–12): 413–46.

Shapiro, Sidney A. "Dying at Work: Political Discourse and Occupational Safety and Health." *Wake Forest Law Review* 49, no. 3 (2014): 831–47.

Shippen, Nicole Marie. *Decolonizing Time: Work, Leisure, and Freedom*. New York: Palgrave Macmillan, 2014.

Smith, Peggie R. "The Pitfalls of Home: Protecting the Health and Safety of Paid Domestic Workers." *Canadian Journal of Women and the Law* 23, no. 1 (2011): 309–39.

Standing, Guy. *The Precariat: The New Dangerous Class*. London: Bloomsbury, 2011.

Standing, Guy. *A Precariat Charter: From Denizens to Citizens*. London: Bloomsbury, 2014.

Stuart, Forrest. "From the Shop to the Streets: UNITE HERE Organizing in Los Angeles Hotels." In *Working for Justice: The L.A. Model of Organizing and Advocacy*, edited by Ruth Milkman, Joshua Bloom, and Victor Narro, 191–210. Ithaca, NY: Cornell University Press, 2010.

Theodore, Nik. "After the Storm: Houston's Day Labor Markets in the Aftermath of Hurricane Harvey." Chicago: Great Cities Institute, University of Illinois at Chicago, 2017.

Theodore, Nik. "The Ballad of Industry: Recuperating Alienated Identities through Day Laborers' Song." *South Atlantic Quarterly* 117, no. 2 (April 2018): 410–19.

Theodore, Nik. "Day Labor in Seattle: Casa Latina's Impact on Wages and Earnings." January 2016. http://casa-latina.org/sites/casa-latina.org/files/documents/Day%20Labor%20in%20Seattle%20March%202016.pdf.

Theodore, Nik. "Generative Work: Day Laborers' Freirean Praxis." *Urban Studies* 52, no. 11 (2015): 2035–50.

Theodore, Nik. "Realigning Labor: Toward a Framework for Collaboration between Labor Unions and Day Labor Worker Centers." Washington, DC: Neighborhood Funders Group, 2010.

Theodore, Nik, and Nina Martin. "Migrant Civil Society: New Voices in the Struggle over Community Development." *Journal of Urban Affairs* 29, no. 3 (2007): 269–87.

Theodore, Nik, Abel Valenzuela Jr., and Edwin Meléndez. "La Esquina (The Corner): Day Laborers on the Margins of New York's Formal Economy." *Working USA: The Journal of Labor and Society* 9, no. 4 (December 2006): 407–23.

Theodore, Nik, Abel Valenzuela Jr., and Edwin Meléndez. "Worker Centers: Defending Labor Standards for Migrant Workers in the Informal Economy." *International Journal of Manpower* 30, no. 5 (2009): 422–36.

Torres, Rebecca, Rich Heyman, Solange Munoz, Lauren Apgar, Emily Timm, Cristina Tzintzun, Charles R. Hale, John McKiernan-Gonzalez, Shannon Speed, and Eric Tang. "Building Austin, Building Justice: Immigrant Construction Workers, Precarious Labor Regimes and Social Citizenship." *Geoforum* 45 (2013): 145–55.

Trautner, Mary Knell, Erin Hatton, and Kelly E. Smith. "What Workers Want Depends: Legal Knowledge and the Desire for Workplace Change among Day Laborers." *Law & Policy* 35, no. 4 (October 2013): 319–40.

Tsing, Anna Lowenhaupt. *The Mushroom at the End of the World: On the Possibility of Life in Capitalist Ruins*. Princeton, NJ: Princeton University Press, 2015.

Tully, James. *Public Philosophy in a New Key*. Volume 1: *Democracy and Civic Freedom*. Cambridge: Cambridge University Press, 2008.

Tully, James. *Strange Multiplicity: Constitutionalism in an Age of Diversity*. Cambridge: Cambridge University Press, 1995.

US Department of Labor. Bureau of Labor Statistics. "Employer-Reported Workplace Injuries and Illnesses—2014." News Release. Washington, DC, October 29, 2015.

US Department of Labor. Occupational Safety and Health Administration. "Adding Inequality to Injury: The Costs of Failing to Protect Workers on the Job." Washington, DC, 2015.

Valdez, Avelardo, Alice Ceneda, Nalini Negi, and Charles Kaplan. "Fumando la Piedra: Emerging Patterns of Crack Use among Latino Immigrant Day Laborers in New Orleans." *Journal of Immigrant & Minority Health* 12, no. 5 (2010): 737–42.

Valenzuela, Abel, Jr. "New Immigrants and Day Labor: The Potential for Violence." In *Immigration and Crime: Race, Ethnicity, and Violence*, edited by Ramiro Martinez Jr. and Abel Valenzuela Jr., 189–211. New York: New York University Press, 2006.

Valenzuela, Abel, Jr., Nik Theodore, Edwin Meléndez, and Ana Luz Gonzales. "On the Corner: Day Labor in the United States." Los Angeles: UCLA Center for the Study of Urban Poverty, January 2006.

Wagner, Heike. "Migration und Gewalt gegen Frauen. Über unsichtbare Migrationsgründe und Neuverhandlungen im Migrationsprozess." *Anthropos* 104, no. 1 (2009): 41–61.

Wajcman, Judy. *Pressed for Time: The Acceleration of Life in Digital Capitalism.* Chicago: University of Chicago Press, 2015.

Walter, Nicholas, Philippe Bourgois, Margarita Loinaz, and Dean Shillinger. "Social Context of Work Injury among Undocumented Day Laborers in San Francisco." *Journal of General Internal Medicine* 17, no. 3 (March 2002): 221–29.

Webb, Darren. "Paulo Freire and 'the Need for a Kind of Education in Hope.'" *Cambridge Journal of Education* 40, no. 4 (December 2010): 327–39.

Weeks, Kathi. *The Problem with Work: Feminism, Marxism, Antiwork Politics, and Postwork Imaginaries.* Durham, NC: Duke University Press, 2011.

Weil, David. *The Fissured Workplace: Why Work Became So Bad for So Many and What Can Be Done to Improve It.* Cambridge, MA: Harvard University Press, 2014.

White, Hayden. *The Content of the Form: Narrative Discourse and Historical Representation.* Baltimore: Johns Hopkins University Press, 1987.

Wilmsen, Carl, Diane Bush, and Dinorah Barton-Antonio. "Working in the Shadows: Safety and Health in Forestry Services in Southern Oregon." *Journal of Forestry* 113, no. 3 (May 2015): 315–24.

Worby, Paula A., and Kurt C. Organista. "Contextual Influences on the Drinking of Male Latino Immigrant Day Laborers." *Substance Use & Misuse* 48, no.5 (2013): 391–402.

Worby, Paula A., Kurt C. Organista, Alex H. Kral, James Quesada, Sonya Arreola, and Sahar Khoury. "Structural Vulnerability and Problem Drinking among Latino Migrant Day Laborers in the San Francisco Bay Area." *Journal of Health Care for the Poor and Underserved* 25, no. 3 (August 2014): 1291–1307.

Yardley, Jim. "Report on Deadly Factory Collapse in Bangladesh Finds Widespread Blame." *New York Times,* May 22, 2013. http://www.nytimes.com/2013/05/23/world/asia/report-on-bangladesh-building-collapse-finds-widespread-blame.html.

Zavella, Patricia. *Women's Work and Chicano Families: Cannery Workers of the Santa Clara Valley.* Ithaca, NY: Cornell University Press, 1987.

Index